LIBERTY.

First published in 2021
This edition published in 2023 by Welbeck
An imprint of Welbeck Non-Fiction Limited,
part of the Welbeck Publishing Group
Offices in: London – 20 Mortimer Street, London W1T 3JW &
Sydney – Level 17, 207 Kent St, Sydney NSW 2000 Australia
www.welbeckpublishing.com

First published in 2013 and 2019 by Carlton Books Limited

A CIP catalogue record for this book is available from the British Library.

ISBN 978 1 80279 607 0

Printed in China

MIX
Paper | Supporting responsible forestry
FSC® C020056

LIBERTY.

THE HISTORY

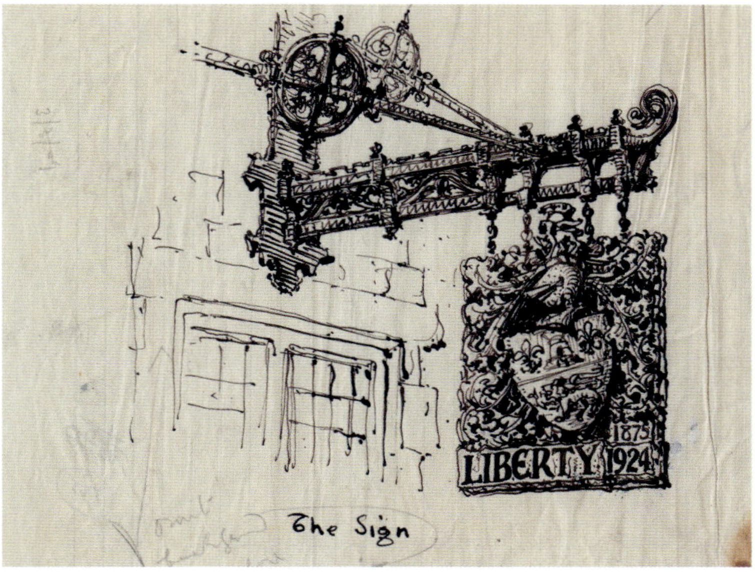

MARIE-THERESE
RIEBER

WELBECK

CONTENTS

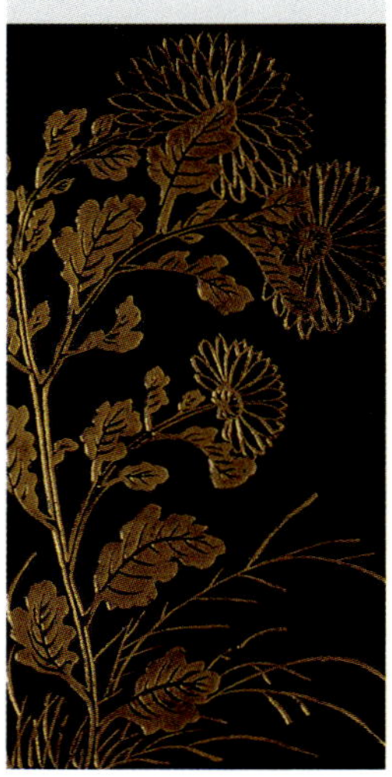

THE EMPORIUM

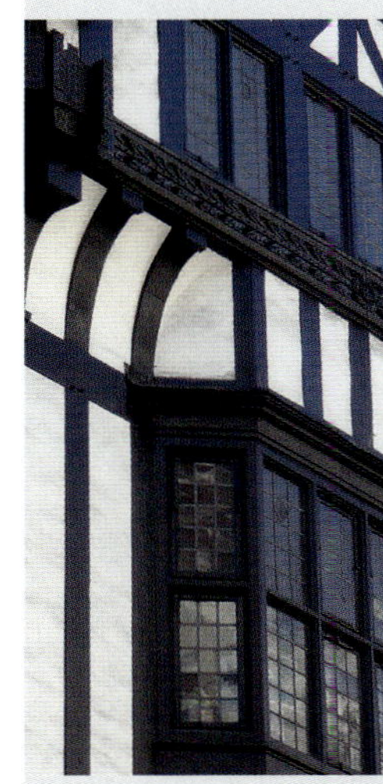

THE ART FABRICS

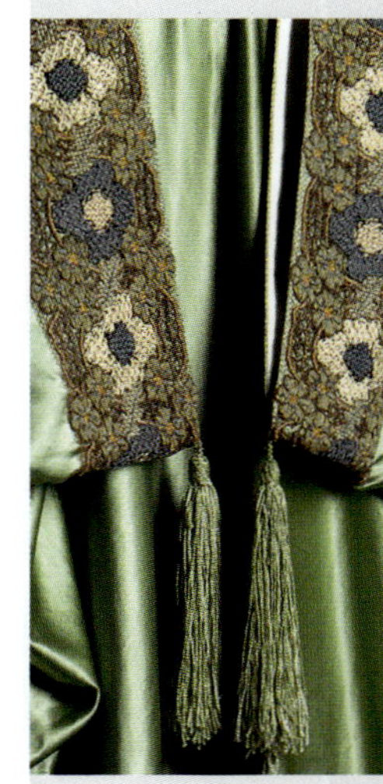

THE DOCUMENTS

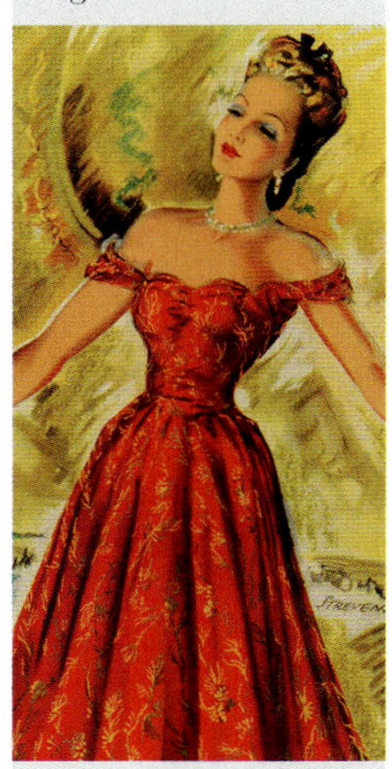

STILE LIBERTY

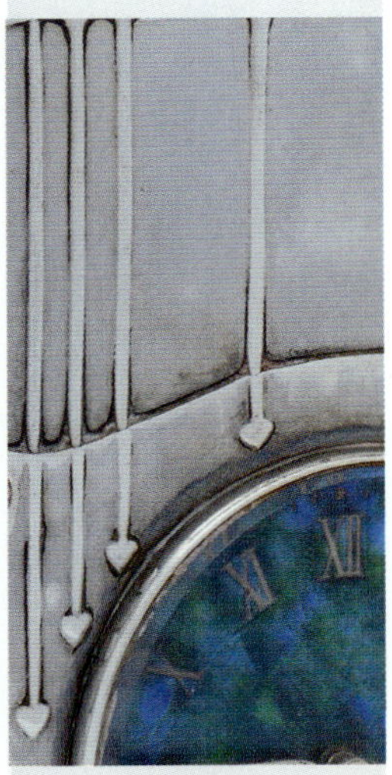

MID-CENTURY

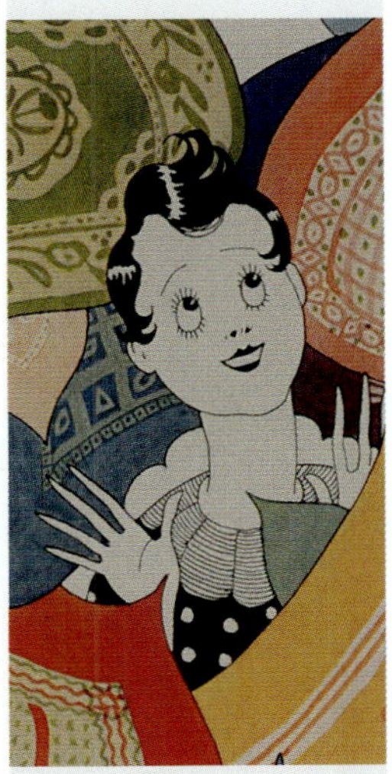

ART NOUVEAU REVISITED

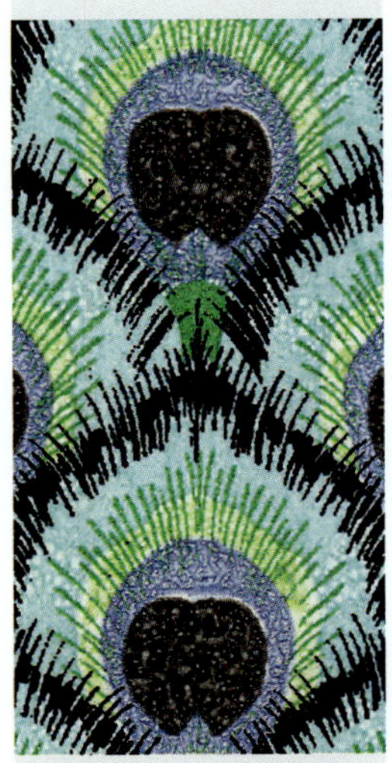

NEW DIRECTIONS

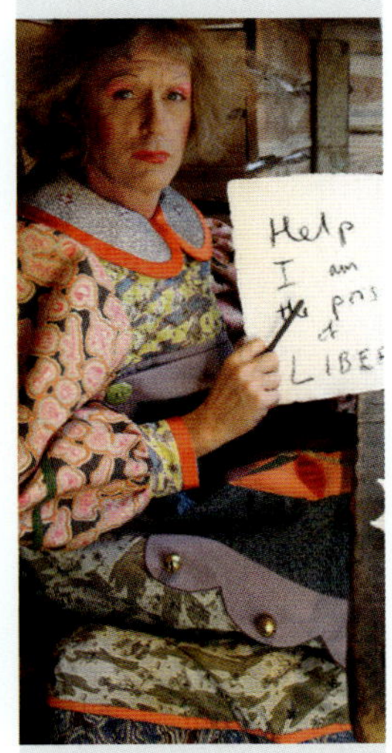

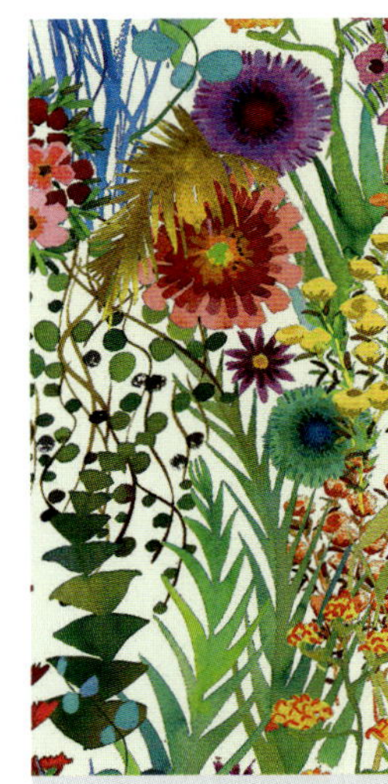

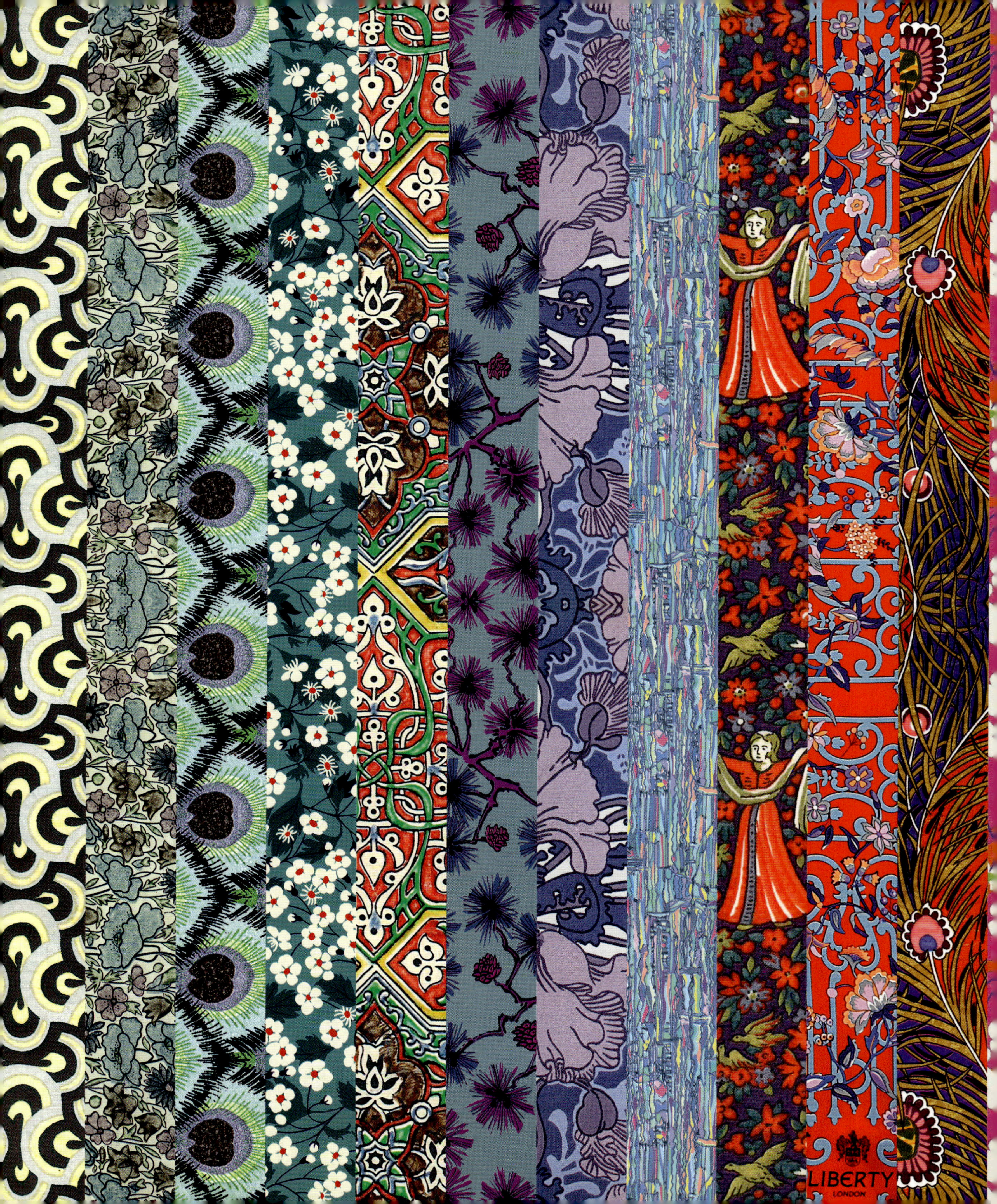
LIBERTY

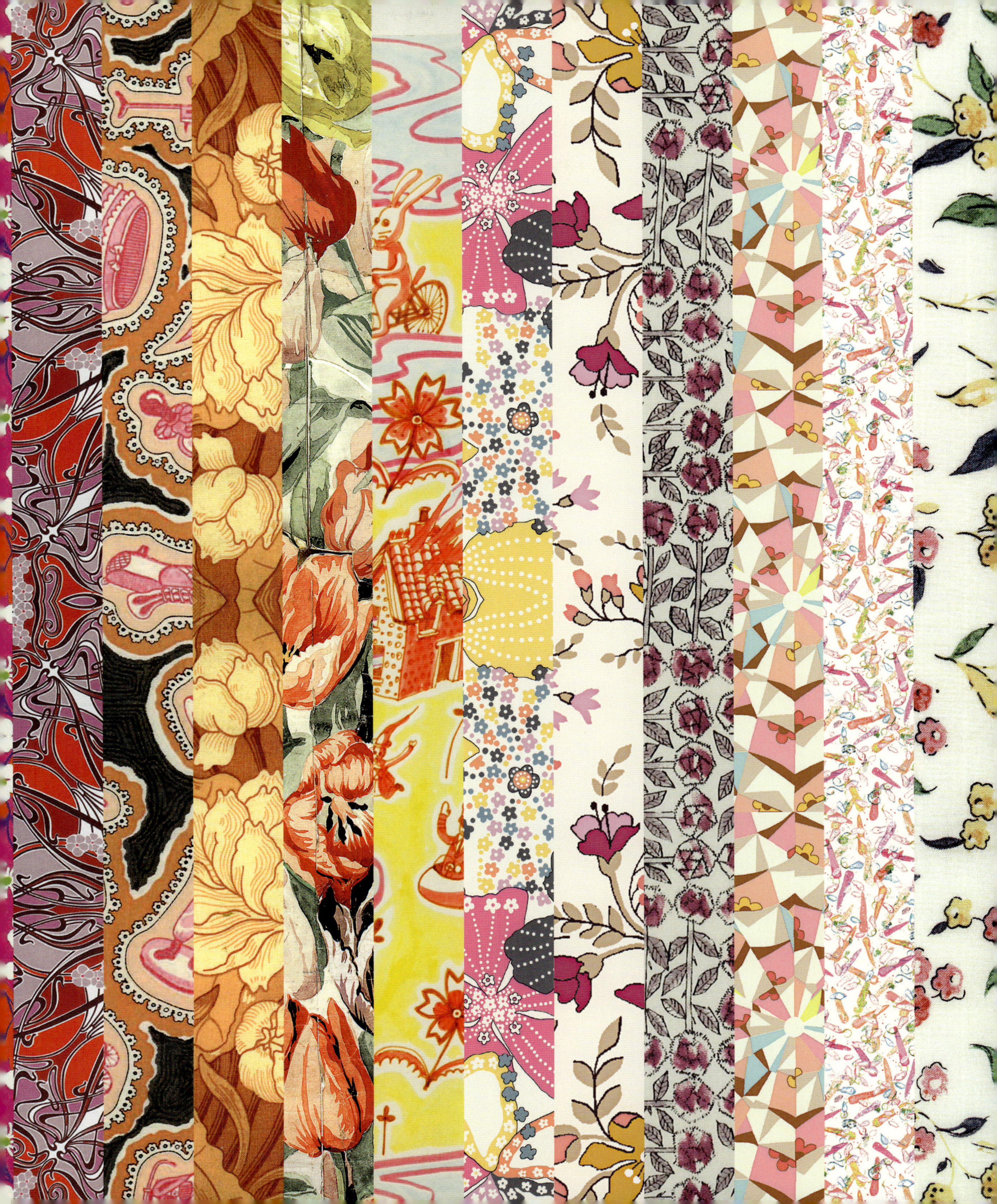

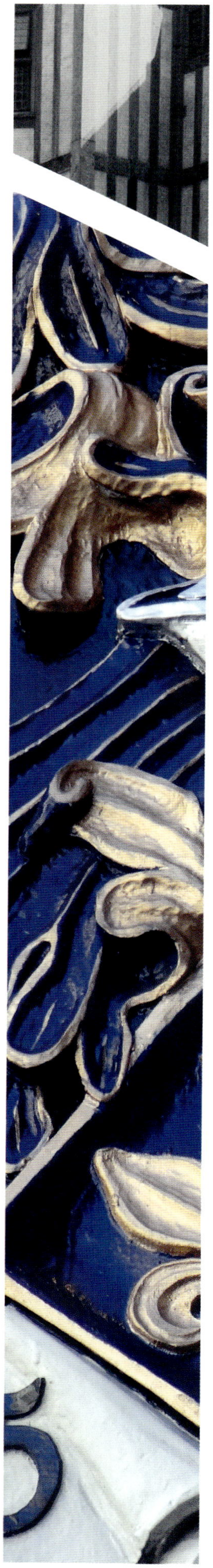

THE EMPORIUM

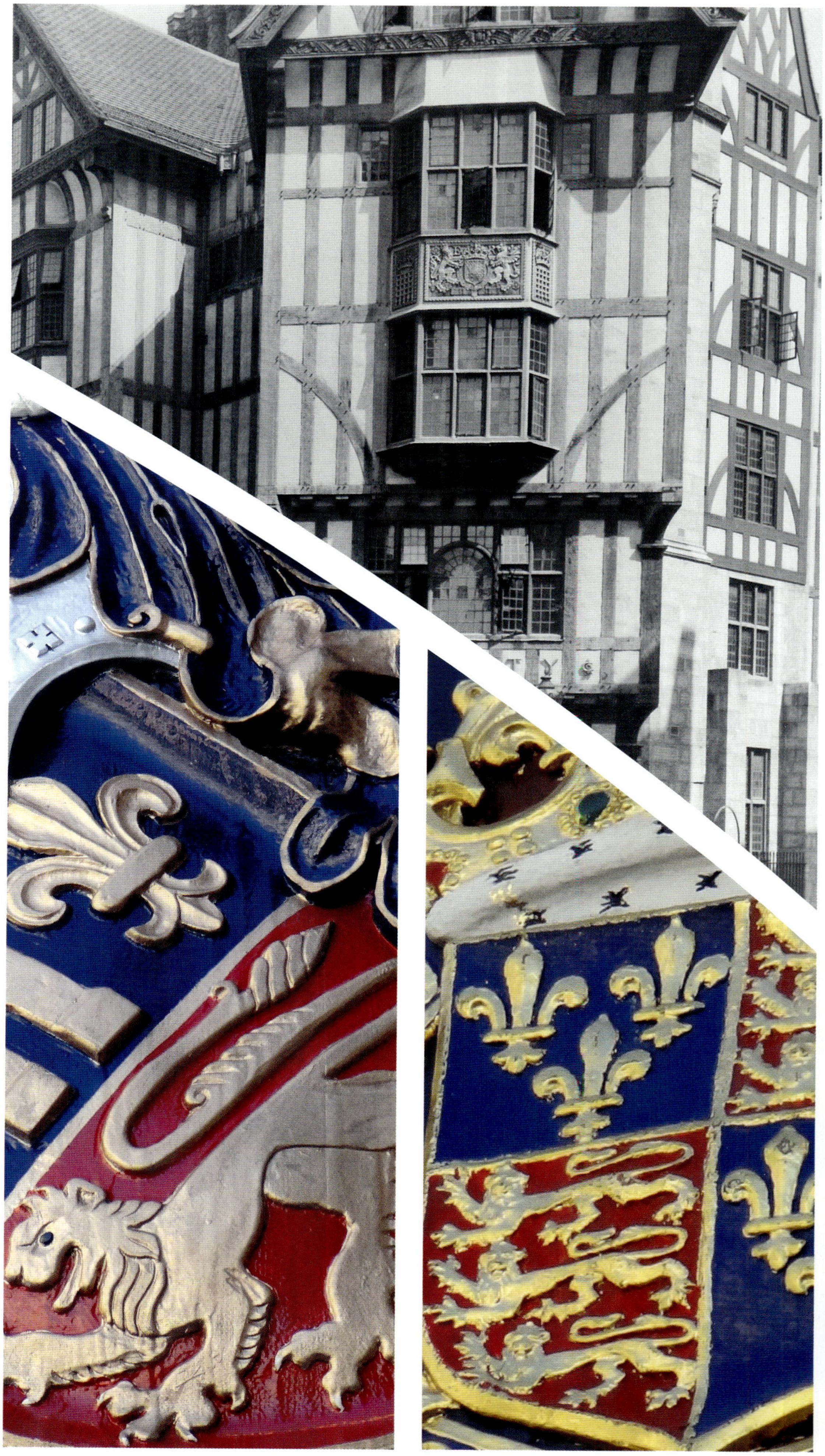

ABOVE AND OPPOSITE
The Tudor Shop, past and present.

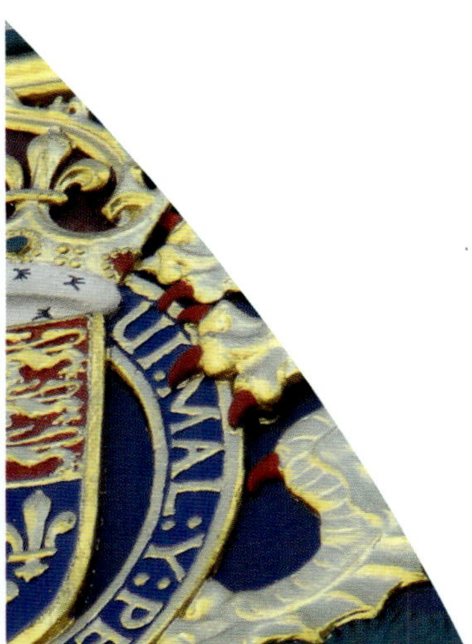
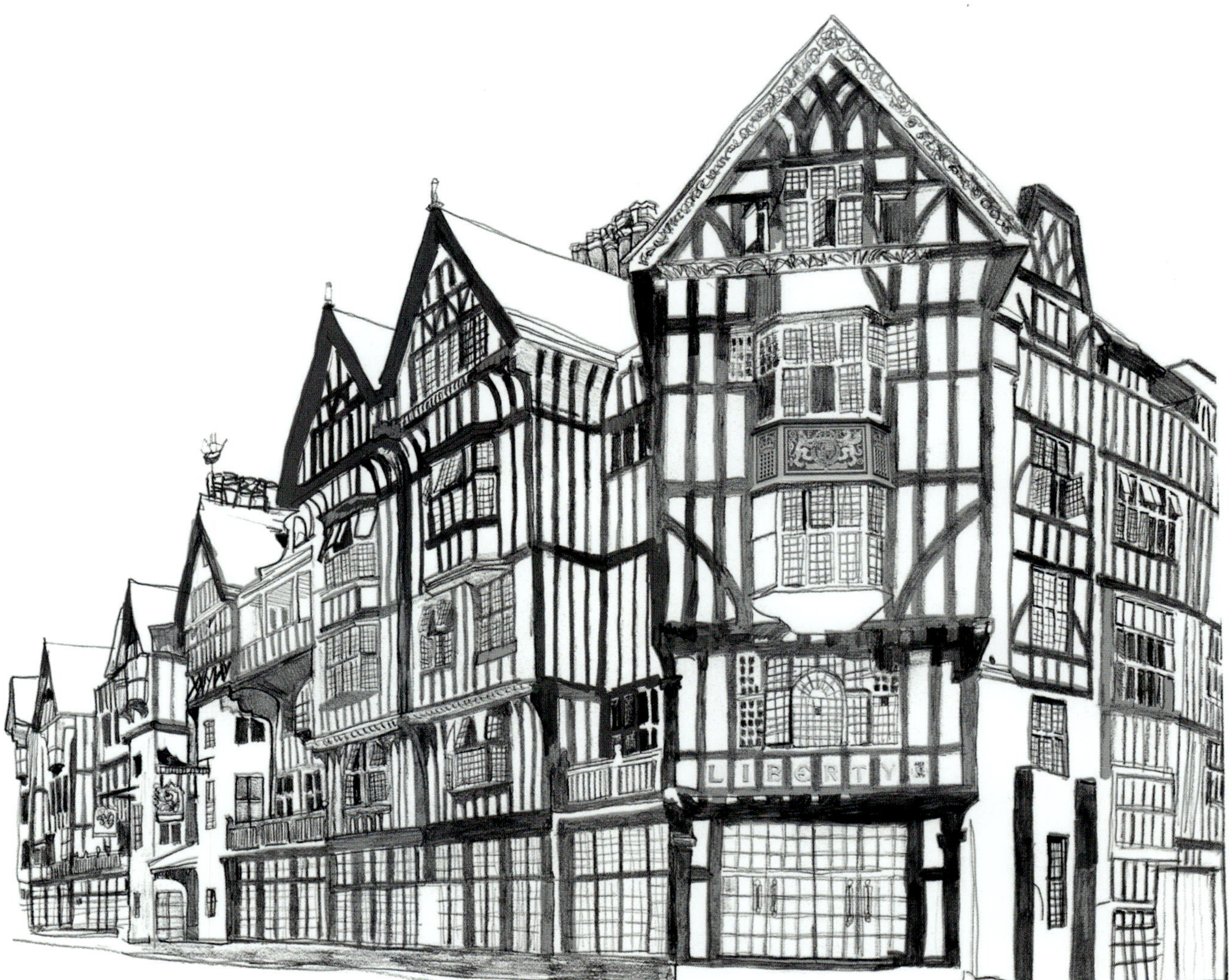
LIBERTY

ARTHUR LIBERTY'S SHOPPING EMPORIUM

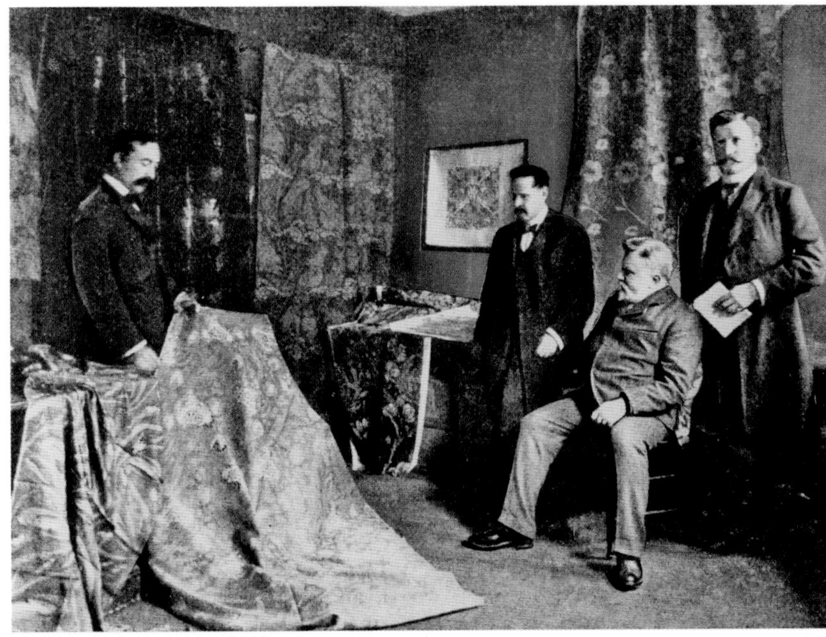

ABOVE *Arthur Liberty (seated) selects silk fabrics being displayed by John Llewellyn in the Trial Studio in the mid-1880s, along with fellow directors William Street and J. W. House.*

Liberty, probably London's best-loved and certainly its most recognizable department store, started life as a small half-shop on Regent Street in 1875. Its founder, Arthur Lasenby Liberty (1843–1917), opened the business selling imported goods from the Far East, tapping into the then current fascination with all things Oriental. A phenomenal success, the rapidly expanding enterprise soon became a byword for a very distinct and highly fashionable style of fabric that is as popular now as it was then.

The eldest of eight children, Arthur Liberty was born in the small market town of Chesham, Buckinghamshire, where his father, also Arthur, was a draper. Following in his footsteps, Arthur was apprenticed at the age of 16 as a draper in Baker Street, London, but after two uninspiring years, found work instead at the highly fashionable Farmer & Rogers Great Shawl & Cloak Emporium on the elegant shopping mile of Regent Street.

Liberty excelled at Farmer & Rogers, and when the store expanded, opening up the Oriental Warehouse next door, he was appointed one of its two employees. Two years later, he was made its manager. The Oriental Warehouse had acquired a considerable number of artefacts from the 1862 London International Exhibition, which they used as their original stock. The exhibition had showcased Japanese arts and crafts, which captured the public imagination, as well as Arthur's. As he later remarked, the Oriental Warehouse was the only shop in London at the time dealing in "things from the East". The shop became a mecca for Pre-Raphaelite artists, delighted to find in the soft imported silks the right material to drape over their models, and also for early collectors of Japanese art and blue-and-white porcelain.

Arthur Liberty not only had a fascination for the Eastern goods he was selling, but he also developed a considerable expertise in them. As a result, he made the acquaintance of some of the most exciting artists, designers and architects of his time, including E. W. Godwin, William Morris, Dante Gabriel Rossetti, Edward Burne-Jones and Lawrence Alma-Tadema.

After 10 successful years running the Oriental Warehouse, Arthur, by then in his early thirties and engaged to Emma Louise Blackmore, asked to become partner at Farmer & Rogers. He was refused but, encouraged by promises of loyalty from his artistic customers, decided to establish his own shop. With financial backing from his future father-in-law, he opened East India House, a rather grandiose title for such a tiny shop, at 218A Regent Street, just across from his former employers. A 16-year-old girl, a Japanese boy and an

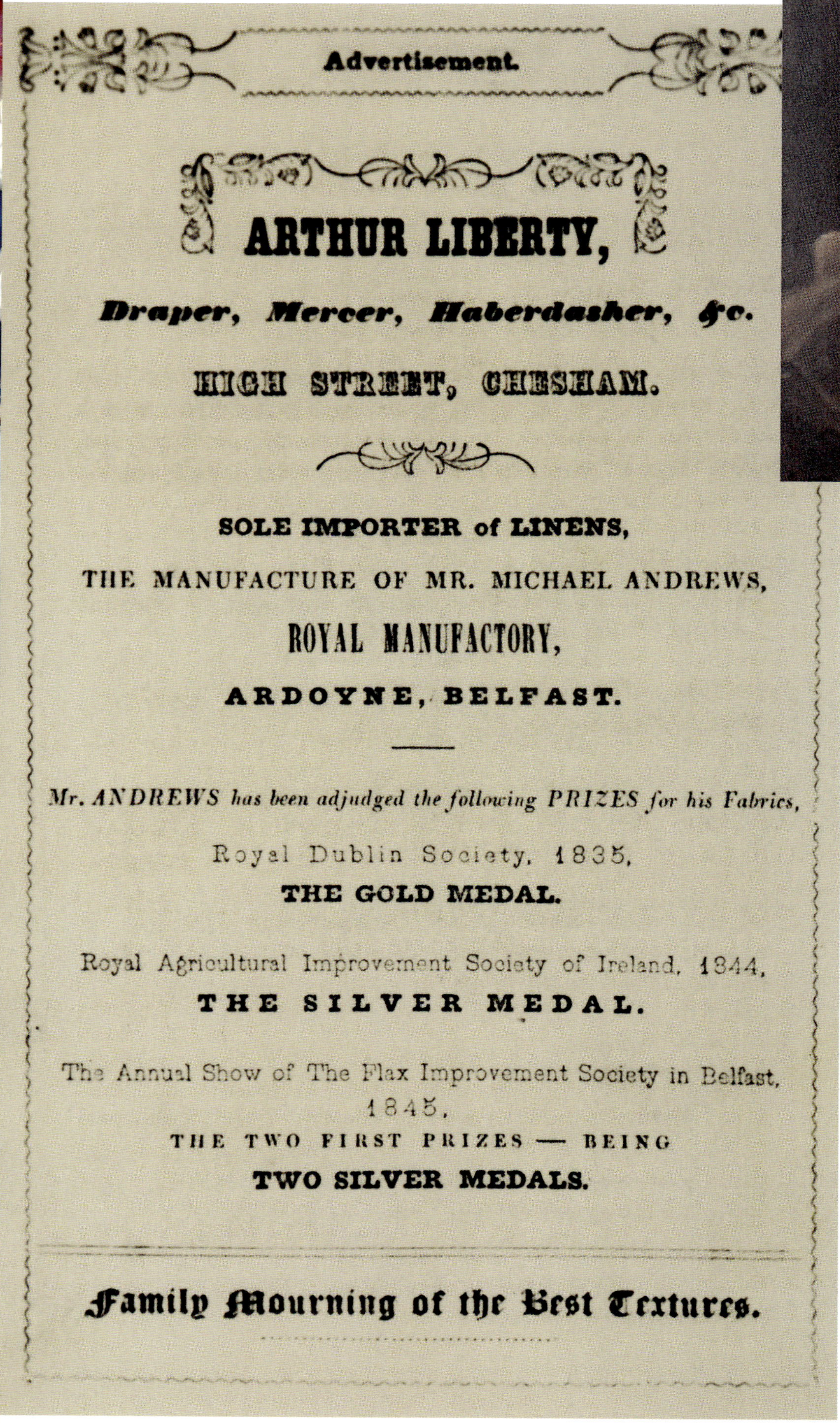

Advertisement.

ARTHUR LIBERTY,

Draper, Mercer, Haberdasher, &c.

HIGH STREET, CHESHAM.

SOLE IMPORTER of LINENS,

THE MANUFACTURE OF MR. MICHAEL ANDREWS,

ROYAL MANUFACTORY,

ARDOYNE, BELFAST.

Mr. ANDREWS has been adjudged the following PRIZES for his Fabrics,

Royal Dublin Society, 1835,

THE GOLD MEDAL.

Royal Agricultural Improvement Society of Ireland, 1844,

THE SILVER MEDAL.

The Annual Show of The Flax Improvement Society in Belfast, 1845,

THE TWO FIRST PRIZES — BEING

TWO SILVER MEDALS.

Family Mourning of the Best Textures.

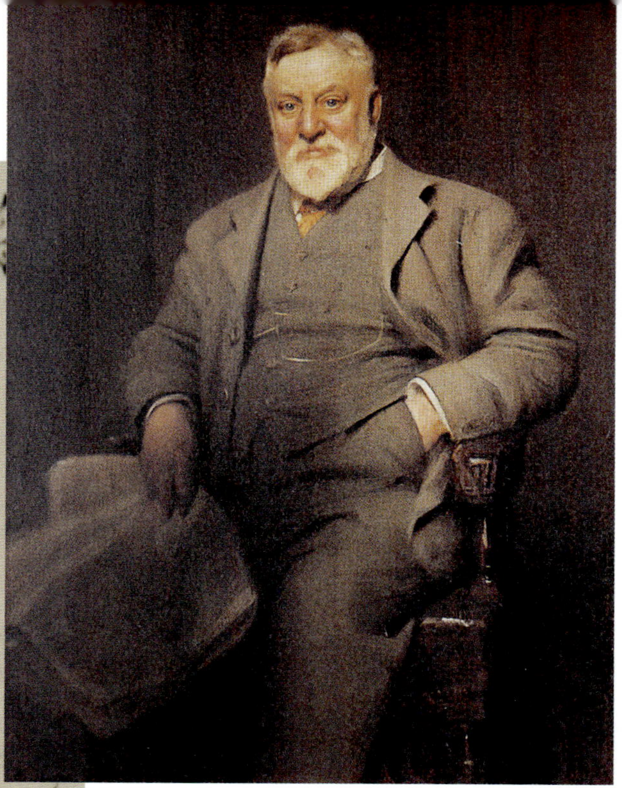

employee from Farmer & Rogers, who had volunteered to work whether he was paid or not, joined him at his new enterprise.

With East India House, Arthur Liberty made his name importing beautiful and high-quality fabrics, particularly silks, from Japan, but also from Persia, India and China. Very soon, his wares comprised an astonishing range of exotic goods, from ceramics, Japanese fans, screens, wallpapers, matting and Oriental carpets to all manner of antiques, curios and *objets d'art*. Arthur's timing could not have been better. He established his business exactly when all things Japanese were in vogue, and also at the height of the Aesthetic movement, which was characterized by the idea of "art for art's sake" and an interest in Japanese, classical and medieval art. He was so successful that he was not only able to pay back his loans in full after only 18 months in business, but to acquire the other half of the premises at 218 Regent Street.

Arthur had stated early on that his ambition was to "change the whole taste of fashion and decoration". Thanks to his great enthusiasm for Eastern arts and crafts, a passion to educate, his keen eye for styles and trends, and an astute talent for business, East India House rapidly became much more than an Oriental bazaar, and Liberty himself a leading

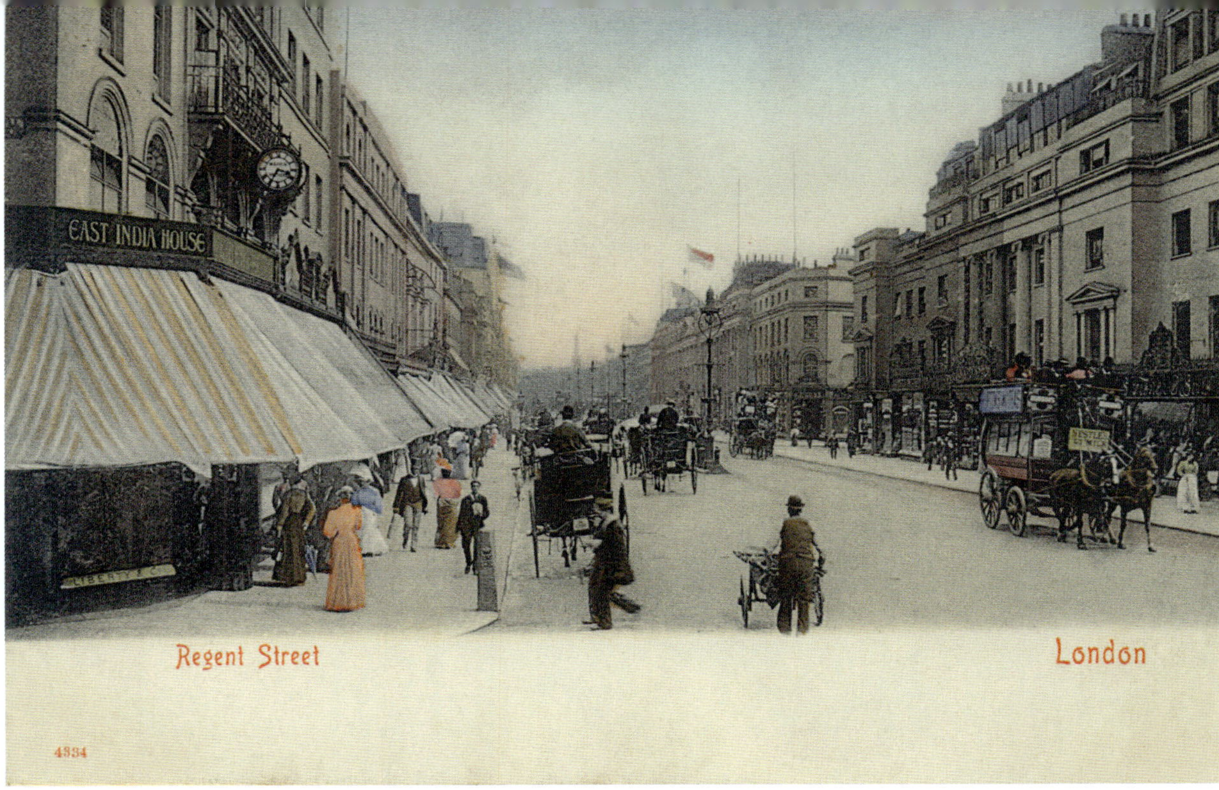

LEFT
A postcard view from 1890 depicting East India House. The uniform awning along the length of the shop front is an attempt to unify the disparate architecture.

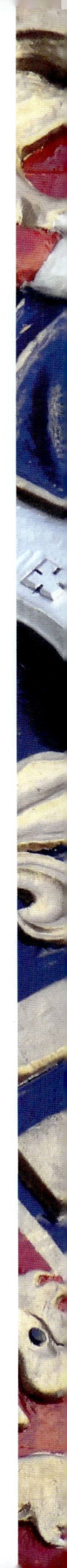

'retail tastemaker'. From the 1890s, the close association with the Aesthetic movement faded, and Arthur effectively created his own distinctive house look, known as the "Liberty Style", or as the Italians dubbed it, "Stile Liberty".

A sociable man, Arthur had moved in advantageous circles from the beginning of his career. He counted many of the key personalities in art and design at the time as his friends and acquaintances, from the avant-garde designer Christopher Dresser, a fellow admirer of Japanese art, and the architect Richard Norman Shaw to the artist James McNeill Whistler. Since these leading figures were customers as well as friends, whom he visited in their studios, Arthur was in an ideal position to know what would excite and tempt them at East India House. He also realized that these artistic trendsetters would draw wealthy middle-class customers in their wake. Gradually, he expanded the scope of his offerings to appeal to this growing clientele.

Arthur soon approached British manufacturers and started to have dress and furnishing fabrics printed, dyed and woven in Britain. Remarkably soft and subtle, in muted but instantly recognizable patterns and colours, these beautiful, high-quality textiles swiftly became best sellers and world-famous as 'Liberty Art Fabrics'.

As the business prospered, so the shop expanded, and from the late 1870s, it became known as Liberty & Co., the destination for the artistic shopper. This led to Arthur Liberty acquiring much larger premises on Regent Street, which he named Chesham House, after his birthplace. This new Eastern bazaar, beautifully decorated with antique Japanese goods and extravagantly lit by electric light, was dedicated to carpets, furnishings and Oriental antiques. Further expansion followed until Chesham House came to span 140–150 Regent Street.

Stepping into this exotic emporium from the busy street, shoppers could feel as if they had travelled to foreign parts of the world and entered an enchanting cave. The many rooms of the sprawling premises were hung with Oriental draperies and decorated with objects of rare beauty. Shoppers were seduced with all their senses. Some of the spaces were decorated thematically, such as the Japanese smoking room, which created a stage for the objects on sale and set them into context. There was also an Arab tea room, where customers could take tea and refreshments, but also buy exotic fare such as Indian condiments, Chinese tea and ginger. These marketing strategies seemed to work. A review from the *British Mercantile Gazette*, January 1884, noted: "This sumptuous

OPPOSITE
A newspaper advertisement for Arthur Liberty's father's Chesham haberdashery, dating from the early nineteenth century.

OPPOSITE ABOVE
An informal portrait of Arthur Liberty dating from 1911, almost four decades after the establishment of Liberty & Co.

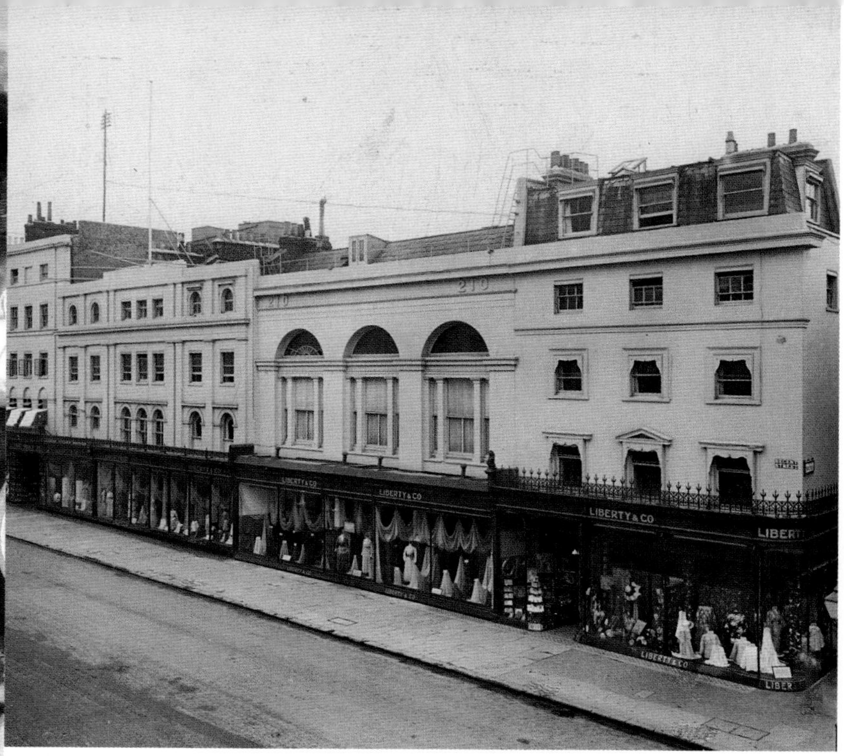

ABOVE *The original premises for Liberty & Co. were known as East India House – an eclectic row of mismatched Georgian buildings on Regent Street, seen here in 1912.*

establishment, or rather establishments, for there are three or four, is crowded daily to the utmost capacity of its 34 or 35 beautiful rooms, as well as its main shop. It is a positive art education to stroll through these treasure-trove receptacles."

The store had a furnishing and decorating studio that undertook commissions from all over the world for entire houses or individual rooms, as well as for balls, exhibitions and bazaars. It began to produce its own furniture in an impressively eclectic range of styles, initially Japanese, Moorish, Egyptian and Classical designs, but later including Gothic and Art Nouveau. From 1884, a costume department catered to the needs of sophisticated ladies aspiring to dress themselves, and their children, in the fashionable Aesthetic style.

Soon, customers could find almost anything they needed to furnish a fashionable "artistic" home at Liberty & Co. as it branched out into the design and manufacture of silver- and pewterware, jewellery, ceramics and glass. It commissioned some of the best designers of the time, and collaborated with world-famous British manufacturers such as the pottery firm of William Moorcroft and the metalware maker W. H. Haseler.

Although Arthur Liberty was always keen to promote British design and support British manufacturing, his love for the exotic and the East never ceased. His company continued to import Oriental antiques as well as modern artefacts, relying on a large network of agents and envoys. And in the old English tradition of merchant adventuring, which he so admired, he travelled on holiday with his wife to several of the far-away countries that were the source of his extraordinary merchandise, including Turkey, North Africa and Japan.

Liberty & Co.'s influence on the decorative taste of the time was unparalleled and the store was financially very successful. By the turn of the century, it had over 1,000 employees and, alongside the shopping emporium in Regent Street, there were thriving branches in Paris and Birmingham, and agents selling Liberty's wares and textiles all over continental Europe, in North America, Australia, China and Japan. Arthur Liberty stepped back from the daily business in 1894, a wealthy man. Three years prior to his death in 1917, aged 74, he was knighted for his services to the decorative arts. As he had no children of his own, he made his nephew Ivor his heir and requested he take on the name of Liberty. It was under Ivor Stewart-Liberty that Liberty & Co. entered the twentieth century, and it was he who commissioned the mock-Tudor building that the store inhabits to this day.

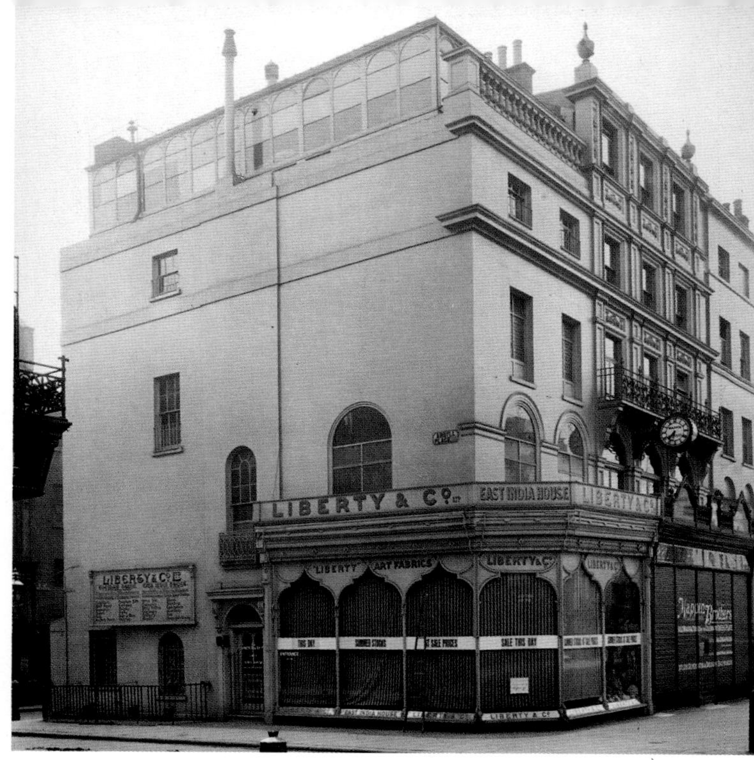

ABOVE *A view of the corner of East India House, looking down Great Marlborough Street (then known as Argyll Place), from the early 1900s.*

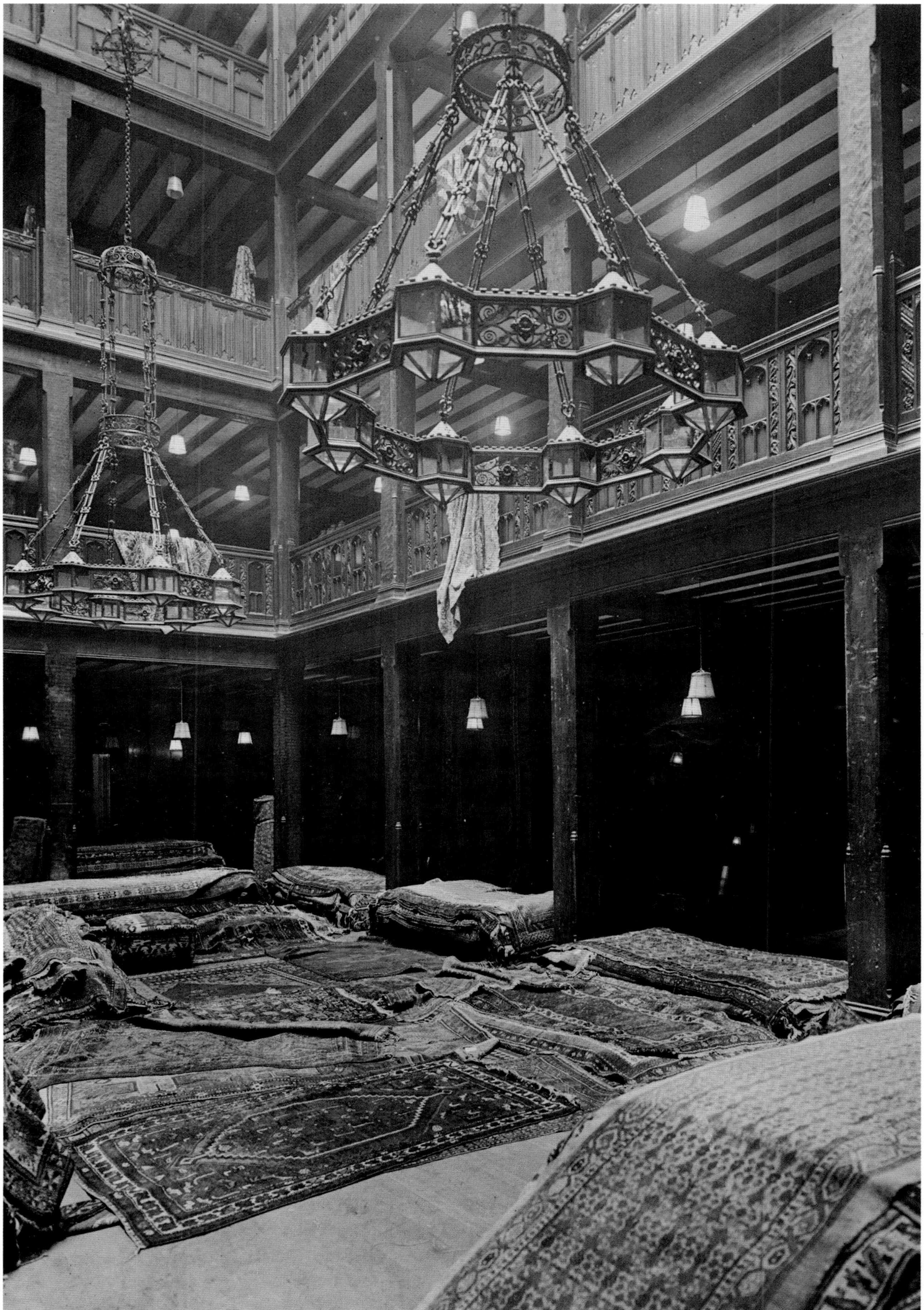

LEFT *The interior of the new Tudor Shop carpet department. The galleried atrium was ideal for displaying large rugs and carpets and provided a focal point for the new building.*

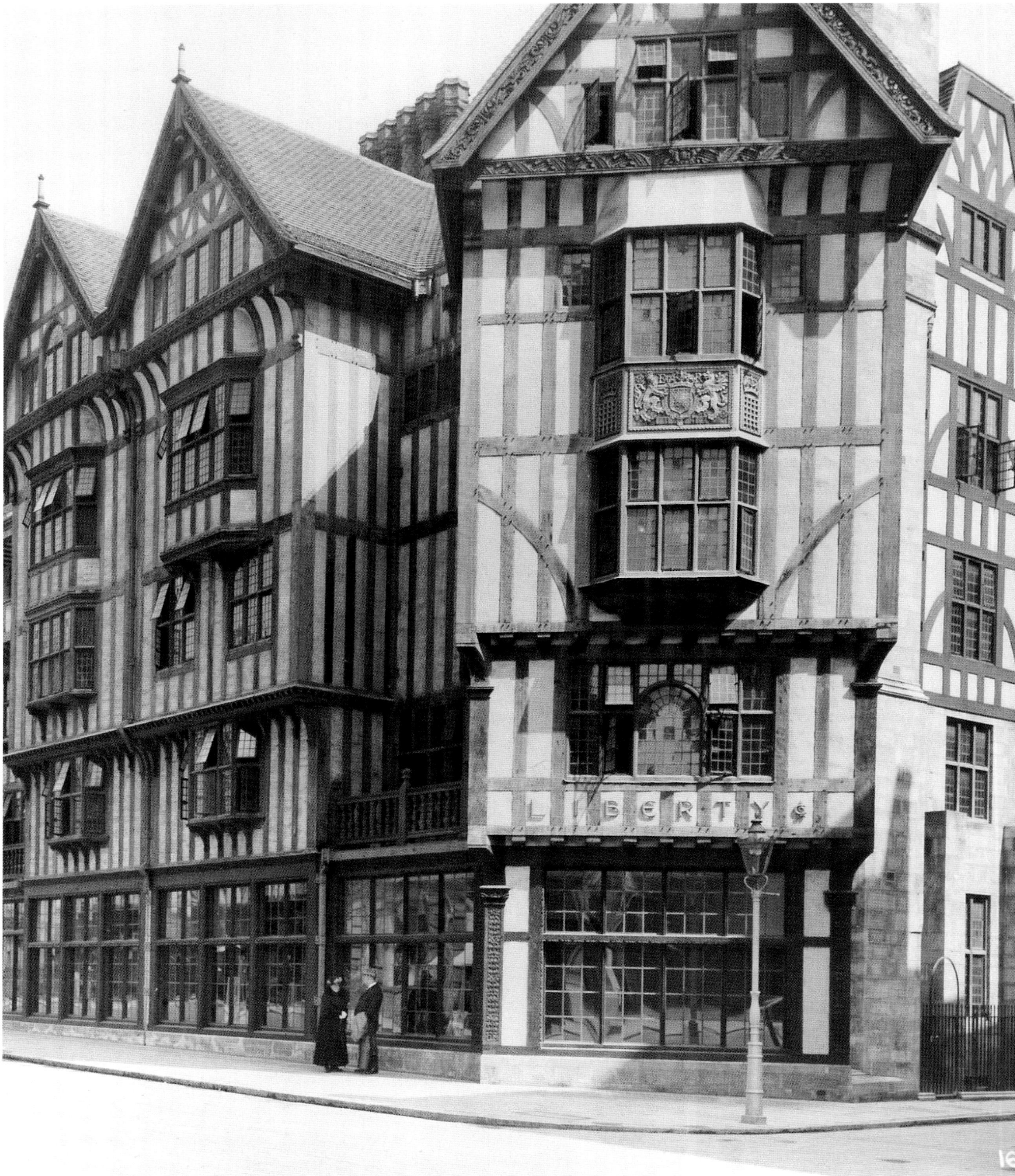
LIBERTY

THE TUDOR SHOP

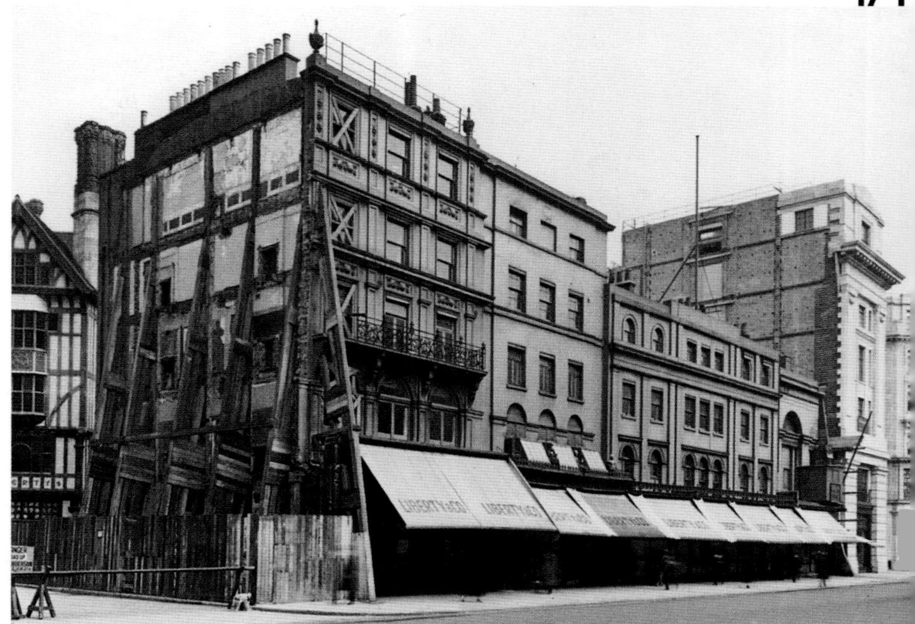

ABOVE *An image of the rebuilding work in progress from the early 1920s, with the partial demolition of the Georgian houses on Regent Street, the completed Tudor Shop to the left and the new south-end bay of East India House to the right.*

When passers-by turn a corner on Regent Street, a striking half-timbered building, that black-and-white landmark that is Liberty's "Tudor Shop" catches the eye. With its dramatic dark beams and gabled windows, the architecture recalls the Elizabethan period, but it was in fact built and first opened its doors to customers in 1924, a bright example of the mock-Tudor style.

The fashion for mock-Tudor or Tudor revival had started in the middle of the nineteenth century and became all the more fashionable in the first decades of the twentieth century, with its reassuringly "truly English" style. It was influenced by the Arts and Crafts movement in its emphasis on traditional craftsmanship and simple, historical forms.

Arthur Liberty had always had a particular liking for the Tudor period style, with its allusion to the merchant adventurers of the time and ancient guilds of craftsmen. He had died in 1917, but Liberty's board of directors, under its chairman Ivor Stewart-Liberty, no doubt aware of the founder's affinity for the style and strongly influenced by the director John Llewellyn, responded to the Crown Estate-mandated remodelling of Regent Street with the decision to build two buildings in two very different styles. The design of the site on Regent Street, a Crown property, adhered out of necessity to the Crown Estate's very strict regulations and was built as a convex classicistic façade in Portland stone, with Ionic pilasters and a large decorative frieze. The other premises just behind Regent Street, however, which had been slowly acquired over the years, were to be designed in an almost provocatively different fashion as a homage to the Tudor style, which Ivor Stewart-Liberty described in a publication of the time as the "most genuinely English period of domestic architecture".

The Tudor Shop, like the East India House on Regent Street, was designed by the father and son architects Edwin Thomas and Edwin Stanley Hall. It was inspired by the famous Rows of Chester and built in accordance with the principles of the Arts and Crafts movement. Fittingly for the construction of a 'flagship' store, timbers from two nineteenth-century Royal Navy battleships, later training ships, the H.M.S. *Impregnable* and H.M.S. *Hindustan*, were used. It was a happy coincidence that one of the ships was the same length and height out of water as the planned building. The interior floors were made of the original deck timbers and were cleaned every night by ex-Royal Navy personnel.

A gabled roofline, Tudor chimneys, leaded bay windows, extensive fine carving around the windows and doors, as well as

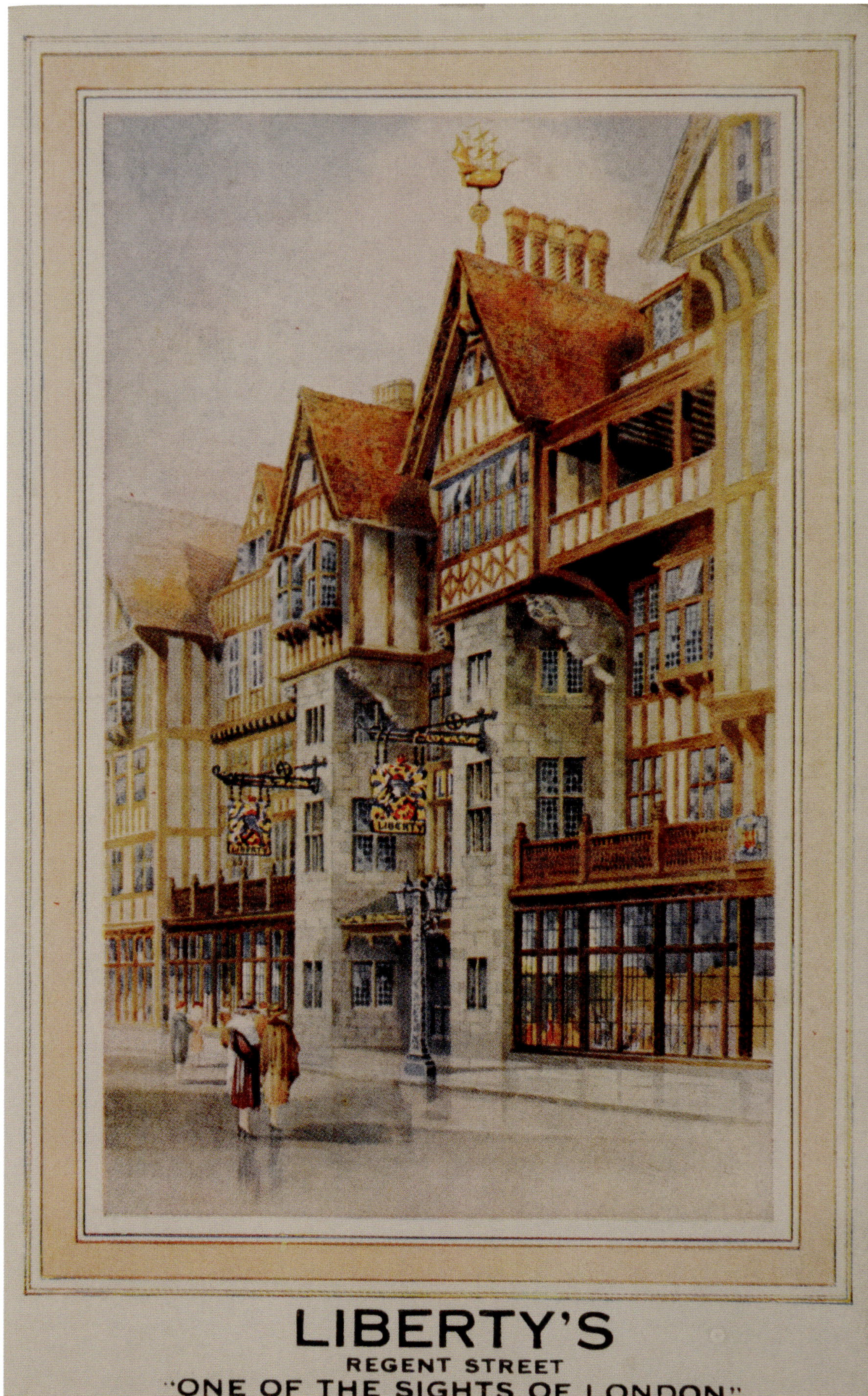

RIGHT *The new Tudor Shop was one of the earliest stores to be promoted as a destination in its own right, for both shoppers and tourists.*

“I was determined not to follow existing fashion but to create new ones”

ARTHUR LIBERTY

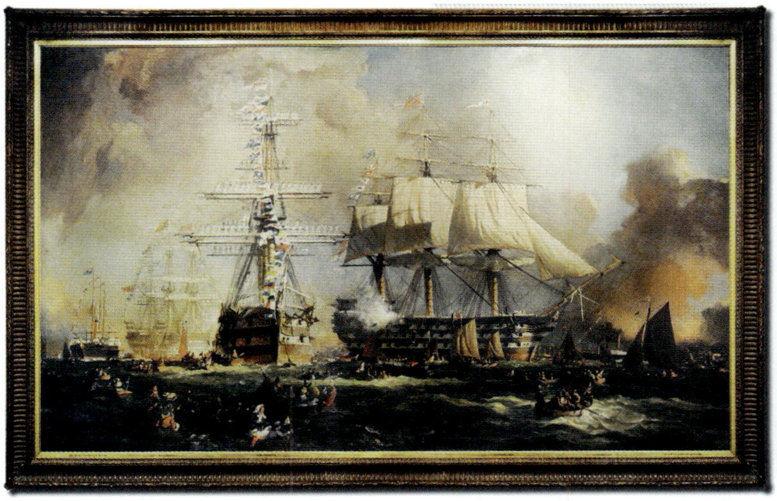

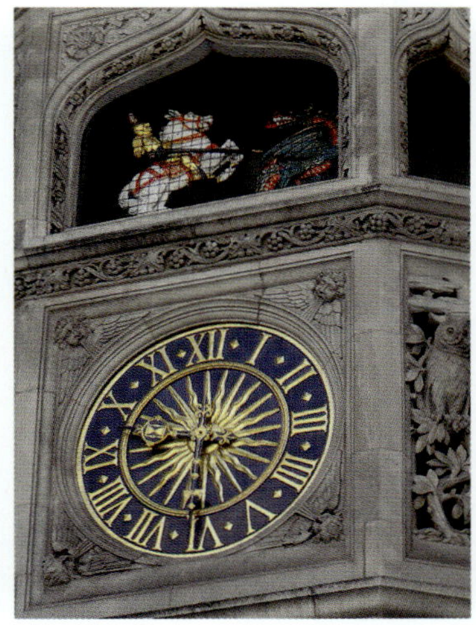

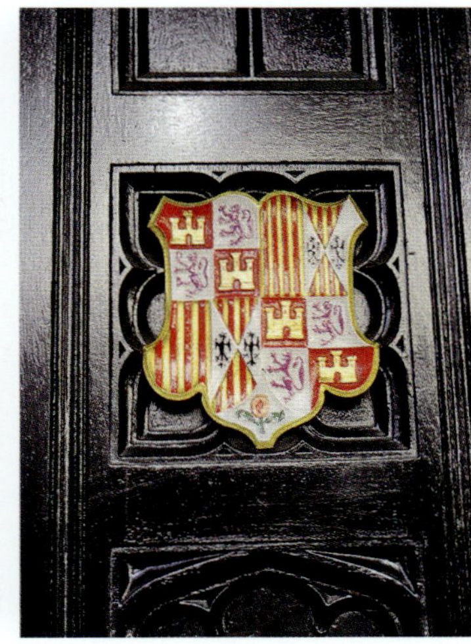

ABOVE LEFT *A 1968 seascape by Leslie A. Wilcox depicts H.M.S.* Impregnable *and H.M.S.* Hindustan, *the two nineteenth-century ships from which timber was plundered in order to build the Tudor Shop in 1924.*

ABOVE MIDDLE *A detail of the clock positioned over the main entrance to the Tudor Shop, erected in 1925. Depicting St George and the Dragon, it was based on the clock at Wells Cathedral in Somerset.*

ABOVE RIGHT *A section of carved panelling, with bright mock-heraldic shields decorated with castles and rampant-lion motifs, echoes the royal coat of arms and provides a vibrant contrast to the dark wooden panelling.*

the use of heraldic emblems and allusions to galleon ships, all combined to create the idiosyncratic charm of the Tudor Shop. The central gable was topped with a gilded weathervane in the model of the ship *The Mayflower*, while a deep relief carving of craftsmen at work was erected over the left side door to Great Marlborough Street. For one and a half years, over 20 carvers worked on the numerous wooden decorative elements. Many of the interior features of the shop were designed and carried out by Liberty’s own studios and workshops, serving as inspiration for customers and as advertising for Liberty’s interior design department.

The inside of the shop was, and still is, arranged around three light wells on four storeys, each surrounded by wood-panelled galleries and even sporting fireplaces, of which some remain to this day. In many ways, Liberty rejected the idea of the more horizontal open-plan American stores that were starting to be built around that time in London, opting instead for a more conservative yet highly individualistic look.

Light wells, for example, were expensive to build and took up a lot of precious floor space, but at the same time became a sign of luxury and of the traditional personal service that Liberty was proud to offer its customers. The design created a welcoming atmosphere ideally suited to its special merchandise, with small, intimate rooms to display its precious goods. As at Liberty’s former location at Chesham House, the wares could be presented in rooms similar in proportion to those in their customers’ homes.

Over the course of the following decades, various refits and minor revamps took place with the result that by the mid-1970s, most of the original panelling was hidden under several layers of more recent coverings. After the great success of the 1975 Centenary Exhibition at the Victoria and Albert Museum, and the corresponding celebrations at the store, it was recognized that the building’s iconic history clearly formed a significant part of the particular appeal of shopping at Liberty. As a result, the original wood panelling was restored to its former glory. Today, the Tudor Shop is a rare example of a store with surviving original features of early twentieth-century shop design.

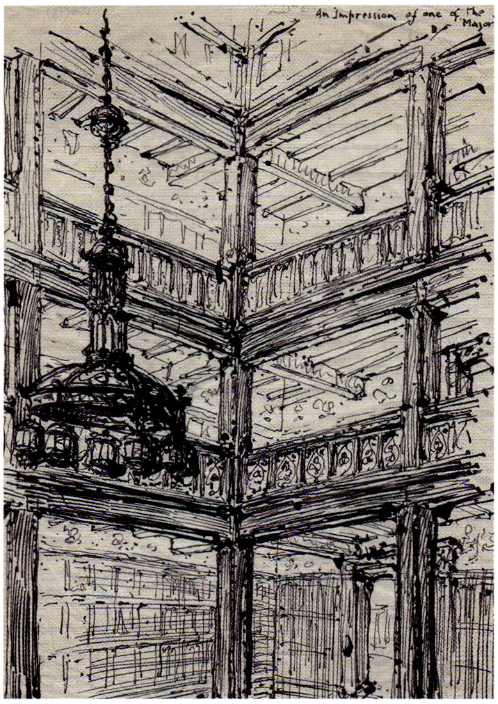

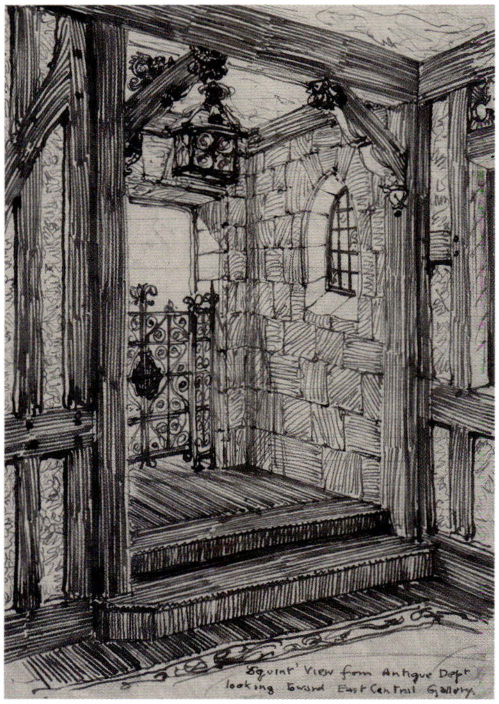

LEFT TO RIGHT *Pen and ink sketches from the 1930s, drawn by Liberty designer E. P. Roberts, depict various views of the new Tudor House interior, including the main galleried atrium at the heart of the shop and the country-house-style staircase and fireplace.*

BELOW *A true sense of the scale, harmony and coherence of style of the Tudor Shop can be seen in this present-day panoramic view of Liberty. The frontage is the same length and height as H.M.S.* Hindustan.

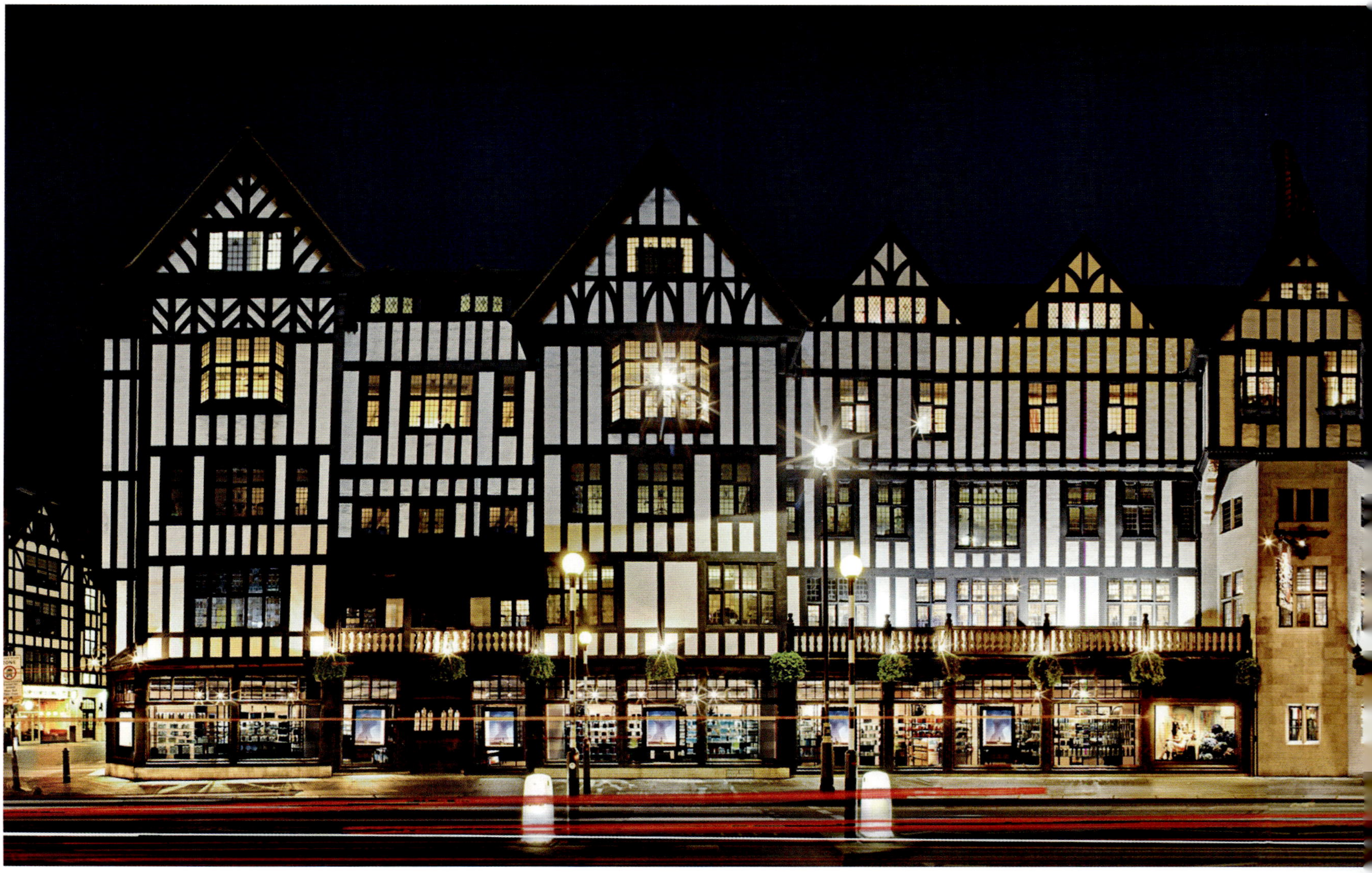

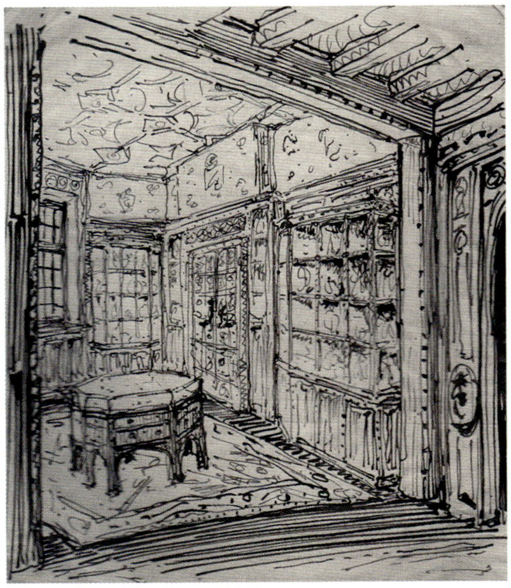

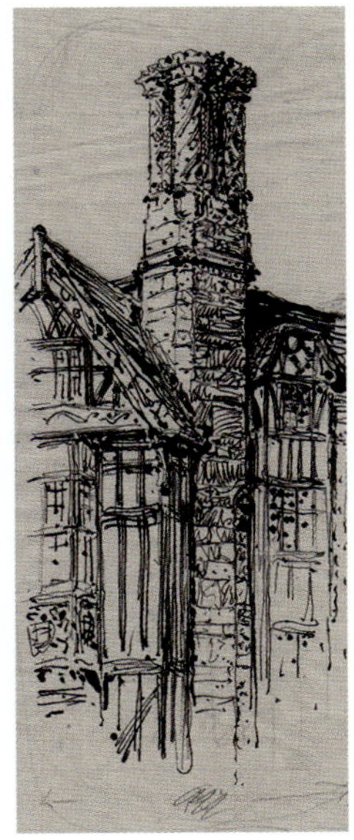

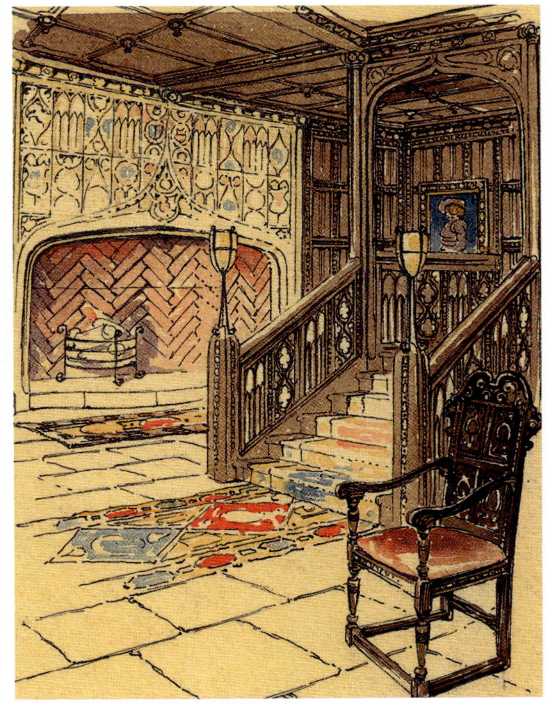

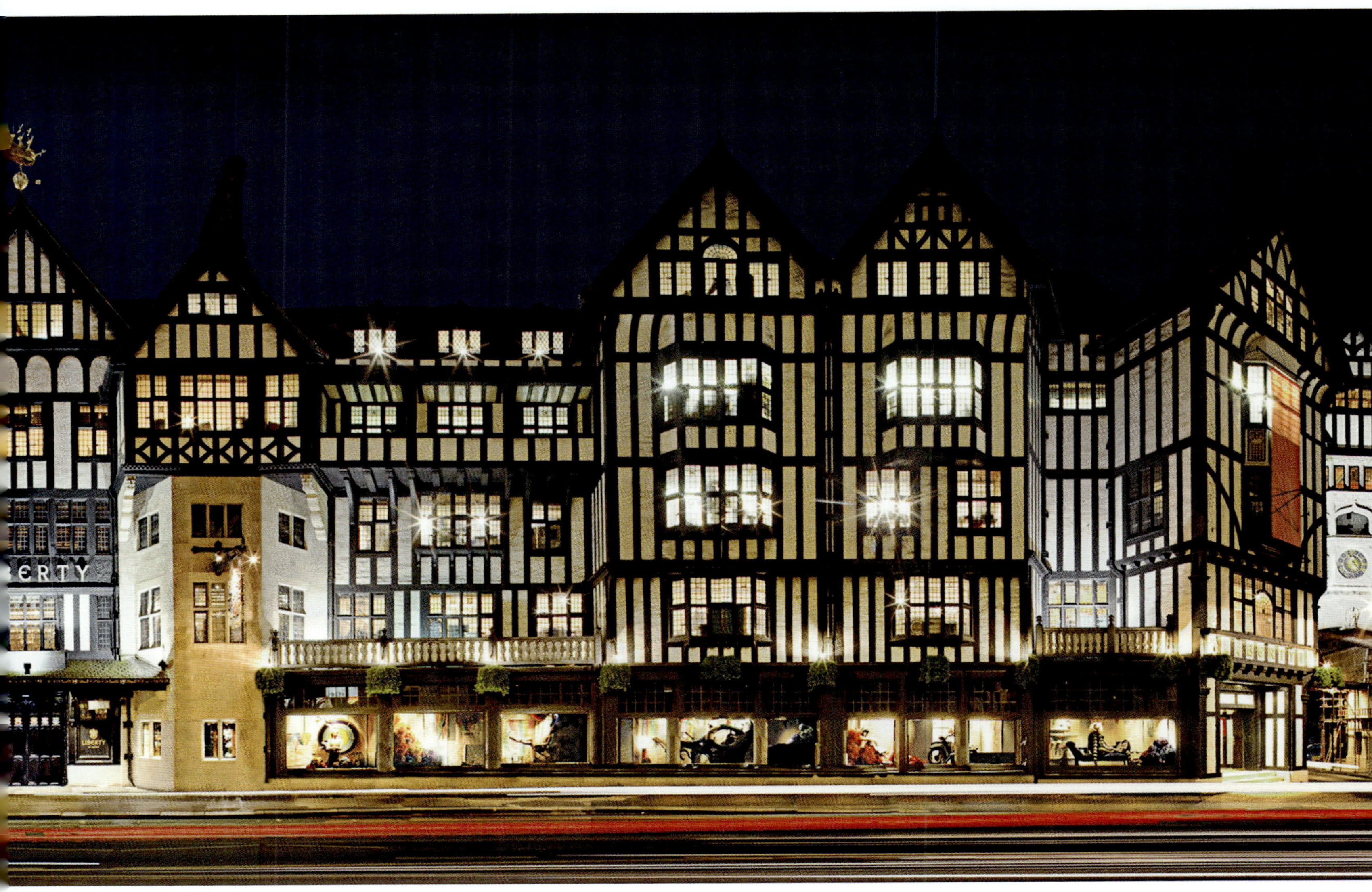
ERTY

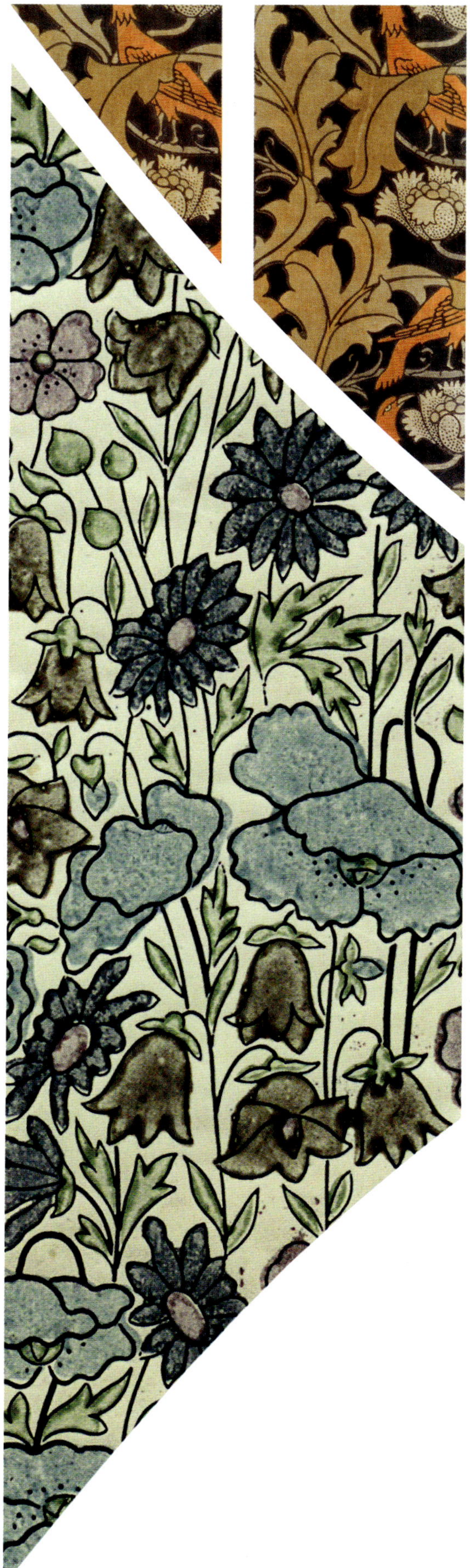

THE ART FABRICS

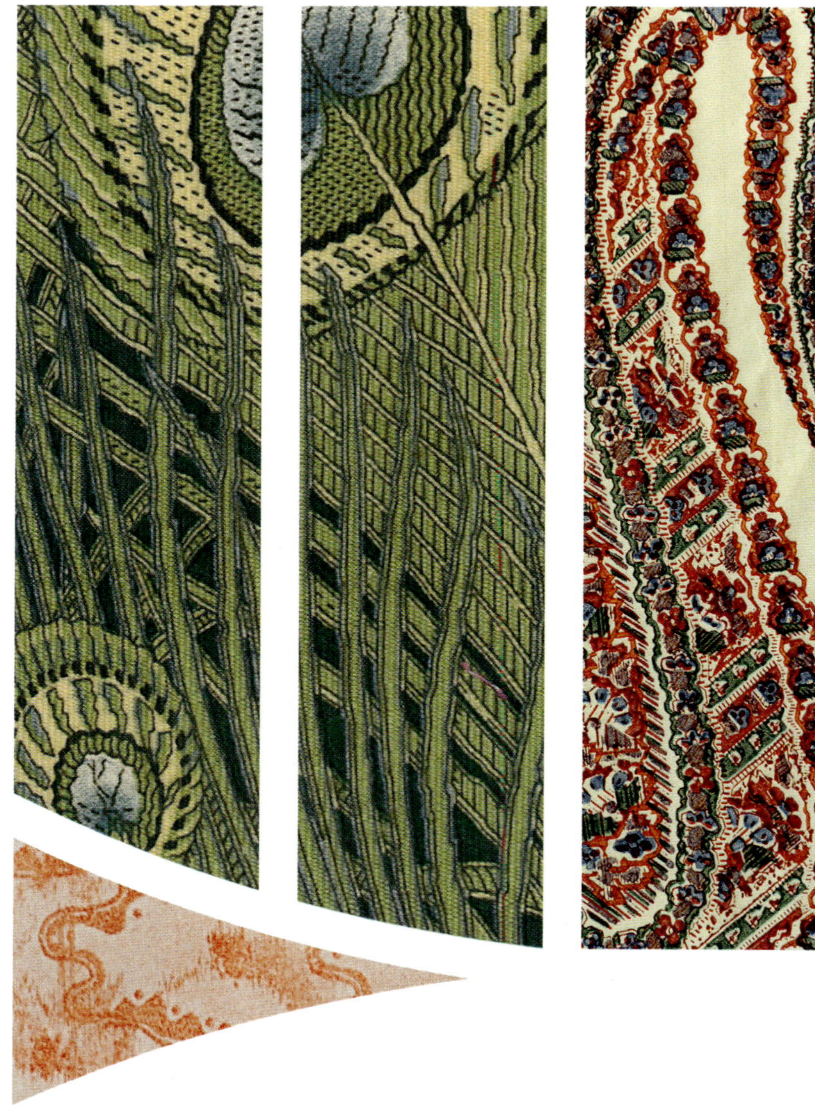

THIS PAGE
Various Liberty Art Fabric prints.

OPPOSITE
Illustration from the 1905 Dress & Decoration *handbook, the Iseult design, based on a fourteenth-century French evening gown.*

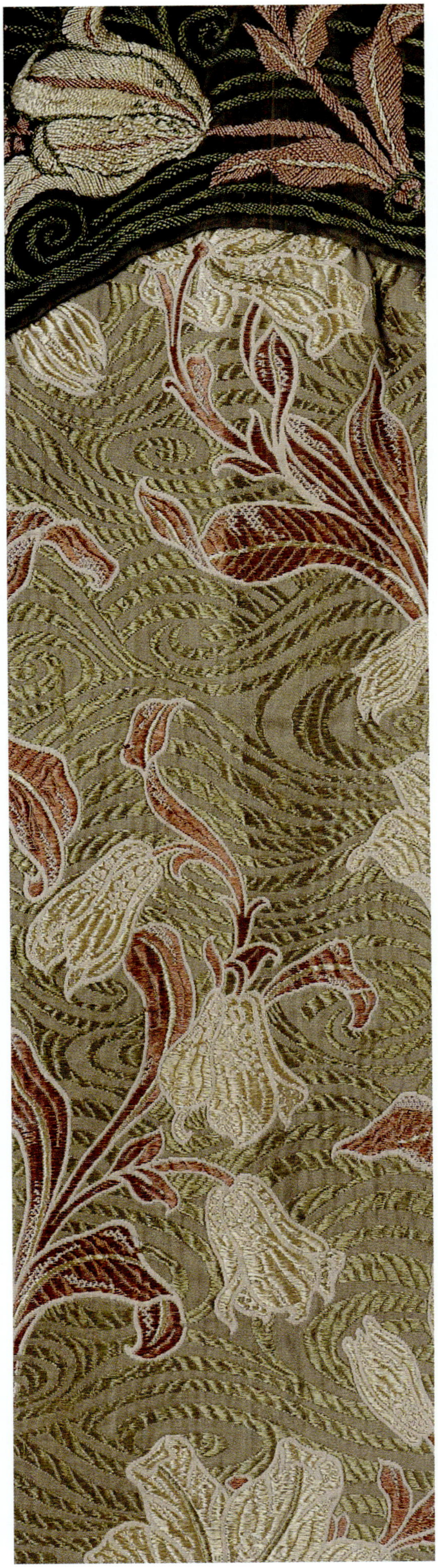
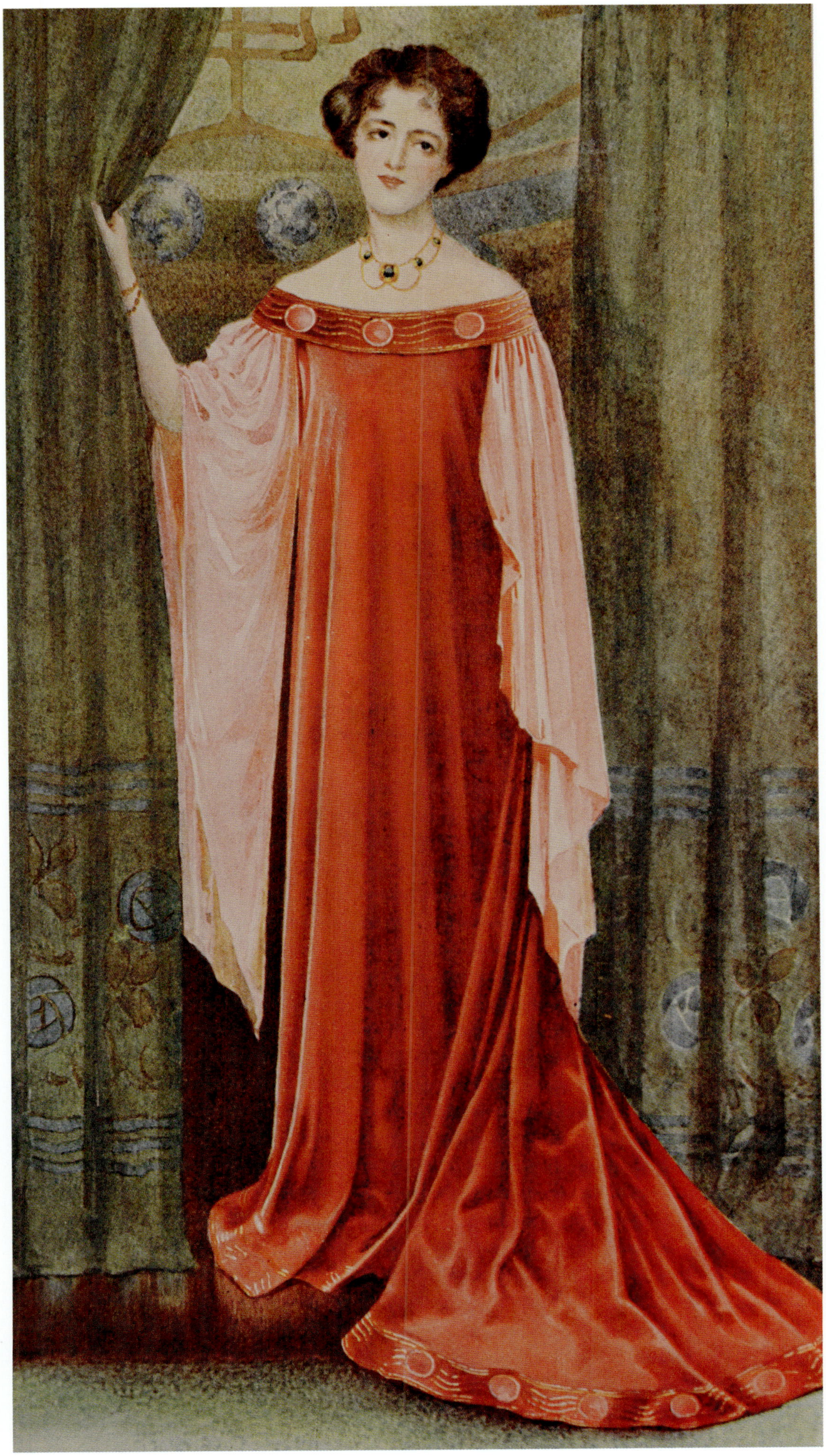

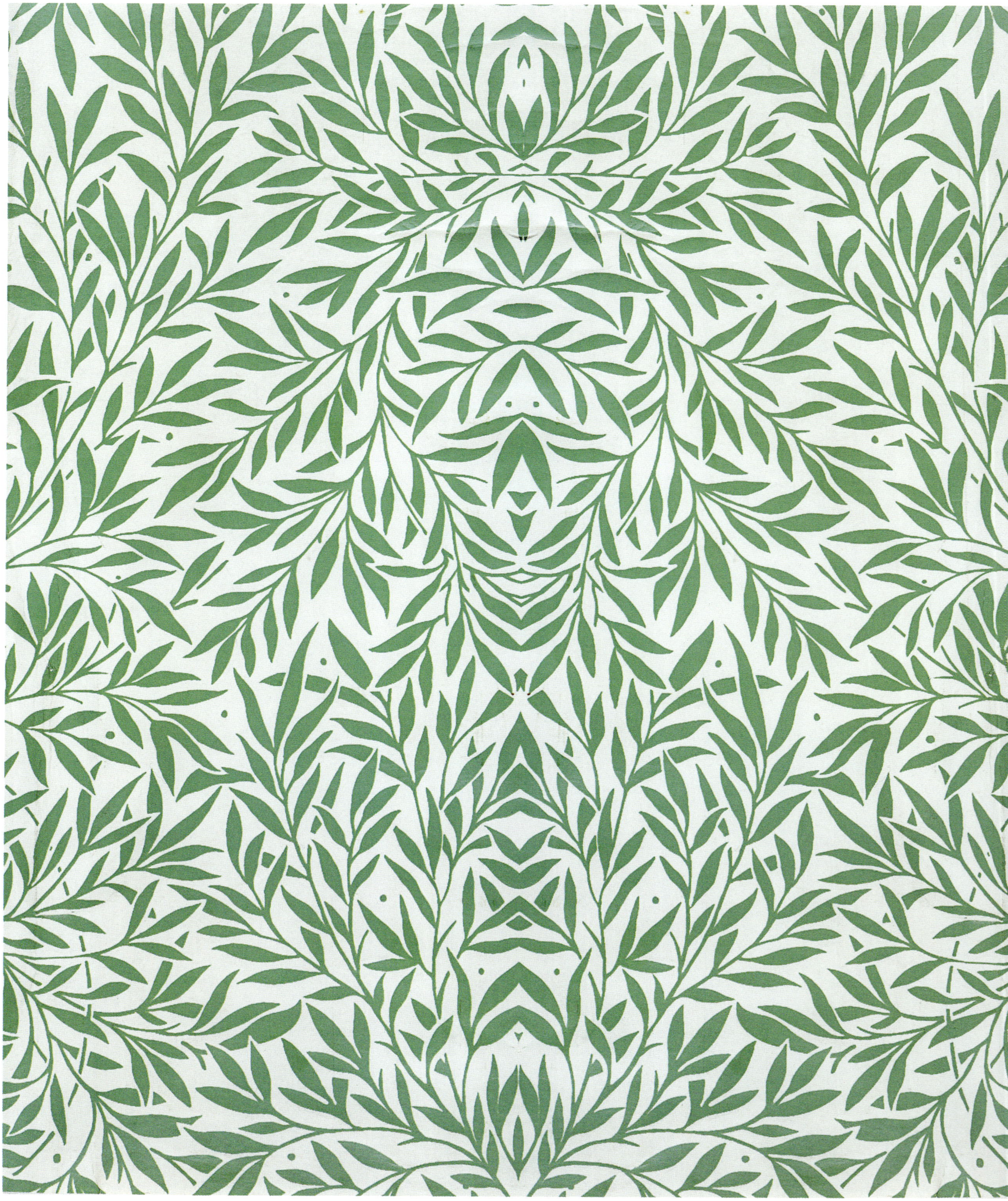

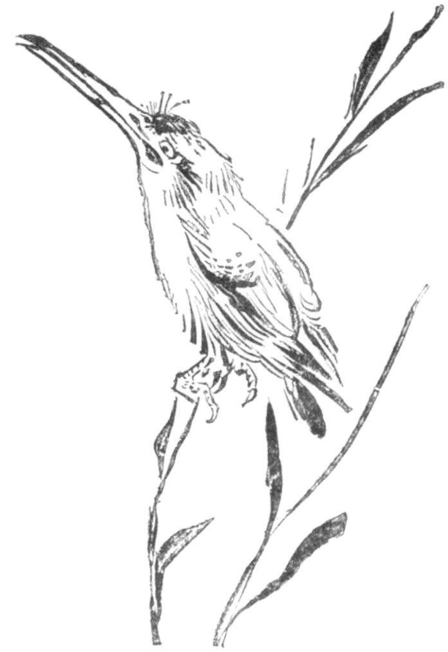

EASTERN INFLUENCES

In the latter part of the nineteenth century, when Arthur Liberty set out to build his design emporium, Britain experienced a renewed wave of Orientalism, a fervent taste for the exotic, and Liberty played a not inconsiderable role in furthering this trend. There had been a fashion for imported, mostly Indian, fabrics, particularly muslin and cashmere, from the late eighteenth century onwards, and a fascination for exotic cultures like China and their artefacts, particularly lacquer and porcelain, which had begun as far back as the seventeenth century, but this had been confined almost exclusively to aristocratic circles. In the mid-nineteenth century, renewed or intensified trading relationships with countries like India, Egypt and Japan, made the import of Oriental goods increasingly possible and, accelerated by the ever-increasing disposable income of the growing middle-classes, Orientalism turned into a full-blown craze in art and design in Victorian Britain, at the time the richest country in the world.

While the vogue for all things Eastern encompassed the crafts and arts of the Far East as well as the Near East and Africa, probably the greatest enthusiasm was aroused by objects from Asia – China, India and Japan. Among these, it was particularly Japan and its artefacts that held a particular fascination, and would prove a key influence for Victorian design – for artists, designers and consumers alike.

As a result of the Treaty of Edo in 1858, Japan opened up its market to trade after more than 200 years of self-enforced isolation, which promised new and mysterious objects for the Victorian fascination with the exotic. In 1862, the Japanese section at the International Exhibition, with over 600 exhibits consisting of artefacts and objects of daily use, stimulated an interest which would turn into a mania over the next few decades. It was the first time a substantial number of Japanese objects were shown in Britain, and, together with the unprecedented arrival of Japanese diplomats in Europe, the Japanese section became something of a sensation and was widely reported on in the press.

The exhibited artefacts made an enormous impression on many artists, architects and designers, and maybe on none more so than J. M. Whistler, E. W. Godwin and Christopher Dresser. These early devotees of the 'cult of Japan' would in turn be very influential in disseminating Japonism in late Victorian Britain. Japanese objects, as well as other Oriental goods, would be treasured for their rarity and romantic associations, for their beauty and artistic design, but also for their quality and handmade origin. The fascination with Eastern objects could be seen as a reaction to the mediocrity, and sometimes sheer ugliness, of the machine-produced everyday objects of the Industrial Age, and maybe even to the uniformity of life in an industrialized nation. Arthur Liberty, when he opened East India House in 1875, catered to this emerging trend and rapidly established his name as a leading specialist in Japanese and other Eastern goods. Less than one and a half years after the first customers had entered the little shop in Regent Street, E. W. Godwin described in an article in *The Architect* the fascinated buzz of customers waiting for a fresh delivery of Japanese fans at the new "Anglo-Japanese" store:

> *"There was quite a crowd when we arrived. A distinguished traveller had button-holed the obliging proprietor in one corner; a well-known baronet, waiting to do the same, was trifling with some feather dusting brushes; two architects of well-known names were posing an attendant in another corner with awkward questions; three distinguished painters with their wives blocked up the staircase; whilst a bevy of ladies filled up the floor space."*

Beautiful silks and other imported fabrics, Japanese fans and mattings, kimonos, folding screens, carpets and rugs, stools, blue-and-white porcelain and other ceramics, artefacts made of lacquer and metal, and various other mysterious curios and *objets d'art* were to be found in what Godwin called "an enchanting cave".

By first mesmerizing the tastemakers and trendsetters of the leisured classes with fine imported goods, as well as putting smaller objects within the reach of most buyers and producing, on a large scale, Anglo-Oriental wares that would go well with the exotic objects, Liberty brought the taste for all things Japanese to a much wider audience. Liberty was soon in the happy position of enjoying a reputation of exclusivity and progressiveness while drawing in an increasing number of middle-class shoppers.

At the height of the Japanese trend, Gilbert and Sullivan's opera *The Mikado*

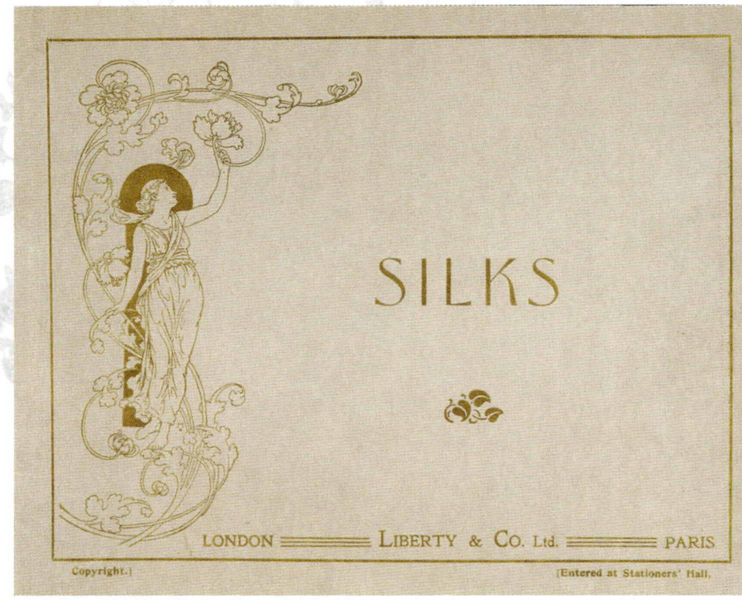

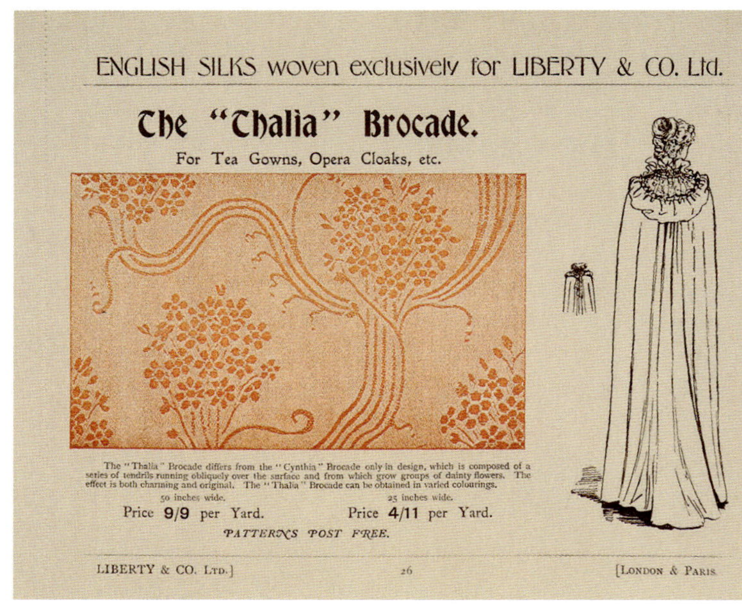

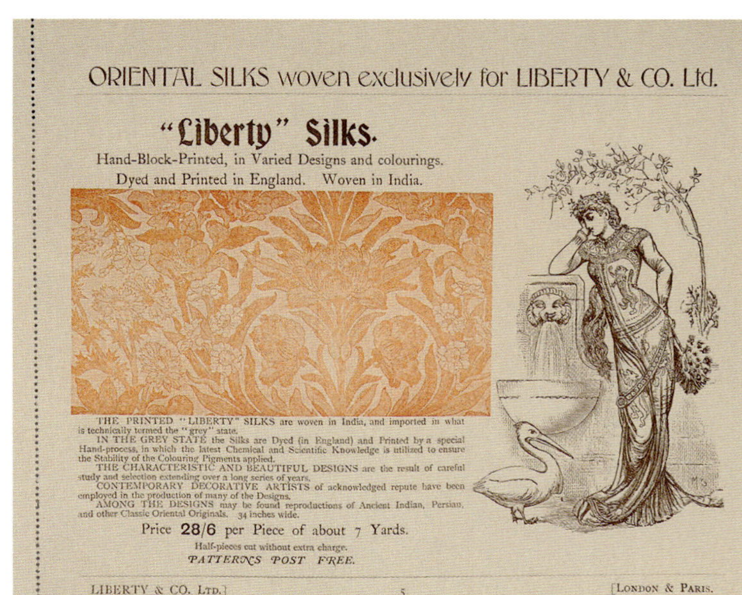

RIGHT *The cover and internal pages from the advertisement catalogue* Silks, Eastern and Western *(c. 1896) produced to publicize fabrics from the new Oriental Warehouse. The figures were drawn by J. Moyr Smith.*

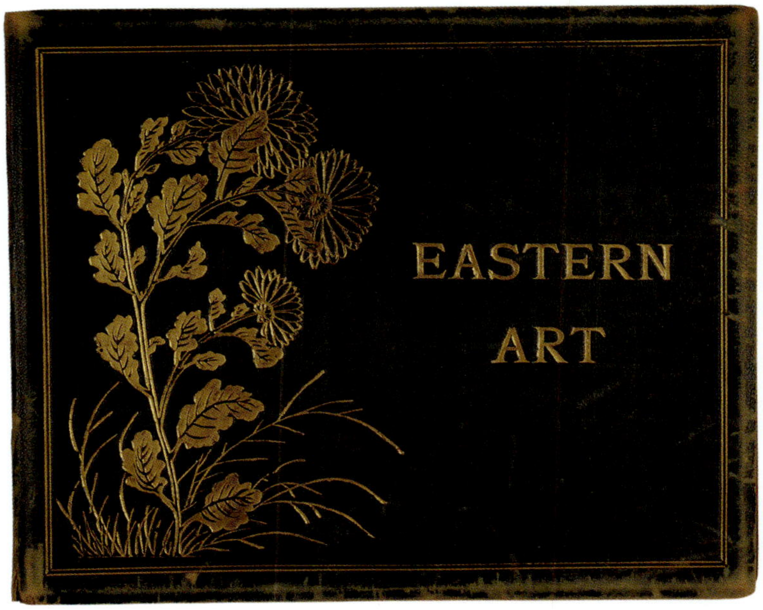

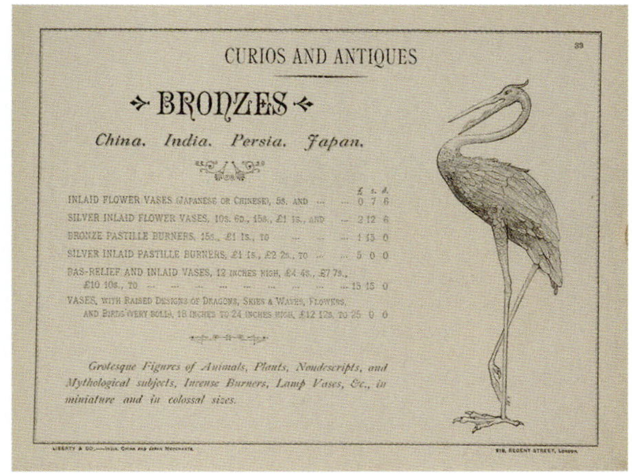

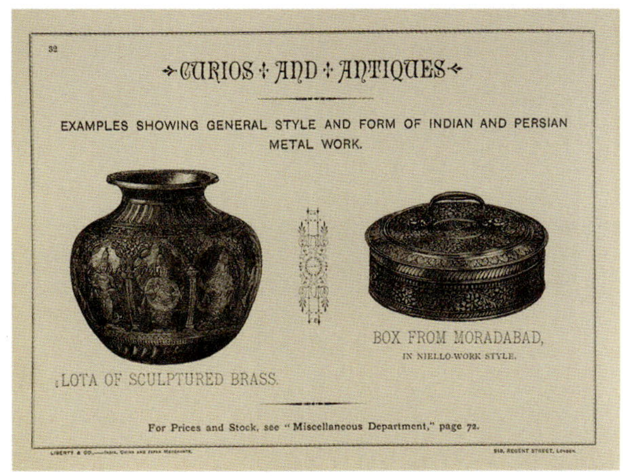

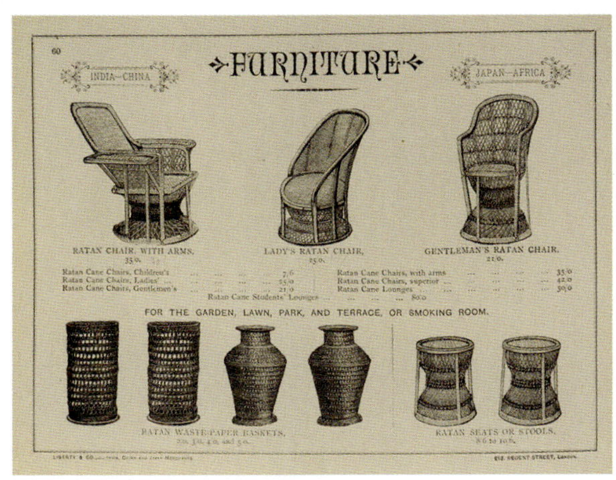

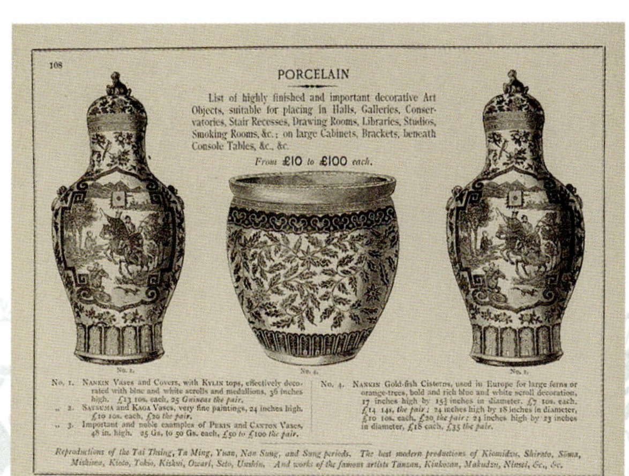

further popularized a romanticized image of Japan, and it was Liberty that designed the opulent costumes from original fabrics, brought back by a special envoy, who was sent to Japan in preparation for the task. In 1889–1890, Arthur Liberty, an enthusiast of Japanese art ever since the International Exhibition, travelled to Japan with his wife Emma and two professional contacts. He visited various manufacturers and gave talks on the art and industrial design of Japan, and the mutual influences of Japanese and Western design, both there and on his return to Britain.

The demand Arthur Liberty himself had created soon posed a problem, as the quality of the imported goods did not always stand up to the uses demanded in the West. He responded to this by cooperating with British manufacturers to produce designs heavily influenced by the Eastern originals. By the end of the century, Liberty offered all the paraphernalia that any discerning member of society needed to suggest that they were cultured connoisseurs of Eastern art and devotees of the Aesthetic movement.

ABOVE AND RIGHT *Liberty produced lavishly illustrated catalogues to advertize their products, including this* Eastern Art *catalogue, c. 1881. Shown here are antique Chinese and Japanese bronzes, Persian metalware, and chairs and porcelain from the Far and Near East.*

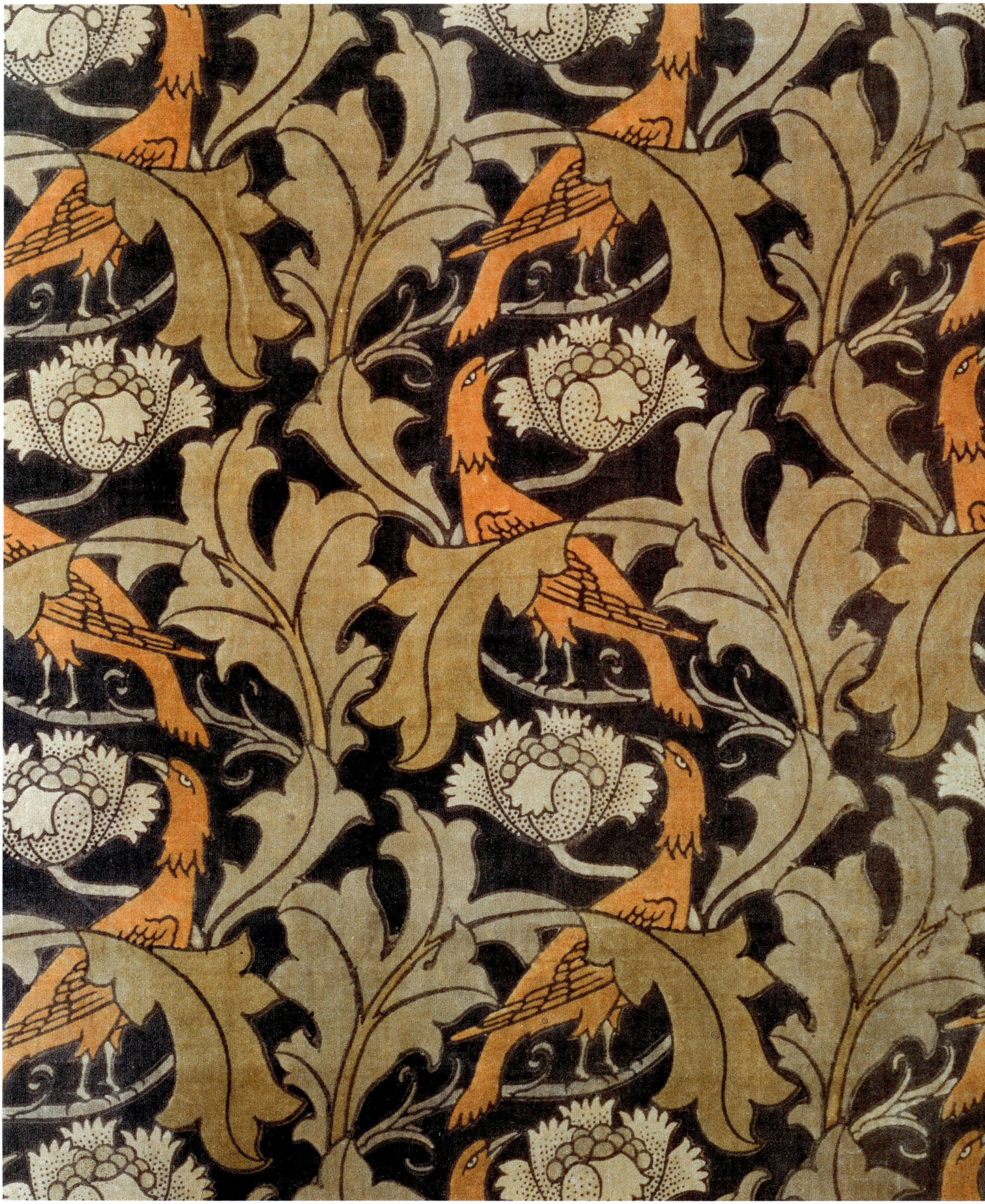

"Liberty is the chosen resort of the artistic shopper"

OSCAR WILDE

THE AESTHETIC MOVEMENT

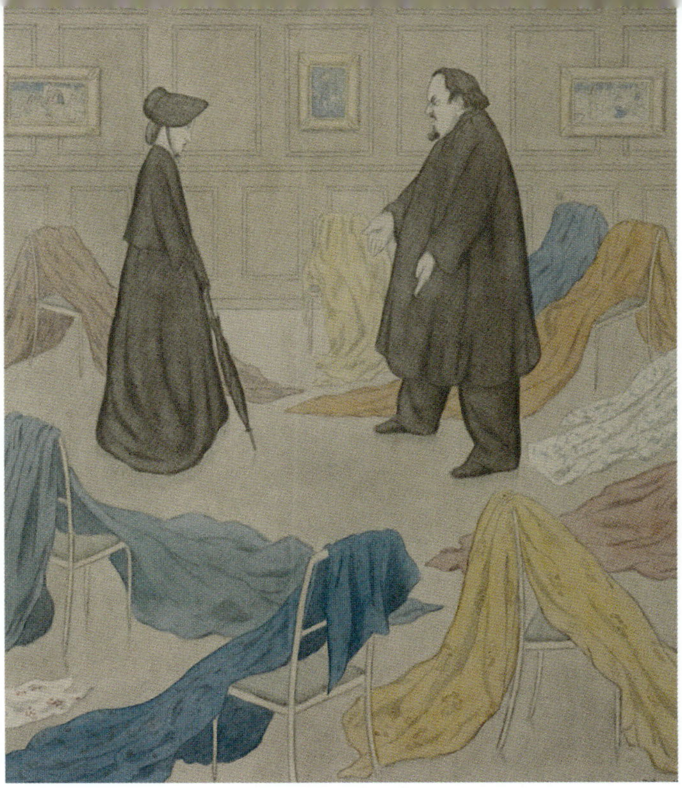

ABOVE *A satirical painting by Max Beerbohm from 1917 depicts the artist Dante Gabriel Rossetti attempting to persuade his reluctant sister to exchange her plain black "pew-opener" garb for livelier Liberty fabrics.*

Aestheticism was an eclectic art movement in literature as well as the visual arts – and to its critics it was, above all, a fashionable world view and decadent lifestyle – that developed in Britain between the 1860s and 1890s. Its unifying principle was the idea of "art for art's sake" which, when applied to the decorative arts, translated into the predominance of beauty and the artistic above all other considerations. For inspiration, the Aesthetic movement drew on an eclectic range of sources, from classical Greece and the Gothic style of medieval Europe to arts and crafts from the Middle and Far East, and Japan in particular. Its main exponents were considered to be the artist J. M. Whistler, the poet and aesthete par excellence Oscar Wilde and the celebrated Shakespearean actress Ellen Terry. All were much admired but also lavishly ridiculed for their attitude, lifestyle and aesthetic attire. Architects and designers, such as Thomas Jeckyll and E. W. Godwin in particular, worked towards a refined and artistic design language, the latter, for example, decorating Wilde's house.

Hand in hand with the Japanese craze, Aestheticism deeply affected Victorian interior design, and the name of Liberty was, for the duration of the trend, closely associated with the fashionably aesthetic, both in interiors and dress fabrics. Benefitting from his closeness to all the top names of Aestheticism and Japonism, Arthur's East India House essentially became a one-stop opportunity to acquire all the hallmarks of an "artistic" way of living.

It was at "the most progressive tradesman in Regent Street" (a quote from *The Furniture Gazette* in 1878) where discerning customers could buy blue-and-white porcelain, all-important Japanese fans and folding screens, peacock feathers (in themselves the emblem of Aestheticism) and, last but not least, the soft and silky fabrics in fashionable "Art" colours that were essential to do up a room artistically. The fabrics sold in enormous quantities and the draperies were often decorated and held up with Japanese fans. That an interest in the artistic or aesthetic style of decoration became a widespread phenomenon rather than the hobby of an elite few was due also to an increasing number of middle- and upper-middle-class consumers in late Victorian Britain who wanted to express their individuality, as well as status, through fashionable and cultured interiors of their houses – conspicuous consumption at its most obvious. They were guided in this consumption by Oscar Wilde, the undisputed prince of aesthetes. One of the subjects on Wilde's American lecture

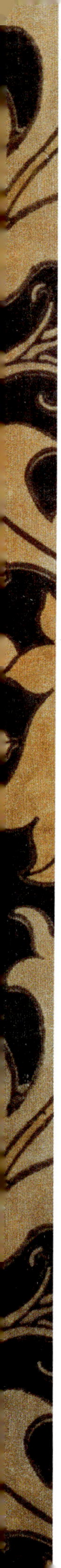

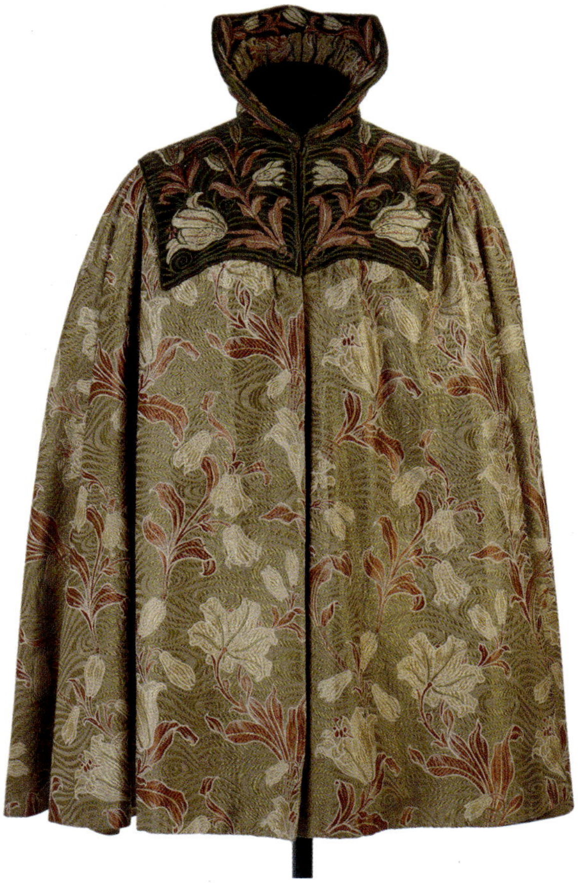

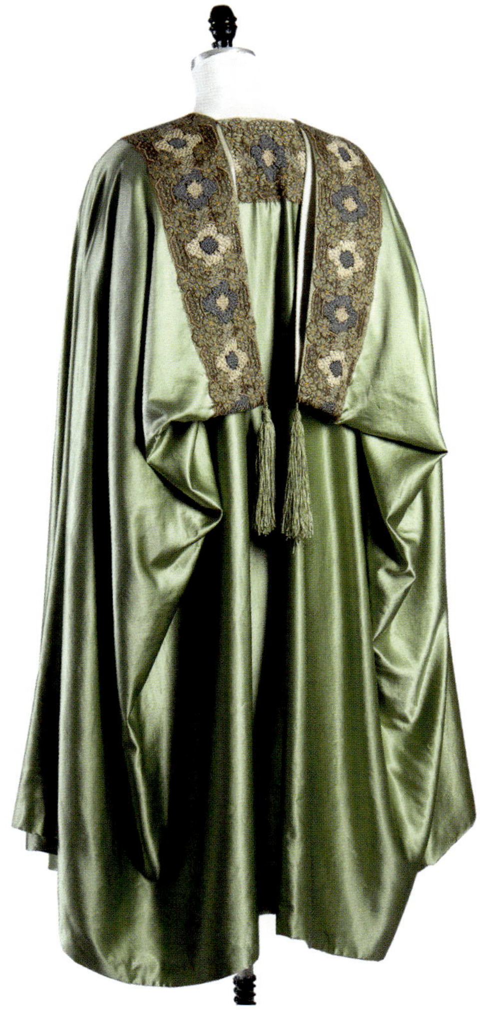

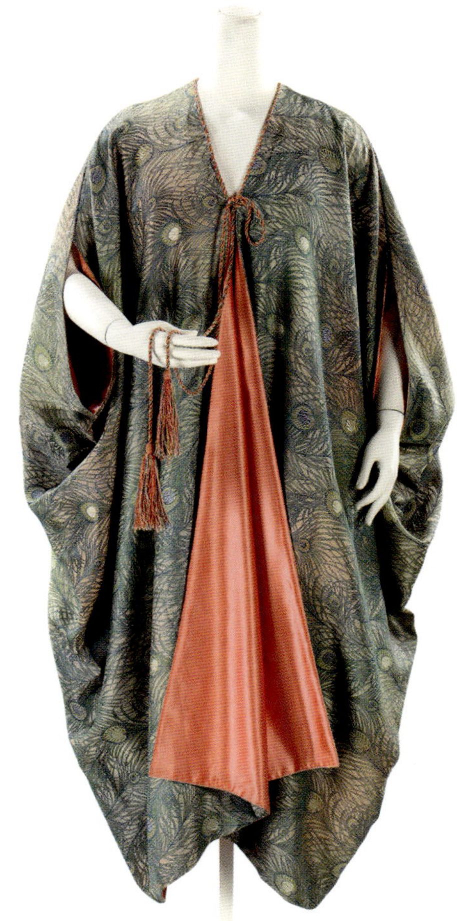

ABOVE LEFT *A cape fashioned from heavy floral brocade Liberty fabric from the late nineteenth century, when the Aesthetic movement was at its height, in the preferred colour palette of "greenery yallery".*

ABOVE MIDDLE *A sea-green silk satin evening cape from 1904 from Liberty, with silk-thread appliqué panels.*

ABOVE RIGHT *A dramatic draped evening coat styled like a medieval gown, c. 1910–1915, in a silk jacquard featuring Liberty's signature peacock feather design.*

tour was "The House Beautiful", and his discourses on taste and decoration proved to be fantastic publicity for Liberty, both in America and in Britain.

The Aesthetic movement and its most fervent devotees were the object of much witty ridicule. George du Maurier had begun his brilliant caricature of the aesthetic "crowd" in the satirical magazine *Punch* in 1877. While it mocked the foppish posturing of aesthetes producing nothing more than sentiment and conversation, it also brought the whole phenomenon to a much wider audience.

In 1881, Gilbert and Sullivan produced their comic opera *Patience, or Bunthorne's Bride*, a very contemporary satire of Aestheticism and its main apostles, assumed by many to be Whistler and Wilde. In a superb publicity coup, Liberty provided the fabrics for this and many other Gilbert and Sullivan operas, and in the operas' programmes Liberty promoted their involvement with prominent advertisements for Liberty Art Fabrics. In an article in the *Daily Chronicle* of 1913, called "The House of Liberty and its Founder", Arthur Liberty later said of the Aesthetic movement:

> *"From the first to the last I was closely associated with that tendency which unfortunately overreached itself, mainly owing to the eccentricities of those who took it up. I felt I was rather 'in it' then and I always took a box for the first night of a Gilbert and Sullivan Opera – for most of which I supplied the costumes."*

Towards the mid-1890s, criticism of the perceived decadence of the Aesthetic movement's most famous followers intensified, and after Oscar Wilde was put on trial and sentenced to prison for homosexuality, Aestheticism lost its momentum and essentially petered out. With his finely tuned antennae sensing a change in taste, Liberty had by then already moved on to create and establish a new style in furniture, metalware, interior design and textiles.

OPPOSITE *Primarily an architect, C. F. A. Voysey was also a distinguished pattern designer. This floral design dates from 1889.*

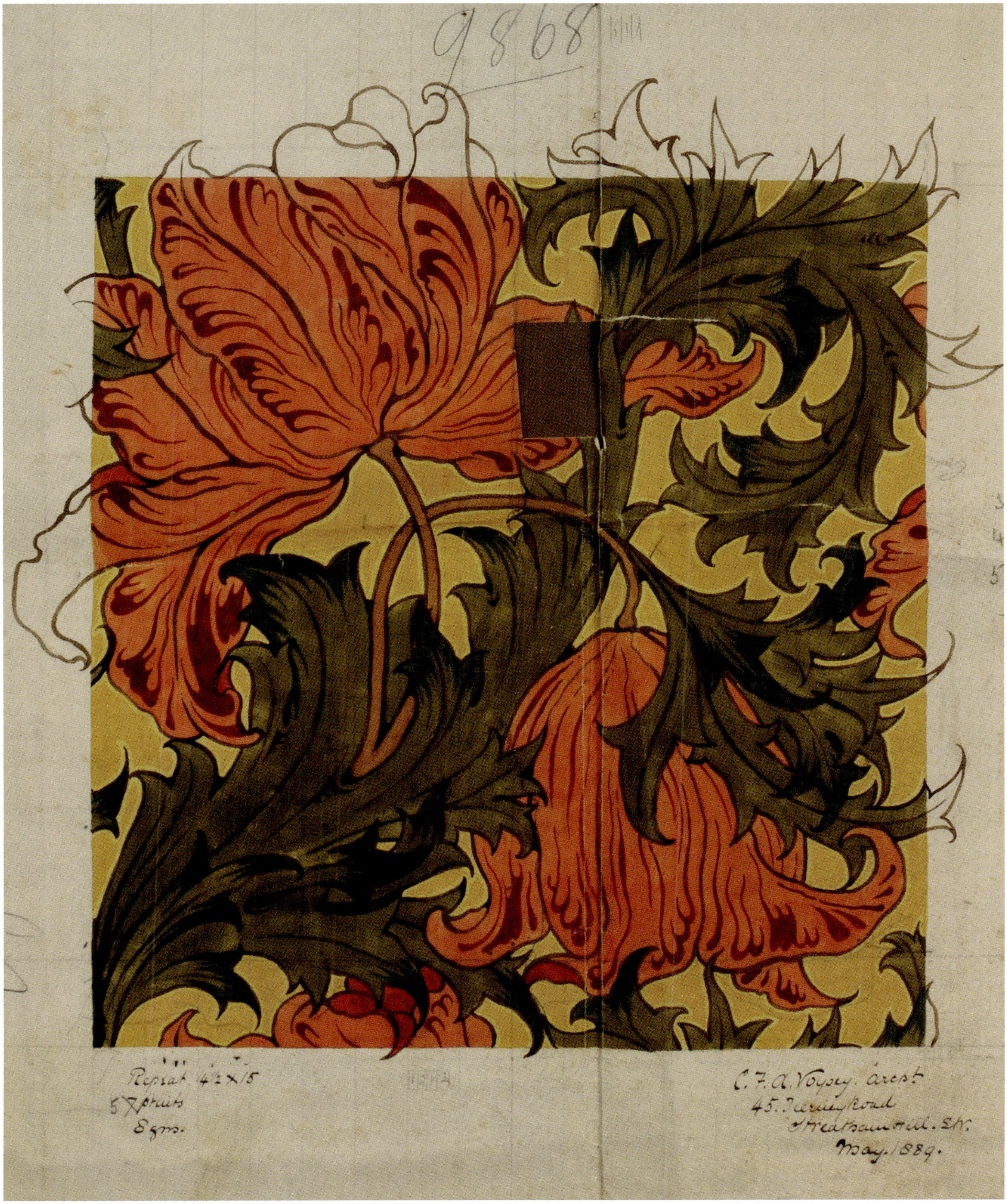
9868
Repeat. 14½ × 15
5 X prints
8 gns.
C.F.A. Voysey. arch
Streatham Hill. S.W.
May. 1889.

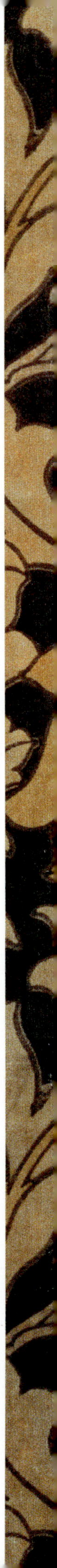

ART FABRIC CARDS, C. 1918
Advertisements for Liberty Art Fabrics and Furniture showrooms, which appeared on programmes for Gilbert and Sullivan operas.

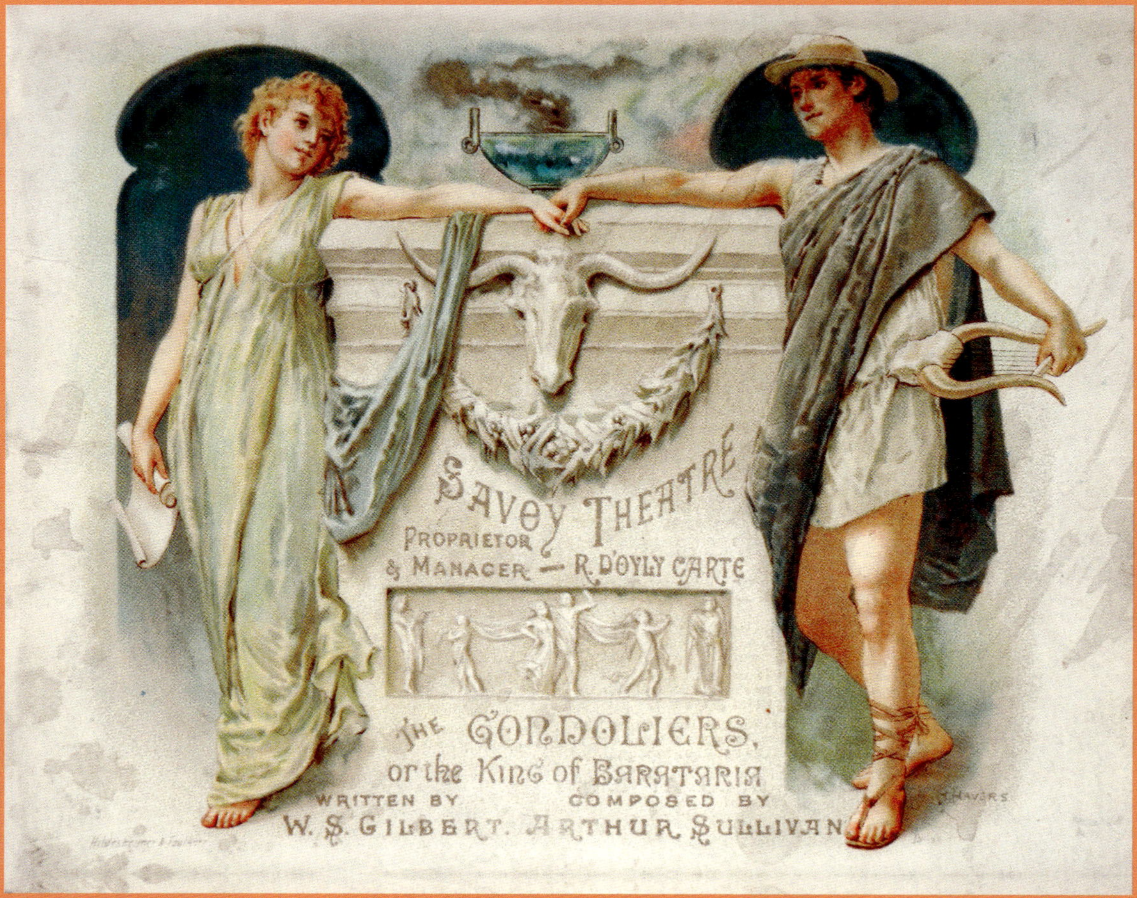

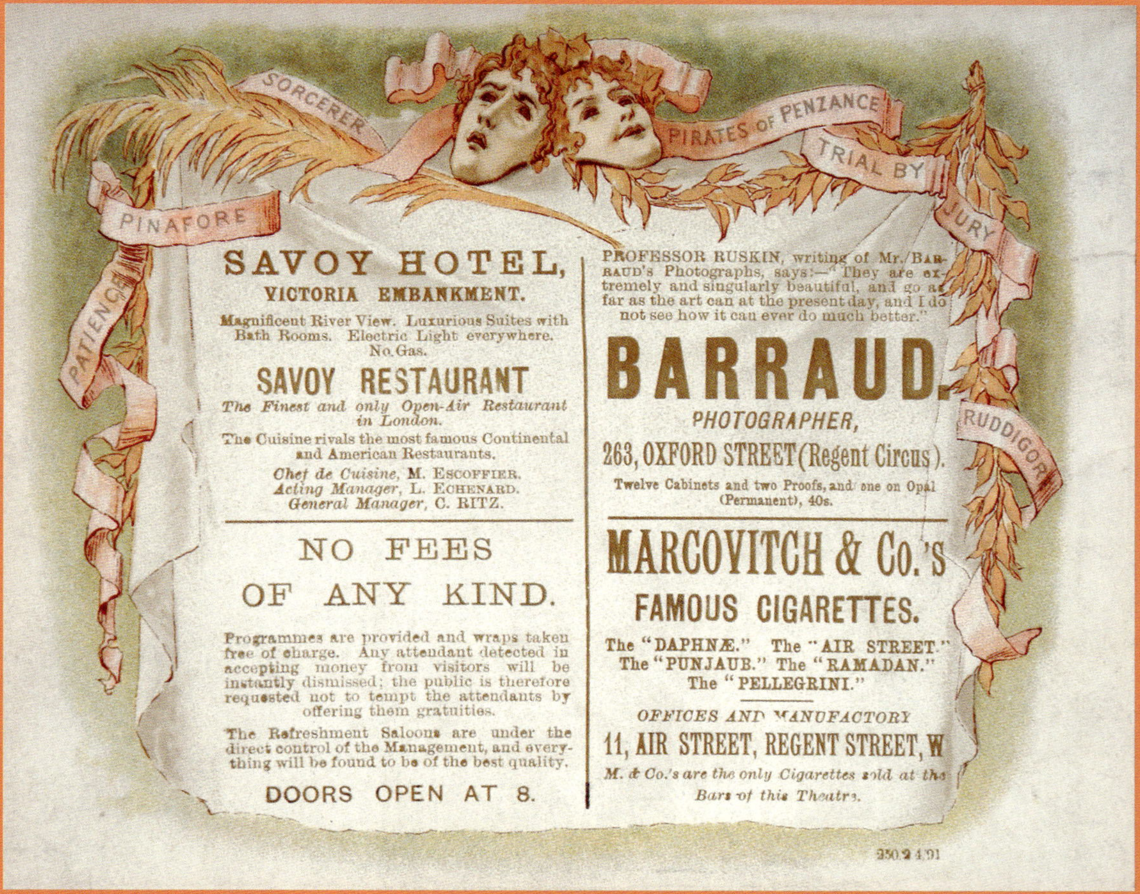

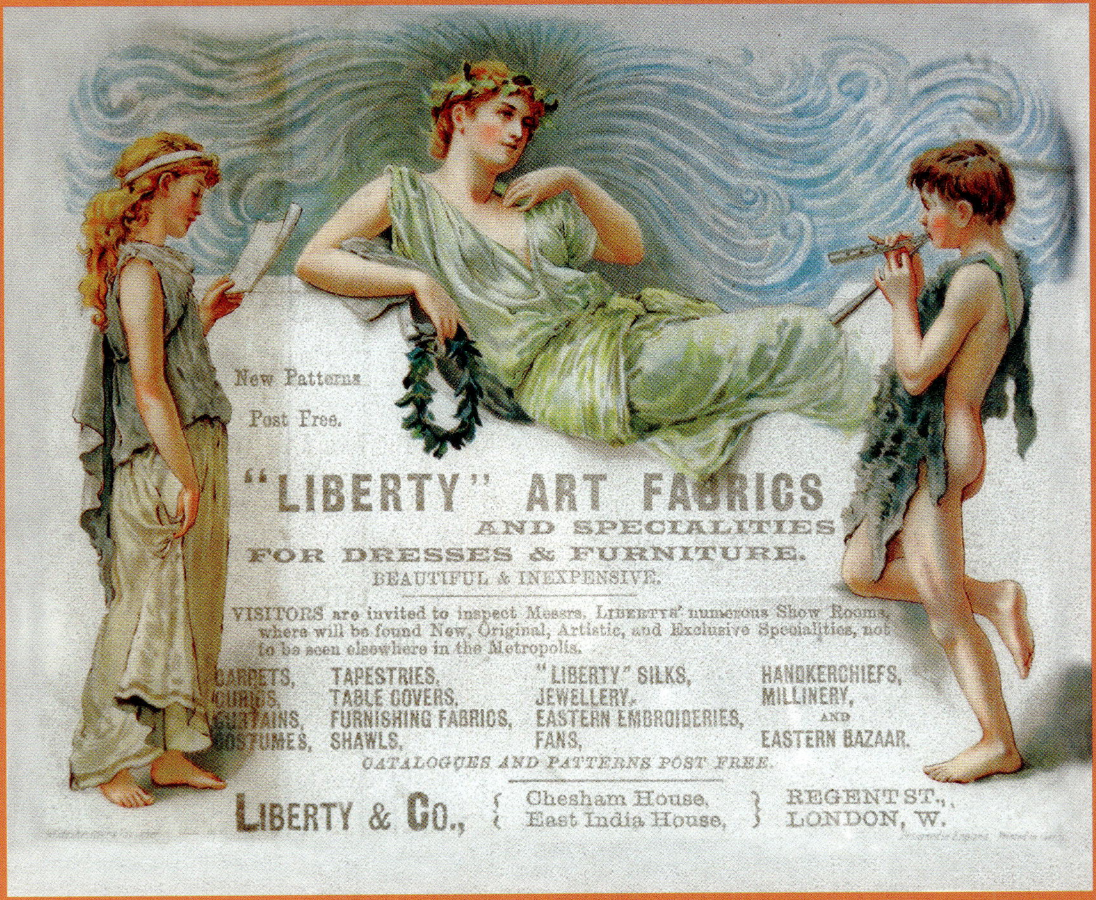
New Patterns
Post Free.
"LIBERTY" ART FABRICS
AND SPECIALITIES
FOR DRESSES & FURNITURE.
BEAUTIFUL & INEXPENSIVE.
VISITORS are invited to inspect Messrs. LIBERTYS' numerous Show Rooms, where will be found New, Original, Artistic, and Exclusive Specialities, not to be seen elsewhere in the Metropolis.
TAPESTRIES,
TABLE COVERS,
FURNISHING FABRICS,
SHAWLS,
"LIBERTY" SILKS,
JEWELLERY,
EASTERN EMBROIDERIES,
FANS,
HANDKERCHIEFS,
MILLINERY,
AND
EASTERN BAZAAR.
CATALOGUES AND PATTERNS POST FREE.
LIBERTY & Co.,
Chesham House,
East India House,
REGENT ST.,
LONDON, W.

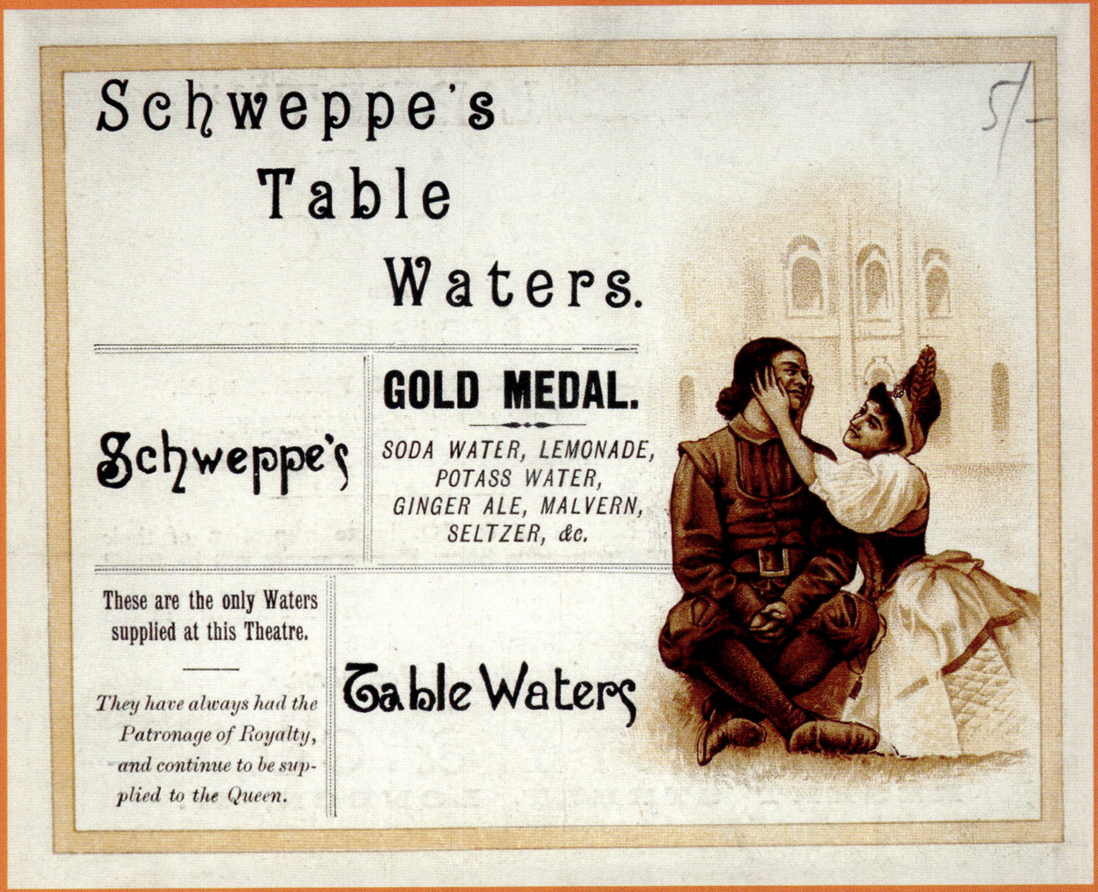
Schweppe's
Table
Waters.
5/-
Schweppe's
GOLD MEDAL.
SODA WATER, LEMONADE,
POTASS WATER,
GINGER ALE, MALVERN,
SELTZER, &c.
These are the only Waters supplied at this Theatre.
They have always had the Patronage of Royalty, and continue to be supplied to the Queen.
Table Waters

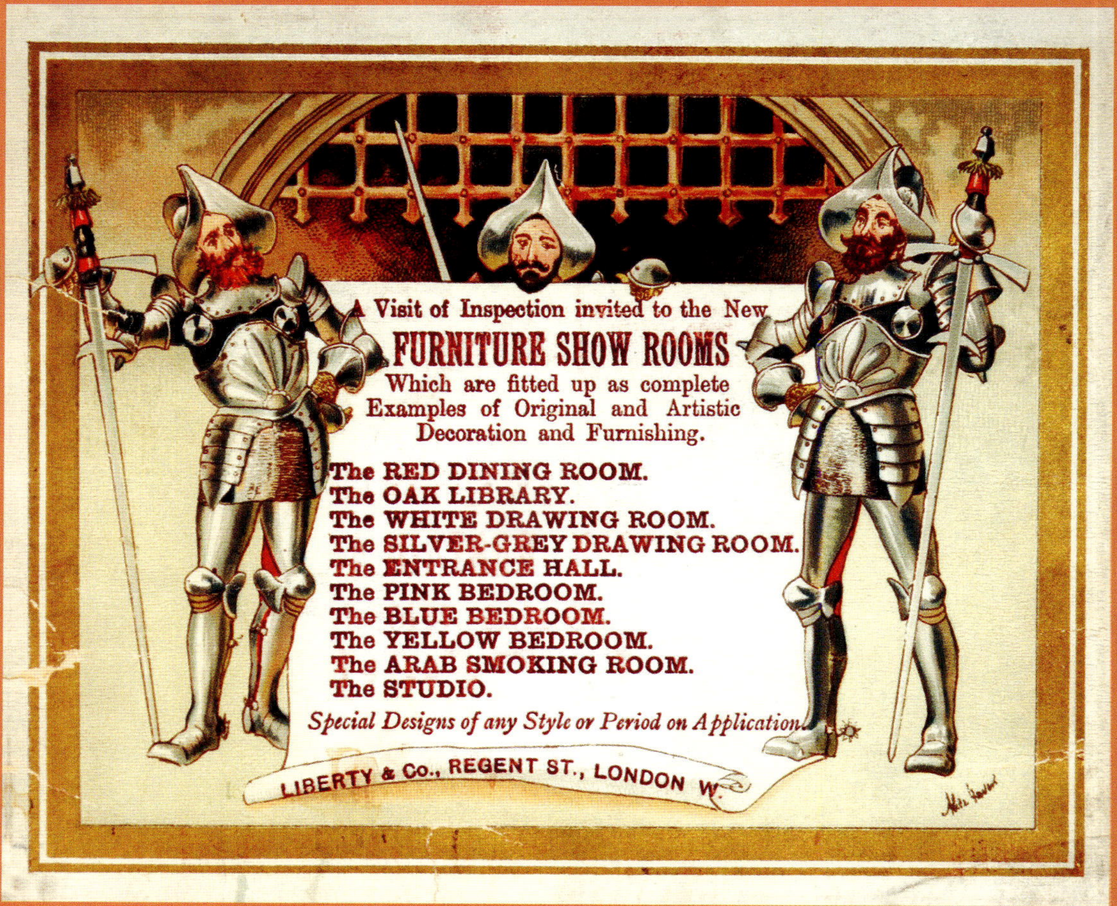

ART FABRIC CARDS, C. 1918
Advertisements for Liberty Art Fabrics and Furniture showrooms, which appeared on programmes for Gilbert and Sullivan operas.

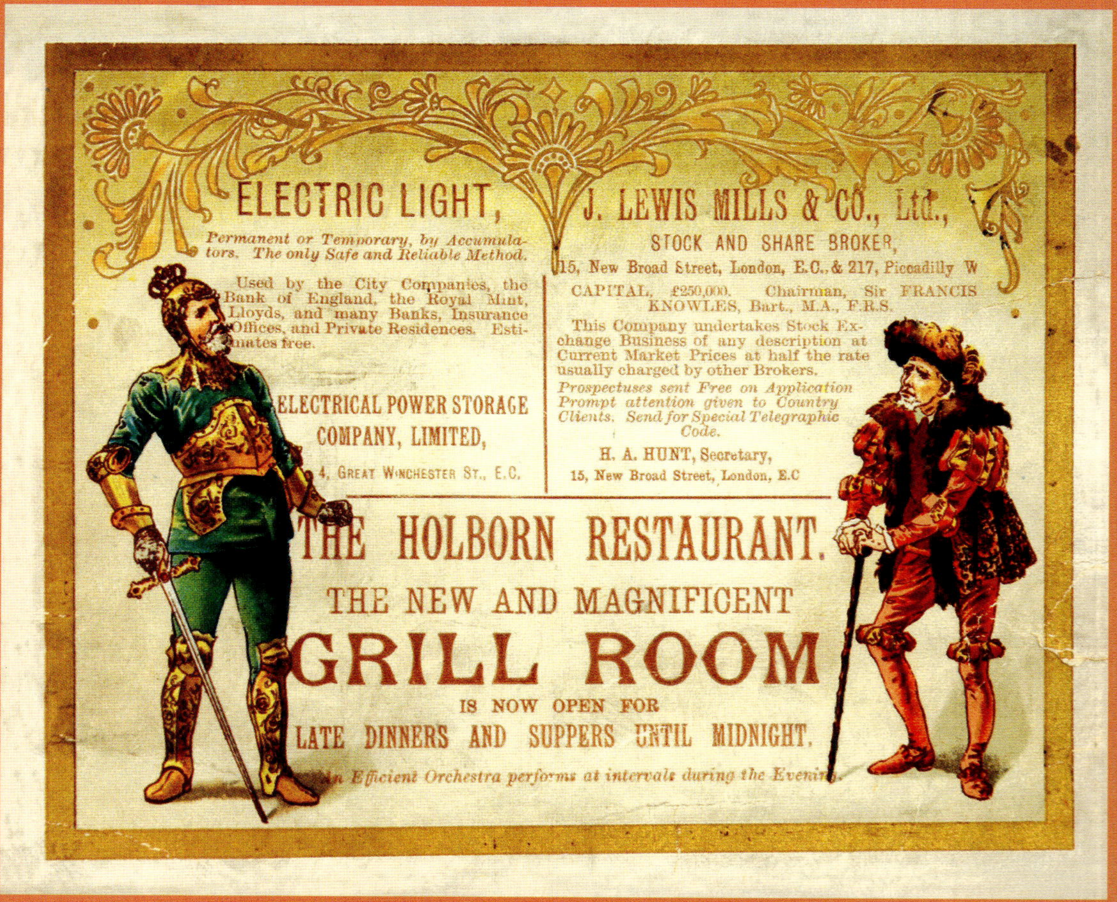

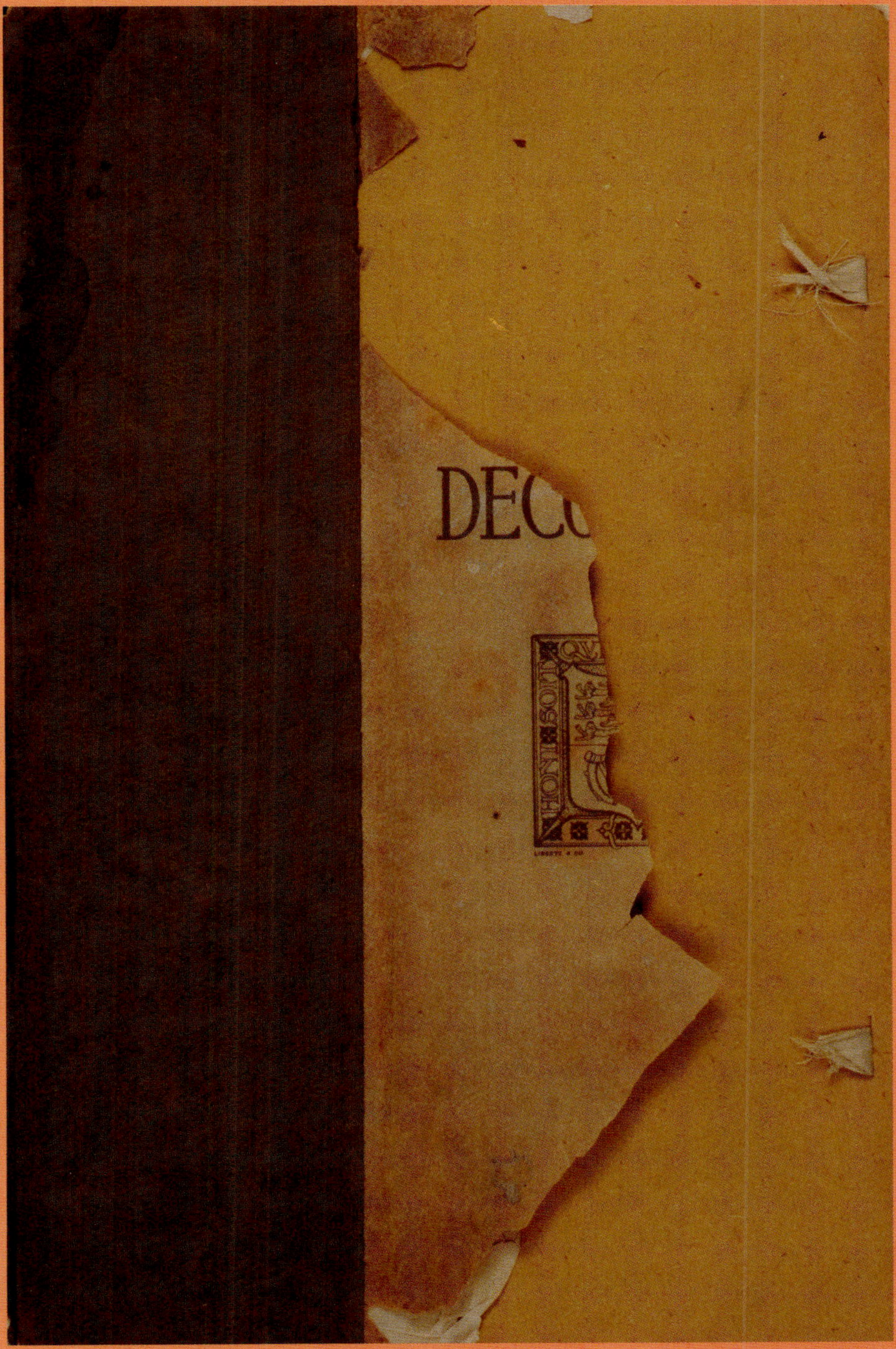

DRESS & DECORATION HANDBOOK, C. 1904

The cover and insides of a trade catalogue, consisting of 13 tipped-in colour plates of female costumed figures in various styles of Aesthetic dress, mostly against backgrounds of Arts & Crafts rooms.

DRESS & DECORATION HANDBOOK, C. 1904

The cover and insides of a trade catalogue, consisting of 13 tipped-in colour plates of female costumed figures in various styles of Aesthetic dress, mostly against backgrounds of Arts & Crafts rooms.

DRESS and DECORATION

THE question of dress has to a large degree, nowadays, become one of individual settlement. For women, while conforming to the prevailing mode, reserve the right to adapt it to their particular tastes and requirements. This emancipation from slavish subjection to passing fashions is a feature of the new century. Together with the renaissance of the decorative arts it was heralded in the closing years of its predecessor. The resultant general effect is that women's dress is more graceful, more refined, and more suited to its requirements than in any previous age. It has been an educational evolution. Not only has the science of hygiene asserted its right to consideration, but the extended knowledge of the laws of decorative art has refined the taste of the nation, and with the refinement of taste has come the discerning power of selection and rejection—selection of what is good, rejection of the bad and offensive.

BEAUTY of material is useless in itself. It is absolutely necessary there should be brought to bear the discernment and taste that are associated with artistic knowledge: familiarity with the grace of line and form, with colour harmonies, with the suitability of the material to its requirements. With women the love of dress is instinctive, and when their individuality is strongly assertive and combined with good taste the outcome is always to the advantage of their appearance. But even these qualities are not sufficient to ensure a completely satisfactory result. Individuality can formulate general ideas, and taste can control them within the right bounds, but there is needed the deeper knowledge that can only be acquired by the specialist to secure the success of the *ensemble*. To attain this end it is axiomatic that appropriateness must be the first consideration, and to this must be added the harmoniousness of colour, and the general questions of environment and pictorial effect. All of which relates distinctly to the expert.

DRESS and DECORATION

ALL that is good in current art is the outcome of the experiments and efforts of past centuries, there is nothing that is absolutely new, it is all a matter of evolution. The influence of long bygone days is still manifest, and the artists of Greece, of the Italian Renaissance and of eighteenth century France can all claim a share in the moulding of art as it is to-day.

THE designs in this volume demonstrate this in respect to costume. Some among them take us back in thought through the ages to the time when the "world was young," and reveal to us the art of those far remote days. In the end it is only the truth that survives, and herein is artistic truth, as fresh and fair as when it was first revealed. It is never old, never out of date. Classic, Renaissance, and Empire styles, developed during long intervening years: absorbed into each other, reincarnated, but never lost, because they were good and true in principle. And so to-day their appeal is as strong as ever.

ARTHUR FISH

IN the direction of refinement of taste in dress Messrs. Liberty have had a powerful effect. They have devoted attention to the home production of silks and other textile fabrics, introduced beauty with variety in design and colouring, and effected the presentation of the complete costume designed and executed on artistic lines.

THEY offer suggestions, based upon a close and intimate study of the history of costume and a definite knowledge of modern requirements. With this purpose in view they place before the public this series of designs, types of many others stored in their portfolios, and drawn upon the experiences of the past, selected from what is worthy of retention, and adapted to the necessities of to-day.

AMELIA" Empire Evening Gown with Coat. Robe of Orion-satin embroidered in harmonious colouring. Coat of silk-velvet lined with satin; collar, cuffs and belt embroidered with silk and appliqué of velvet.

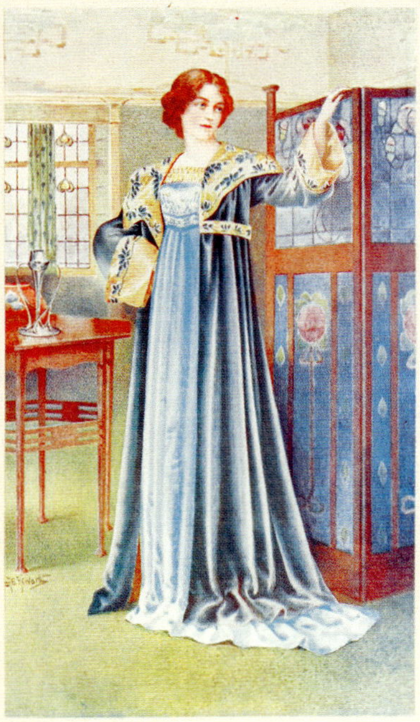

ISEULT" French 14th Century Evening Gown. Robe of soft velveteen finished with hand-embroidery and appliqué work. Sleeves of silk gauze in harmonized colouring.

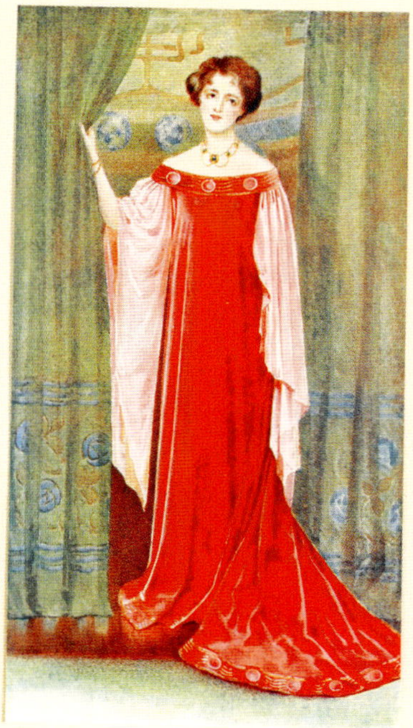

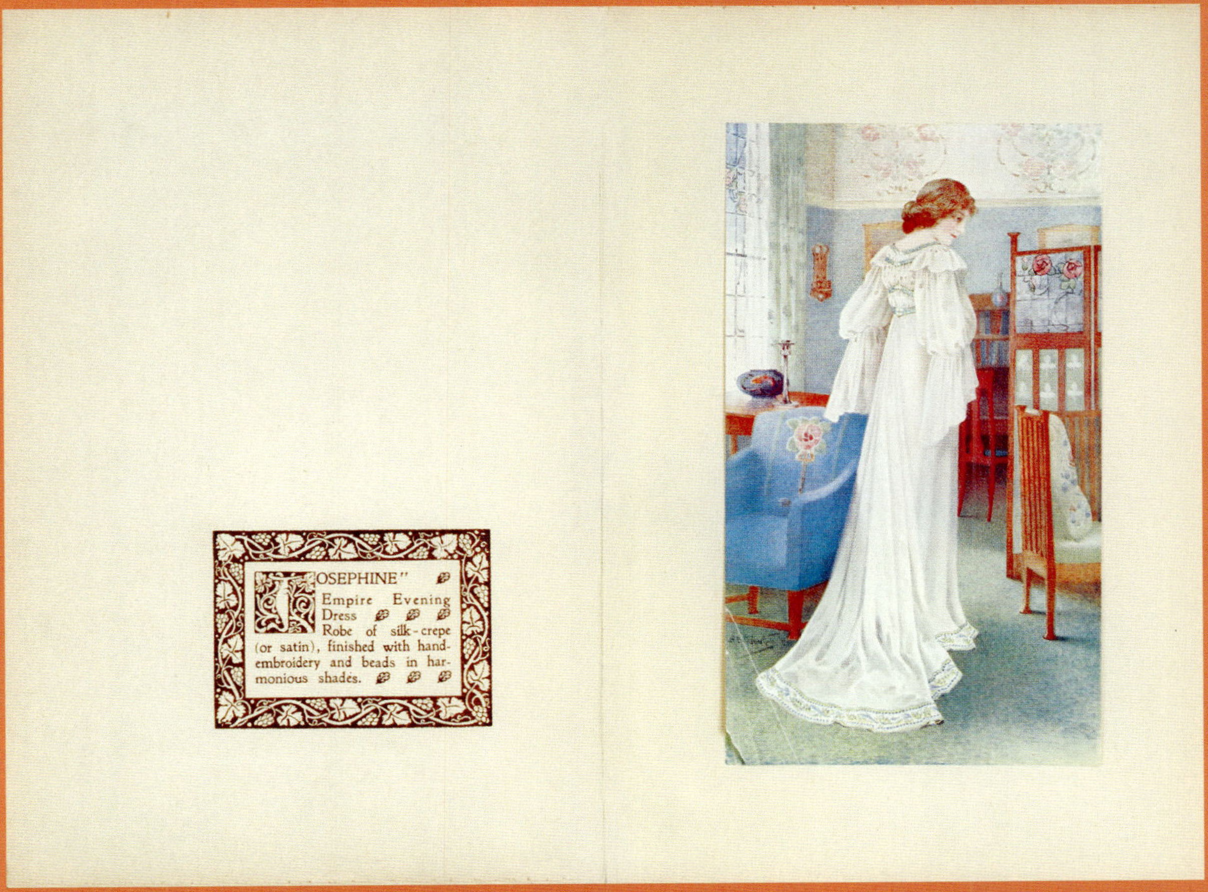

DRESS & DECORATION HANDBOOK, C. 1904

The cover and insides of a trade catalogue, consisting of 13 tipped-in colour plates of female costumed figures in various styles of Aesthetic dress, mostly against backgrounds of Arts & Crafts rooms.

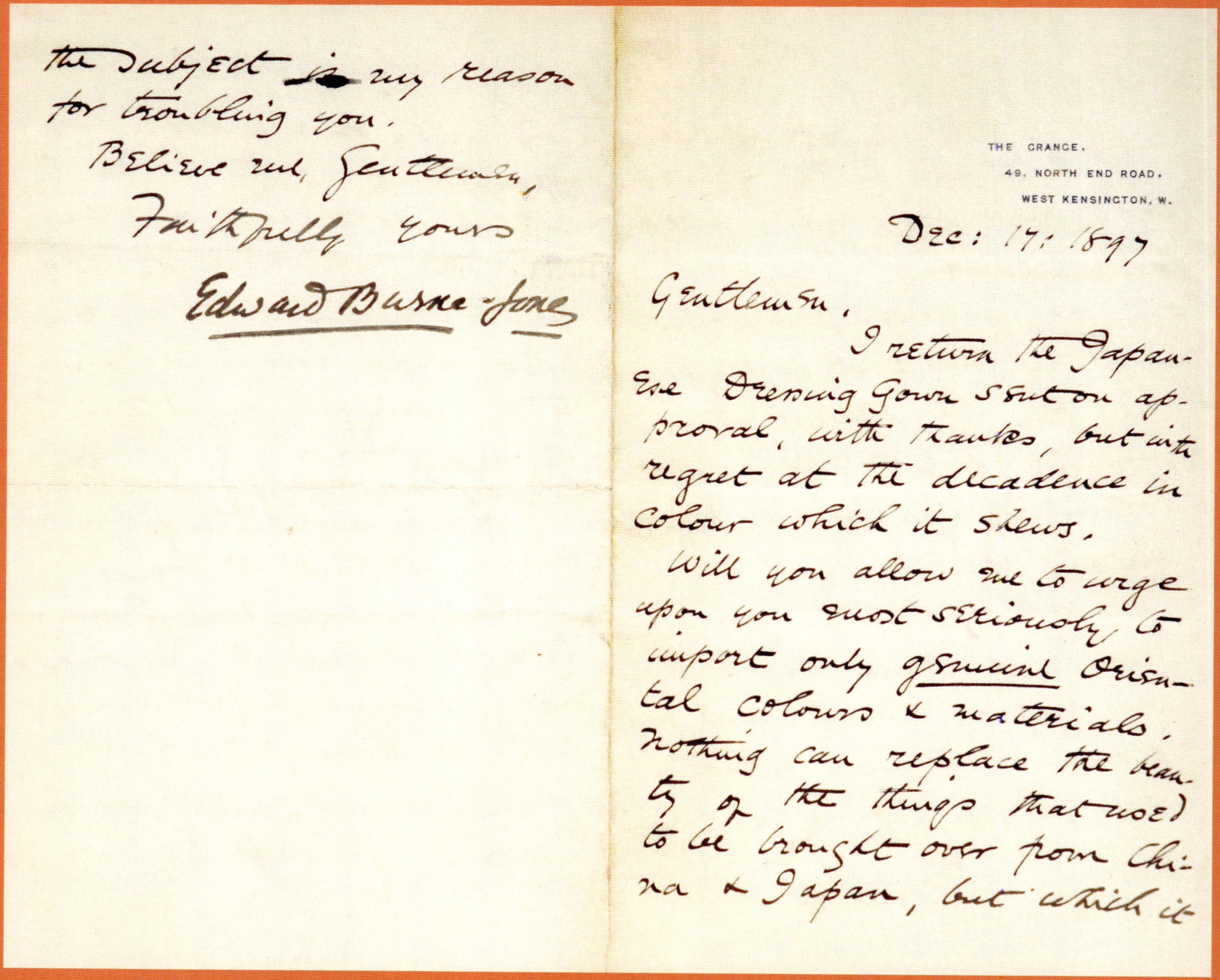
THE GRANGE.
49, NORTH END ROAD.
WEST KENSINGTON, W.

Dec: 17: 1897

Gentlemen,

I return the Japanese Dressing Gown sent on approval, with thanks, but with regret at the decadence in colour which it shews.

Will you allow me to urge upon you most seriously, to import only genuine Oriental colours & materials. Nothing can replace the beauty of the things that used to be brought over from China & Japan, but which it

the subject ~~is~~ my reason for troubling you.

Believe me, Gentlemen,

Faithfully yours

Edward Burne-Jones

EDWARD BURNE-JONES LETTER, 1897

Letter from the Pre-Raphaelite artist to Arthur Liberty, imploring him to use only authentic Oriental colours and materials in his dressing gowns.

is almost impossible to find in the market now. Your assistant's recommendation, "They are our <u>own</u> colours," accounts for the fact: it is impossible at the present time for the West to dictate colour to the East without fatal results.

With gratitude for what you have done in the past by bringing lovely and precious materials & colours over, I cannot withhold the expression of my deep disappointment at the level to which both have fallen, under the influence of demands made for cheapness & for assimilation to our own lower standard of beauty.

In a short time it will be too late to correct this – but even now I am sure a return to the original colours might be made – if we would trust the oriental workman as he deserves in that matter.

The importance of

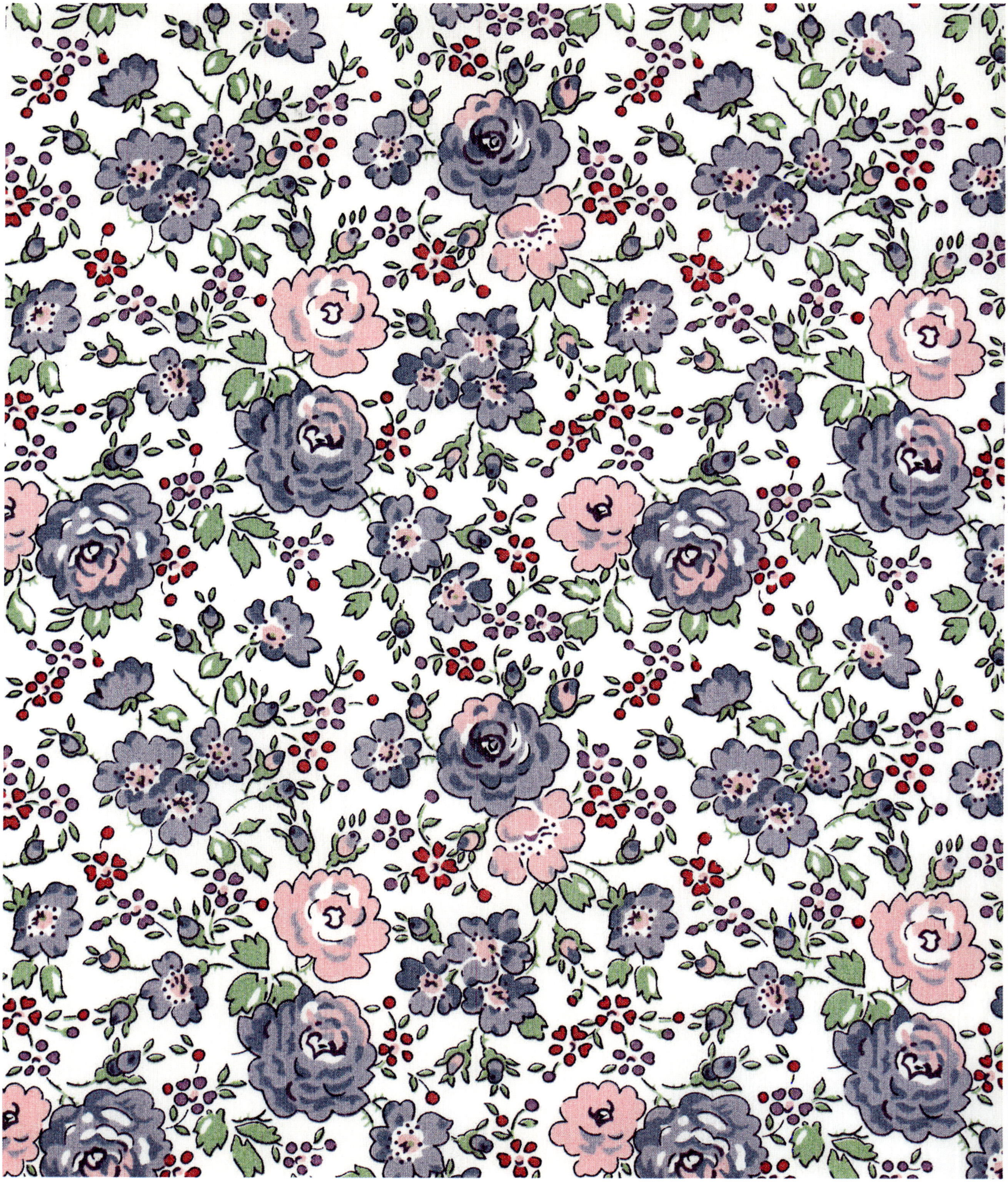

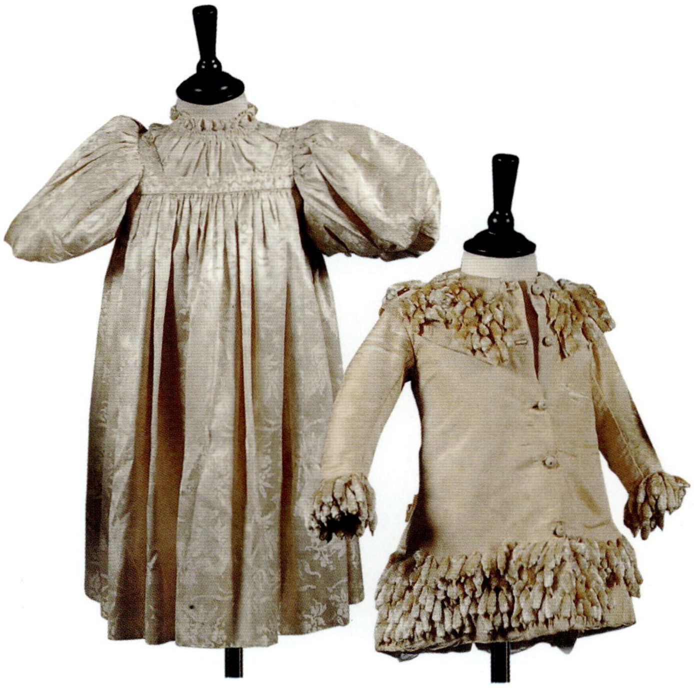

THE COSTUME DEPARTMENT

The soft silks and cashmeres that lent themselves so perfectly to being draped on artists' models, and which excited and seduced Victorian shoppers accustomed to stiff and coated fabrics, were nevertheless problematic when it came to dressing the fashionable ladies who shopped at the Regent Street emporium.

Arthur Liberty himself later explained in the *Daily Chronicle* article, "The House of Liberty..." (1913), why the costume department was introduced:

> *"In those days we were in a difficulty with regard to soft fabrics, because the British dressmaker was deadly opposed to them. She was accustomed to work on hard stiff lines, and the new material (cashmere) gave her more trouble ... It was a great drawback from a commercial point of view because when our artistic friends bought material they generally came back and said "my dressmaker will not touch it". The only way out of this difficulty seemed to me to turn dressmaker myself."*

So, in 1884, Arthur Liberty decided to open up a costume department, responding to the growing trend of female devotees of Aestheticism wanting to dress like the fashionably languid figures in the paintings of Burne-Jones or Albert Moore. The Artistic and Historic Costume Studio was intended not only to afford its "artistic" customers the opportunity to dress in a style as artistic and unconventional as the aesthetically decorated home, but was indeed conceived as a clear statement for dressmaking on a 'hygienic, intelligible and progressive basis'. This was directly opposed to the conventional fashion of stiff and glaring silk dresses, with tightly laced corsets and prominent bustles, and was aimed at challenging the perceived predominance of French taste, and the Parisian couturiers' liking for significantly more rigid materials and lines.

From the beginning, Arthur Liberty had sold Japanese kimonos, antique Chinese and Japanese embroidered coats and robes and Turkish veilings and shoes, but his objective with the new dress department was not to faithfully reproduce exotic costumes from the Near and Far East. The idea was to make historically inspired dresses, adapted to artistic sensibilities, but also to the practical needs of the late nineteenth century. The styles were appropriate to the fashionable aesthetic look, but also appealed to adherents of the dress reform movement, for once united in the desire to free up the waist, and in their taste for high-quality materials.

ABOVE *A Chinese silk damask child's dress from around 1910, and a silk faille coat with an elaborate chenille trim from the same period.*

RIGHT *Typical of the 'Directoire' style, this wrap front coat from Liberty & Co. in heavy black satin with white embroidered detailing is from the early twentieth century.*

FAR RIGHT *Customarily worn for informal occassions, this tea gown dates from 1885. The delicate colours, soft lace collar and sleeves, and ruched torso create the romantic silhouette favoured by Arts and Crafts followers.*

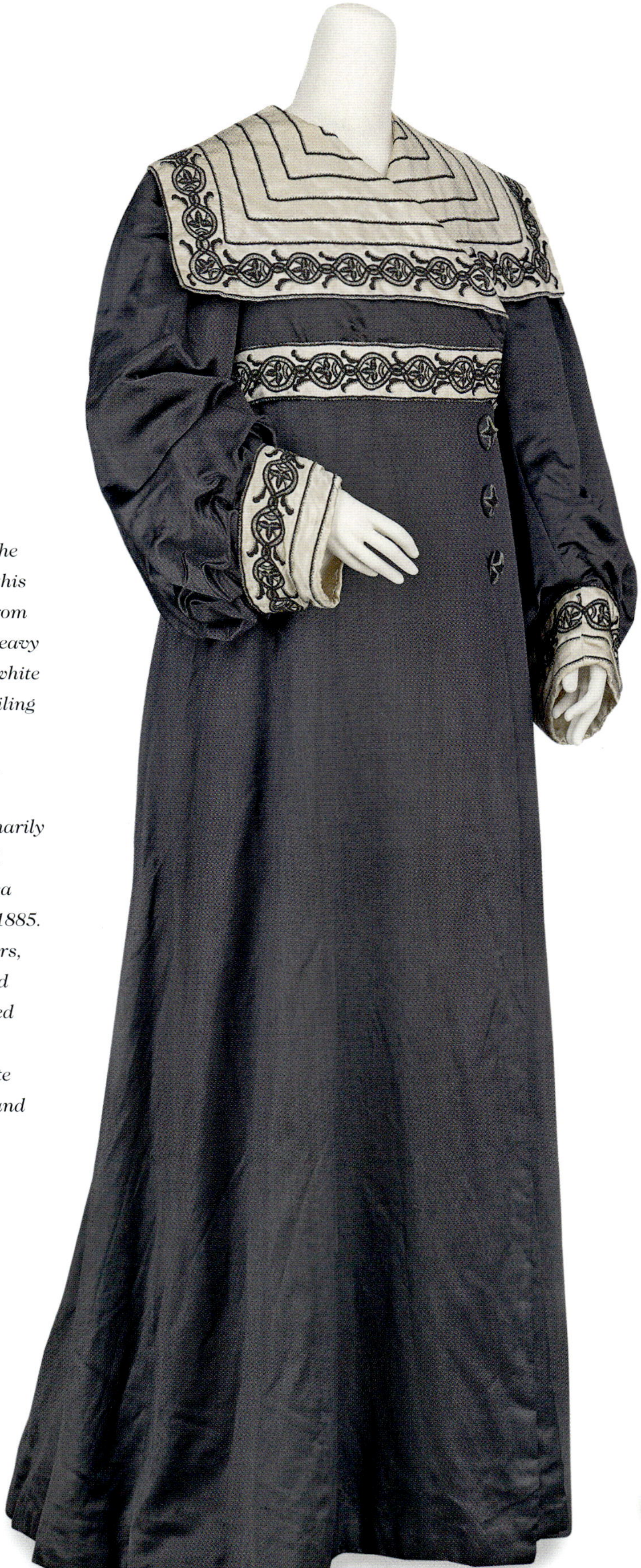

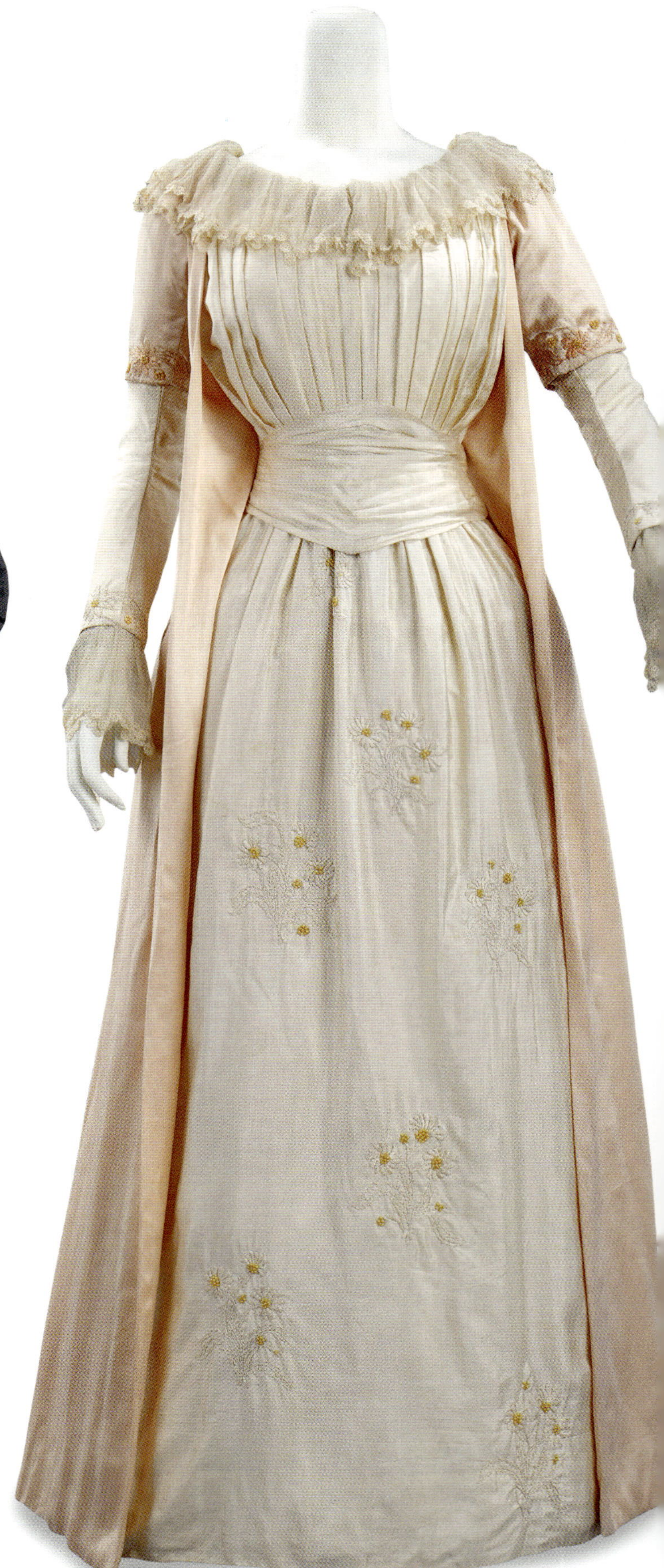

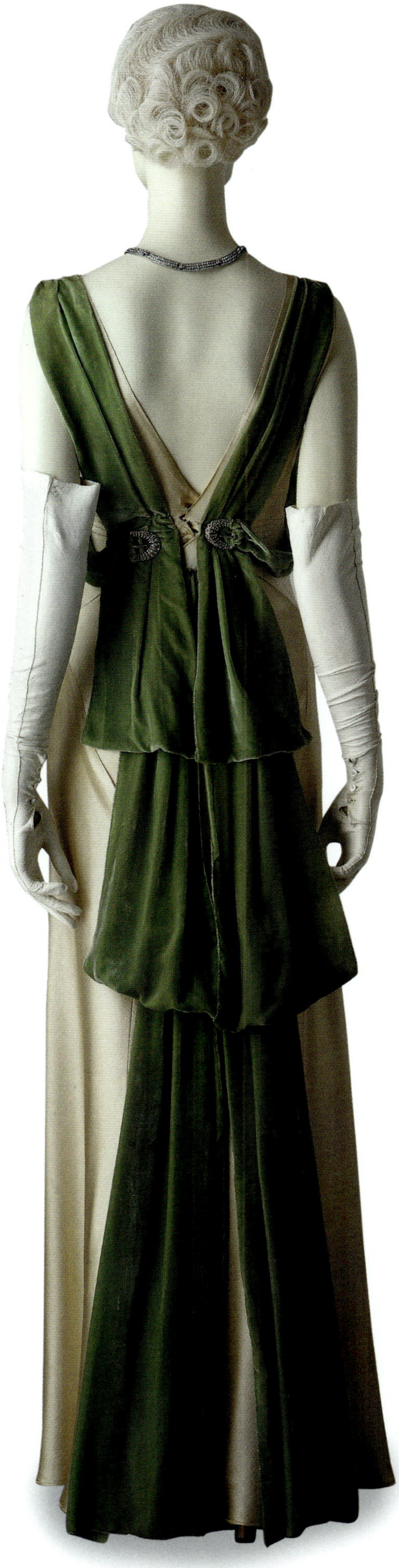

LEFT *In 1933, Liberty commissioned a number of designs by Paul Poiret for its Model Gown Salon. This bias-cut ivory satin evening gown with green velvet cascade is typical of Poiret's style with its emphasis on back detail.*

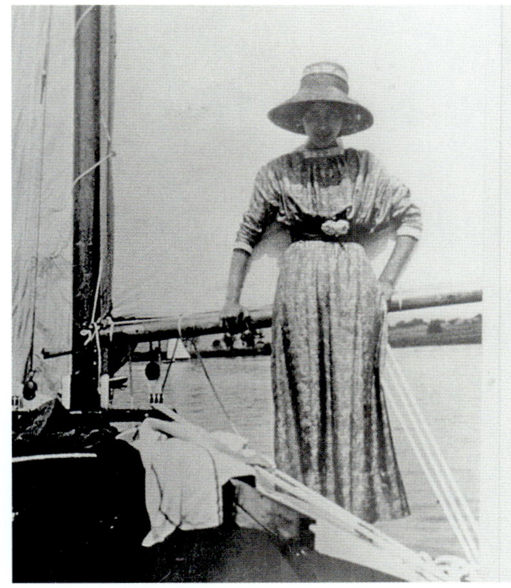

LEFT *Modelled by the fashion designer Paul Poiret's wife, this Liberty-print day dress is gathered simply at the waist in the loose, uncorseted style synonymous with the House of Poiret.*

Head consultant designer and supervisor of the new department was to be E. W. Godwin, the celebrated architect and designer, and well-known historic dress specialist, who had lectured on 'Dress and Its Relation to Health and Climate', convinced that true beauty was to be found in the past. He was also an old friend of the well-connected Arthur Liberty. Godwin had already designed much-admired stage costumes for famous actresses, Ellen Terry among others. Apart from Godwin's specialist knowledge and past experience, hiring him must have been very good publicity for Mr Liberty's new enterprise, linking it firmly with the Aesthetic ideal, and long after Godwin's death in 1886, the costume department continued to work in accordance with his ideals.

Liberty had a considerable influence on late nineteenth-century fashion in Britain, reaching the leisured and artistic as well as the aspiring middle classes. The draped fabrics and delicate colours changed the colour spectrum and quality of elegant textiles, but while the Empire line became quite fashionable in certain circles, in mainstream fashion, however, the cinched waist would not be on its way out for some years to come.

What is probably most remarkable is that Liberty had in fact created a unique style that would come to be so closely identified with its own name. A Liberty dress, with its flowing lines and faded colours, became a highly recognizable fashion statement.

For those with a taste for the artistic, from actress Ellen Terry and dancer Isadora Duncan to society ladies like the Countess of Aberdeen or Mrs Andrew Carnegie, Liberty was definitely the place to go. An article in *Women's World* in 1888 (edited at that time by Oscar Wilde) noted, 'Liberty's is the chosen resort of the artistic shopper'. Customers could choose to appear in a kaleidoscope of historical styles – anything from a Greek Hera dress to models inspired by medieval France based on twelfth-century figures from Chartres Cathedral, or gowns alluding to Stuart times, to dresses in the Empire style of the late eighteenth and very early nineteenth centuries. They could also, at no additional cost, have dresses made after their own designs. Over the years, with the Aesthetic movement beginning to lose steam, the designs proposed showed the influence of the Arts and Crafts movement and later of Art Nouveau. More conventional styles would also be introduced alongside the historical ones.

The historic and artistic costume department offered its customers not only inspirations and models from which to choose, but was also intentionally aimed at educating its potential customers' taste.

LEFT TO RIGHT *A collection of four ready-to-wear day dresses, typical of the elongated silhouette of the period, from an early 1930s* Liberty Costume Studios *catalogue.*

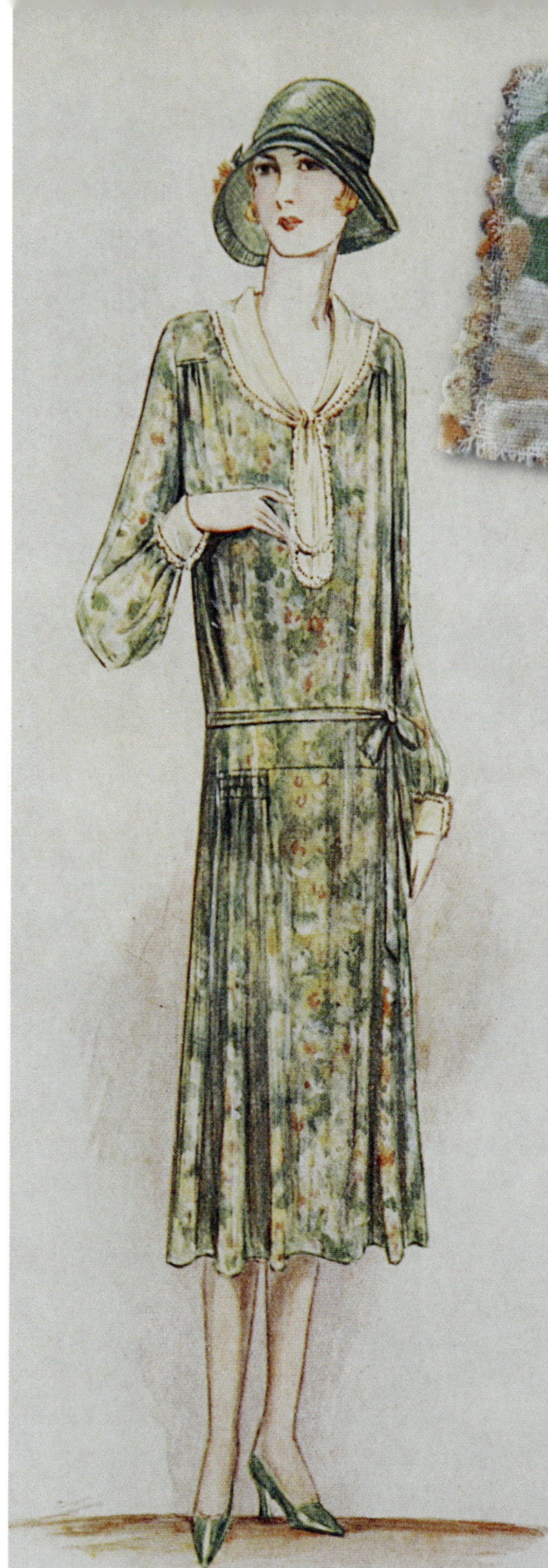

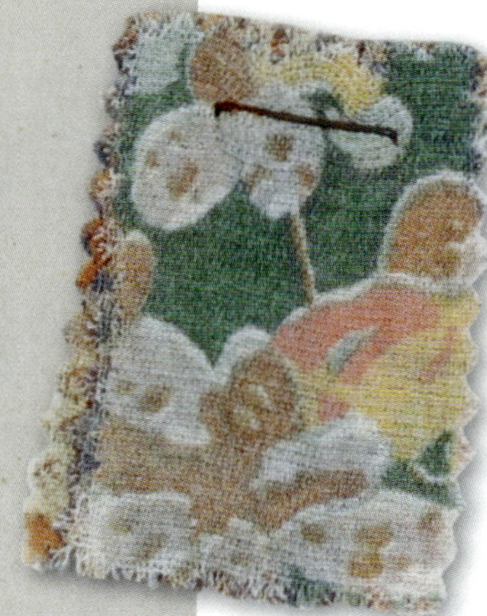

***1.** Model 21 Printed cotton georgette with net collar and cuffs, edged in lace.*

Explanatory booklets elaborated on the various desirable historical periods and their styles in dress. This educational, almost missionary zeal, was not limited to the artistically inclined lady but was intended to educate the dress trade in general. Liberty also offered lessons, especially in embroidery, which, influenced by the ideas of the Arts and Crafts movement, became a feature of many of their designs.

The silks, in their soft and delicate colours, already enjoyed a great success in Paris, to the point where softly coloured silks were generally being called "*soies Liberty*". In 1890, Liberty & Co. opened up a branch, the Maison Liberty, in the French capital at 38 Avenue de l'Opéra, selling the famous Liberty fabrics and dresses made in their costume studio. The Children's Salon, selling Liberty smocks and dresses modelled on Kate Greenaway's enchanting drawings, became the destination of choice for elegant mothers dressing their chic little *Parisiennes*, mirroring the craze for Kate Greenaway children's clothes that had engulfed London.

But while Liberty enjoyed commercial success in Paris, bringing about an acceptance of Empire-style dresses, the most influential *élégantes* continued to look to the grand French fashion houses for the most fashionable designs. Nevertheless,

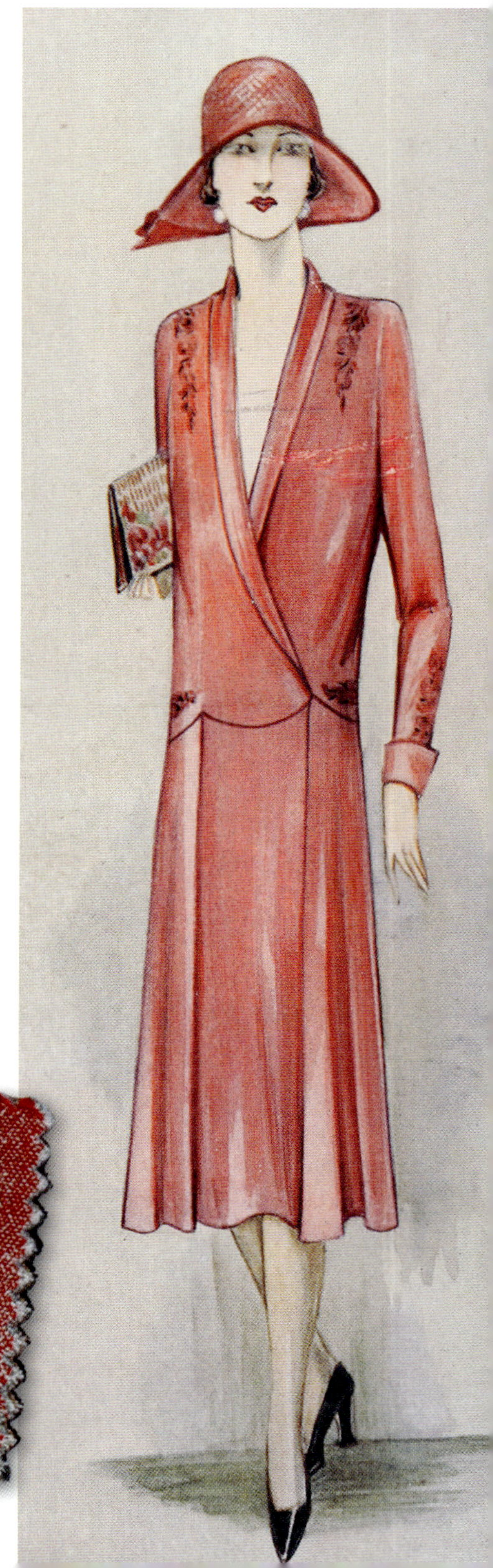

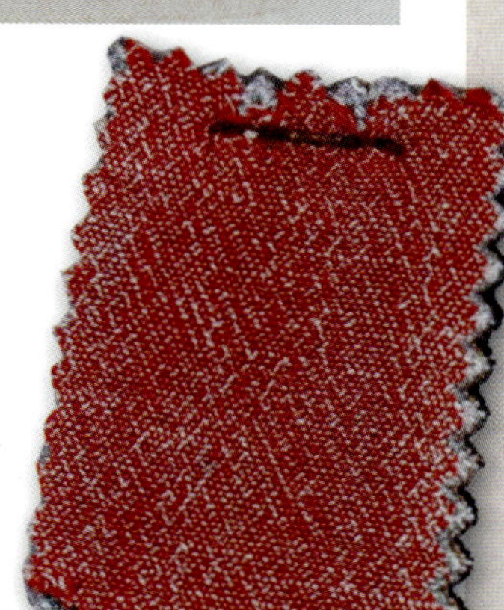

***2.** Model 66 Red Yoru crepe dress, with intricate embroidery at the shoulder.*

3. *Model 37*
Hand-printed Tyrian green silk dress with silk georgette details.

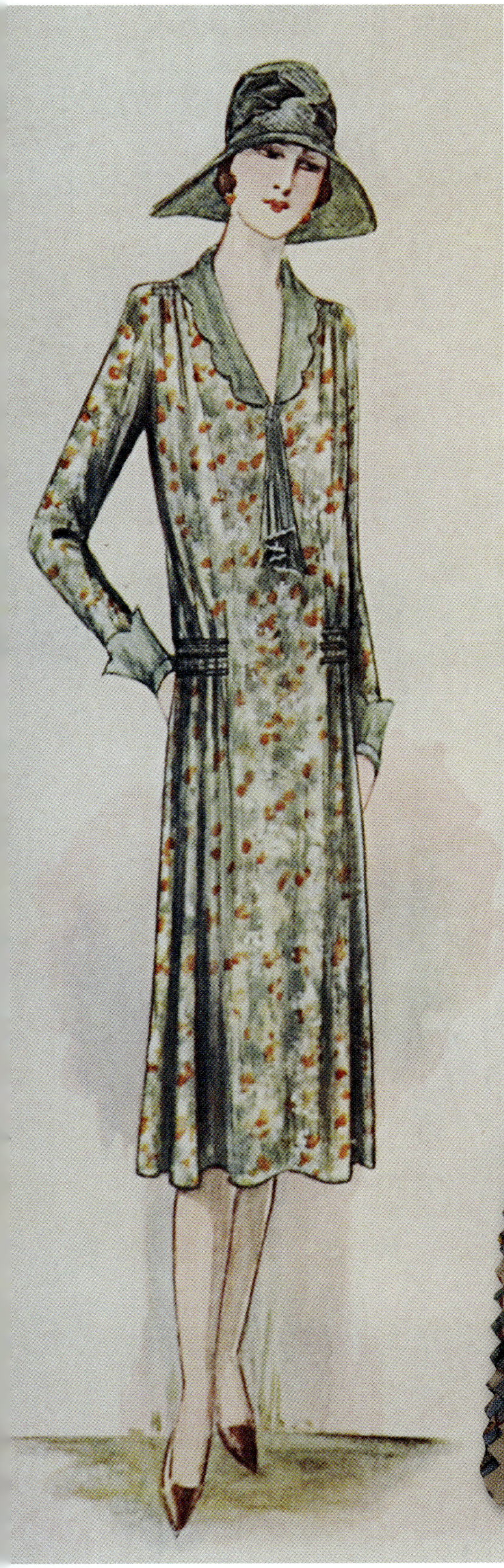

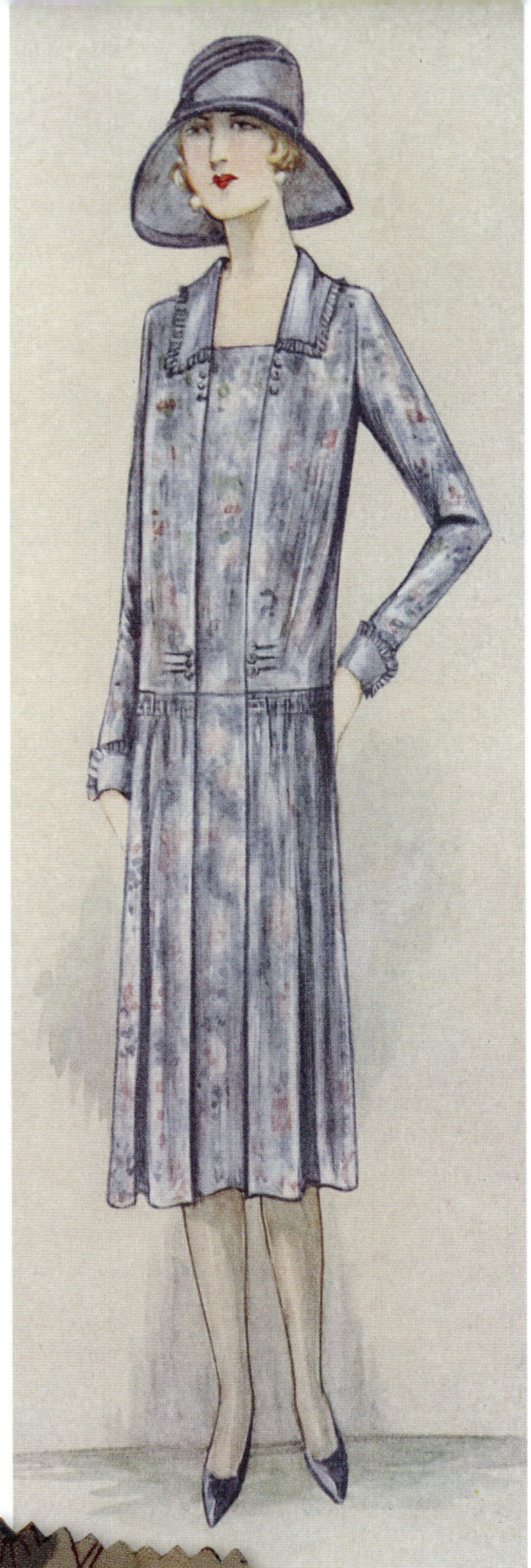

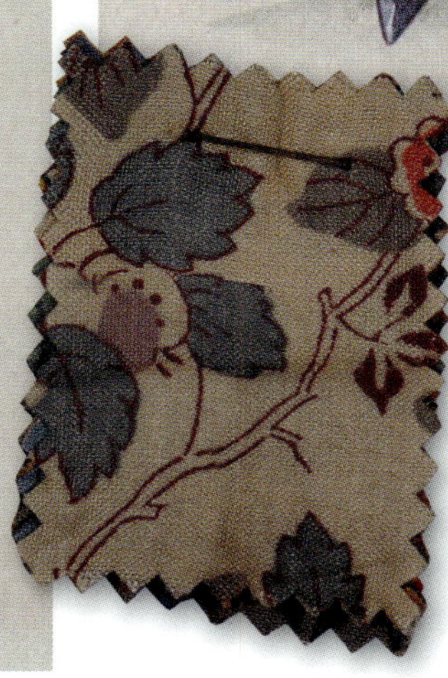

4. *Model 38*
Hand-printed purple Tyrian silk dress with plain silk collar and cuffs.

Liberty exerted considerable influence on French high fashion more indirectly but, as a result, all the more powerful: a young and experimental Paul Poiret worked with Liberty silks extensively when he opened his own fashion house in 1903. Poiret, influenced by Art Nouveau but also, possibly, by the Empire line that Liberty had reintroduced to Paris fashions in the late nineteenth century, created a new silhouette that became the height of fashion and was the death-blow to the corseted figure, irreversibly changing the course of twentieth-century fashion.

Thirty years later, the Maison Liberty in Paris had already closed down in the dire economic climate of the time, and Paul Poiret was sadly no longer the avant-garde designer he had been in the Edwardian era. He had failed to adapt to the changed world of fashion in the 1920s. Perhaps out of respect for past, shared glories, but maybe also themselves slightly out of touch with the current mood, Liberty's board decided to hire Poiret to design four collections for them.

After many years of adhering to their own, very specific vision of the Liberty look, from the 1920s and 1930s onwards, Liberty's dress department started to respond increasingly to changing tastes and to a now more conservative clientele.

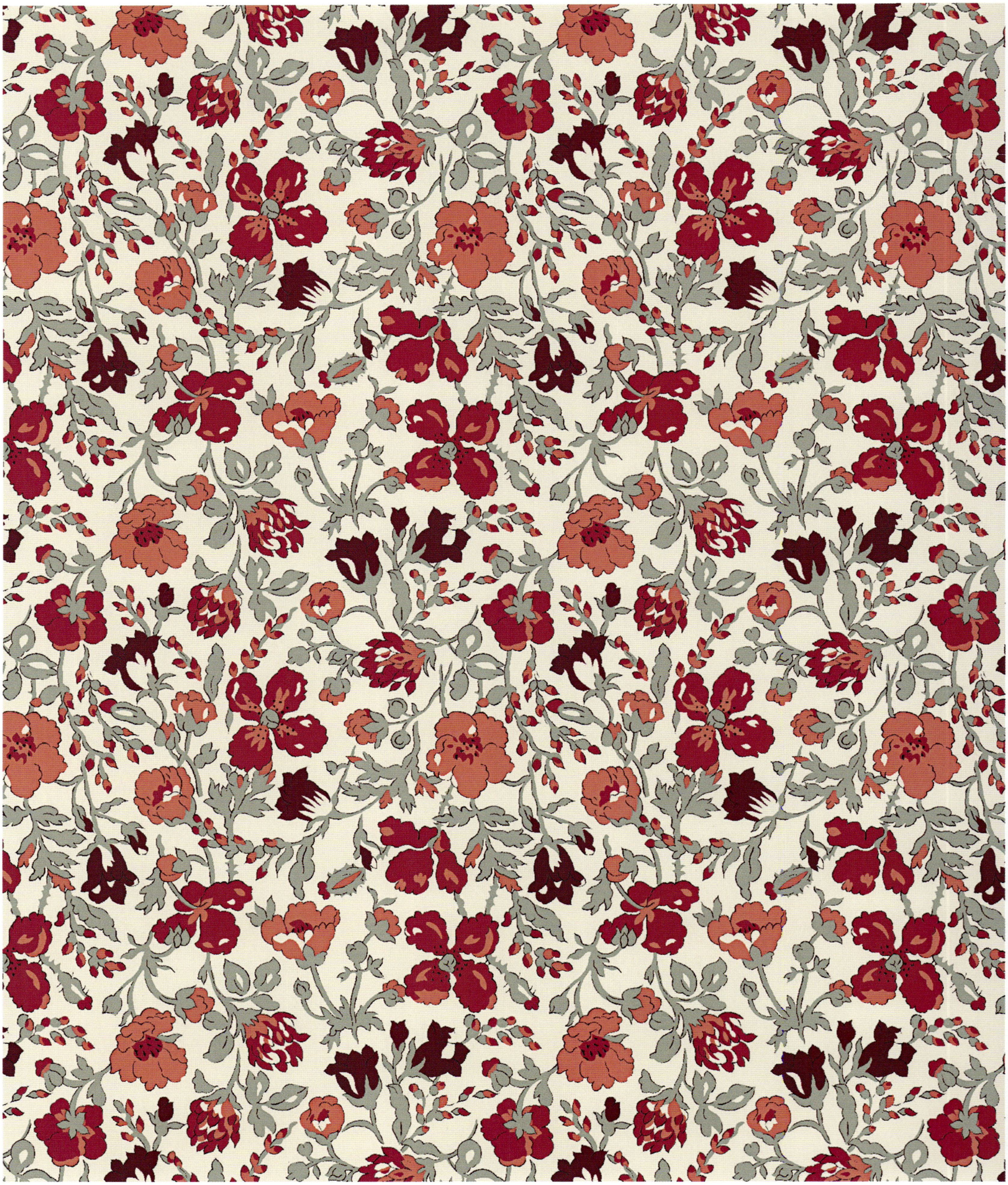

LIBERTY COLOURS & TANA LAWNS

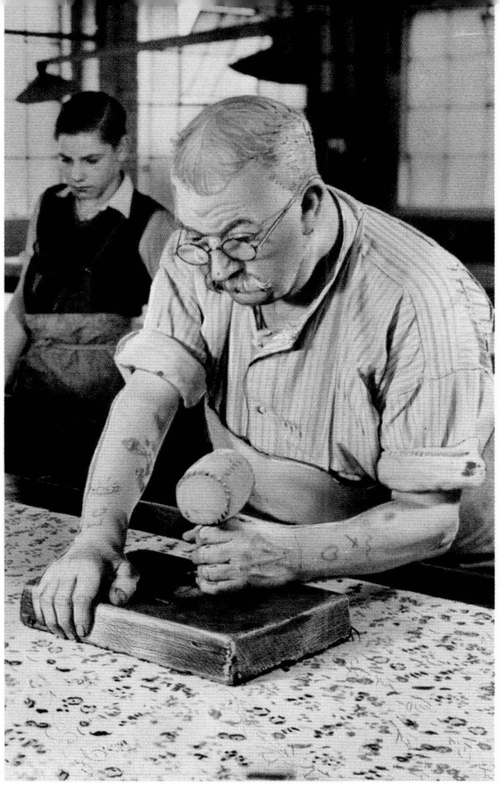

LEFT *Fabrics were block-printed by hand, a time-consuming process. Here, a Merton printer is seen tapping the wood block onto the fabric to ensure an even print of the repeat.*

Merton Abbey, in south-west London, had been a centre of printing and dyeing for several centuries when Liberty first began to trade in 1875. With Edmund Littler setting up his factory in the early 1800s and William Morris establishing his own workshops in 1881, the area had become synonymous with the highest levels of craftsmanship by the time Liberty acquired the Littler workshops in 1904. The artisan skills deployed at the Abbey were increasingly valued in an age of the burgeoning mechanization of the printing process, and the prices of the fabrics were correspondingly high.

As well as establishing a reputation for hand-printed fabrics, Arthur Liberty also saw an opportunity to exploit Liberty's reputation as a manufacturer of high-quality products with the introduction of 'Art Colours', which came to be known as 'Liberty colours'. These were a range of subtle silk dyes, created in collaboration with Thomas Wardle of Staffordshire, which proved extremely popular with the Aesthetic movement. The methods of producing these specialist dyes were thought to be a secret known only to the Chinese, but Liberty and Wardle managed to discover the process.

Throughout the twentieth century, Liberty's perennially popular sprigged-floral Tana Lawn fabric was a mainstay of its textile business and was one of the key hand-printed textiles produced in Merton. Strictly speaking, the name refers to the particular type of cloth registered by Liberty, but the term is now generally understood to also include any small-scale, all-over delicate floral design.

The original Tana Lawn fabric patterns were created by William Haynes Dorell in the early 1930s. For such a quintessentially English aesthetic, the etymology of the word is seemingly exotic, being named after the fine cotton yarn produced around Lake Tana, in Ethiopia. The 'lawn' refers to the sheen texture applied to the fabric, giving it a crispness that perfectly showcases the delicate florals with the small stylized flower motifs.

Tana Lawn was almost exclusively used for childrenswear until the advent of 'youthquake fashion' in the 1960s, when designers such as Gerald McCann and Mary Quant appropriated the fabric for their designs. The most long-standing partnership, however, was with Cacharel, whose romantic silhouettes married perfectly with the sweet floral print. At the height of this partnership, in the mid-1970s, Cacharel bought almost a million metres of fabric from Liberty.

OPPOSITE *An original 1930s floral design, Meadow, was printed as a woodblock print at Merton, revived by Susan Collier in the 1970s and has been on classic Tana Lawn since 1986.*

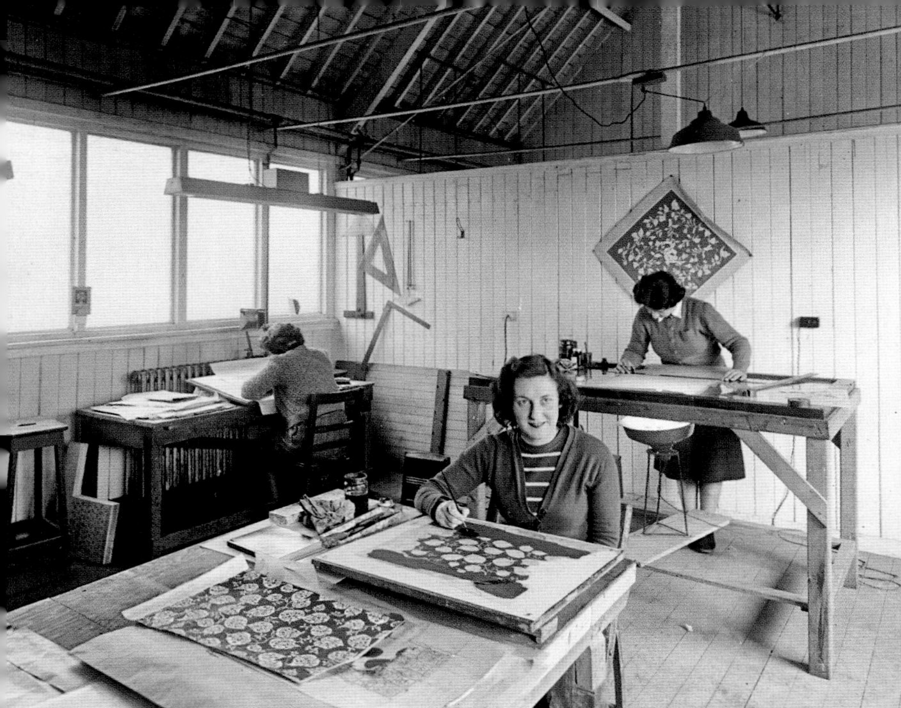

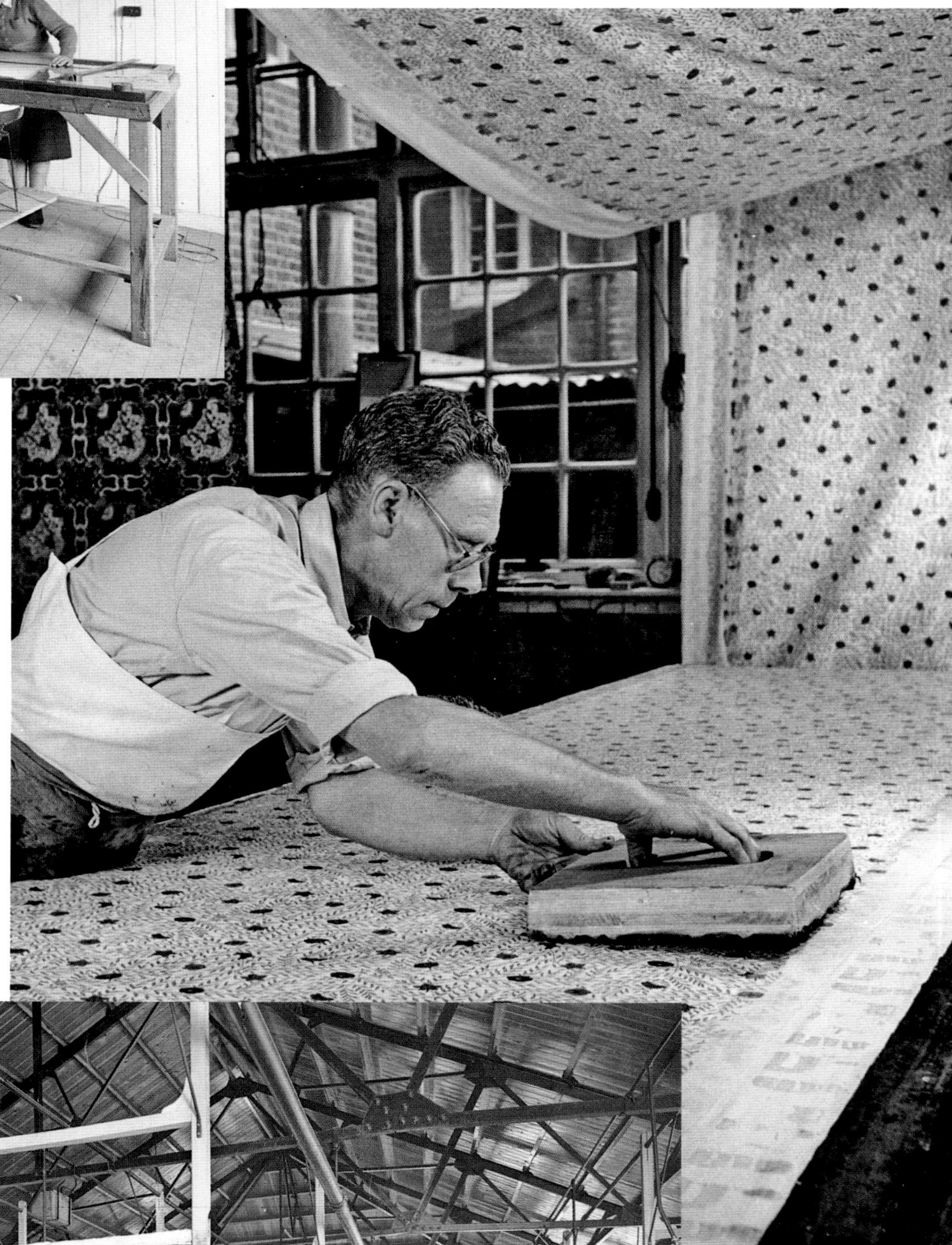

FROM TOP *Preparing a silkscreen for a printed design at the Merton factory in the 1950s; a printer, wearing a waistband apron to protect the print from smudging, positions the woodblock onto the fabric to create a repeat of this design; the Merton factory interior during the 1930s, showing an overview of the print tables.*

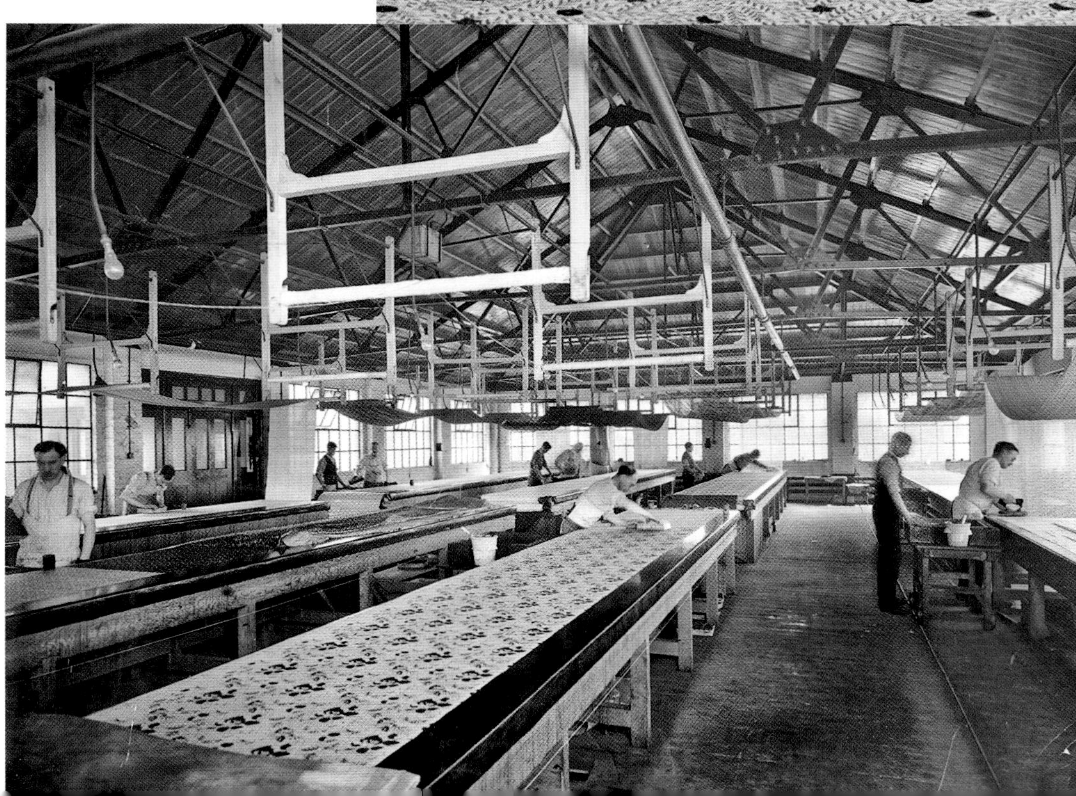

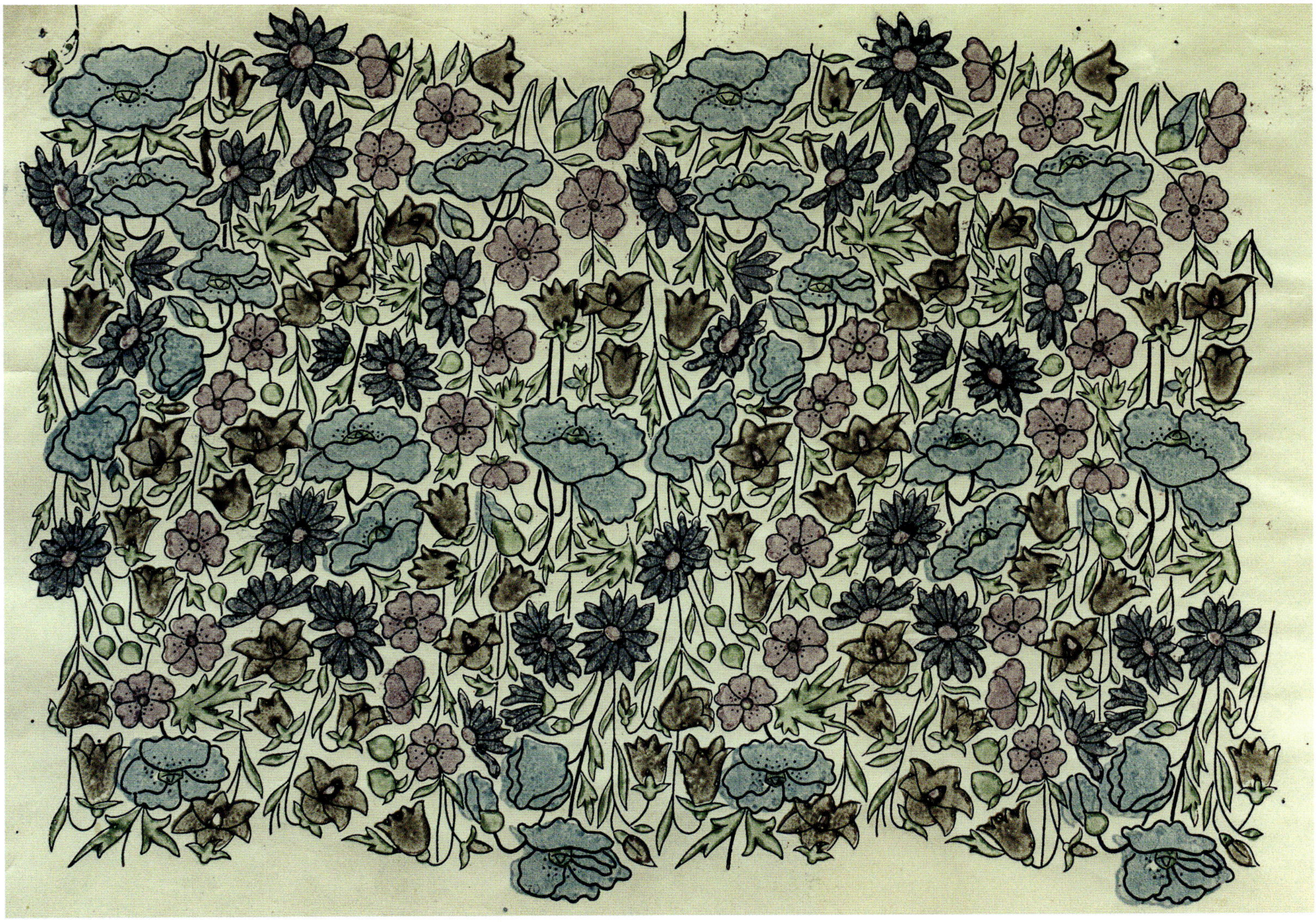

ABOVE *Original print impression for the Poppy & Daisy fabric print, in production from 1917 until the mid-1950s.*

RIGHT *Originally a classic Tana Lawn print in a yellow, pink and blue colourway, this design, Felicite, was created in 1933.*

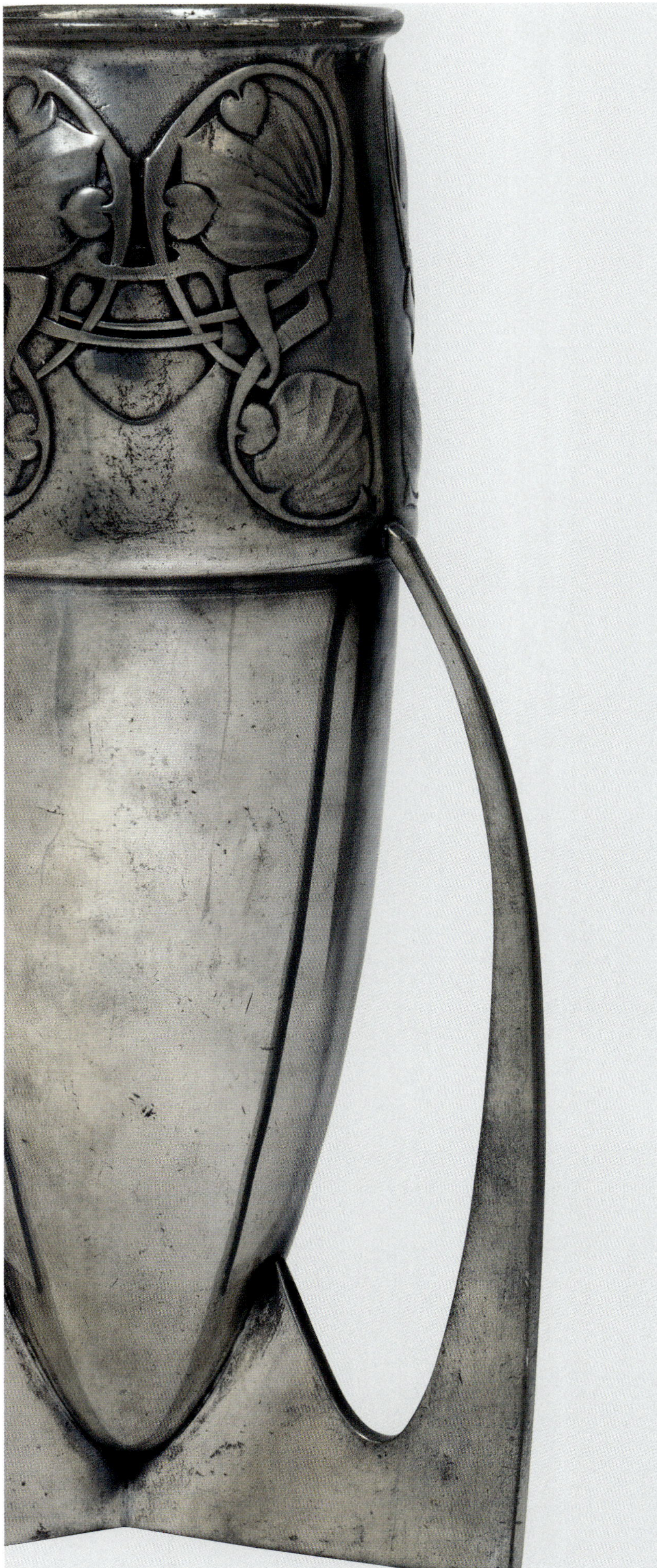

STILE LIBERTY

LEFT
Pewter vase, design attributed to Archibald Knox, produced by W. H. Haseler for Liberty, 1906–1909.

OPPOSITE
Details of furniture, silverware, pewter and ceramics, and sketches from the Liberty archive sketchbooks.

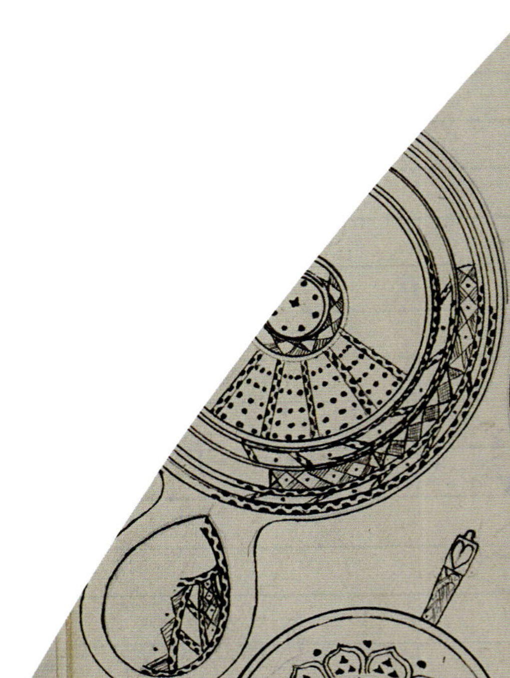

JEWELLE
SKETCH
Buttons
Blotters
Boxes
Buckles
Cigarette
Card
Caddie
Cruets
Clasps
Clocks
Cups
Cushion
Chalice &

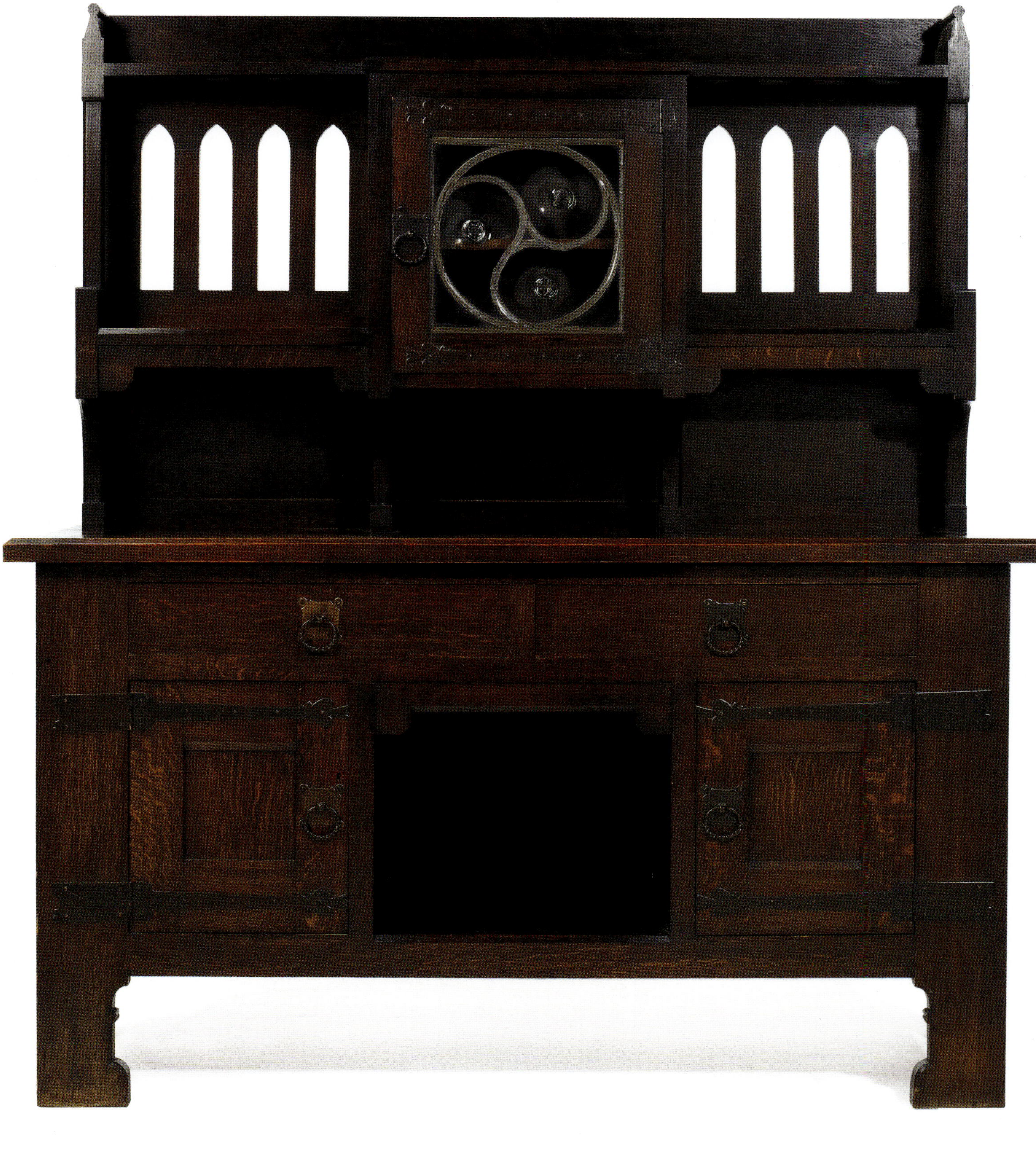

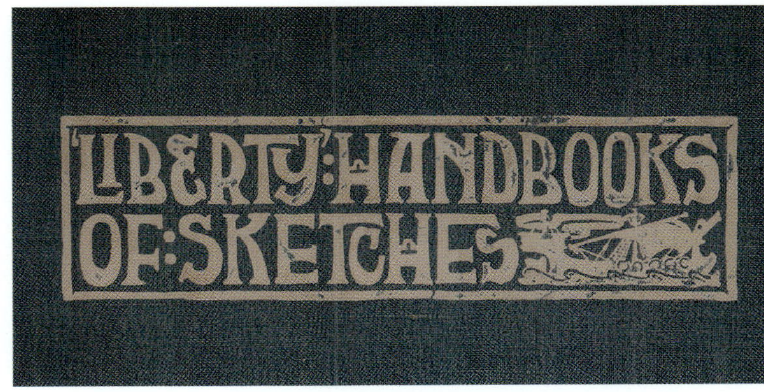

ABOVE *Cover from the Liberty* Handbook of Sketches, *printed in 1890.*

INTERIORS & FURNITURE

The Furnishing and Decoration Studio was established in 1883, at the very height of the Aesthetic movement, when Liberty expanded into their new and larger location at Chesham House on Regent Street.

The studio was put under the direction of Leonard F. Wyburd (1865–1958), who was just 18 years old when he was first employed by Liberty. Wyburd, a painter, architect and designer, was the son of a well-known genre painter, Francis John Wyburd, who exhibited at the Royal Academy, and it was perhaps through his father that the connection to Arthur Liberty was first established. Clearly, Arthur must have considered the young designer to be very talented. Leonard Wyburd stayed with the firm for 23 years, and at Liberty's Furnishing and Decoration Studio, Wyburd developed a furniture style that was highly fashionable, very influential and integral in establishing Liberty as a leading 'Art' furniture manufacturer. Apart from his design work for Liberty & Co., Leonard Wyburd was a painter in his own right. Under his direction, the studio grew from year to year in importance: it both provided designs for Liberty's ranges of furniture to be sold at the shop alongside the imported Oriental wares, and was responsible for the bespoke interior decoration services that Liberty offered its most exclusive clientele.

In the premises at East India House as well as at Chesham House, Liberty had created a series of themed rooms which would allow customers to see the exotic items in the appropriate settings and, like the Japanese smoking room or their popular Arab tea room, they also provided inspirations as to how the shopper's own home could be decorated in an elegant and stylish fashion.

In the early years, when Aestheticism and its craze for exotic interiors was at its zenith, the Furnishing and Decoration Studio made its name by designing spectacular room settings in many of the Oriental styles that were so incredibly fashionable at the time. A Japanese drawing room, halls decorated in the style of an Indian palace, a smoking room in the very popular Moorish and Arabian idiom, or even an Oriental room combining some or all of these styles – Liberty could provide the fitted interior, bespoke Anglo-Oriental furniture and antiques, as well as all of the fabrics and *objets d'art* needed for the decoration of their customers' homes.

When, in 1889, the Marchioness of Aberdeen had the music room at her Grosvenor Square house redecorated as an elaborate 'Eastern dream', an article in the press of 1889, and quoted in Liberty's *Handbook of Sketches*, 1889–1890,

OPPOSITE *This wooden cabinet from the turn of the century is executed in the Arts and Crafts style, with a treskelion motif glass door panel at the centre.*

THE following sketches of work which has been carried out by Messrs. LIBERTY are not intended to represent a complete Catalogue, but merely to illustrate a few especially selected and approved types of Decoration and Furniture.

A selection from a large number of Water-colour Drawings of complete and original schemes of Decoration for rooms of every description, can be sent on application by return of post. Skilled assistants are also sent to wait on customers at any address in the United Kingdom or Abroad. They are prepared to receive instructions on the spot, or to submit subsequently suggestions, designs and estimates for any description of artistic interior decorative, or furnishing work, from the simplest to the most elaborate treatment.

REVISION · OF · BUILDER'S · PLANS.

Messrs. LIBERTY would respectfully suggest to those contemplating artistic structural, or decorative additions, or alterations to their houses, that they should be allowed to see the builder's plans before work is commenced, as it is often possible, by means of a slight variation, to obtain far greater comfort and "style" without materially affecting the original estimate. The character and individuality thus gained cannot, of course, be secured subsequently except at a greatly increased expenditure. They are always prepared to do this free of cost, whether the carrying out of the Interior Decoration is, or is not, afterwards entrusted to their care.

HALL · AND · STAIRCASE (JACOBEAN).

THE "Jacobean" style which prevailed in England during the first half of the 17th century, is perhaps the most ENGLISH in its characteristics of all those which grew out of the classic Renaissance, and is in many respects most suitable to our climate, tastes and habits. Though affording full opportunities for treatment of the greatest magnificence, where expense is of no moment, it may yet be most satisfactorily carried out at a moderate outlay, while retaining its distinctive features.

The illustration shews an alteration at a Country House recently designed and carried out. The Hall was entirely remodelled—a new and dignified staircase substituted for an old narrow and commonplace one, and the partition wall of a small room leading out of the Hall removed. This latter was formed into a commodious "Ingle Nook" with fireside seats, etc.

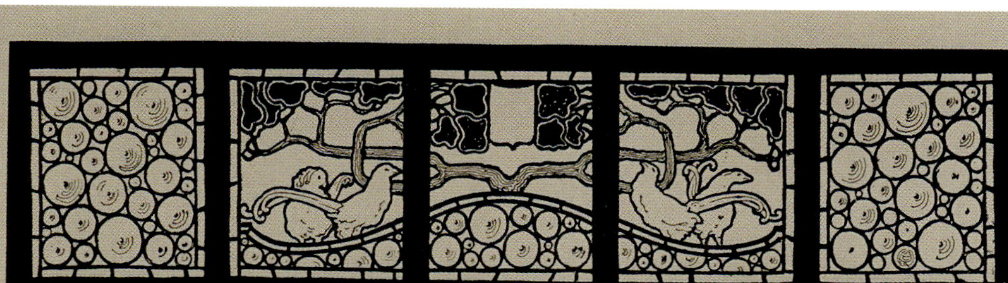

described it as '... a triumph of taste and a monument to "Liberty" enterprise and art. The ceiling panels are modelled from windows around the tombs of the queens of Shah-Ahmed at Ahmedabad; the leaded glass from the tombs of Yufus Mooltan; the exquisite lattices hail from the Punjab; the fire dogs from Nepal; and the tiles from Mooltan. Pure and perfect Orientalism are supreme in this exquisite room.' While exotic interiors continued to have their place in Liberty's catalogues, a variety of historical Old English styles were becoming increasingly fashionable towards the last decade of the century.

In the *Handbook of Sketches* – a catalogue of sorts which gave illustrated inspirations for room settings in the various styles but also provided didactic information on taste and even historical background – Oriental styles share a space with Jacobean entrance halls or Cromwellian dining rooms. Over time, the handbook showed an increasing number of drawings for rooms and sometimes also houses designed in a modified Arts and Crafts style, which evoked a sense of the simple life in the English countryside. Perhaps because of its very Englishness, the work of Liberty's Furnishing and Decoration Studio enjoyed a remarkable success internationally. Between about 1895 and the outbreak of World War I, Liberty's decoration contracts were executed for high-society clients from all over the world – in Europe and Canada, where English taste had become the epitome of stylishness, but also as far as South Africa and India, where rajahs and princes commissioned large interior schemes. Contracts for the ill-fated Archduke Franz Ferdinand of Austria,

LEFT *Pages from the Liberty* Handbook of Sketches, *including two descriptive interior pages and the design for a stained-glass window.*

OPPOSITE *Pages from the* Handbook of Sketches; *an elaborate Tudor-style staircase hallway and an Art Nouveau light fitting.*

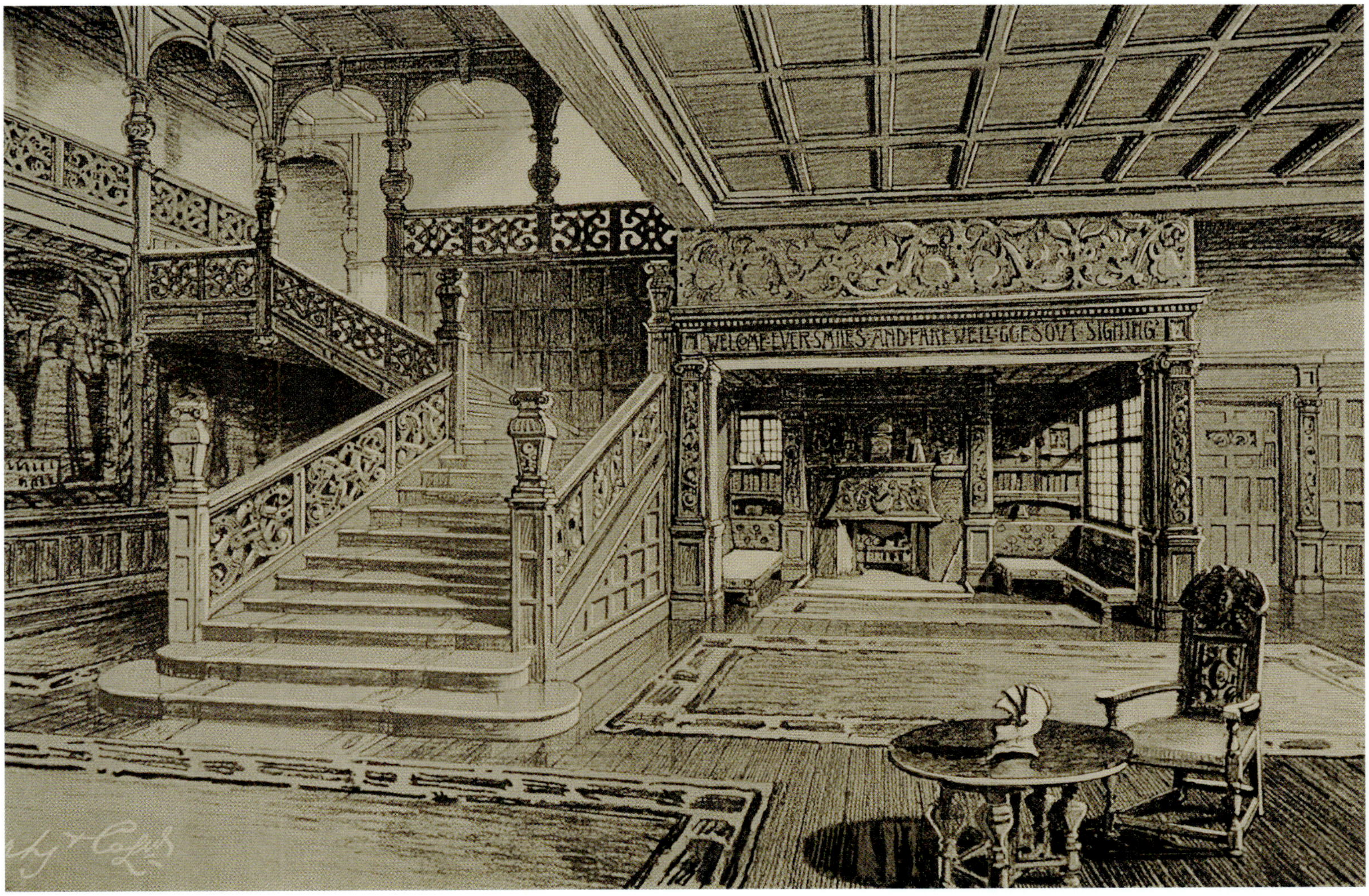

the King of Serbia and even a proposed contract for the Tsar were brought to a halt by the outbreak of World War I but would have added further to Liberty's long list of aristocratic and royal clients.

If the interior design studio's sophisticated bespoke work was beyond the reach of the majority of Liberty's customers, their furniture offering was aimed at a much wider public and always included at least a few items that were much more affordable, but nonetheless of comparable quality.

The stock of furniture had gradually grown since the early days of the shop when E. W. Godwin had bemoaned the fact that there was no 'decent furniture' to be had at the Regent Street emporium, and by the early 1880s, furniture – mostly imported smaller items and Anglo-Oriental bamboo furniture made for Liberty in Soho – occupied several floors of East

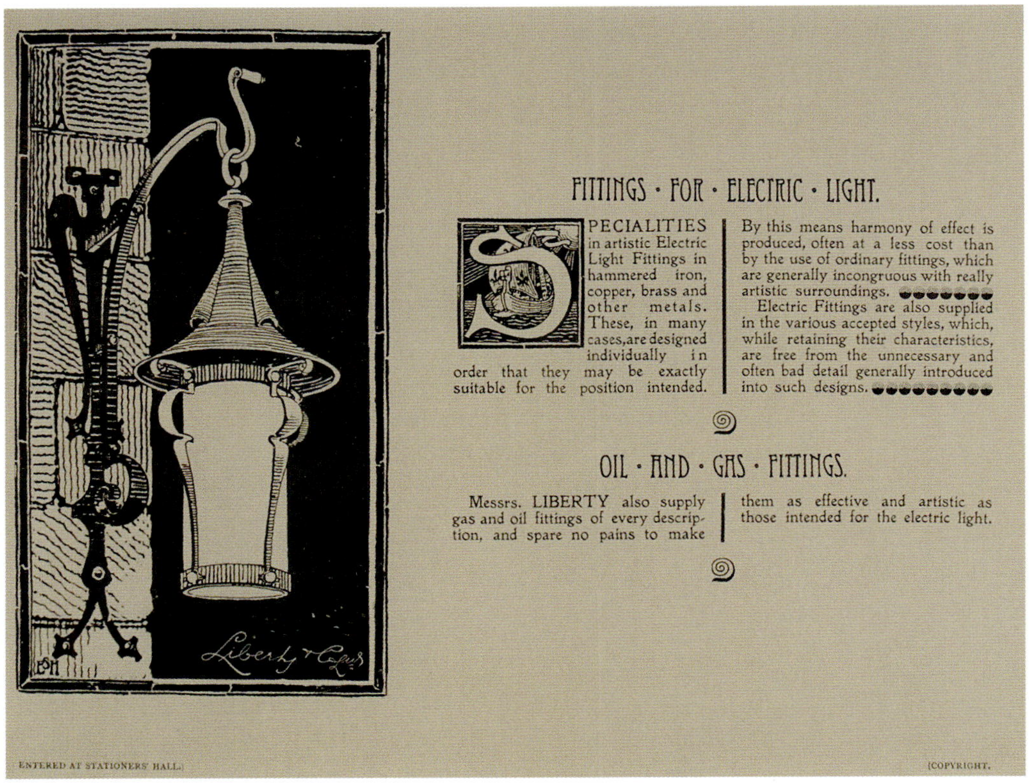

FITTINGS · FOR · ELECTRIC · LIGHT.

SPECIALITIES in artistic Electric Light Fittings in hammered iron, copper, brass and other metals. These, in many cases, are designed individually in order that they may be exactly suitable for the position intended.

By this means harmony of effect is produced, often at a less cost than by the use of ordinary fittings, which are generally incongruous with really artistic surroundings.

Electric Fittings are also supplied in the various accepted styles, which, while retaining their characteristics, are free from the unnecessary and often bad detail generally introduced into such designs.

OIL · AND · GAS · FITTINGS.

Messrs. LIBERTY also supply gas and oil fittings of every description, and spare no pains to make them as effective and artistic as those intended for the electric light.

ENTERED AT STATIONERS' HALL. [COPYRIGHT.

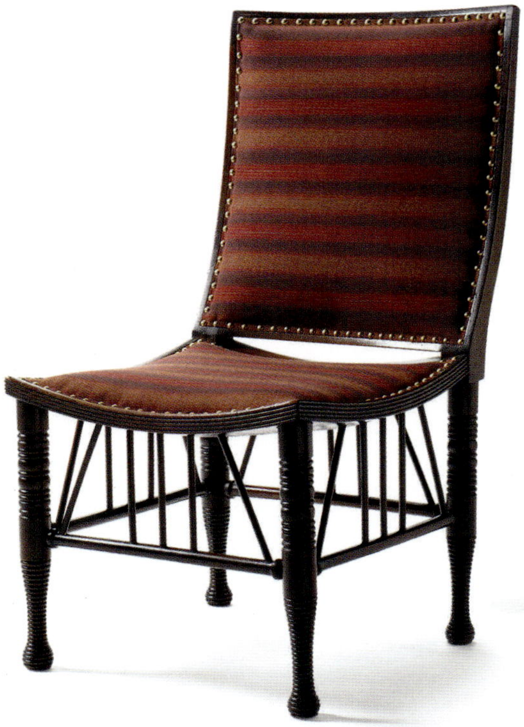

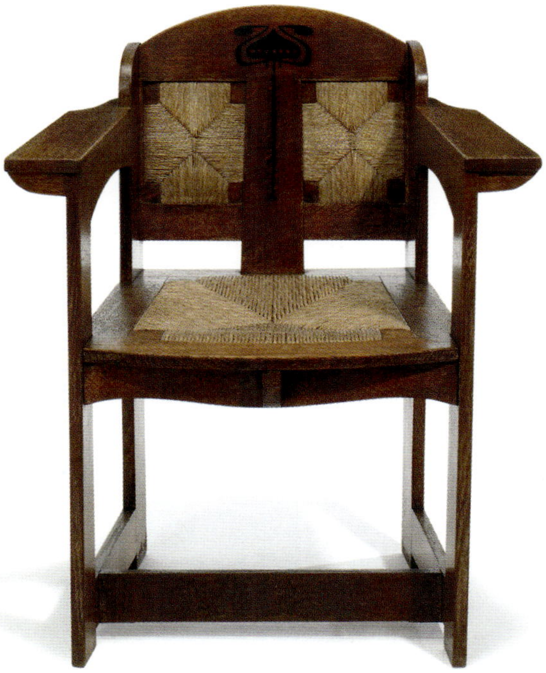

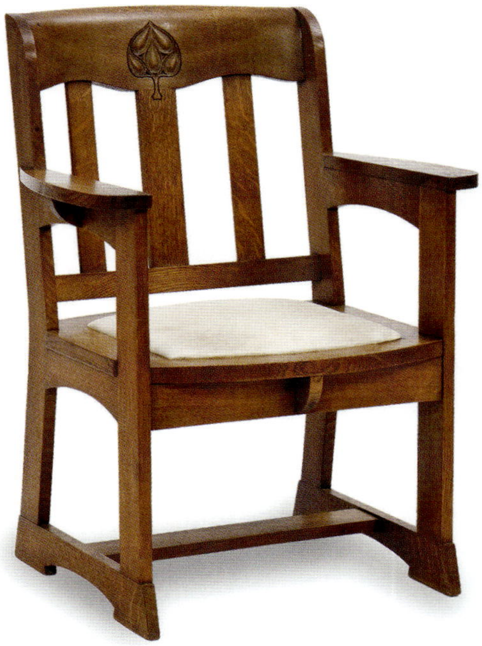

ABOVE *A four-legged, mahogany version of the Thebes chair, inspired by an Egyptian stool in the British Museum and produced by Liberty in the early 1890s.*

India House. With the move to Chesham House and the establishment of Leonard Wyburd at the helm of the Furnishing and Decoration Studio, Liberty & Co. began its own production of Art Furniture, which in the period up to World War I generated many different styles and a wide variety of furniture.

Even though over the years several designers made their contribution to Liberty's furniture venture, the company's general marketing policy of not naming the designers of their products often makes it difficult to attribute the individual designs to their creators. In contrast, Wyburd's contribution and key importance for the development of Liberty's furniture is more clearly visible in the many sketches and designs which appeared, sometimes with his initials, in the company's advertorial publications. Progressively from the mid-1880s, Wyburd's designs for furniture evolved into the avant-garde style that became internationally recognizable as Liberty's own.

Wyburd's earliest designs were in the fashionable Oriental vein. Particularly inspired by the artistry of Arabian furniture, he developed his own designs in the Moorish style, an 'adaptation of Arabian art', in Liberty's words. He often employed Mashrabiya latticework and arches in both his interior decoration schemes, particularly fashionable for smoking rooms, and in his furniture designs, which were described as 'light and elegant'. Wyburd's Moorish designs continued to be part of the Liberty range for many years to come, obviously still popular even after the craze for the exotic had long abated.

One of the first pieces produced after Wyburd had come on board was the Thebes Stool, which came in both a three- and four-legged version. The stools were closely based on ancient Egyptian models that had already inspired a number of artists and designers like Christopher Dresser and E. W. Godwin. Liberty's patented versions were to prove highly popular, and remained in production well into the twentieth century. In 1895, a decade after the first Thebes Stool was launched, Siegfried Bing chose it as part of his stock of the very best of 'advanced decorative art' to be sold in his influential Maison de l'Art Nouveau, and several European museums bought the Thebes and other Liberty furniture as prime examples of contemporary design.

With changing fashions, the popularity of Oriental decor decreased and other

ABOVE MIDDLE *Manufactured by William Birch in his workshop in High Wycombe, Liberty stalwart E. G. Punnett designed this Arts and Crafts oak chair in 1901.*

ABOVE RIGHT *This solid oak armchair featuring a simple leaf motif on the back is designed by E. G. Punnett and dates from 1900.*

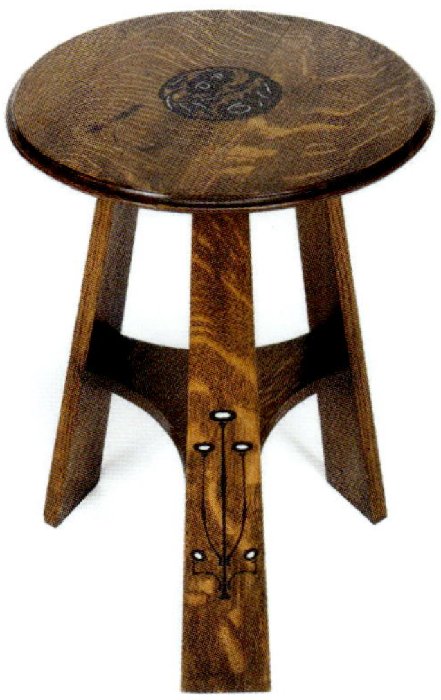

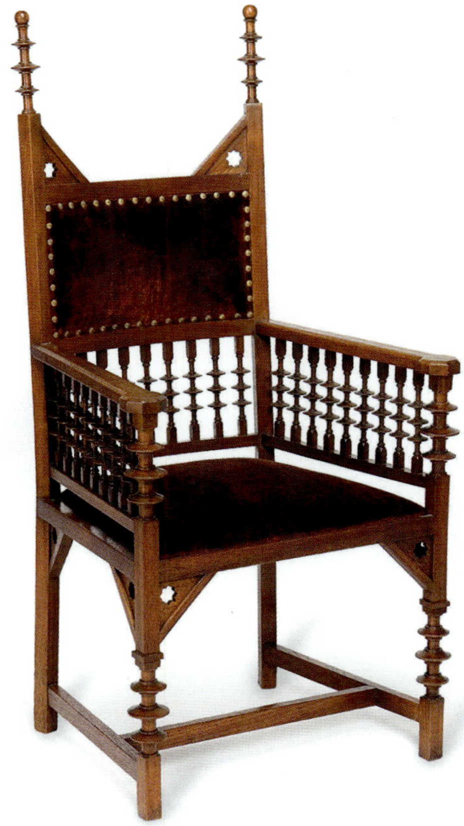

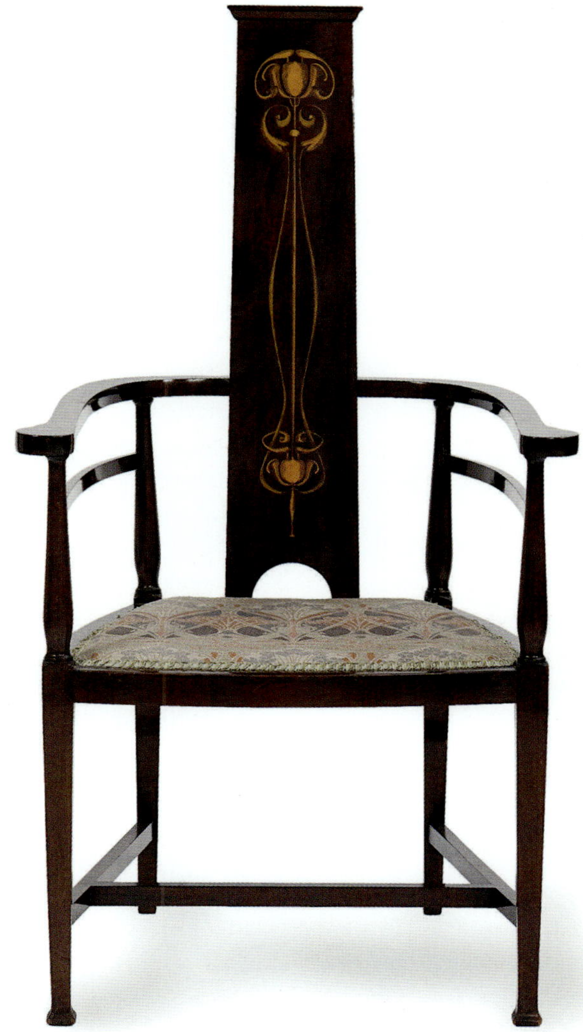

ABOVE LEFT *An Arts and Crafts side table inlaid with a pewter and ebony floral design by E. G. Punnett.*

ABOVE MIDDLE *A velvet-upholstered armchair, redolent of an ecclesiastical chair or throne, with elaborate turned wooden spindles in the arms and back.*

styles came more into favour, particularly traditional, simple country furniture in the style of Morris & Co., and a whole assortment of historical English and European revival styles, which ranged from Jacobean, Elizabethan and English Renaissance to styles called Domestic Gothic, German Gothic or Flemish. These styles evoked a romantic sense of bygone times and the traditional quality of Old English furniture. Jacobean was considered particularly worthy of a resurrection and described in the catalogue as 'perhaps the most English in its characteristics'. Arthur Liberty, in his lecture to the Society of Arts on English furniture in March 1900, held the opinion that the Jacobean was the finest period of English furniture, until the 'Gothic revival brought us back to first principles of construction and directness of design'.

The Old English furniture styles, as well as the traditional country furniture that featured increasingly in the catalogues from the late 1880s and early 1890s onwards, appealed to those interested in the ideas and aesthetics of the British Arts and Crafts movement, which advocated a return to the traditional craft methods of pre-Industrial times.

Gradually, Wyburd's designs evolved from these historical revival styles to designs which became progressively original. By the mid-1890s he had developed his own and innovative idiom that combined elements of the Arts and Crafts style with his own take on an imagined medieval past. In this period, Wyburd designs in Liberty's Art furniture catalogues were characterized by sturdy oak pieces in geometric, often tapering shapes, with a substantial, medieval character, and embellished with prominent decorative metal hinges and handles. Typical elements included the use of heart piercings and hand-beaten copperware – features which were, or were to become, typical vocabulary of the Arts and Crafts-style language. Another recurring feature that started to appear was the application of mottoes or quotations to furniture and panelling: a beaten copper band at the top of a bookcase, for example, held the inscription 'Read not to believe & take for granted but to weigh & consider' (a Francis

ABOVE *This lightweight armchair from around 1900 has an elongated back panel with stylized floral inlay. The seat is upholstered with a typical example of the Art Nouveau print fabric for which Liberty was so famous.*

BELOW LEFT *A side table from the Saracen collection dating from the 1890s, with yellow and green decorative tiles and typically Moorish arches on the base.*

BELOW RIGHT *This delicate walnut side table with ogee arch legs was produced in 1890 in the style of Aesthetic movement designer E. W. Godwin.*

Bacon quotation) and a smoker's cabinet sported the mysterious motto "The man who smokes thinks like a sage and acts like a Samaritan".

The furniture on offer encompassed everything needed for the decoration of an artistic, fashionable home, from imposing sideboards and bookcases to tables, chairs and settees, to bedroom suites and dressing tables. The furniture pieces, representing the very latest in modern design at the time, were paradoxically given archaic-sounding names, like Athelstan, Ethelbert or Lochleven, evoking images of medieval kings and the Age of Chivalry. Wyburd's original interpretation of the Arts and Crafts aesthetic made Liberty's Art Furniture all the rage, both at home and abroad, and because of the resounding success, it became widely known as the Liberty Style.

From its origins as an Oriental Warehouse, Arthur Liberty's namesake store – shaped by the founder's infallible sense for the innovative art and emerging design trends of the time, as well as his astute business acumen – went from strength to strength and by the 1890s, had become a byword for a new and distinctive style of its own. An article called "The Liberty Art Movement", published in 1894 in the magazine *British Warehouseman*, praised Arthur Liberty and his "unique business" for having "created an entirely new taste in fabrics, dress, and interior decoration, the word Liberty having become descriptive of the style...". "I was determined," Mr Liberty said, "not to follow existing fashions but to create new ones."

Liberty's energetic and effective marketing strategies were a key element in this. Its innovative use of catalogues and mail order, elaborate and exciting 'in-shop' exhibitions, and a major presence in the most important and influential contemporary publications on design, such as *The Studio*, spread and popularized the Liberty Style in furniture as well as Liberty's other design ventures. Through these strategies, a wider market for the Arts and Crafts aesthetic was created. Shrewdly, the company strove to appeal both to the very top end of the market with its avant-garde design and exclusive high-end products, and through offering smaller, moderately priced but stylish items, to appeal to the much wider market of middle-class customers. The growth of the middle classes in the later Victorian era, and their steadily increasing spending power, meant that Liberty's potential customer base grew in tandem. For the middle classes, having a fashionably and suitably furnished artistic home had become an important indicator of status. Liberty had become the destination of choice for the aspirational Victorian shopper.

More significantly, Liberty had established a reputation for promoting the best of contemporary design, as a feature in the *Art Journal* of 1900 enthusiastically noted, describing Liberty's position in a highly complimentary way: "it opened up an immense series of possibilities for all

BELOW LEFT *A square walnut side table from around 1890 with a dramatically angled base in the Moresque style embraced by the Aesthetic movement.*

BELOW RIGHT *An Aesthetic movement-style painted side table with the Mashrabiya latticework on the base, as favoured by Leonard Wyburd.*

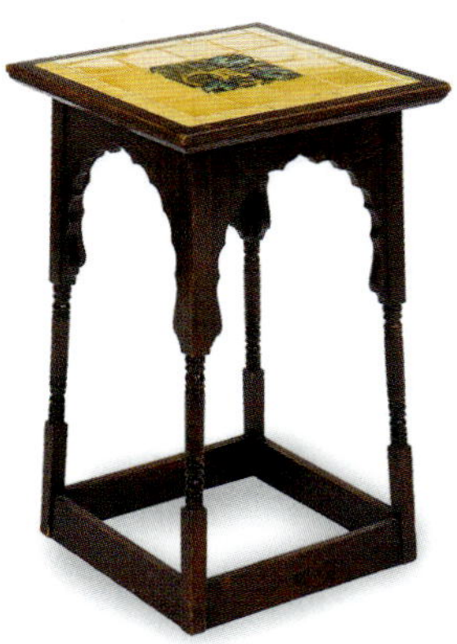

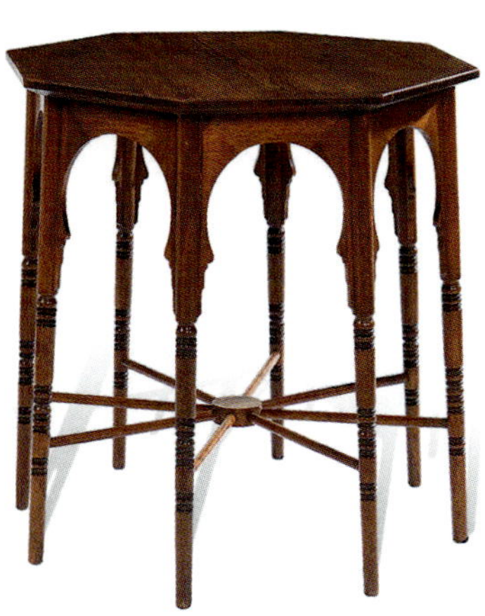

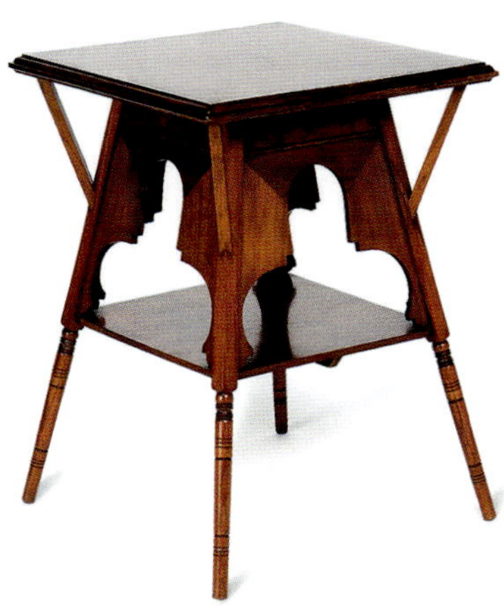

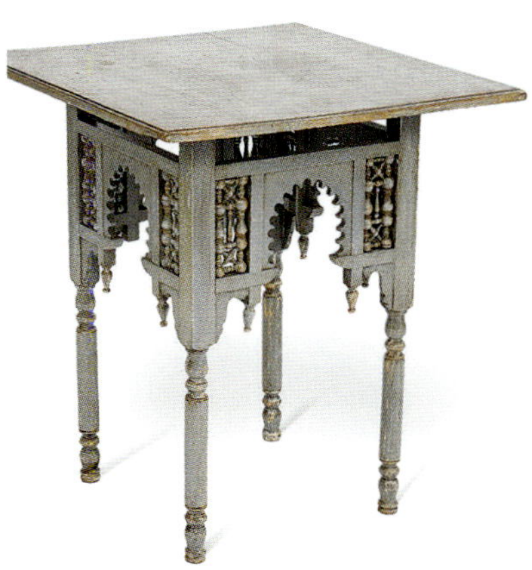

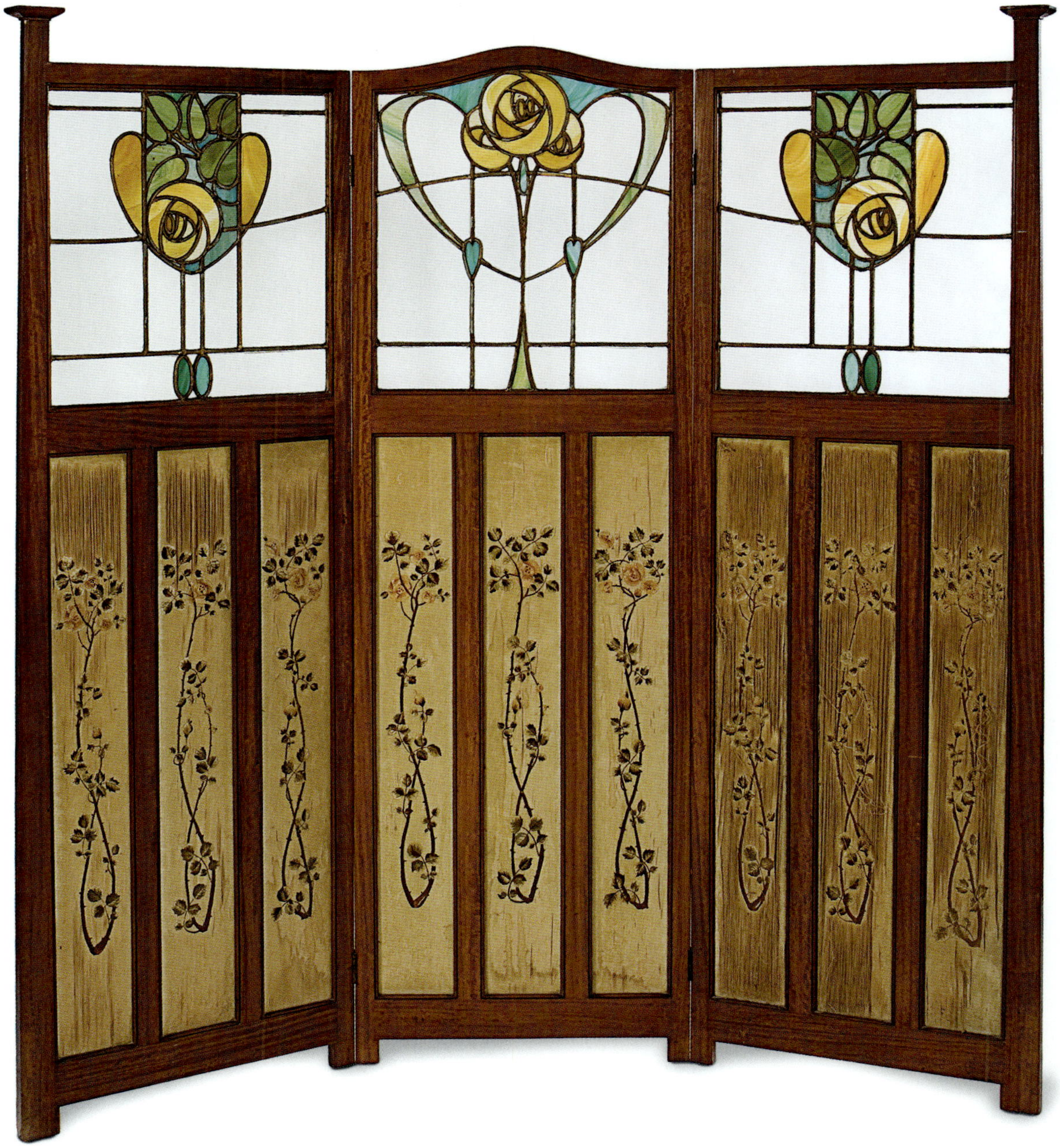

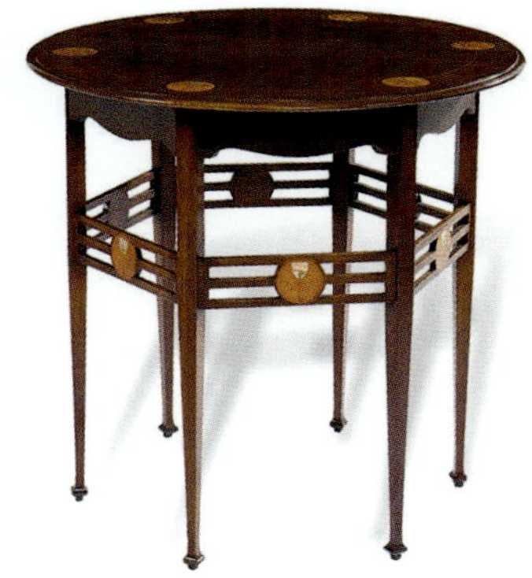

ABOVE *A side table with tapered legs encircled by a hexagonal band and inlaid circular motifs in the Art Nouveau style, produced at the turn of the century.*

LEFT *Glasgow School branch of Arts and Crafts design, headed by Charles Rennie Mackintosh, produced distinctive pieces such as this light satin-wood screen with stained glass and embroidered panels.*

lovers of decorative opportunities" and had "become a huge art centre where the furnishing and fitting up of houses on sound artistic methods is undertaken, where decorative accessories of all kinds may be procured".

A sign of success is when the avant-garde becomes mainstream, and Liberty's furniture venture was no exception to this rule. It had helped to popularize the aesthetics of Arts and Crafts, and more and more furniture makers began to make furniture in an artistic vein, quite clearly inspired by the Liberty Style.

The importance of Arts and Crafts themes in Liberty's furniture began slowly to fade after Wyburd left the company around 1905, and, mostly through the designs of George Walton (1867–1933), lighter pieces with a certain "Glasgow Style" element made their appearance. After 1910 and into the 1920s and 1930s, reproductions of historical styles began to dominate the Liberty catalogues alongside contemporary pieces that were altogether plainer and simpler, and it was not until after World War II, in the 1950s, that Liberty & Co. was to reclaim its position as arbiter of the best in contemporary furniture design.

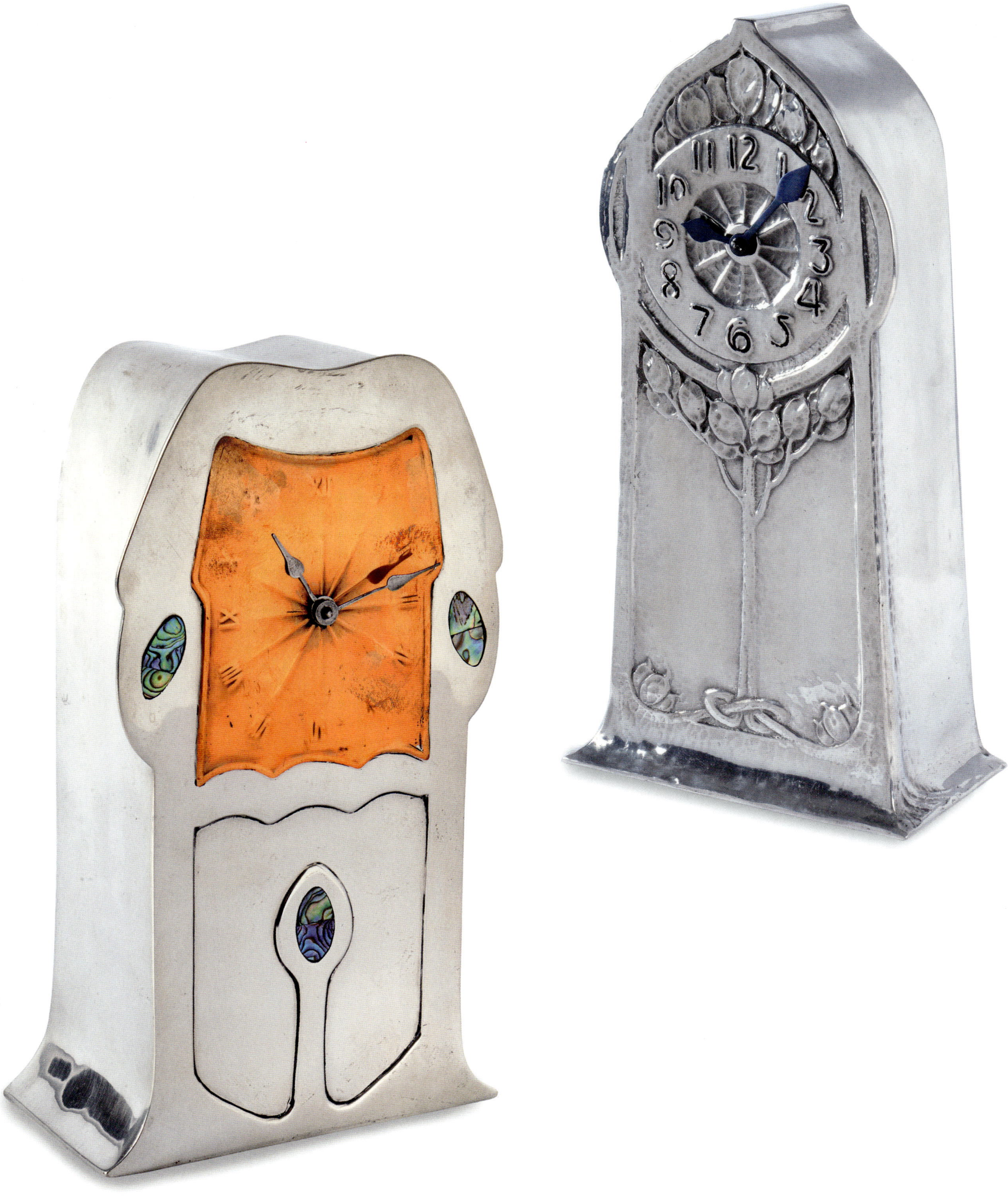

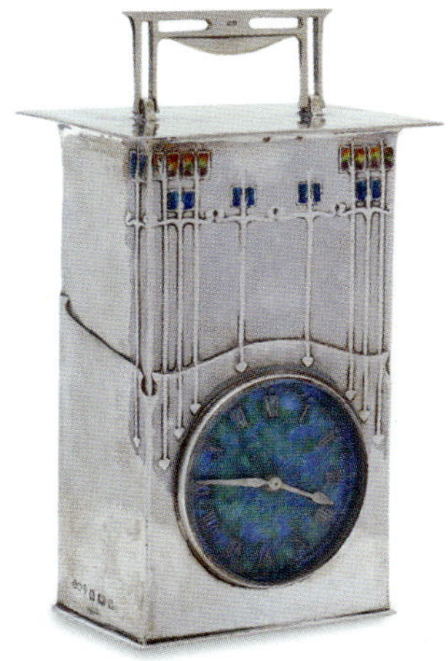

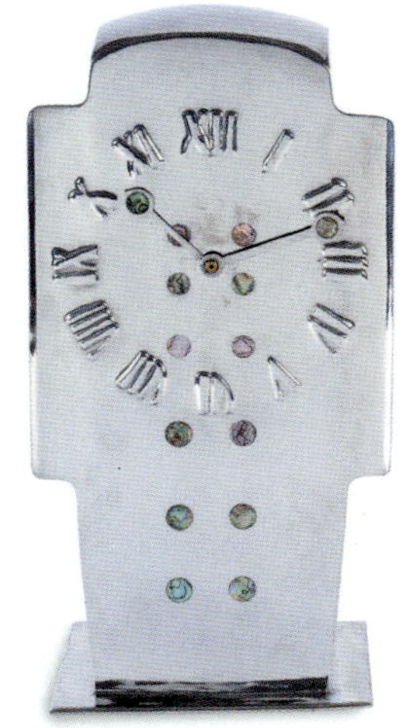

METALWORK

Together with Liberty's Art Fabrics and its output of furniture, the firm's efforts in silver and pewter were key elements in its own idiomatic design amalgam that would become known as Liberty Style, or "Stile". Until the late 1890s when Liberty & Co. would launch its own ranges of metalwork, the Regent Street shop's speciality lay in the incredible variety of exotic silver, brass and copper objects and jewellery from the Near and Far East that it had on offer, as befitted its origins as an Oriental emporium. Many of the pieces, both antique and modern, were Japanese, and they included bronze vases, statues or candlesticks, and small iron cabinets damascened in gold, intricate silver teapots and spoons, as well as antique swords and sword guards. There was also Indian enamel, brass and copper and a large range of Near Eastern metalwork which would particularly find favour in the Moorish smoking rooms that were the height of fashion at the time.

Liberty also carried products from Britain and the Continent, particularly the cloisonné enamel of the Swiss-based firm of the English artist Clement John Heaton (1861–1940) and beaten copper pieces by the craftsman John Pearson. Curiously, given his otherwise close connection to the firm and its founder, it seems only one of Christopher Dresser's many designs for metalwork was sold by Liberty – the Kordofan candlestick, in brass, polished or painted in Art colours.

The guilds of handicrafts of the Arts and Crafts movement, which had sprung up in the 1880s and 1890s, produced metalware of refined design but, with their insistence on the handmade and on traditional techniques, the pieces were mostly far too expensive for anyone but the most affluent to buy. Arthur Liberty's business philosophy to produce "useful and beautiful objects at prices in the reach of all classes" had been applied to textiles and furniture already, and now, towards the end of the century, the company turned their attention to the possibilities in metalware.

Arthur Liberty and John Llewellyn, the director whose artistic guidance since joining the firm in 1889 had exerted such a productive influence on the company's ventures, sensed the need for innovation. With Liberty generally keen to promote British avant-garde design and British manufacture, they decided to start designing and making their own in-house range of silver and jewellery. The collection of Art silverware (which also included some gold jewellery) was launched in a small exhibition at the Regent Street shop in May 1899, and in a nod to Llewellyn's Welsh roots and intended to evoke a sense of the archaic, it was marketed under

OPPOSITE ABOVE *David Veasey began working for Liberty's metalwork department in the 1890s. This pewter Arts and Crafts style clock with a Tree of Life motif dates from around 1903.*

OPPOSITE BELOW *The lines evocative of nature and the colourful abalone inlays on this silver and copper-faced clock are typical of Archibald Knox's Cymric designs created in the Silver Studio in the early 1900s.*

ABOVE LEFT *This Magnus silver carriage clock from 1902, attributed to Knox, is decorated with a green enamel clock face and stylized floral motifs.*

ABOVE RIGHT *A cruciform clock from the Tudric range – the pewter equivalent of the Celtic-influenced Cymric designs – with abalone shell circles on the body of the clock and on the hands.*

RIGHT *Nine original clock designs from the* Silver Sketchbook 1900–1912 *and the* Pewter Sketchbook 1900–1912.

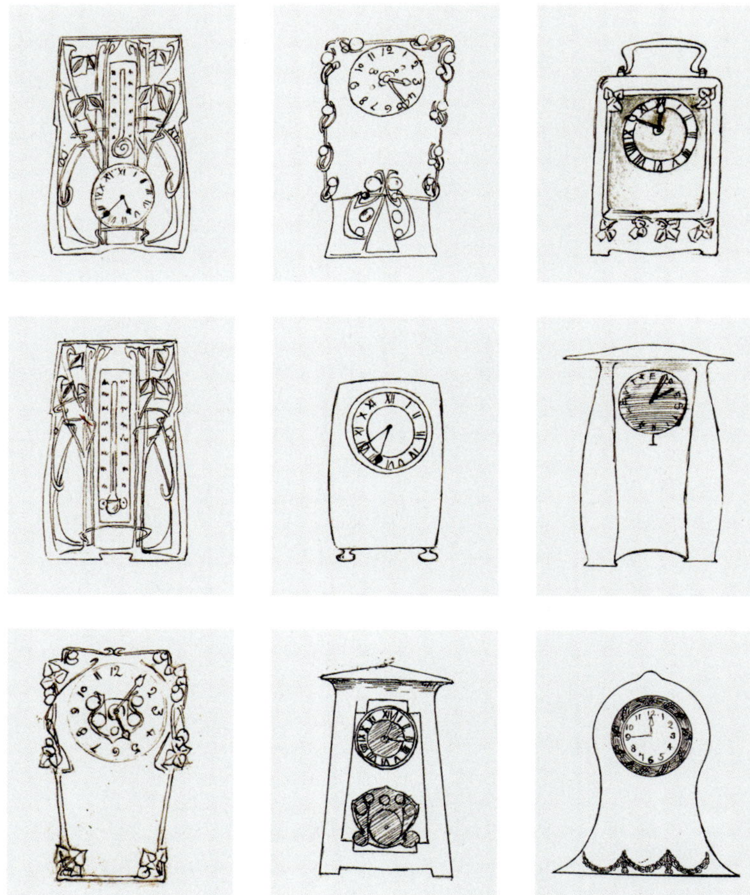

BELOW *A footed bowl executed in hammered silver with vibrant green and blue enamelling, evocative of a classical landscape. Designed by artist Eleanor Fortescue Brickdale in 1899.*

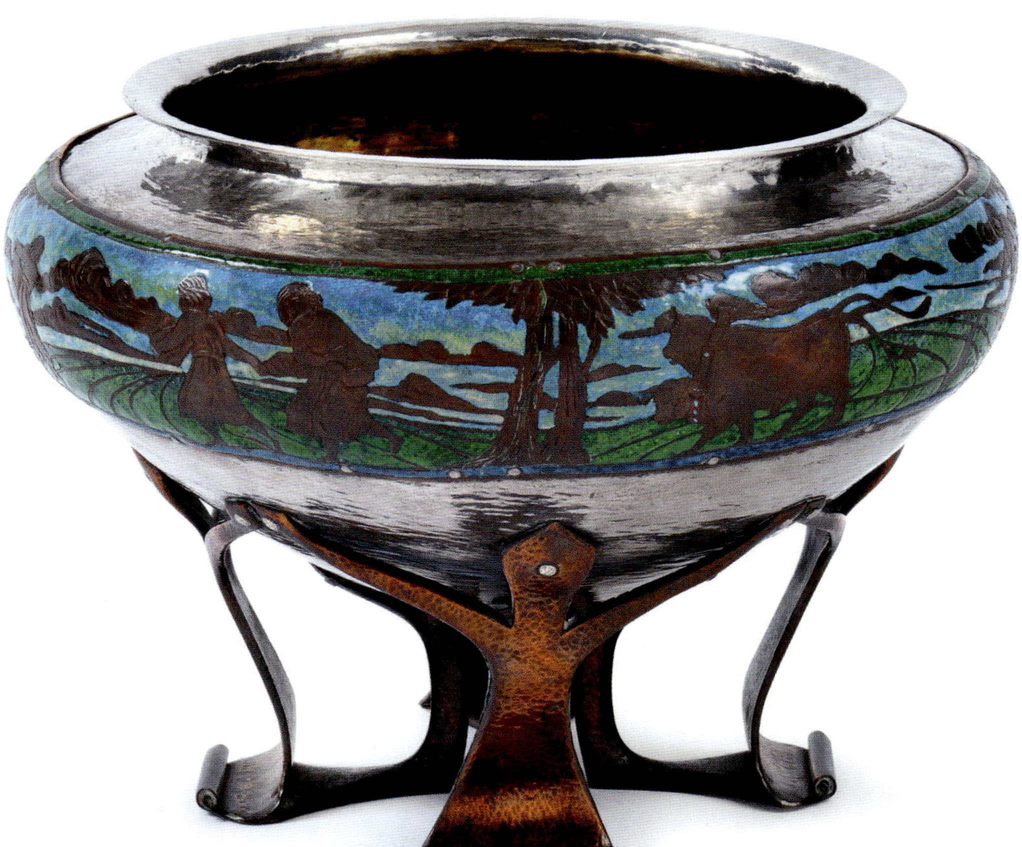

the Welsh moniker "Cymric", with the individual pieces being given historical or romantic names such as Edred, Clywin or Avalon. Initially, Cymric gold and silver pieces were made entirely by hand, but for them to be produced on a large scale economically, the range would soon be manufactured with the help of automated techniques, spinning and die-casting, and then finished by hand to give it the desired hand-wrought look. Cymric's earliest designs were executed by various workshops in Soho, which was the traditional centre of the silver- and goldsmith trade, but before long, W. H. Haseler, the Birmingham firm of manufacturing goldsmiths and jewellers who had been involved in the scheme from the beginning, took over almost the entire production of the range, and a joint venture between Haseler and Liberty followed in 1901. Haseler would continue to manufacture silverware for Liberty until the late 1920s. Through the Haseler connection, designs for the new metalwork venture came from several designers associated with the local Birmingham Arts and Crafts movement, including Arthur and Georgina Gaskin, Oliver Baker and Bernard Cuzner.

However, the bulk of the designs, and really the key influence on the very distinctive direction Cymric was to take, came from the Silver Studio, the design group that already provided some of the most interesting and influential designs for Liberty's Art Fabrics, and especially from one particularly brilliant designer working for the studio, Archibald Knox (1864–1933). The son of a marine engineer, Archibald Knox was born on the Isle of Man in 1864. He had studied and later taught at the Douglas School of Art, where he specialized in Celtic art and ornament, which was to remain a lifelong interest. While on the Isle of Man he worked for a time for the architect Mackay Hugh Baillie Scott and when he moved to London in 1897, it is likely that he was also briefly employed at Christopher Dresser's design studio. However, from 1899 onwards, Knox, through his work for the Silver Studio, would be responsible

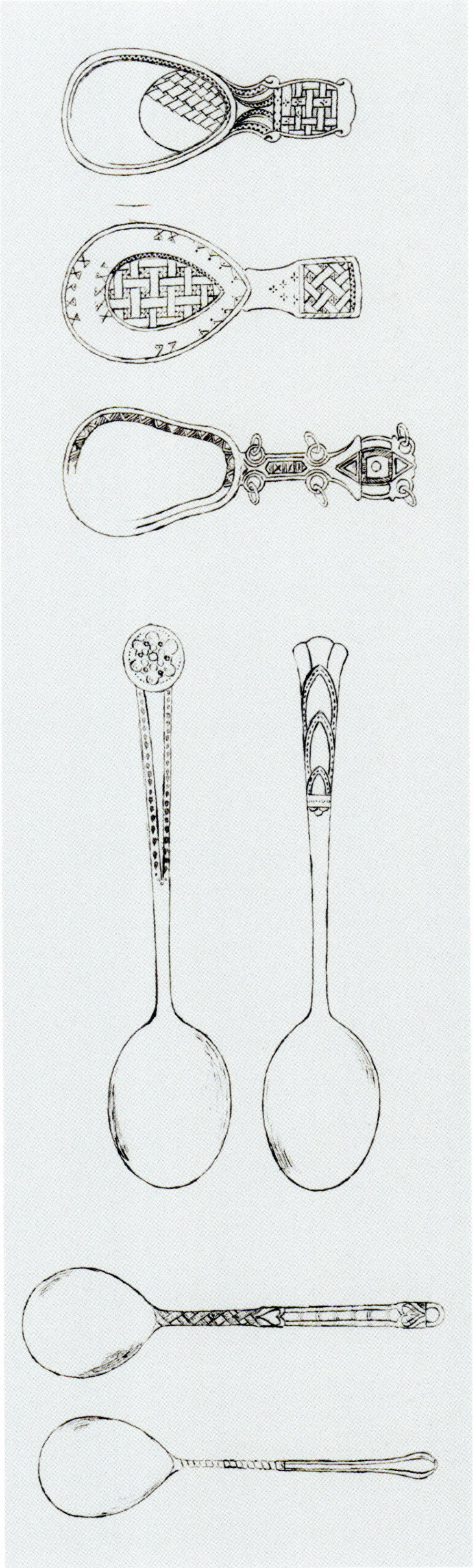

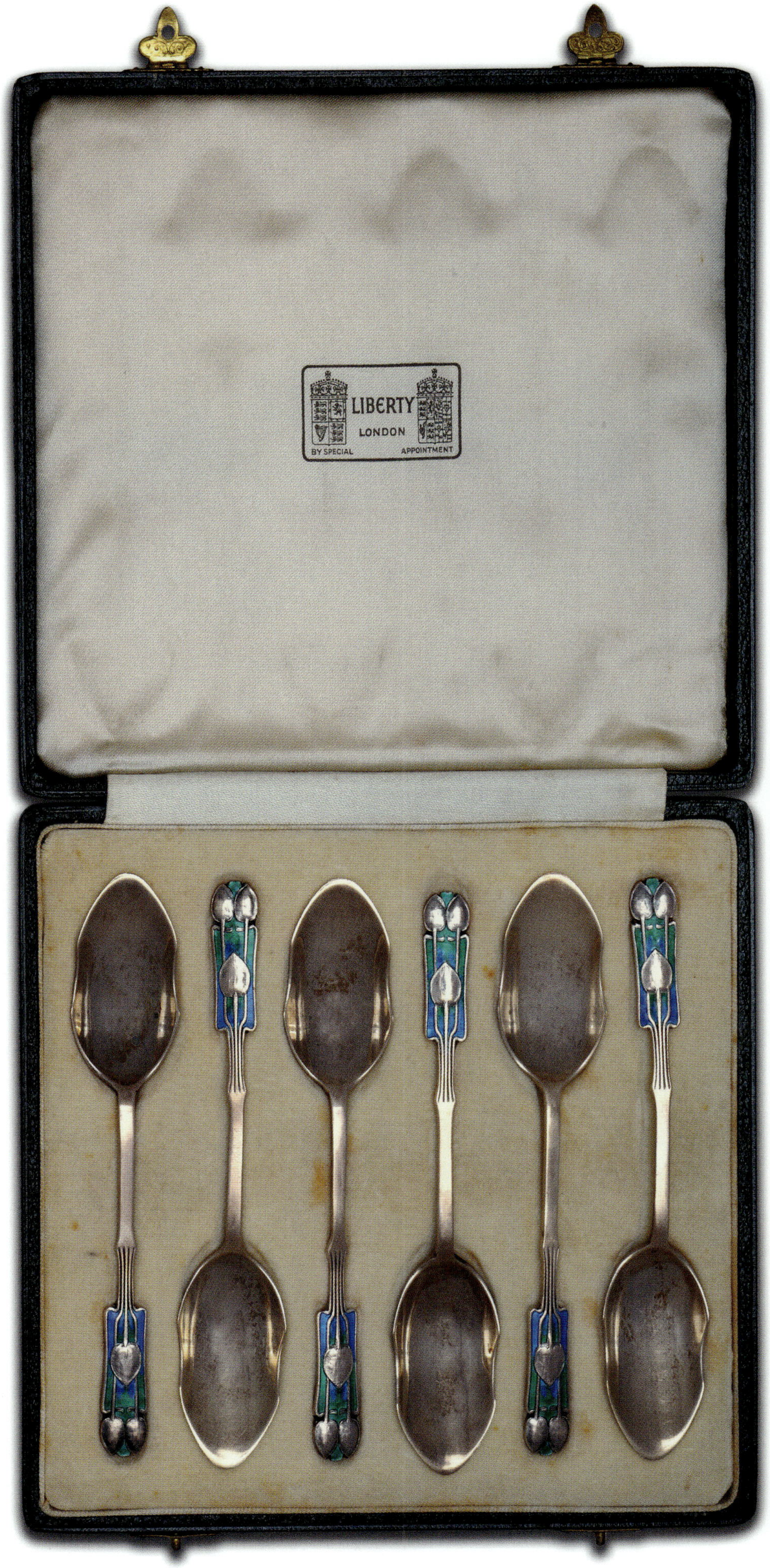

ABOVE AND RIGHT *Original sketches for seven teaspoons from the* Silver Sketchbook *and a set of six silver teaspoons of similar design produced in 1935 and attributed to Archibald Knox.*

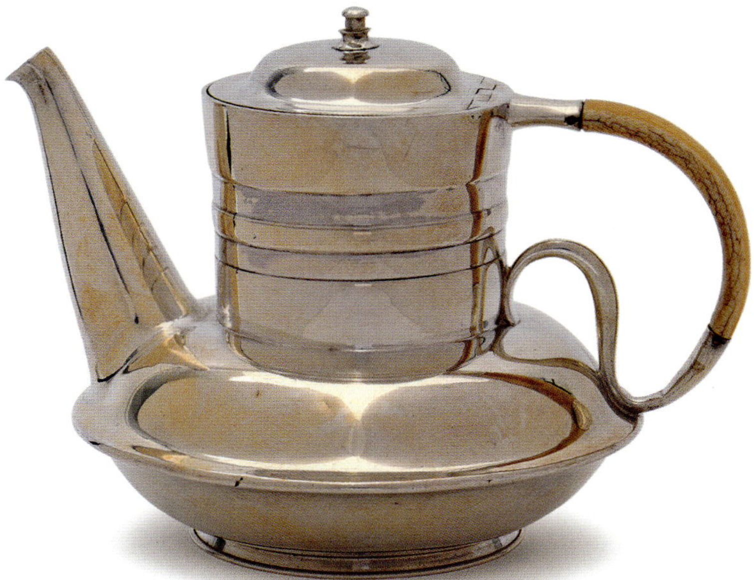

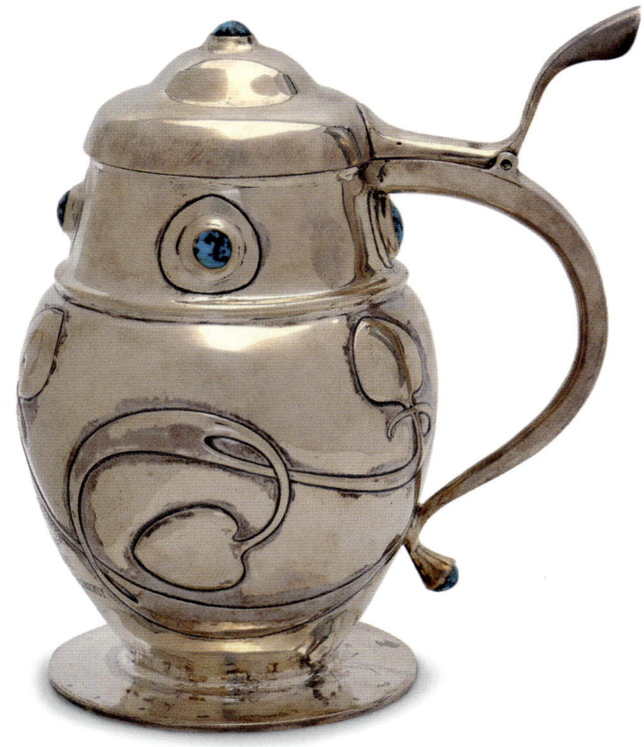

ABOVE *Evocative of the squat style of Japanese teapots, this simple silver and ivory piece was designed by Archibald Knox in 1906.*

ABOVE *Produced in 1901, this silver tankard by Archibald Knox is decorated with stylized foliage and turquoise cabochons.*

for many of the iconic silver and jewellery designs for the Cymric venture, and it was Knox, too, who was so influential in adding that specific Celtic element to Liberty's silverware. Knox's designs for Liberty were not limited to metalware, they also included carpets, textiles and terracotta garden ornaments.

His most prolific period spanned the years from 1903 to 1906, and in the decade he worked for Liberty, Knox supplied over 400 unique designs ranging from tea and coffee services and vases and candlesticks to clocks and jewellery in both the silver and the later pewter ranges. The treatment of ornament varies accordingly, and stylized plant forms, spade and heart shapes featured alongside the Celtic knots. Many of the pieces were decorated with inlays of enamel, pearl or semi-precious stones and showed hammer marks – both very characteristic features of Arts and Crafts. The lines and shapes appear also to correspond to the silverwork of Art Nouveau and Jugendstil on the Continent, even though Arthur Liberty and many of the designers working with him expressed a strong distaste for what they perceived as the design excesses in Art Nouveau.

Other notable decorative artists who supplied metalware designs to Liberty, and many of whom were also associated with the Silver Studio, included Harry Napper, John Illingworth Kay and Harry Silver (the brother of Rex), as well as the head of the studio, Reginald "Rex" Silver who had taken over the role after his father's death. Jessie Marion King designed jewellery, buckles and waist clasps, and elegant silver toilet sets of brushes, mirrors, powder boxes and combs. It is often very difficult to establish who created the original designs, as both the Silver Studio, which simply ascribed all of the artwork leaving the studio to the head of the firm, and Liberty & Co. did not credit the individual designers.

Encouraged by the success of the silverware, this approach was extended to a separate range made entirely of pewter. In 1898, Liberty had begun to import contemporary pewterware from J. P. Kayser & Sohn of Krefeld, as well as from other German firms that were exponents of Jugendstil's rediscovery of pewter. Long considered merely a pale imitation of more precious materials, pewter had seen a considerable re-evaluation of its qualities. It was relatively easy to cast, even in the elaborate forms which Art Nouveau favoured, and as such was perfectly fitted to the new design aesthetic. The

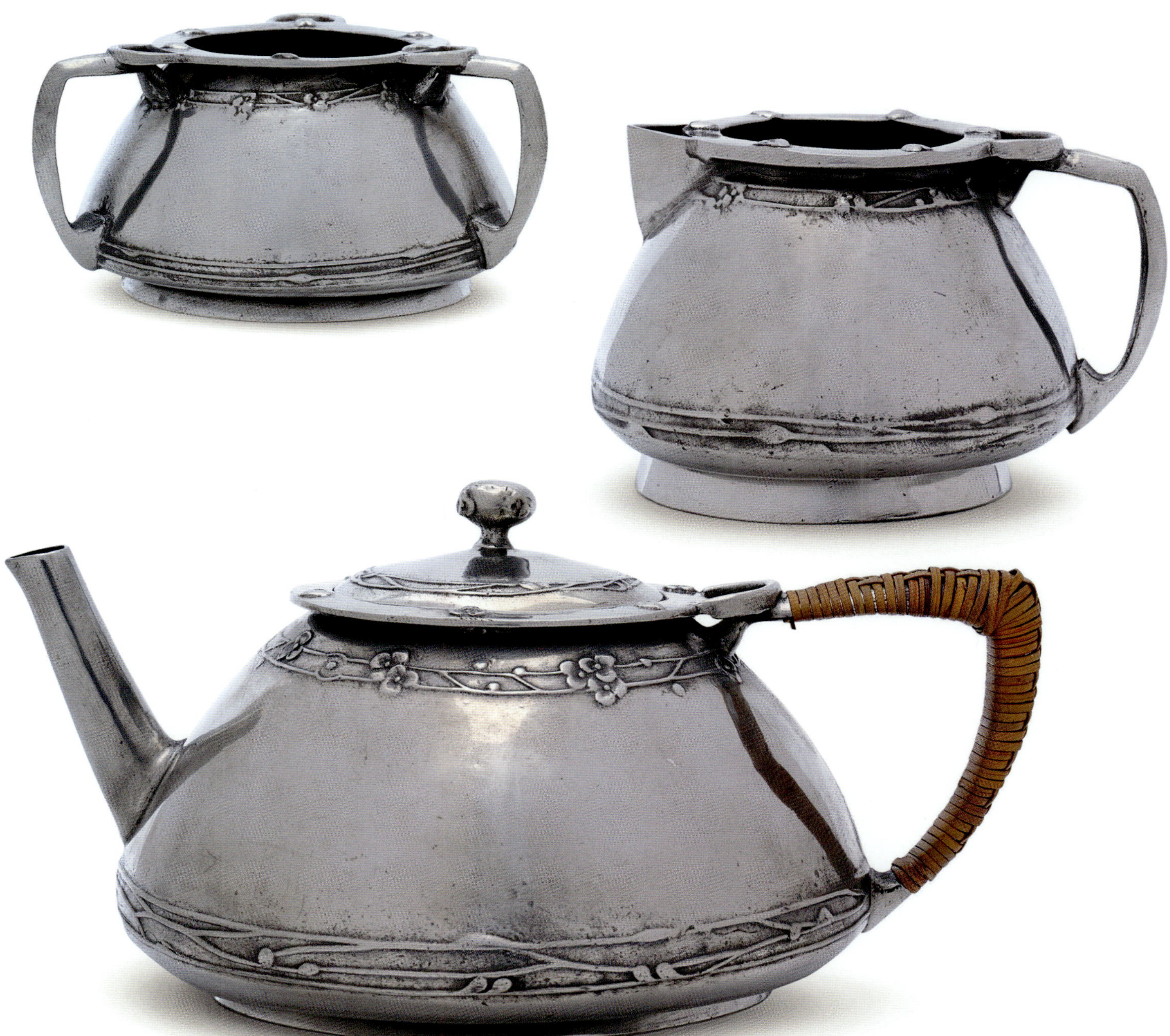

ABOVE *A Tudric tea set in the Art Nouveau style, comprising a teapot, milk jug and sugar bowl designed by Jessie M. King, a designer widely known as a children's book illustrator.*

lower price of the material and the mass production it allowed meant that here was at last one way of offering stylish design at affordable prices. Kayserzinn, the range from J. P. Kayser & Sohn, was considerably cheaper than Liberty's Cymric silverware and seeing the commercial success of the German pewterware in the Regent Street shop, Liberty launched its own line, "Tudric", in 1901, also produced by W. H. Haseler. The bulk of the manufacturing process for the range was done as far as possible through iron-mould casting. The designs, most of which again came from Archibald Knox and the Silver Studio, tended to be simpler, with modifications of Celtic and floral forms. The range's reputation reached its zenith in the years between 1901 and World War I, continuing to be produced, if on a lesser scale, until the outbreak of World War II.

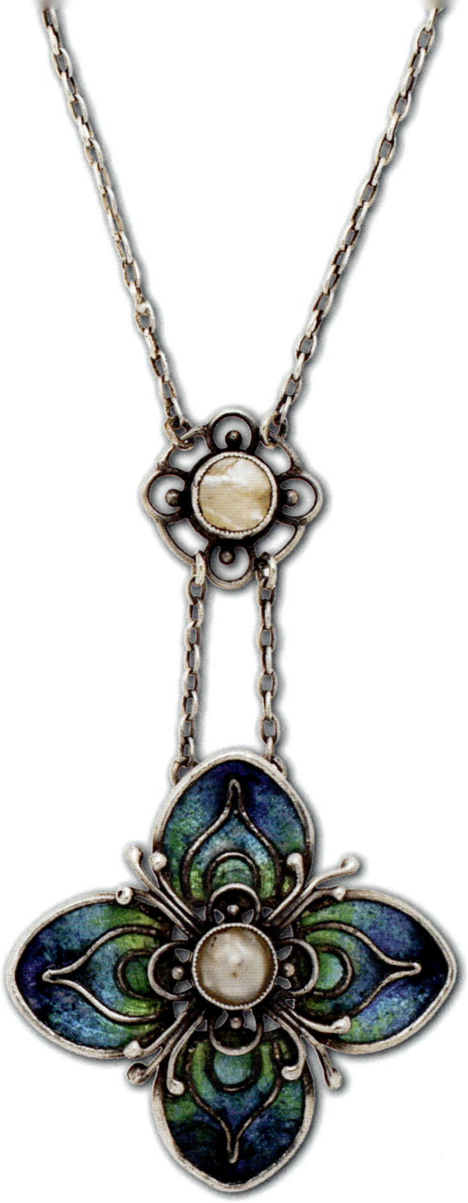

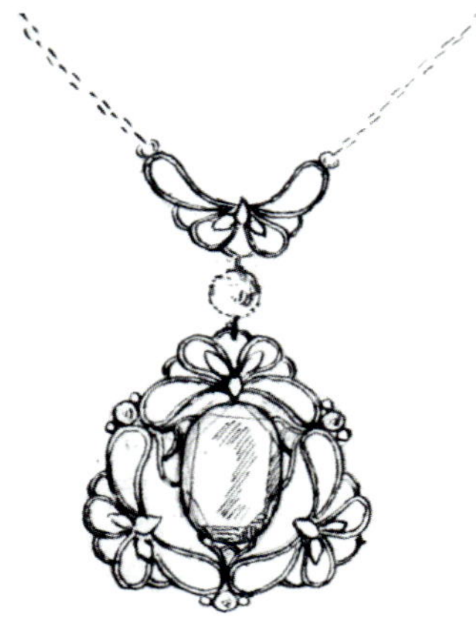

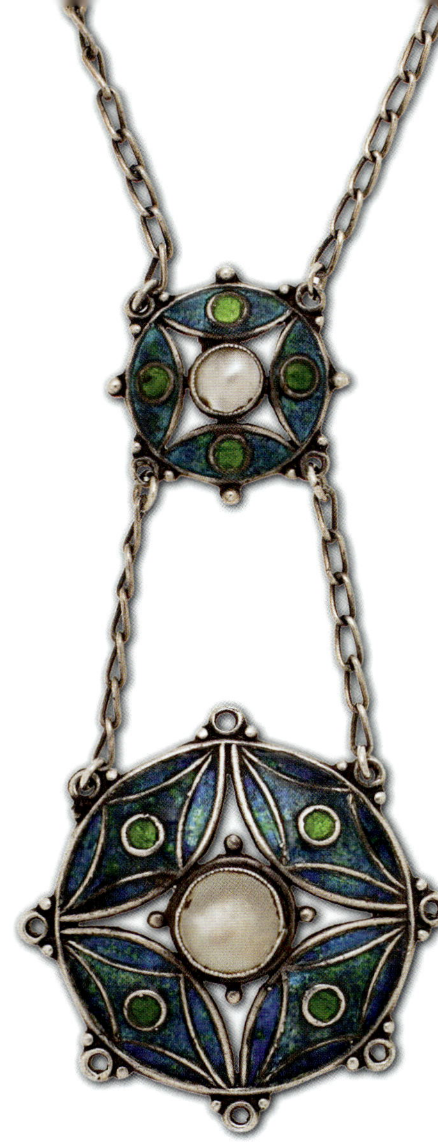

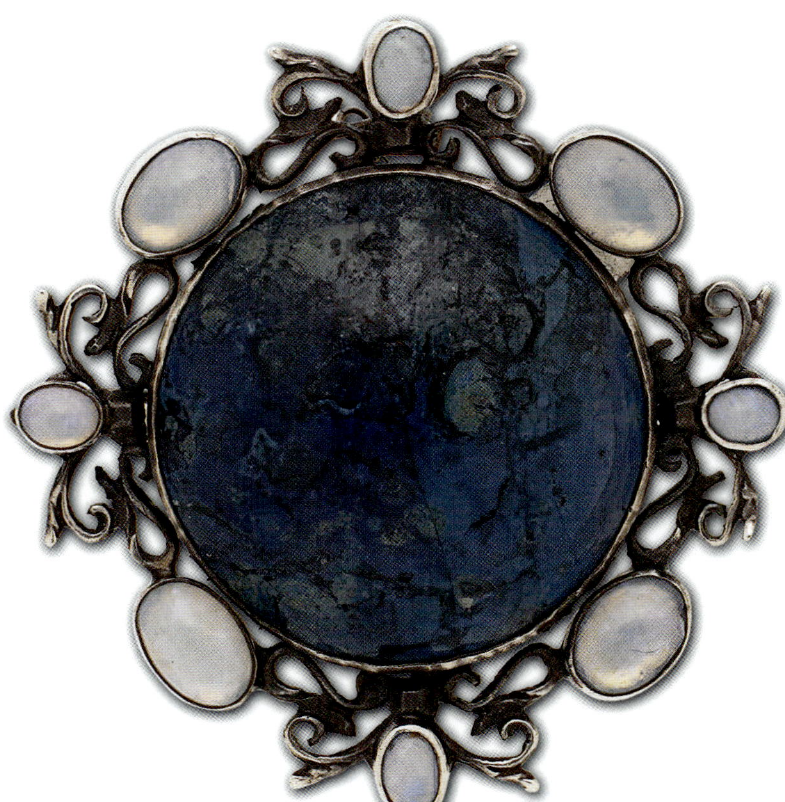

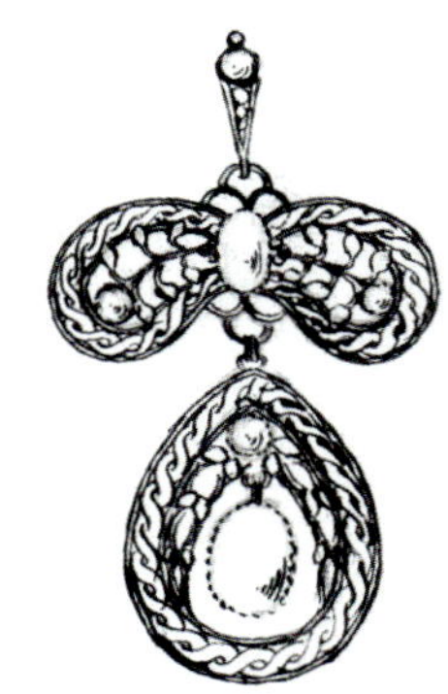

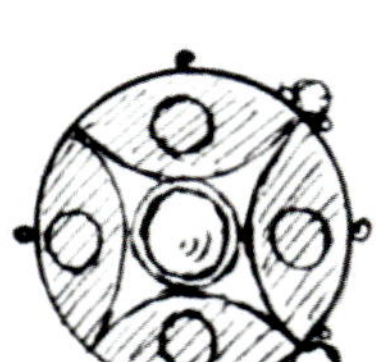

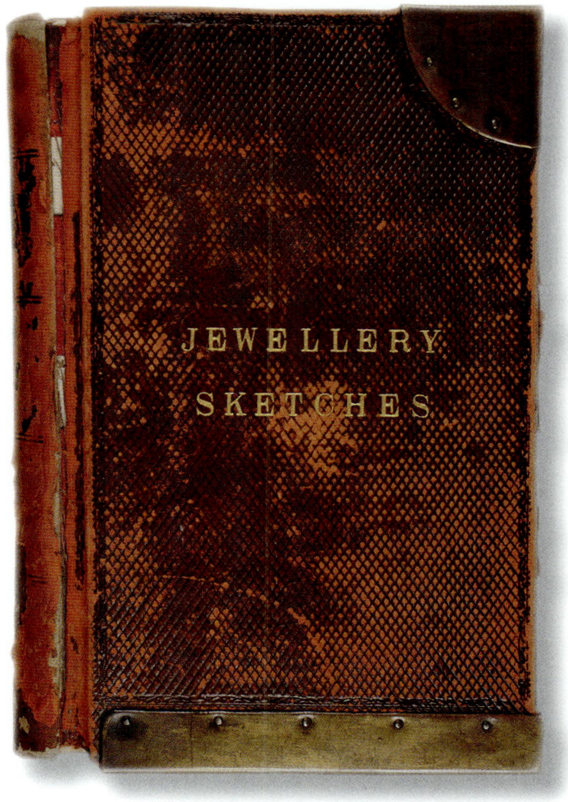

JEWELLERY

Both the Tudric and the Cymric ranges were sold in Liberty's jewellery department, which had existed since 1883 and had originally specialized in jewellery and bijouterie of Oriental origin, from Indian work of gold and precious stones to antique jade and amber. As was the case in most of Liberty's other departments, rare and antique pieces featured alongside much more affordable articles sourced from all over the world. These "art novelties for personal attire" were sold rather like costume jewellery might be sold today, even if the materials used were still genuine, and they included everything from reproductions of archaic Etruscan rings to Fijian moonstone jewellery.

As the century was drawing to a close, Liberty ushered in a new direction for its jewellery design that was attuned to the Arts and Crafts aesthetic. As part of Liberty's Cymric range, jewellery in both gold and silver was showcased at the store. The collection included brooches and necklaces, as well as buckles and waist clasps, and was very much aimed at artistic tastes. Many of the pieces were in a contemporary but restrained Celtic style and, like the silverware range, often stemmed from Archibald Knox and various other designers of the Silver Studio or from Jessie M. King. King, born near Glasgow in 1875, had studied at the Glasgow School of Art from 1892 to 1899, and adapted the school's Art Nouveau style into a more delicate version of her own. She designed jewellery, silverware and textiles for Liberty, and contributed very elegant, delicate designs, which were slightly more organic and tended to use filigree floral and plant ornaments.

Enamel and semi-precious stones, opals, moonstones and blister pearls featured heavily and were set in intricate designs, often with a hammered surface to suggest its hand-wrought quality. The art aspect was emphasized by self-assuredly treating the exhibits not as commercial products but as actual pieces of art. As the 1905 *Liberty Jewellery & Silverware* catalogue advised its customers, "The stock in the showroom is practically a fine art exhibition on a small scale, showing the most recent developments in the Jewellers' and Silversmiths' craft. The goods are marked in plain figures and the assistants are instructed not to solicit visitors to make purchases." Despite, or even because of, these innovative, "reverse" retail tactics, Cymric jewellery became an integral part of Liberty's style.

ABOVE *Cover of* Jewellery Sketches 1900–1912.

OPPOSITE *Pendants and brooches from the turn of the century, including two silver and enamel double pendants with pearl insets (top), and a 1920s silver brooch with agate inset and opal surround designed by Sybil Dunlop (bottom).*

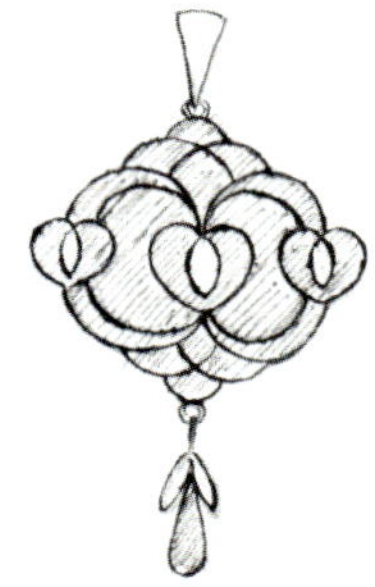

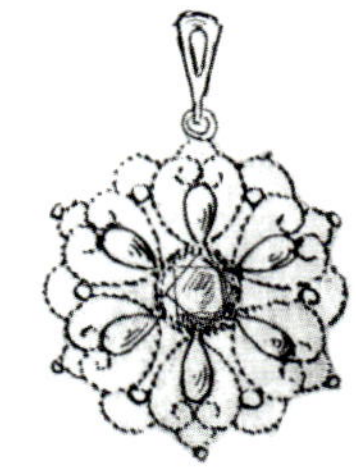

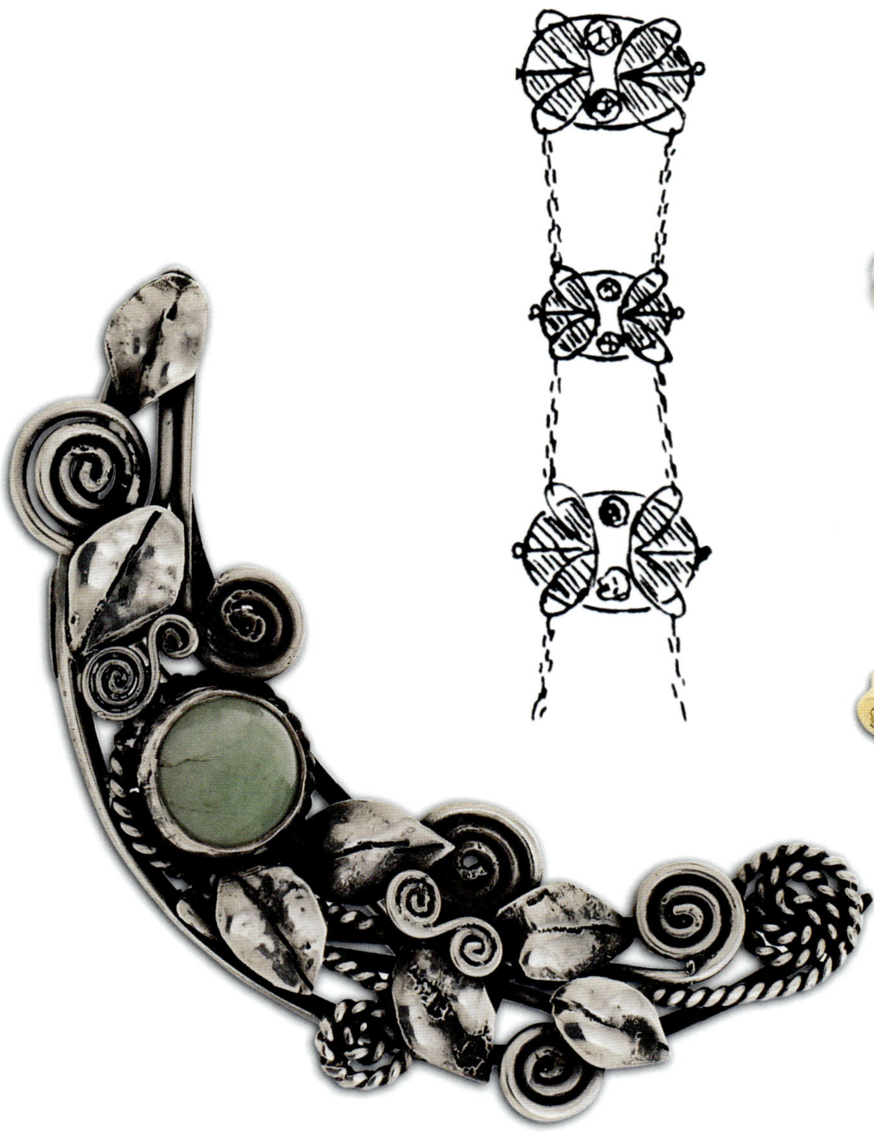

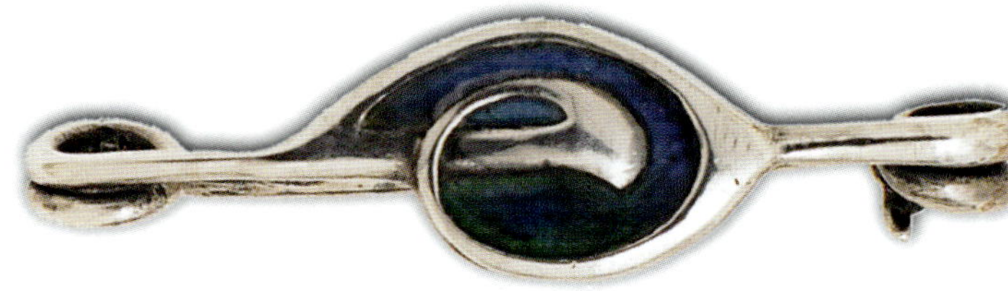

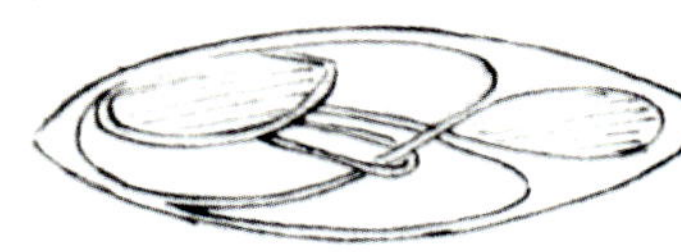

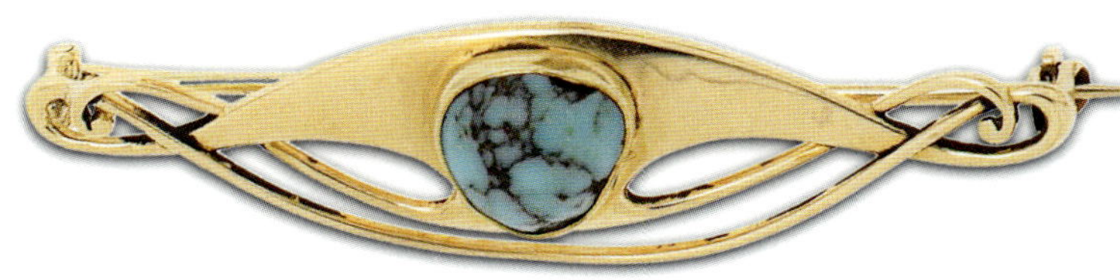

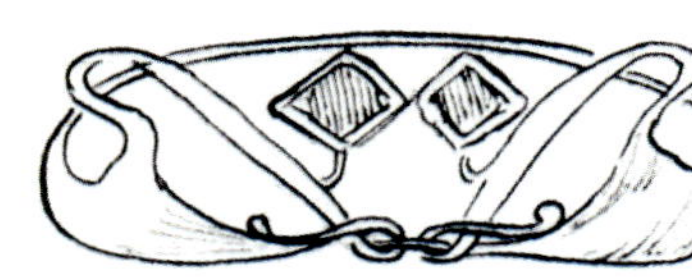

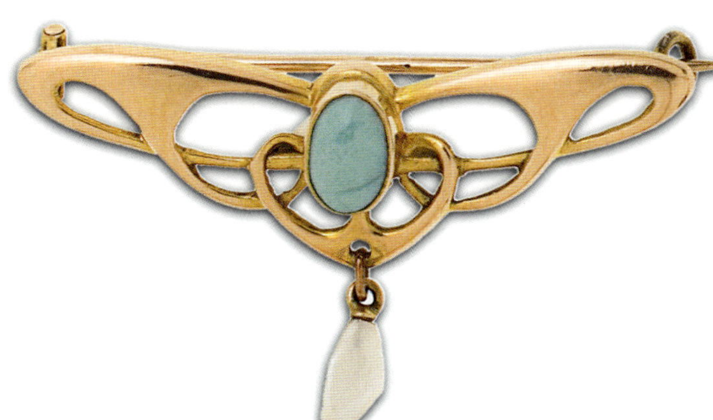

THESE PAGES *Various pendant and brooch designs from the turn of the century, including a gold and matrix turquoise pendant designed by Murrle Bennett (opposite top).*

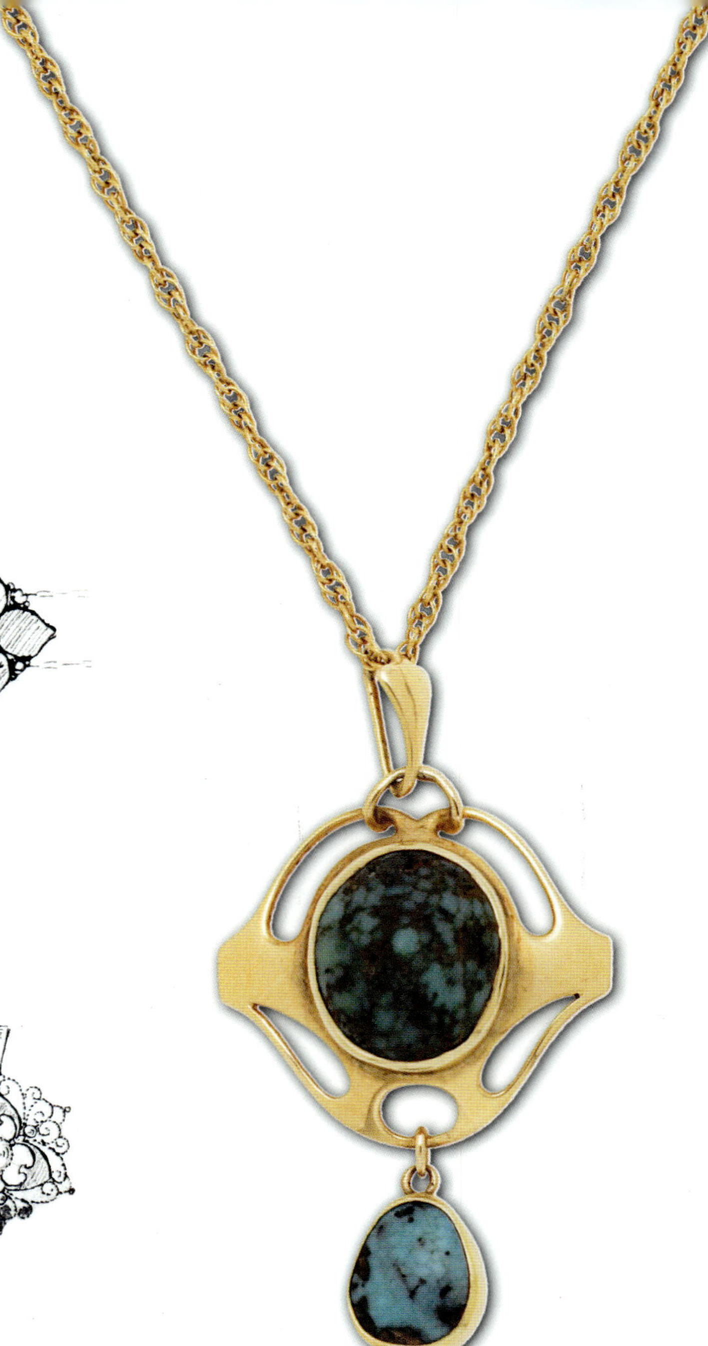
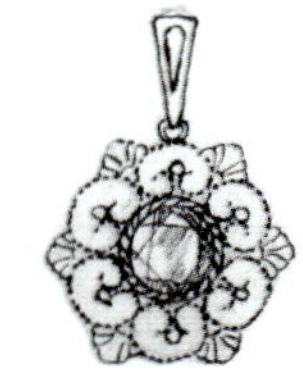
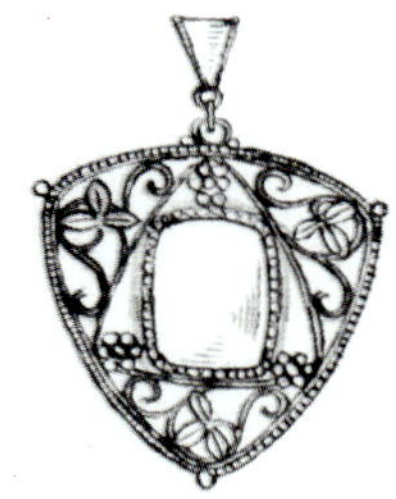
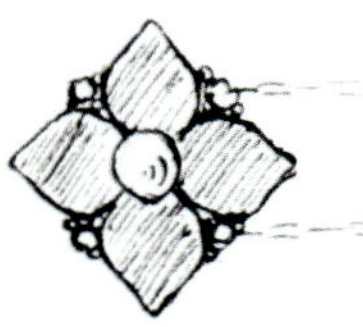
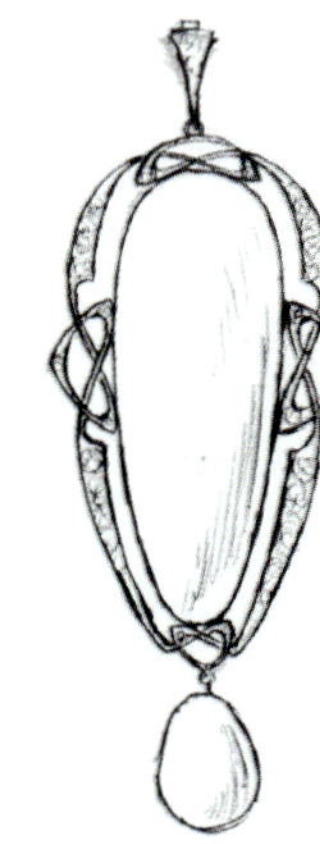
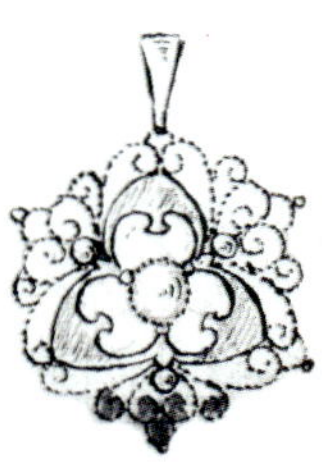
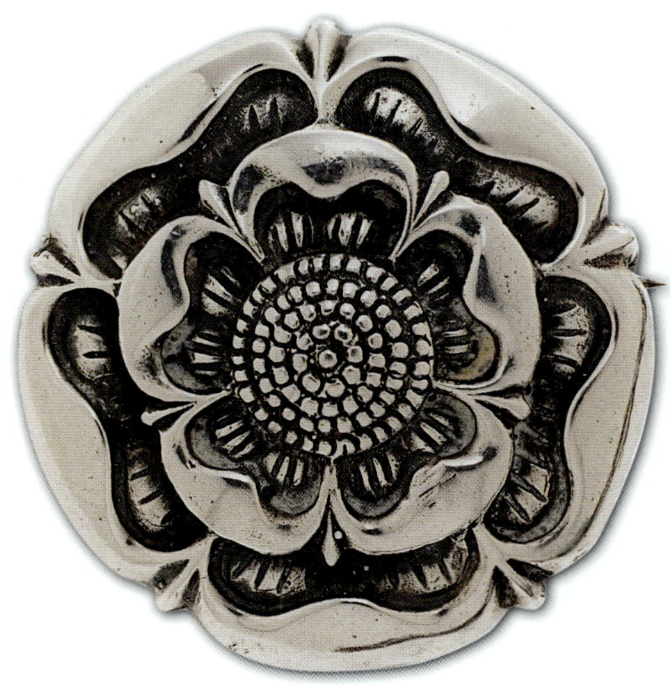
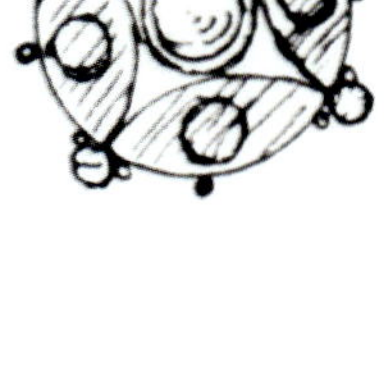

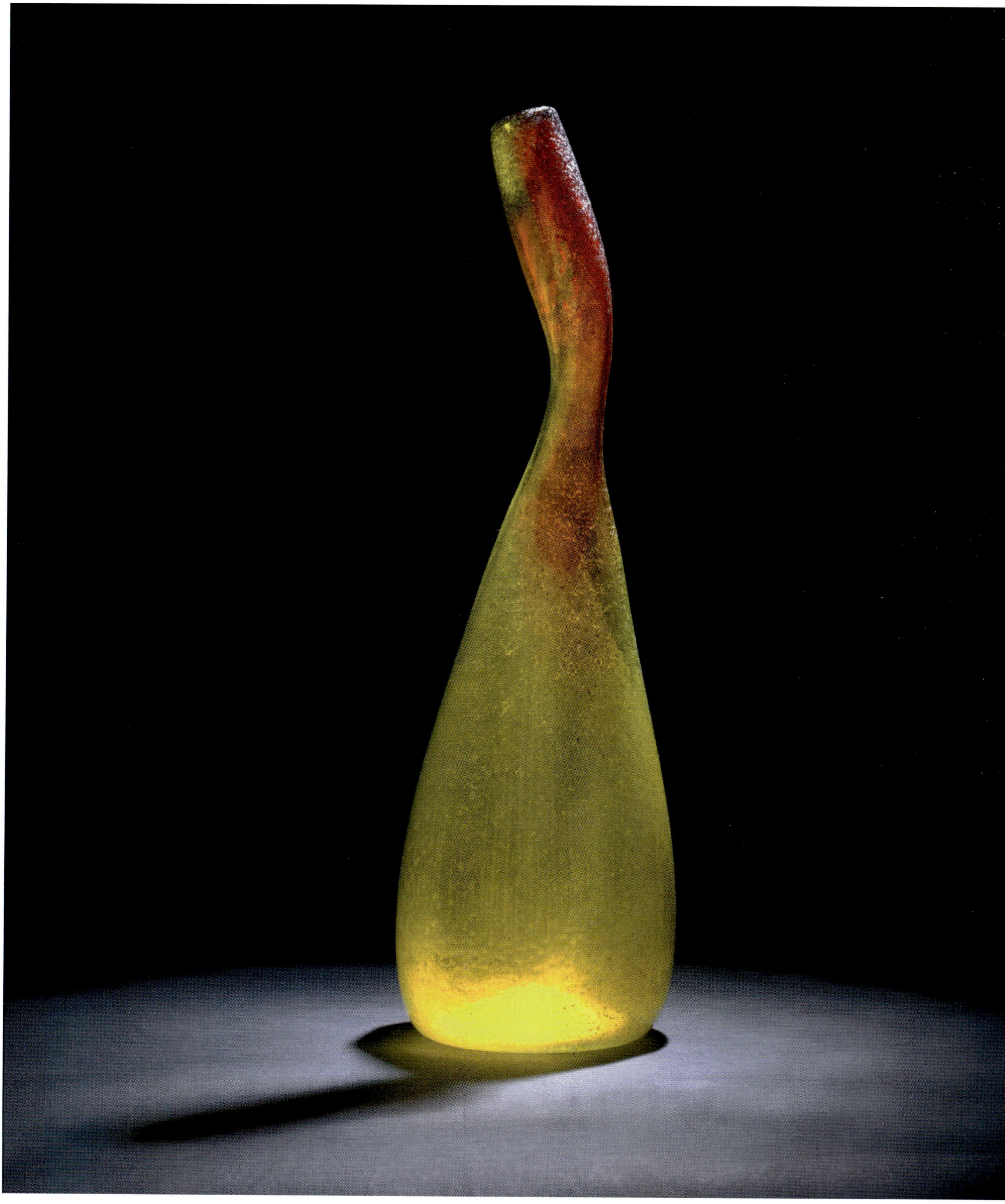

GLASSWARE & CERAMICS

OPPOSITE *This hand-blown Clutha glass vase was designed by Christopher Dresser and made by James Couper & Sons around 1885. Dresser was a proponent of embracing the natural flaws of the material and the handmade process, as demonstrated by the uneven colour and shape of this vase.*

Initially, Liberty mainly offered the Far Eastern ceramics that were so highly prized by the shop's aesthetically driven clientele. The craze for blue-and-white porcelain, which George du Maurier dubbed "acute Chinamania", had enthralled fashionable London society from the 1870s onwards and the search for another piece of what Liberty called "Old Nankin China" probably led many of these discerning enthusiasts to the front doors of the Regent Street shop. Liberty offered precious antique pieces from China and Japan, as well as much more affordable modern items, and to a lesser extent, also precious old Dutch delft and Grès de Flandres, as well as modern Indian and North African pottery.

From the early 1880s Liberty began to supplement their offerings of Oriental pieces with an assortment of contemporary British ceramics from local firms. Ever on the lookout for attractive, artistic wares at relatively low prices to offer to their customers, and a keen supporter of local British manufacturing, Liberty patronized local country potteries which, often themselves influenced by a generation of young art school graduates, started to turn out so-called "Art" pottery. Among others, Liberty sold ceramics by the Aller Vale Pottery, the Della Robbia Pottery and The Farnham Pottery. The popular Royal Barum earthenware of Charles Hubert Brannam first appeared in Liberty's catalogues in the mid-1890s. Selling in large numbers, too, were the Bretby Art Pottery ranges, established in 1883 by William Ault and Henry Tooth, the former manager of Linthorpe Art Pottery, where Christopher Dresser had been art director. Their earthenware was heavily influenced by Japanese and Middle Eastern ceramics and the designs often came from Dresser's studio. Like Linthorpe's pottery, Bretby's ceramics range was relatively inexpensive.

The eclectic variety of Liberty's pottery included a range of Celtic-inspired garden items made by Mary Watts, the widow of the painter George Frederick Watts, at her Compton Pottery near Guildford. While most of the designs were her own, several of the Celtic designs are attributed to Archibald Knox.

In the area of ceramics, it was, however, the association with the renowned artist-potter William Moorcroft (1872–1945) that proved to be the most important and long-lasting relationship for Liberty. Moorcroft, who ran the pottery business of James Macintyre & Co. at Burslem, Staffordshire, became close friends with Arthur Liberty and his wife. He produced "Art" pottery with stylized floral designs in a distinctive Art Nouveau style, and Liberty remained a loyal and important client of his right up until his death in 1945.

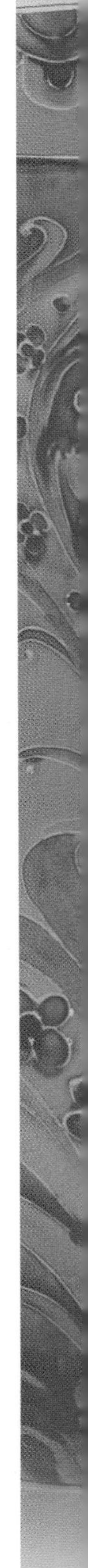

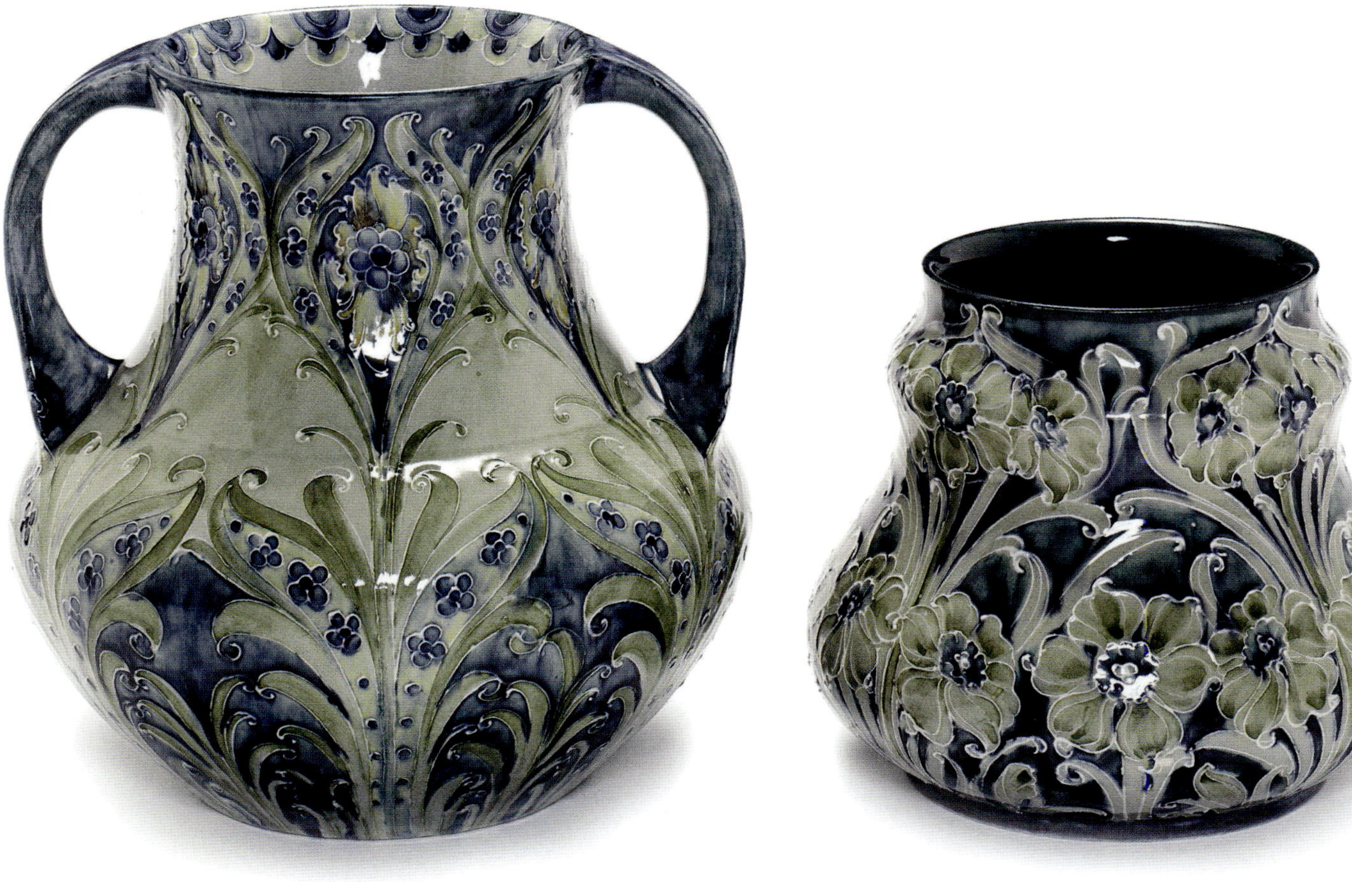

Perhaps most prominent was the new Florian Ware range, which was introduced in 1898. Often in shades of blue or green, it was decorated with delicate designs executed in white slip and a translucent glaze. Moorcroft continued to produce a variety of registered designs for Liberty well into the twentieth century and, after setting up his own pottery factory in 1913, he went on to launch the Moorcroft Blue range – dark-speckled tableware with a distinctive mid-blue glaze. It appealed to a simpler attitude to design, and Liberty used Moorcroft Blue in their Tudor tea rooms when the new shop opened its doors in the 1920s.

While Moorcroft designs remain an important range for Liberty to this day, pieces were certainly not limited to British designs and by the 1890s the company started stocking ceramics and glassware from a selection of Continental firms which produced some of the most distinguished designs of their time. These imported wares included the celebrated Art Nouveau pottery of Max Läuger (1864–1952) from the Kandern ceramic factory in Karlsruhe, Germany. Liberty was the first to import his wares and it was from Liberty that the Victoria and Albert Museum purchased its own examples of Läuger's work in 1898 and 1900.

Other noteworthy imported ceramics included the earthenware of the Florentine Giuseppe Cantigalli, and the lustred Art Nouveau pottery of Zsolnay from the Hungarian town of Pécs. Lustred ceramics proved to be particularly appealing and so-called "Breda Ware" was exclusively produced for Liberty in Holland. Highly intricate Art Nouveau pieces by the French potter and glassmaker Eugène Rousseau (1827–1891), and later, the more affordable, but similar-looking glassware made by his assistant Ernest Baptiste Leveillé, as well as the iridescent glassware of Johann Lötz Witwe of Klostermühle in Austria, added to the remarkable variety on offer at Liberty.

Liberty's Clutha glass, designed by Christopher Dresser for James Couper & Sons of Glasgow, was a widely admired example of British glassware. Introduced in the 1880s and initially sold at Dresser's own Art Furnishers' Alliance, it proved a great success at Liberty. Clutha was, it has been suggested, either the ancient Celtic word for "cloudy" or for Glasgow's river Clyde – and the name (just like Cymric silver and Tudric pewter) was intended to evoke a sense of archaic, nobler times and the idea of a national British art. The range, with its bold, multi-coloured art shades, alluded to an archaic aesthetic, with deliberate imperfections, bubbles and streaks, and the shapes modelled on antique glass, particularly following Dresser's interest in Roman, Egyptian and Near Eastern glass design.

At Liberty, a synthetic approach to design prevailed across the different departments and the catalogues emphasized the highly decorative value of the pieces on offer. A catalogue from 1890, for example, describes Läuger's glassware as "exceedingly effective for sideboard decoration, overmantels, etc". Taken as a whole, the glassware and ceramics sold by Liberty added greatly to what came to be perceived by the public as the Liberty Style.

OPPOSITE *Two examples of the distinctive Florian Ware ceramics designed by William Moorcroft and manufactured by James Macintyre & Co. The two-handled vase and the flower pot were both produced around 1905.*

RIGHT *A hand-thrown stoneware vase from the Hazeldene range designed by Moorcroft in 1902. The decoration was achieved by painting on raised lines of slip to prevent colours from running.*

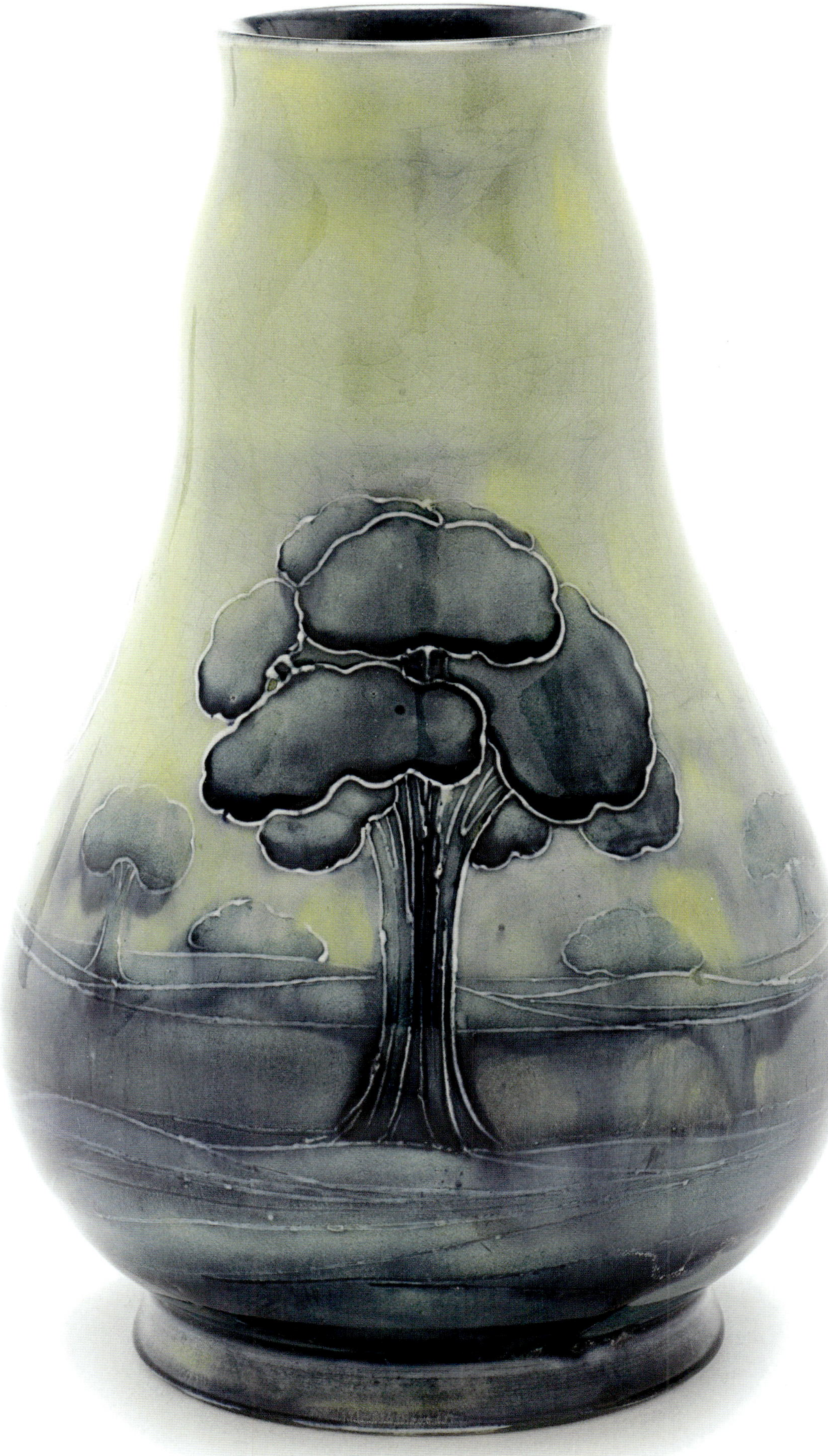

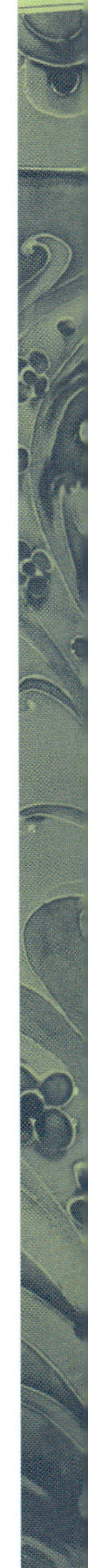

MID-CENTURY

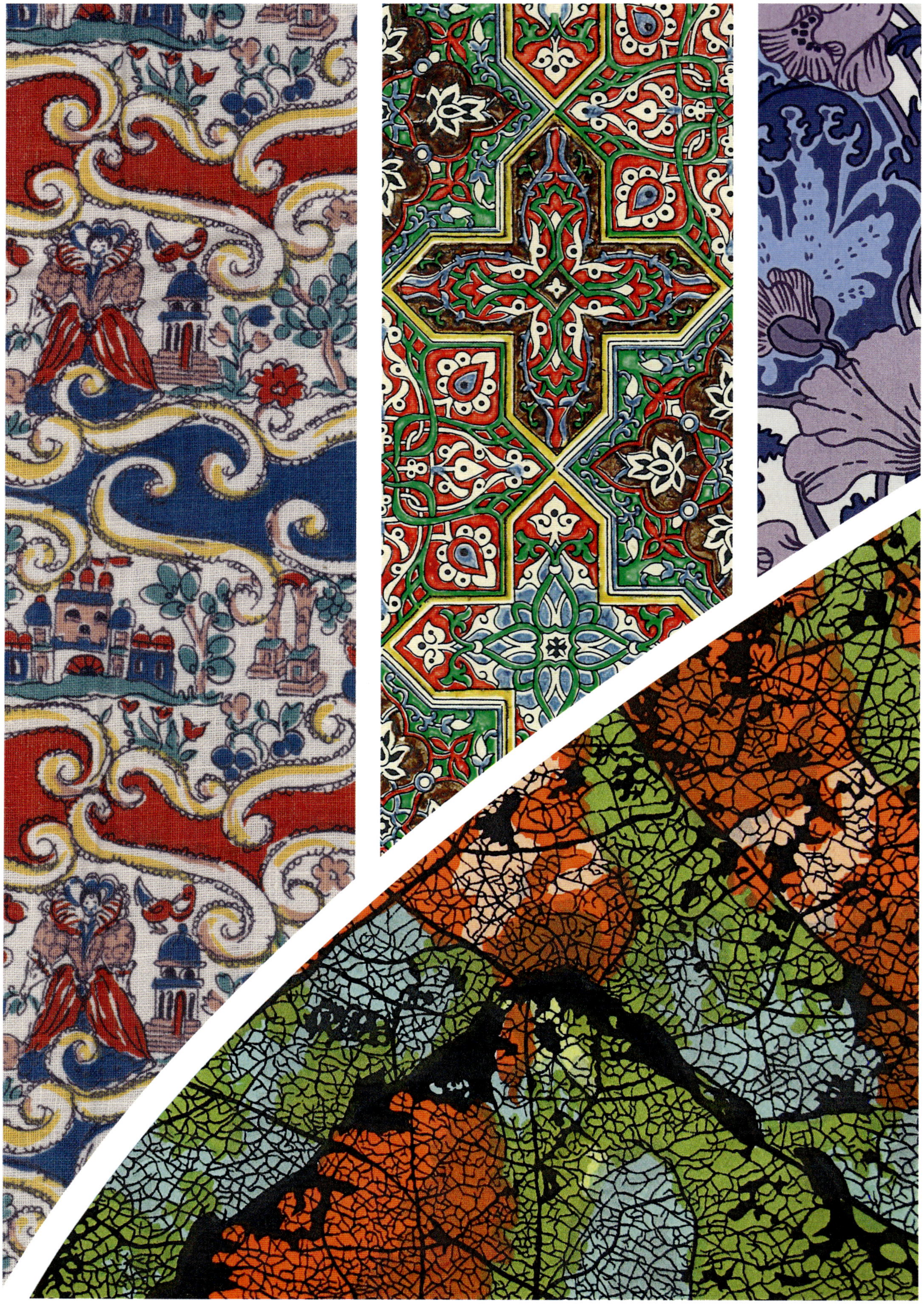

LEFT
Details of Liberty prints from the 1940s to the 1950s. Clockwise from left are: print by Lily Weinman, 1948; print from the Silver Studio, 1946; Clementine, an Art Nouveau design revived in 1958; and Malinda by Gwenfred Jarvis, 1958.

OPPOSITE
Sunman by Robert Stewart for Liberty, 1950 (reprinted in 1992).

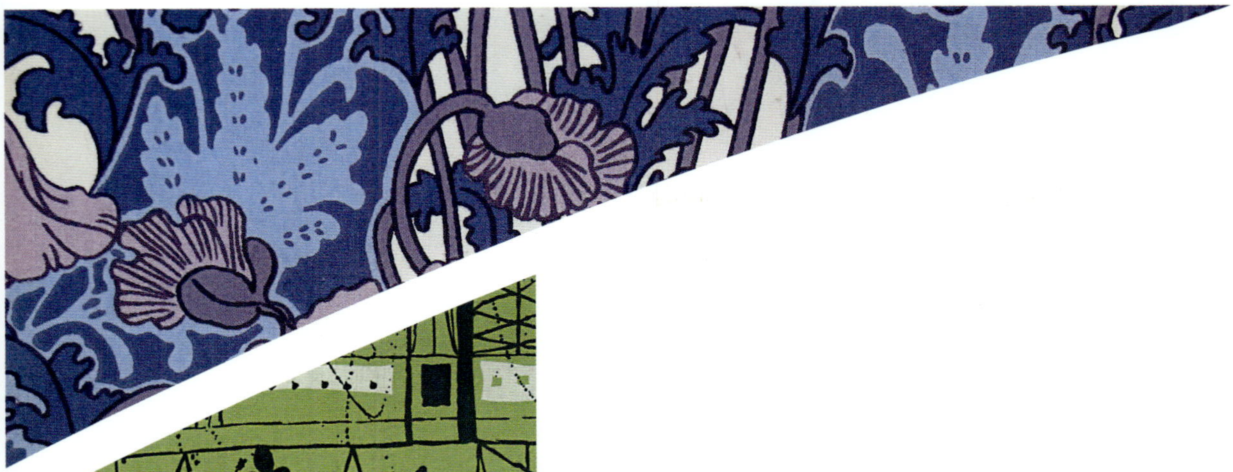
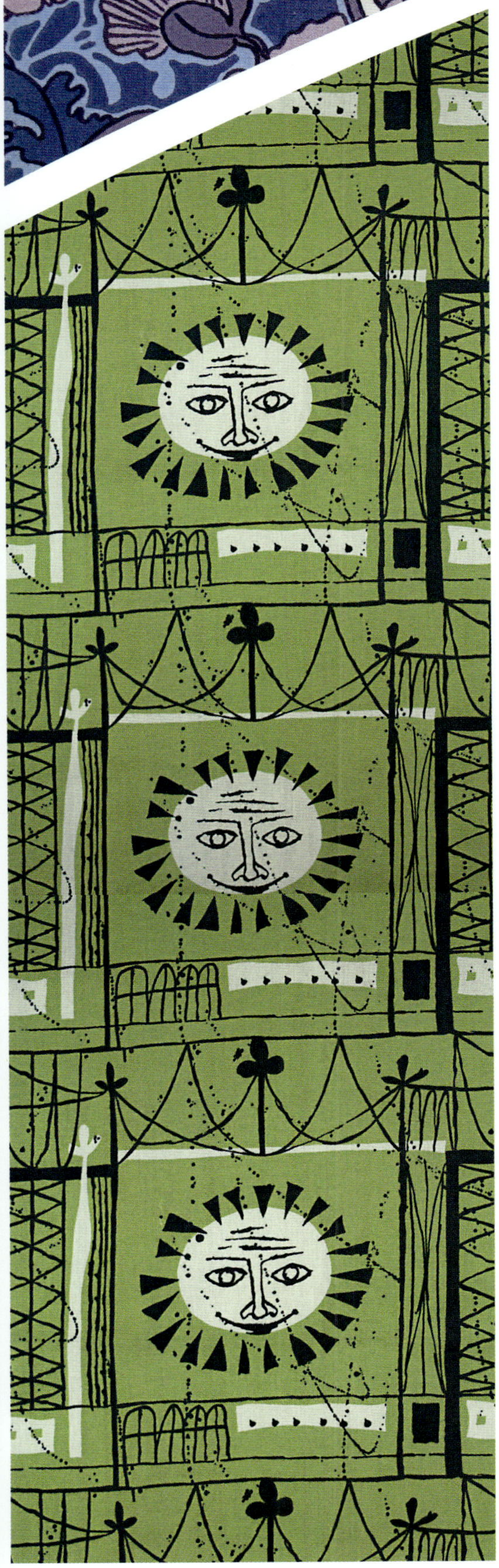

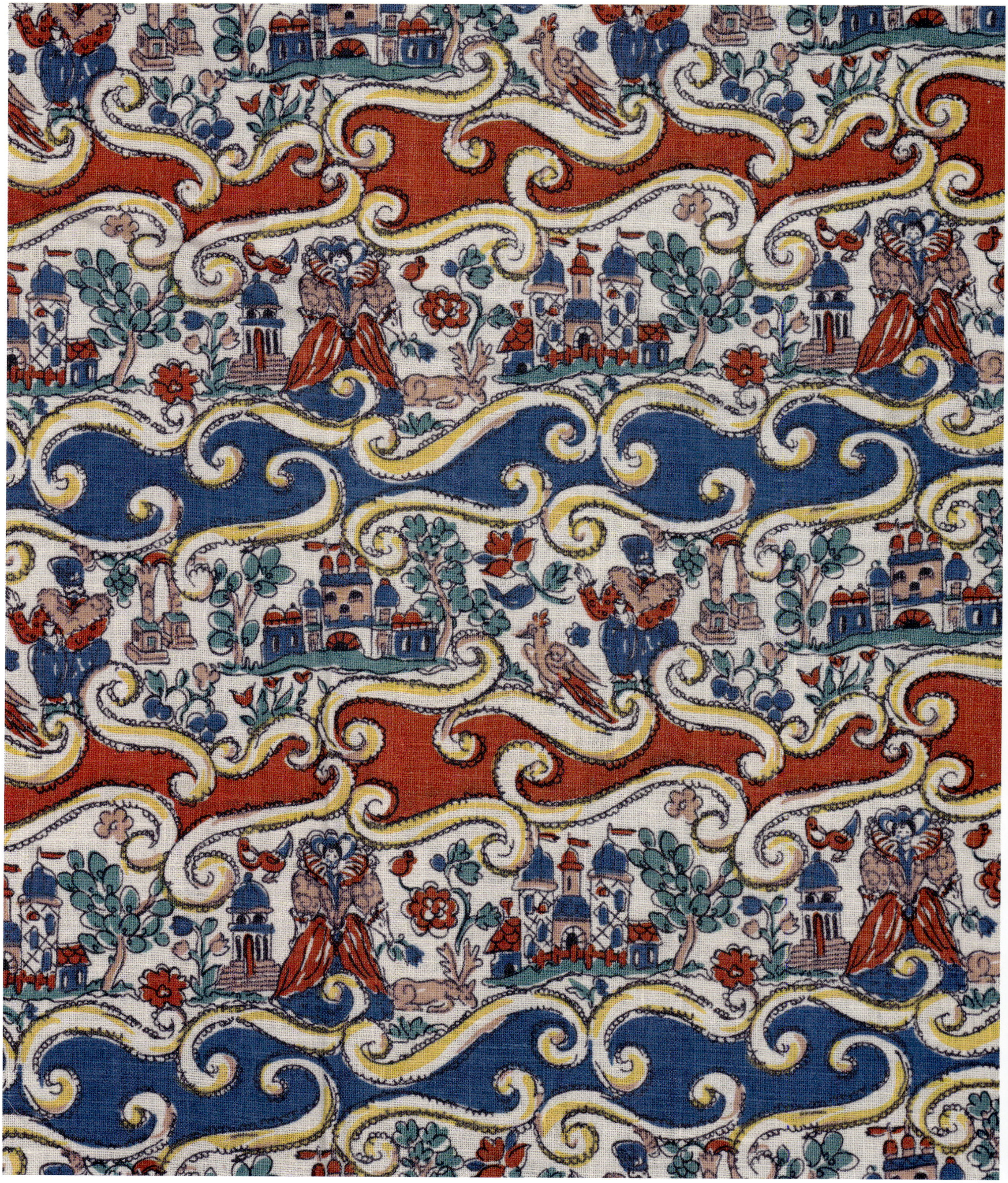

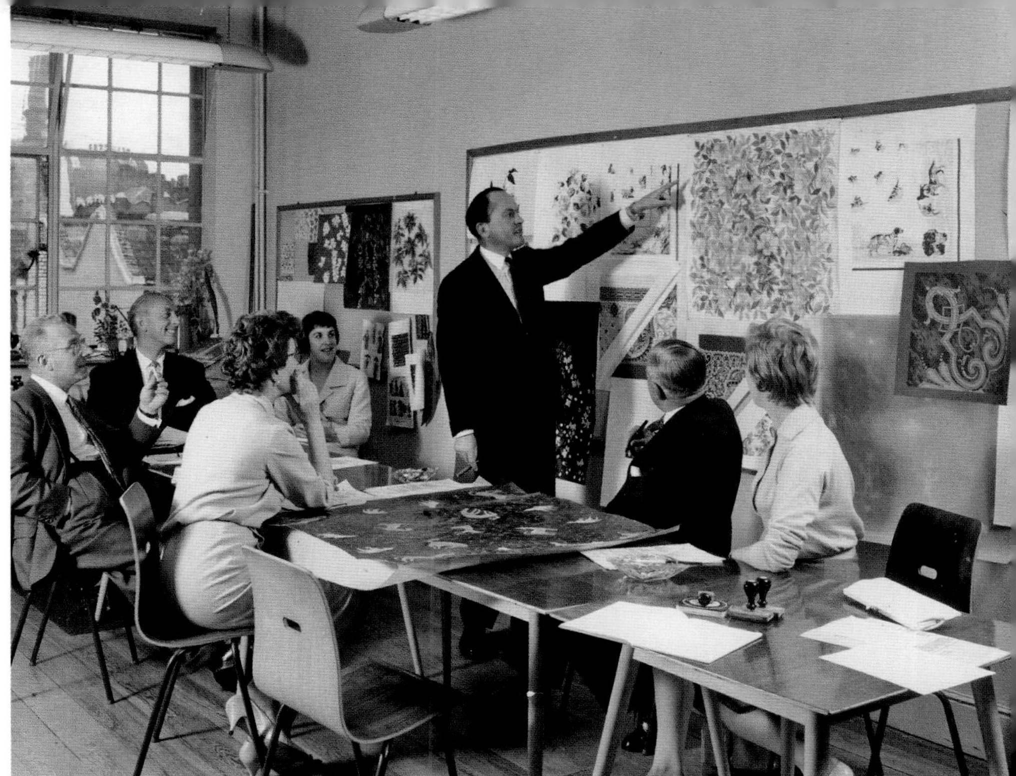

YOUNG LIBERTY

ABOVE *Members of the Design Committee meet to discuss which prints to put into production, c. 1953. Left to right: Mr Browning, Hilary Blackmore, Rosemary Borland, Carole Thomas, Arthur Stewart-Liberty (standing), William Dorrell and Colleen Farr.*

Post-war Britain, tired of austerity and rationing, eagerly embraced a new aesthetic, exemplified by the 1951 Festival of Britain – a celebration of contemporary British design and culture held on London's South Bank and throughout the country. Designers keen to experiment created a new idiom of design that was both quirky and idiosyncratic, with vibrant colours and unconventional motifs. They were also beginning to emulate the contemporary art that was being produced – with the colours of Paul Klee and Jackson Pollock and the lines of Wassily Kandinsky and Joan Miró being particularly inspiring.

In 1949, in an attempt to harness this new energy and vibrancy, Liberty sought to widen its appeal to the younger, more design-conscious demographic by establishing the "Young Liberty" boutique. Young Liberty featured designs by many key figures in 1950s design, including Lucienne Day and Terence Conran, but arguably the most influential designer at Liberty during this period was Robert Stewart. His bold, colourful and figurative designs, executed in a contemporary style, were widely embraced and disseminated by the newly popular household style magazines such as the British periodical *House & Garden*.

Stewart's first design for Liberty was the Beefeater print of 1951, created to commemorate the Festival of Britain. However, his most well-known print was Machrihanish – a prime example of the ebullience and playfulness of his aesthetic. Stewart was extremely prolific, producing over 130 new designs for Liberty alone.

The other important designer during this period was Colleen Farr. Having worked as a freelancer for the company, she was invited by Liberty to set up an in-house design studio in 1952. This marked a turning point in the company's history, as it had, up to that point, only ever used freelance designers or bought in prints from other companies. During Farr's decade-long tenure, she produced and bought in several seminal designs, including the award-winning Atalanta from 1961. Her young, fresh eye brought a new lease of life to the traditional cotton ranges, introducing lively new geometric and abstract prints. Her stylized florals, including the popular Lucilla, were executed with a lightness of touch that chimed perfectly with the spirit of the age. One of her greatest successes was her prize-winning Blackberry design of 1955 – bought in large quantities by the couturier Jean Muir. Together, Stewart and Farr's work in the 1950s was instrumental in placing Liberty at the forefront of printed textile design in Britain.

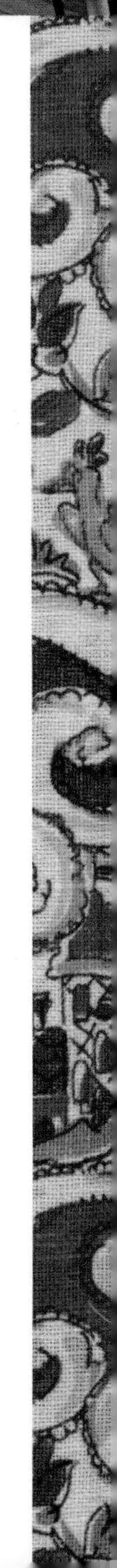

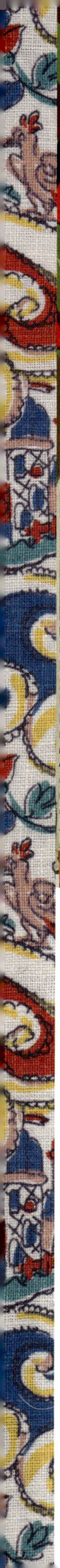

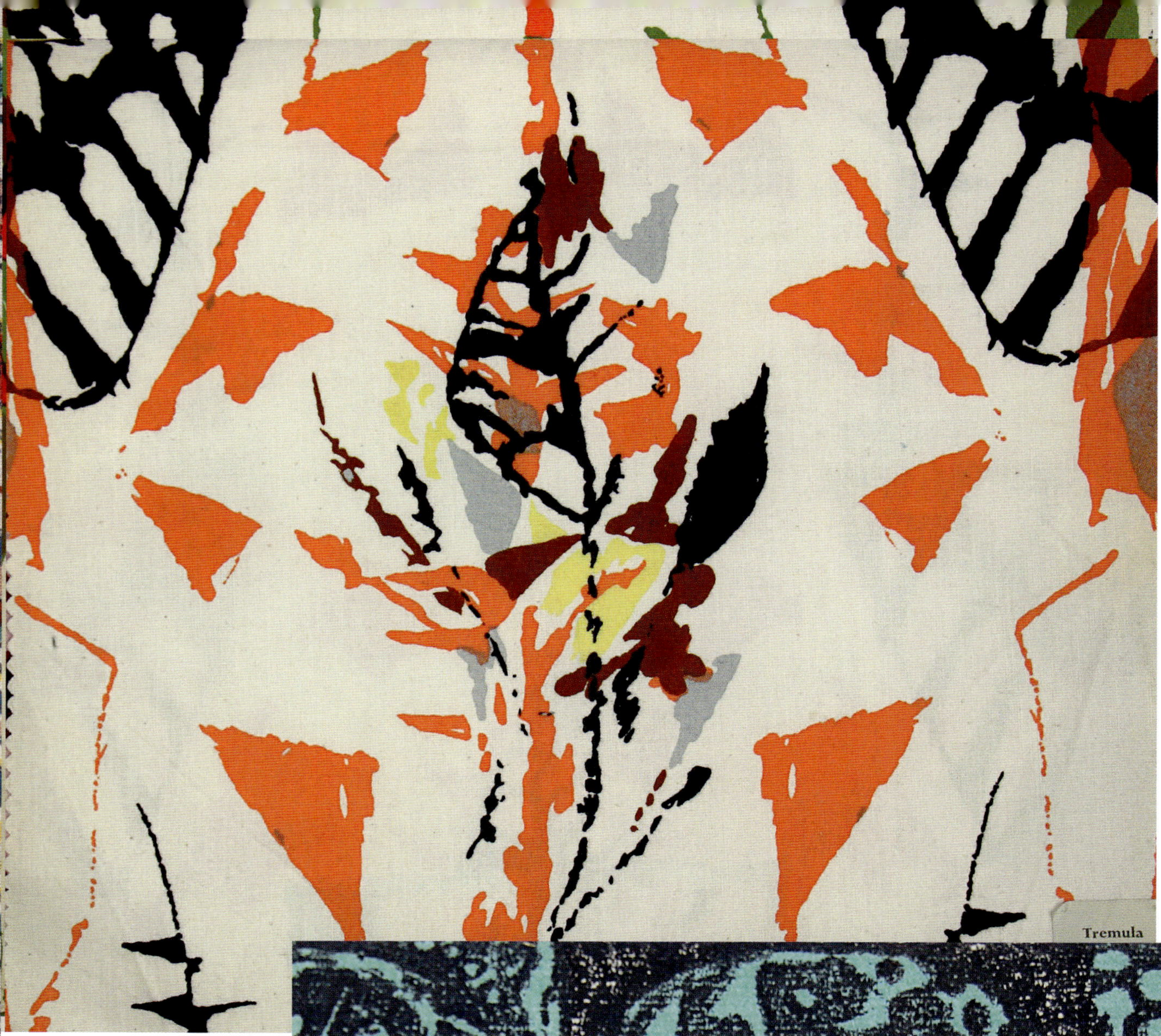

THESE PAGES
Abstraction of patterns from natural phenomena, such as stylized plant forms, were a feature of mid-century print design, seen here in Tremula by Helen Dalby, mid-1950s (left); Denarii by Anthony Levett-Prinsep, 1956 (below); and Fruit Delight by Robert Stewart (opposite) for the Young Liberty label, 1951.

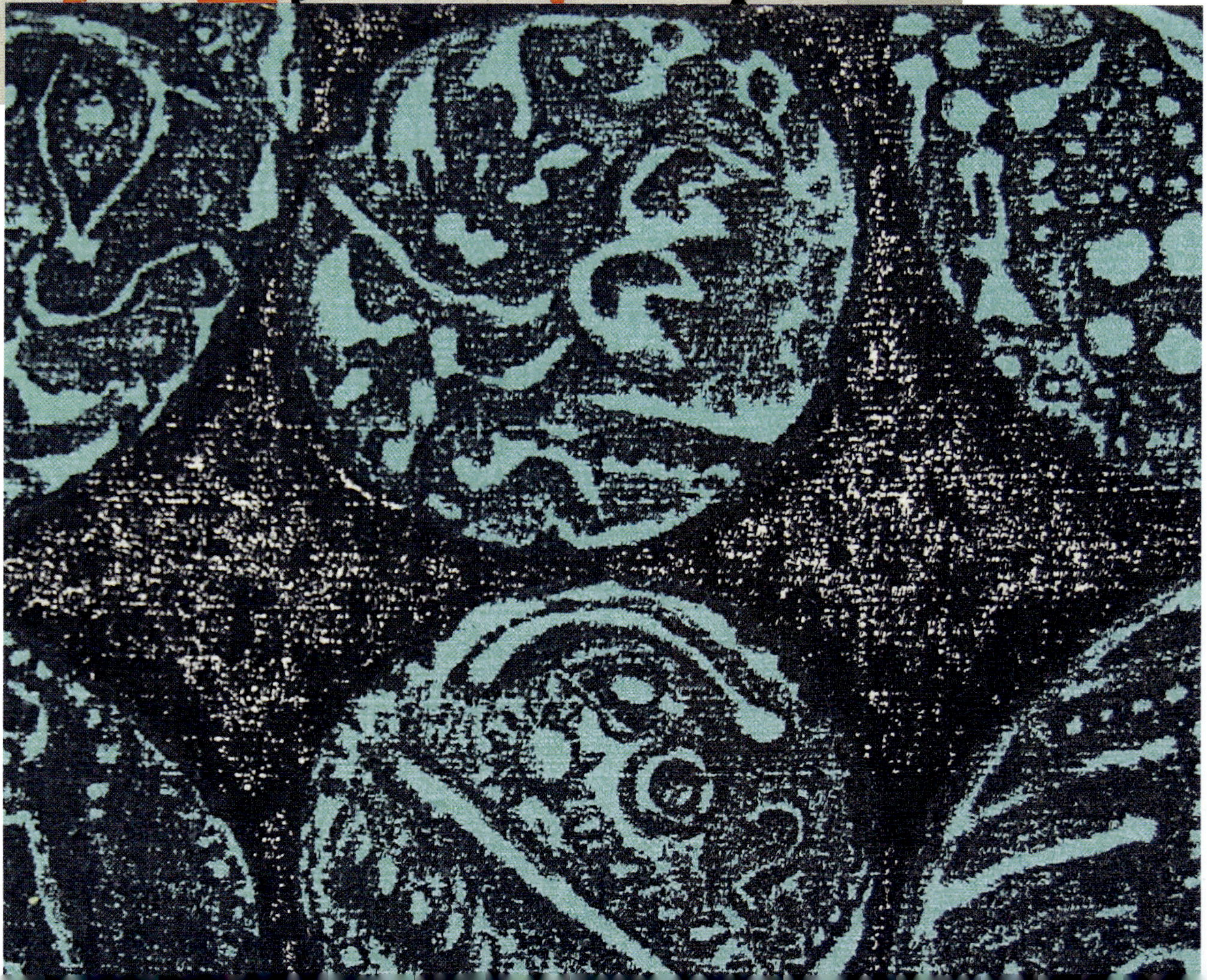

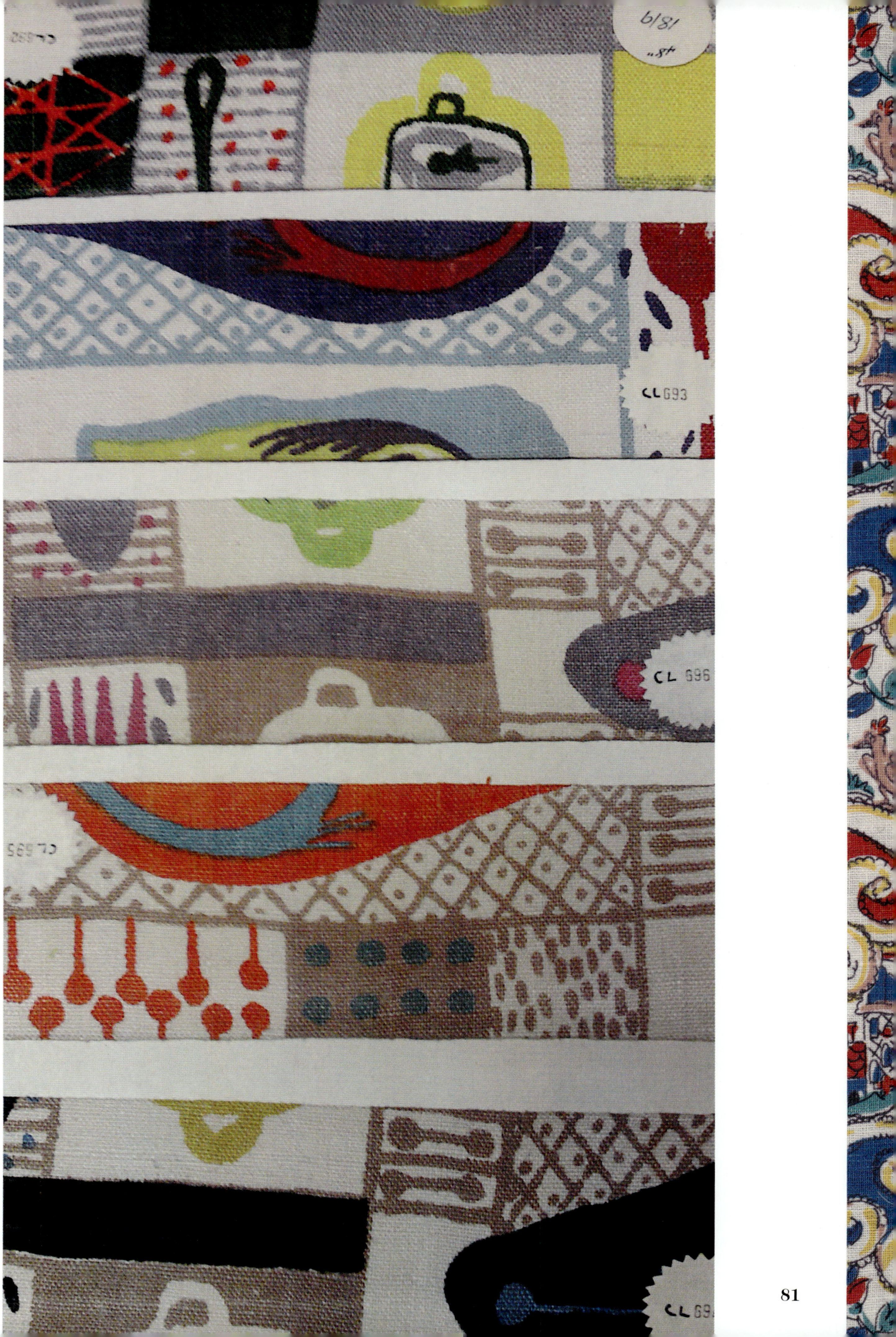
CL693
CL 696

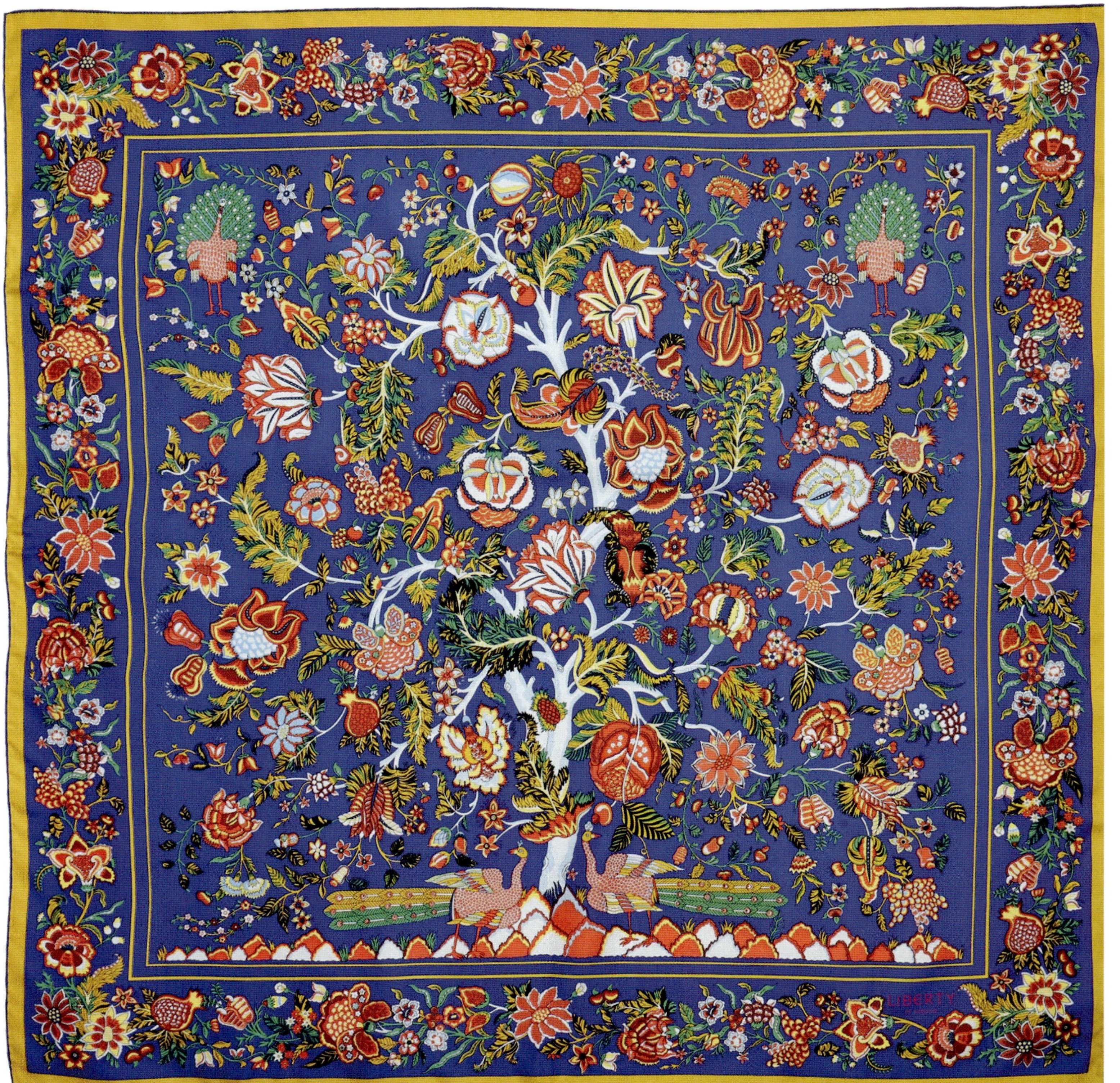
LIBERTY

THE LIBERTY SCARF

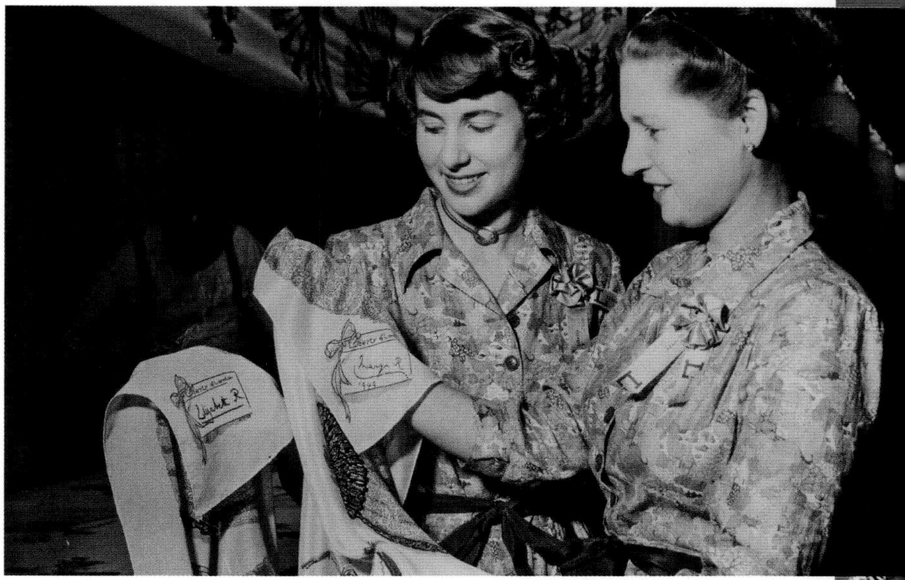

ABOVE *In an attempt to revitalize the craft of hand-block printing at Merton after World War II, a promotional exhibition of various items was mounted, including Liberty scarves. Arnold Lever, also the company designer for Jacqmar, designed this fan print.*

It is impossible to discuss the history of Liberty without addressing the phenomenal success of the Liberty scarf, never more popular than during the mid-twentieth century – a time when the scarf was an intrinsic part of any female wardrobe. The vibrant modernist prints, graphic experimentation and colour explosion of a newly optimistic post-war Britain lent themselves perfectly to the medium of the small silk square. Whether it was Abstract art or Fauvism, the drawings of Cocteau, or chinoiserie and paisleys that mimicked Eastern patterns – all were successfully reworked and reinterpreted.

An eminently accessible means of buying into the brand, a Liberty scarf was a relatively affordable and "safe" way of experimenting with print, adding a perfect shot of colour and vibrancy to an outfit. A new Liberty scarf from the latest season was also an opportunity to update a look, without having to buy a whole new wardrobe, and a means of expressing an interest in current trends.

During the early 1900s, Liberty sold imported woven shawls, an essential accessory for followers of the Aesthetic movement. By the 1920s, however, lighter silk scarves were produced, designed to be worn as a decorative accessory in their own right rather than as a covering. Up until 1953, scarf production had been a complex part of the business, with each type of fabric having its own buyer. However, all this changed with the advent of the Design Committee, set up to provide a sense of unity for the various departments.

The large number of scarf designs required – customers expected a wide variety of prints every season – meant both the in-house design team and freelancers, including Richard Stewart, worked all year round on producing new prints. Liberty also engineered occasional high-profile collaborations with couturiers such as Balmain or Givenchy. Key mid-century designs include those inspired by the Festival of Britain in 1951 and the coronation of Elizabeth II in 1953, including John Wright's playful design of stylized Elizabethan lace on a grey background with the insignia of ER, which was a particular standout.

The silk scarves were printed either at Liberty's mill in Merton or in Lancashire and were hand-printed until the 1960s. Usually made as a delicate silk square but occasionally executed in soft wool or chiffon, the Liberty scarf was a beautiful, compact piece of design. Today, a dedicated accessories department launches new designs and reworkings of archive prints every season.

OPPOSITE *Tree of Life scarf, 2013.*

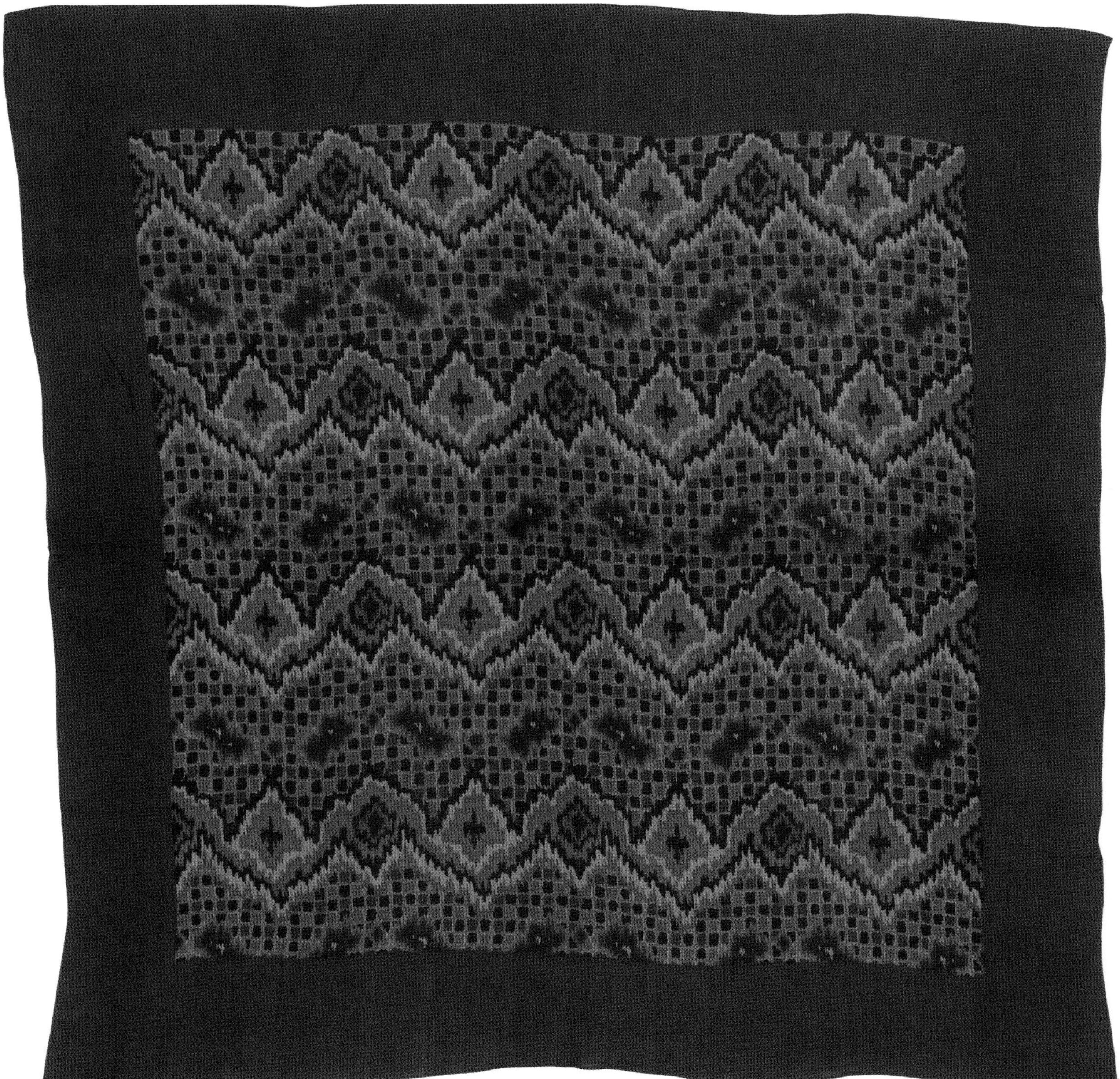

ABOVE

Liberty print scarf, hand block-printed at Merton, c. 1928–1932

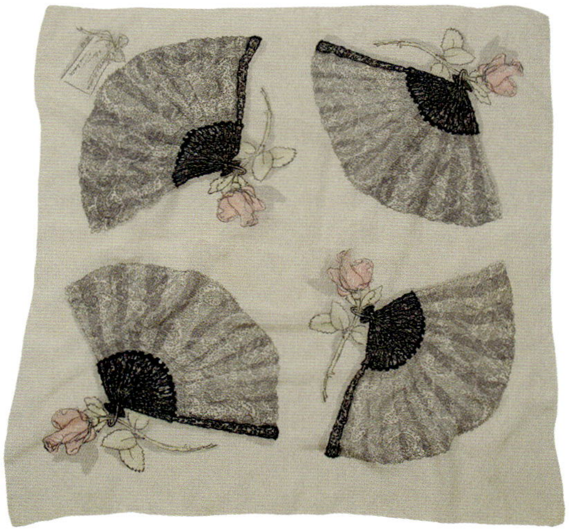

ABOVE

Arnold Lever's fan print scarf.

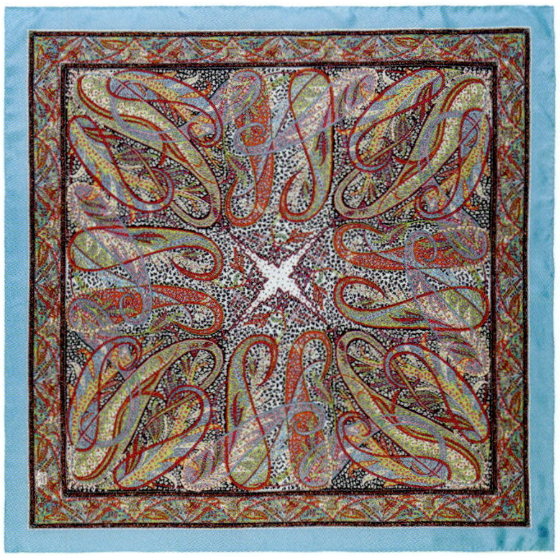

ABOVE

Blue Swirling Paisley scarf, 2012.

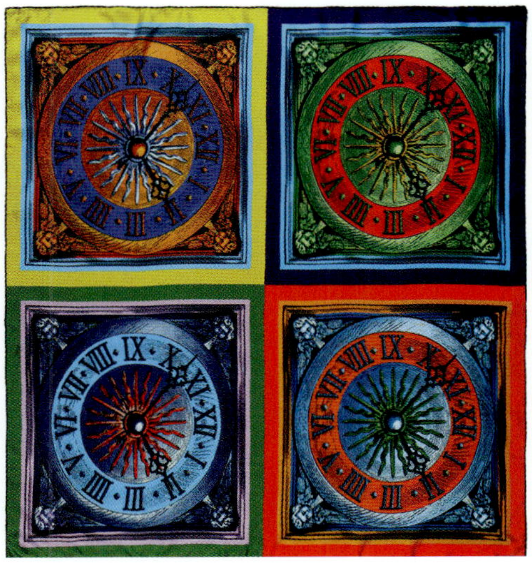

ABOVE

Quadrant Clock scarf, 2012.

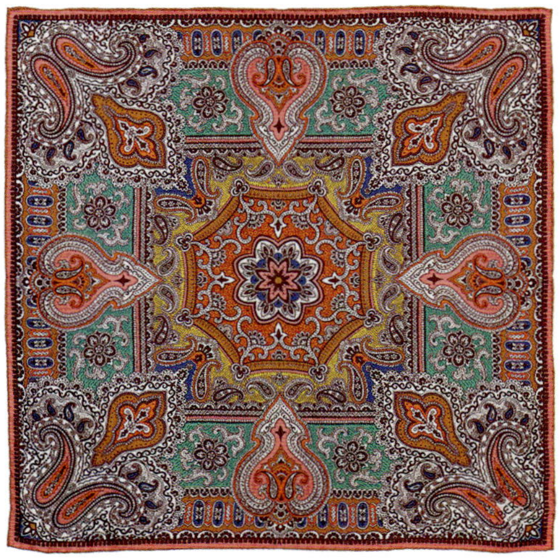

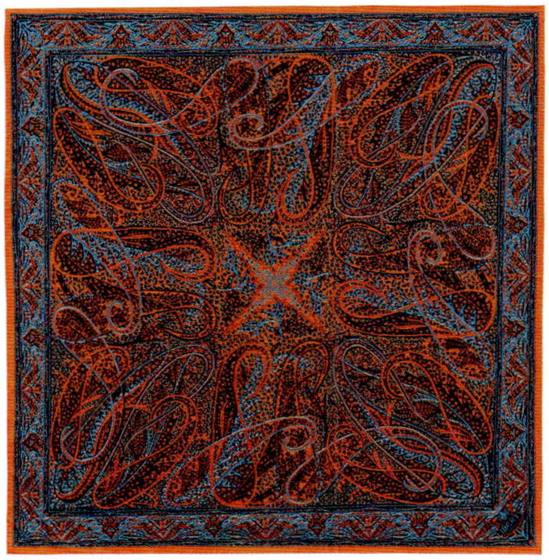

ABOVE

Orange Paisley archive scarf (top) and 2012 Swirling Paisley (bottom).

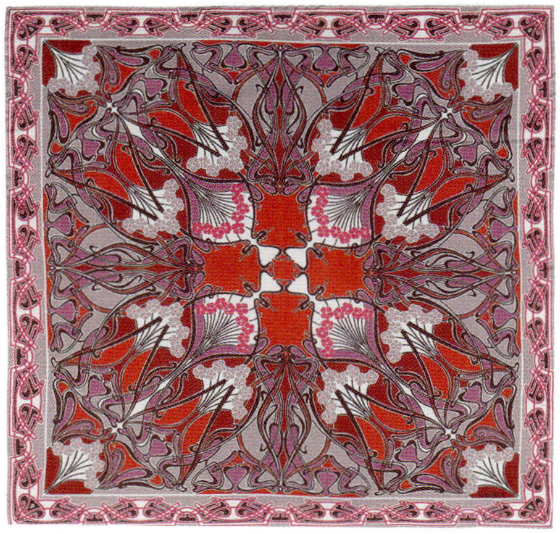

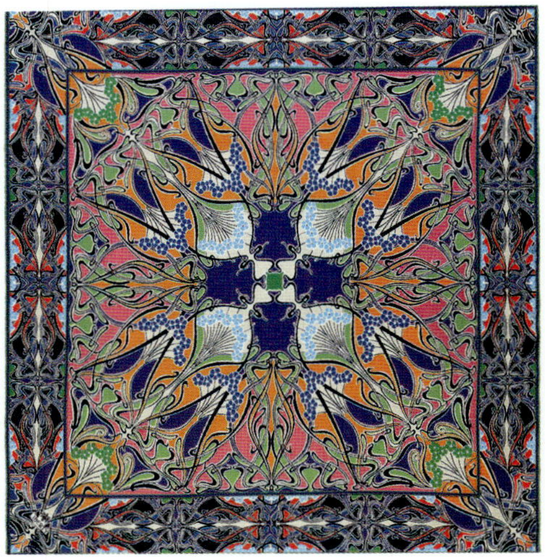

ABOVE

Ianthe archive scarf (top) and 2012 version (bottom).

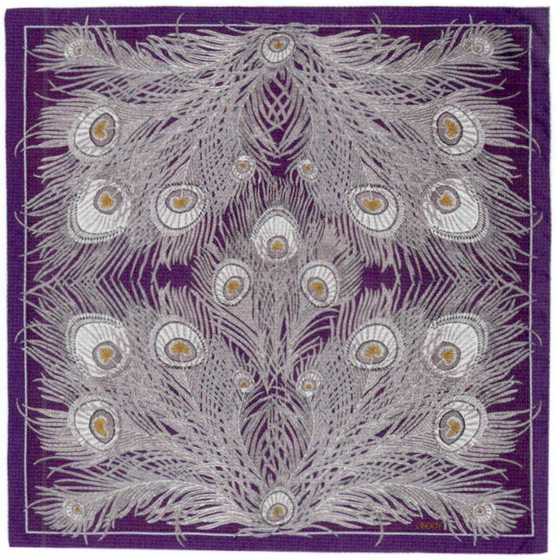

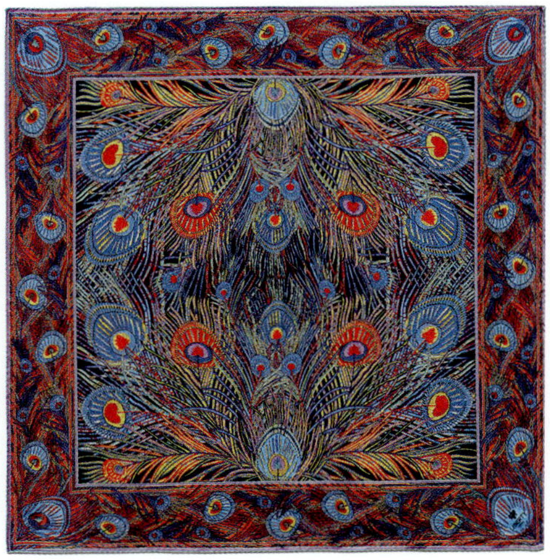

ABOVE

Hera archive scarf (top) and 2013 version (bottom).

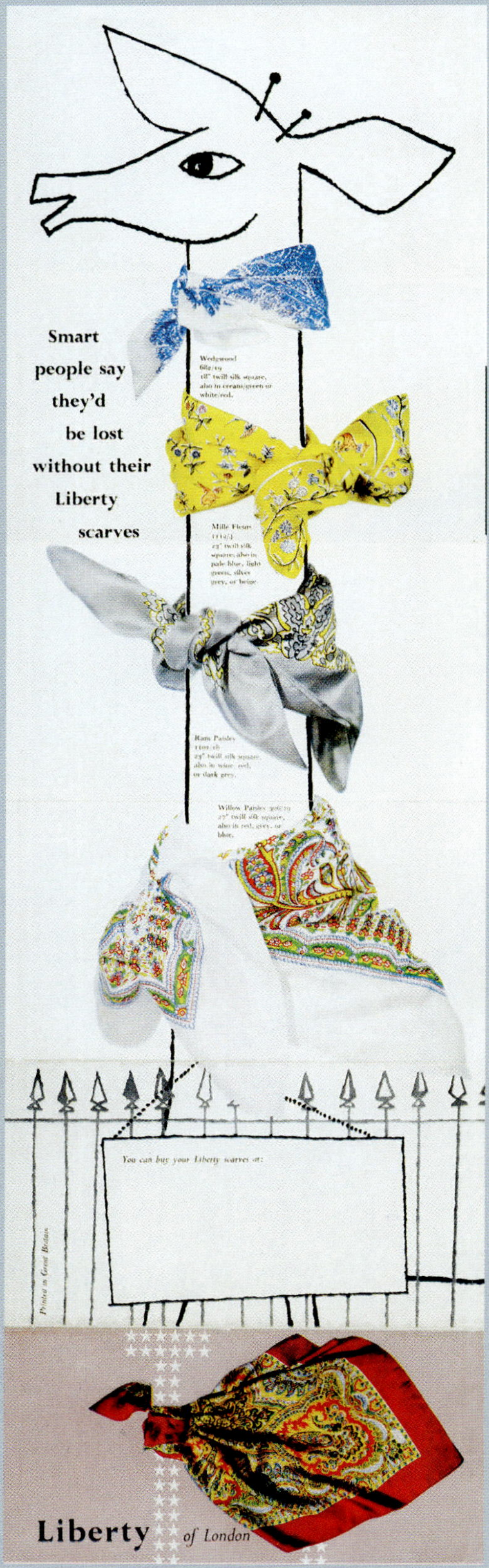

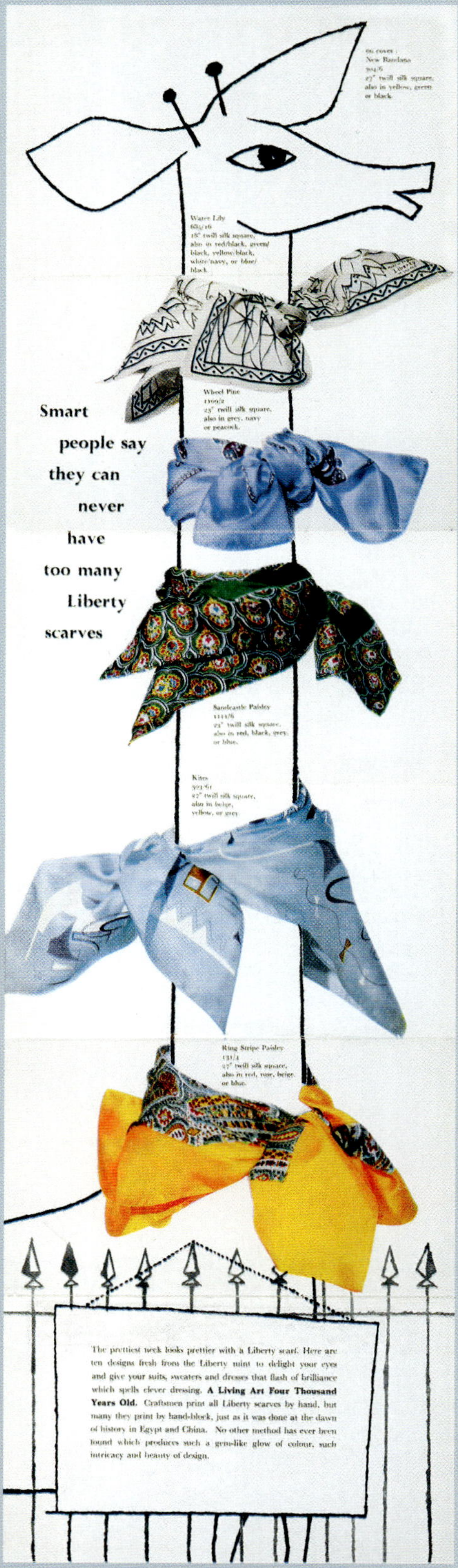

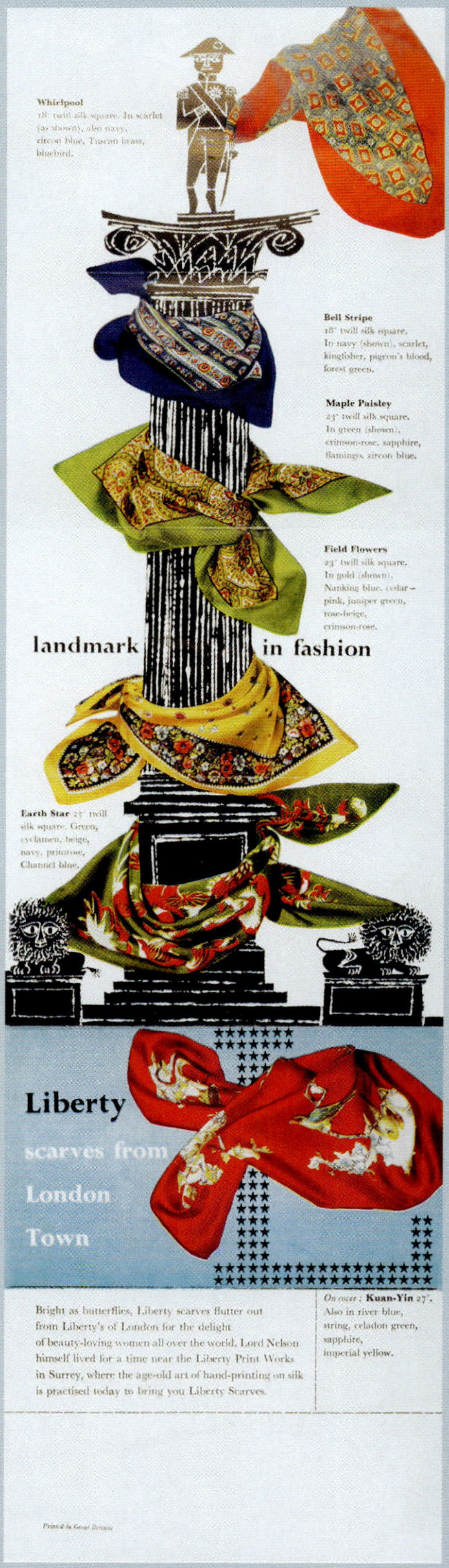

ADVERTISEMENT C. 1956

Illustration of a giraffe's neck decorated with Liberty scarves with the motto: "Smart people say they can never have too many scarves".

ADVERTISEMENT C. 1950

Illustration of Nelson's Column decorated with Liberty scarves with the motto: "Liberty scarves from London Town".

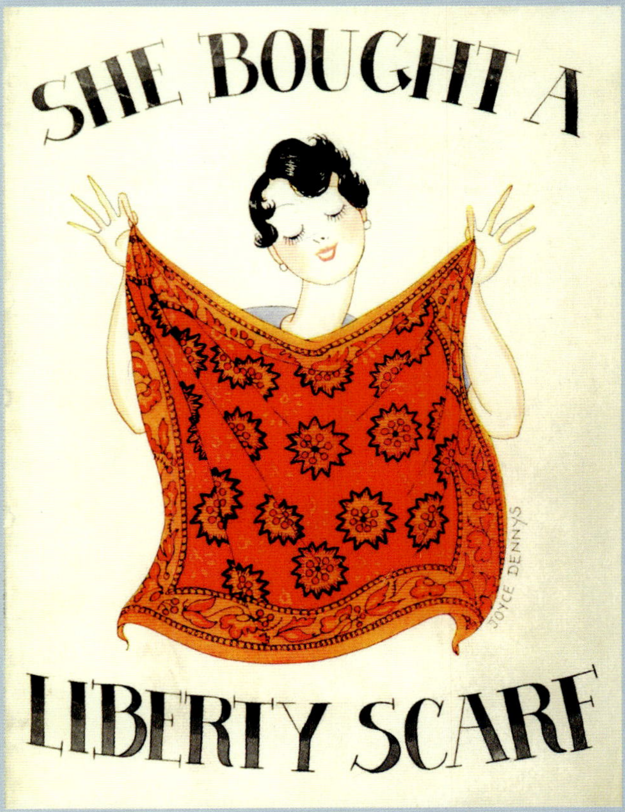

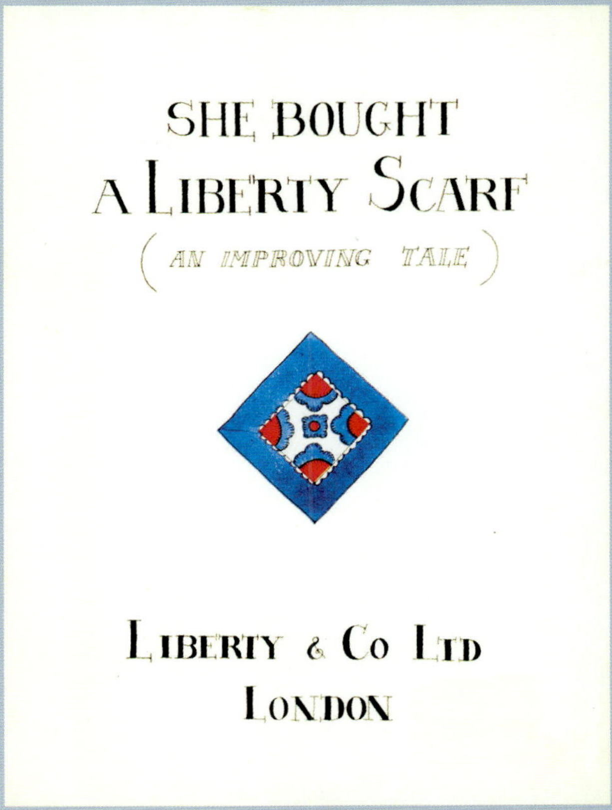

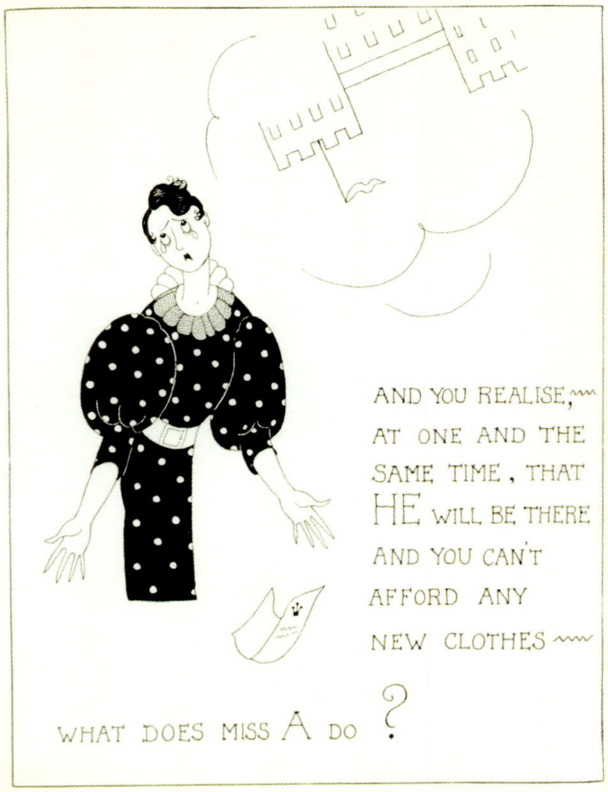

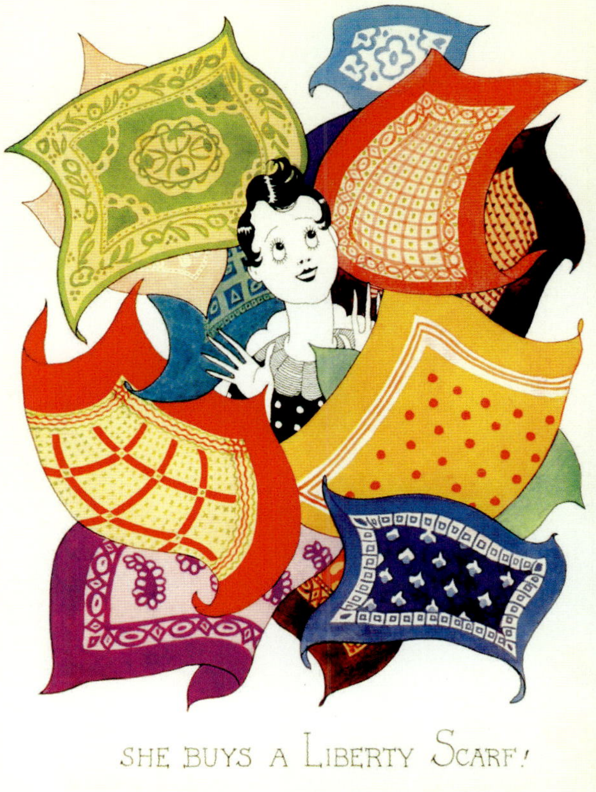

BOOKLET C. 1935

She Bought a Liberty Scarf (An Improving Tale), *with illustrations by Joyce Dennys, is a charming 1930s story of the versatility of the Liberty scarf.*

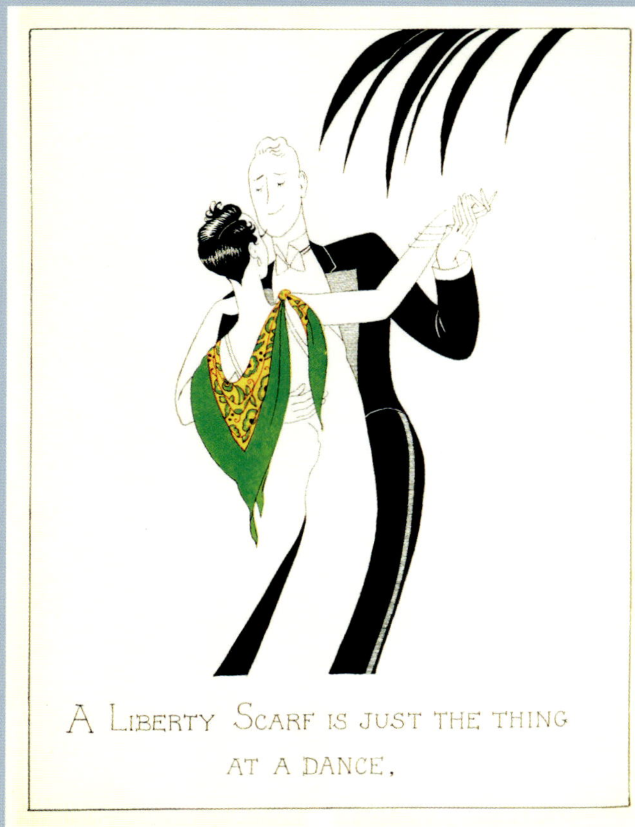
A LIBERTY SCARF IS JUST THE THING AT A DANCE.

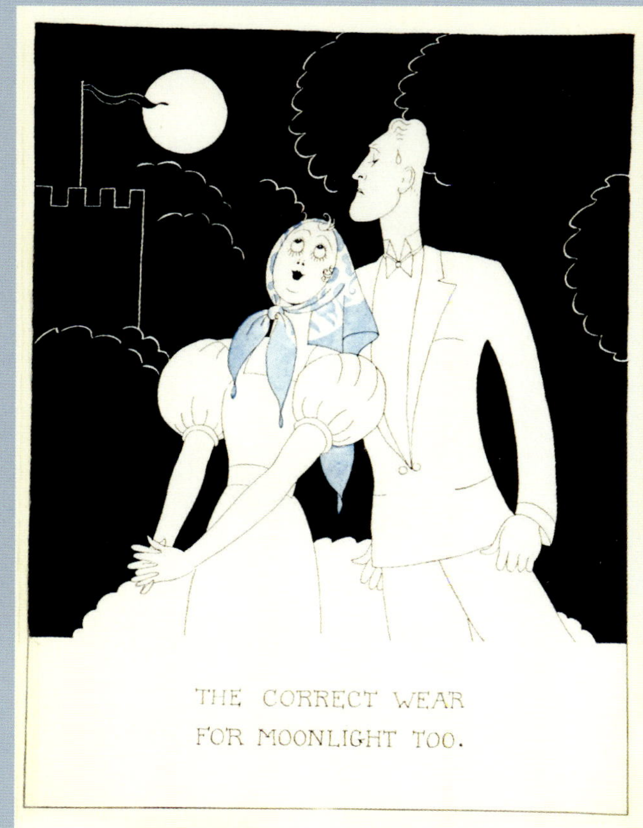
THE CORRECT WEAR FOR MOONLIGHT TOO.

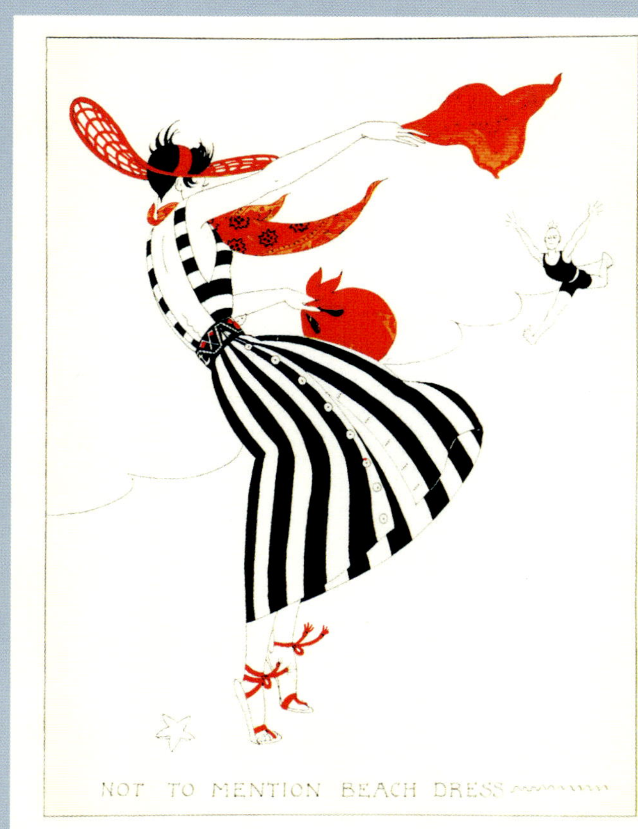
NOT TO MENTION BEACH DRESS

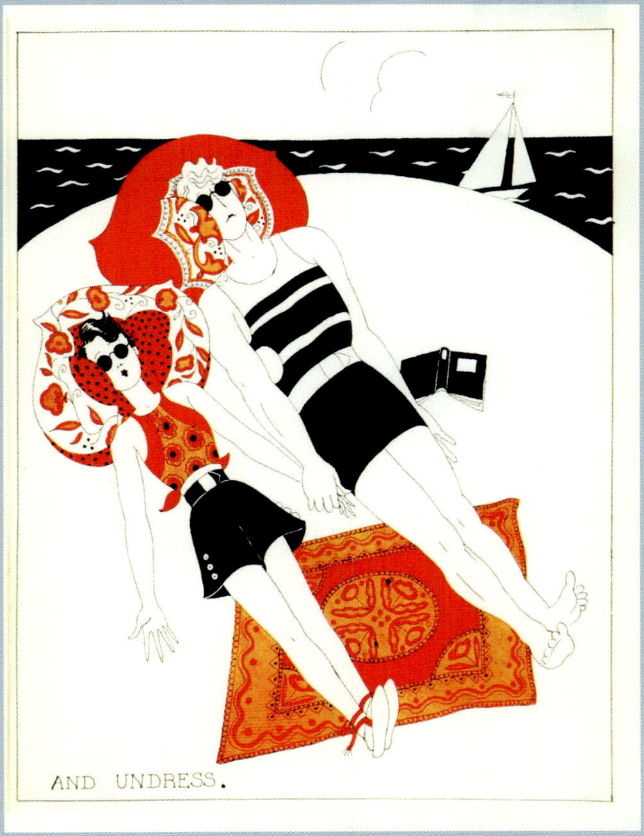

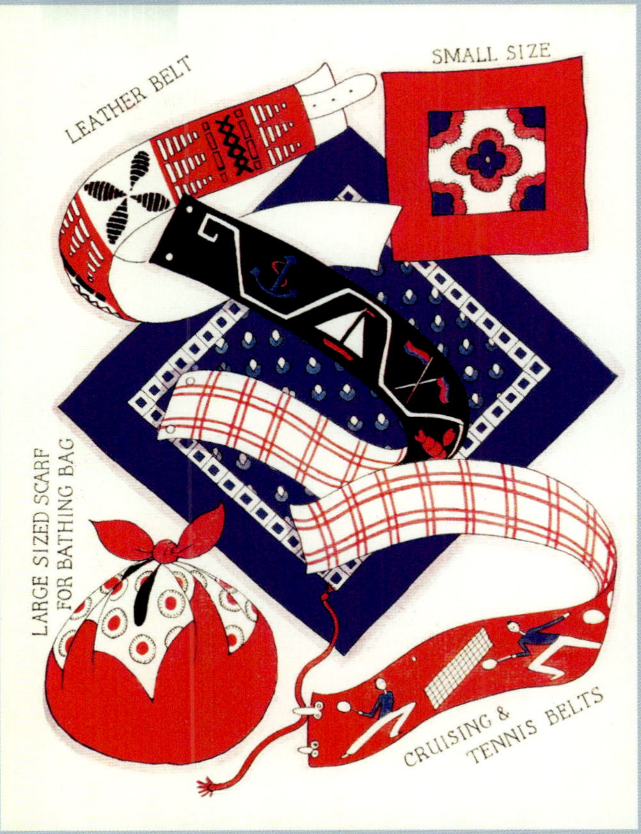

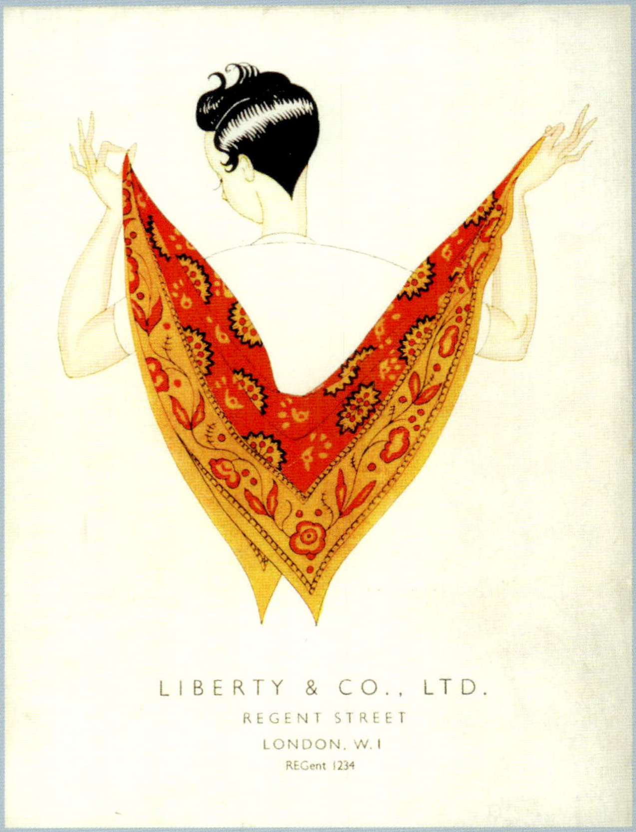

BOOKLET C. 1935
She Bought a Liberty Scarf (An Improving Tale), *with illustrations by Joyce Dennys, is a charming 1930s story of the versatility of the Liberty scarf.*

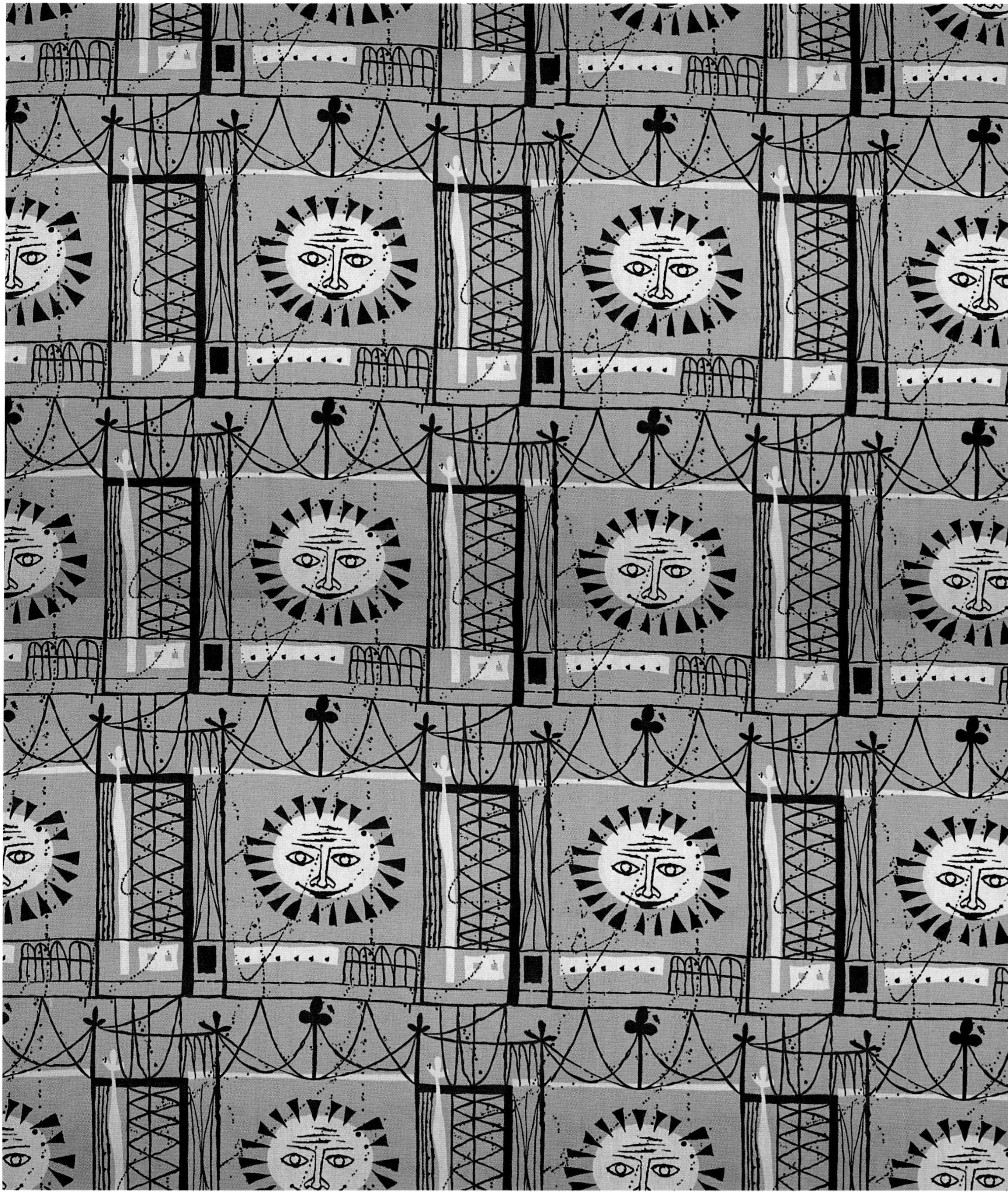

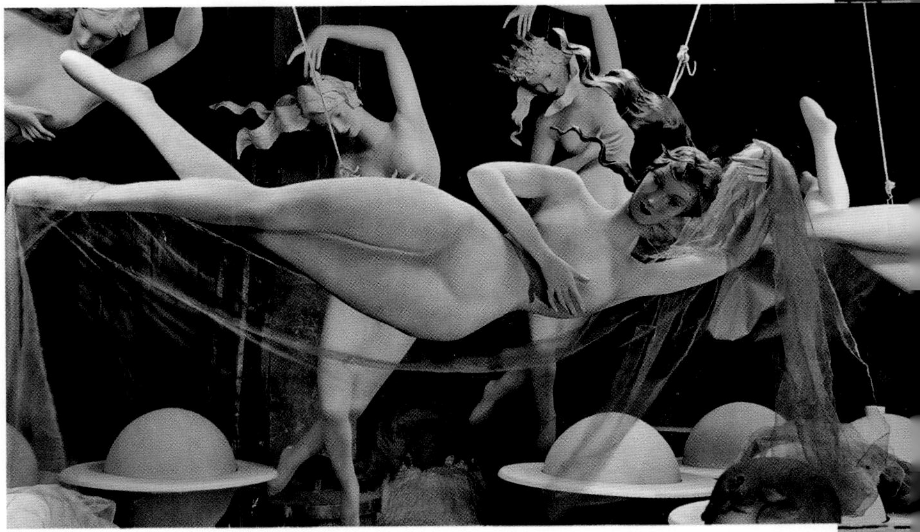

THE ART OF THE WINDOW DISPLAY

When Arthur Stewart-Liberty, Ivor's successor, returned to work in the family store after World War II, it was obvious that the limitations of austerity Britain were reflected in the restricted product lines on offer within the store. Inexperienced in retail, he was still able to recognize that the shop and its products needed revitalizing. One of the first things he addressed was the store's ability to publicize and display its range of goods. It was clear to him that a store of this size required a dedicated window-display department – a team of professional window dressers who could work as a coherent whole, rather than the pre-war system where each department set up their own wares for display in an ad-hoc fashion. The team would also be responsible for advertising and publicity, making sure there was a common purpose across all aspects of the retail business.

Stewart-Liberty was fortunate enough to meet Eric Lucking (1908–1985) just as he was looking for someone to set up the display department. Lucking had been working for various department stores, including the Army & Navy, since before the war. Acknowledged as a leading practitioner in the art of window display and a pioneer in terms of his use of ingenious display techniques, his innovations included spot lighting to highlight certain products, photographic backgrounds to create realistic room settings, and the use of invisible nylon thread in order to suspend objects within the window space. Using these techniques, Lucking created arresting and witty displays that showcased Liberty products with panache. Led by Lucking, the new window-dressing team consisted of many talented designers, including Phyllis Richards, a model-maker who provided imaginative mannequins for display. One of Lucking's most successful windows, and one which contained many of his signature motifs, was the award-winning window created to celebrate the Festival of Britain in 1951. This scene had a headless mannequin sitting in a blank white space surrounded by suspended Boomerang tables that were designed by British designer A. M. Lewis. In the publicity that arose, the April 1951 edition of *Fortune* magazine declared that,

> *"Lucking, a leading light in the modern display world, makes of each window a unified composition of form and colour, symbolic, sophisticated, classically simple or dreamily fantastic, sometimes bizarre and surrealist, but always original and imparting to the West End something of that inventive chic belonging to the smartest Continental houses."*

By the time that the Young Liberty label was established in 1949, the window-display department was perfectly positioned to showcase these new designs in an appropriately exciting and innovative way, a tradition that continues today.

ABOVE *This provocative window display contains several identical Venus figures floating in space and surrounded by planets. It is typical of Lucking's playful use of surrealism for effect.*

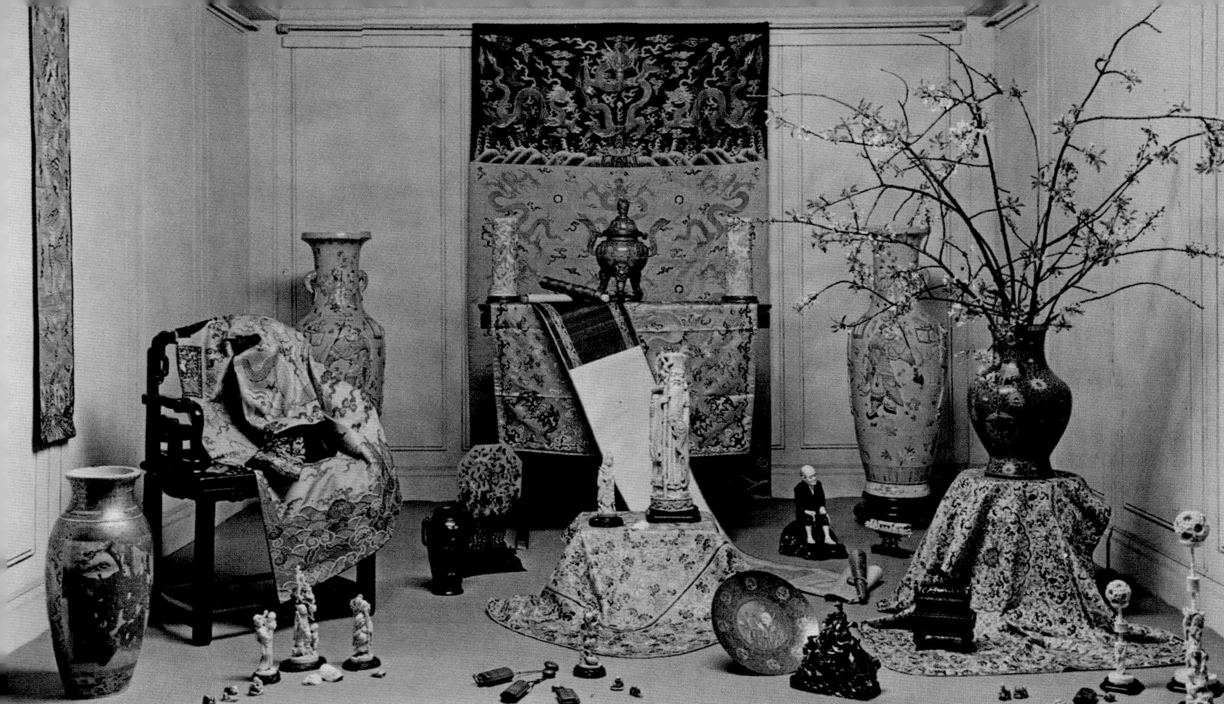

LEFT *Eric Lucking, leading practitioner of the art of window display, groups a collection of chinoiserie objects in his version of a room setting.*

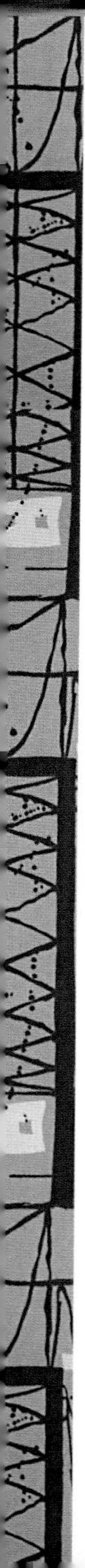

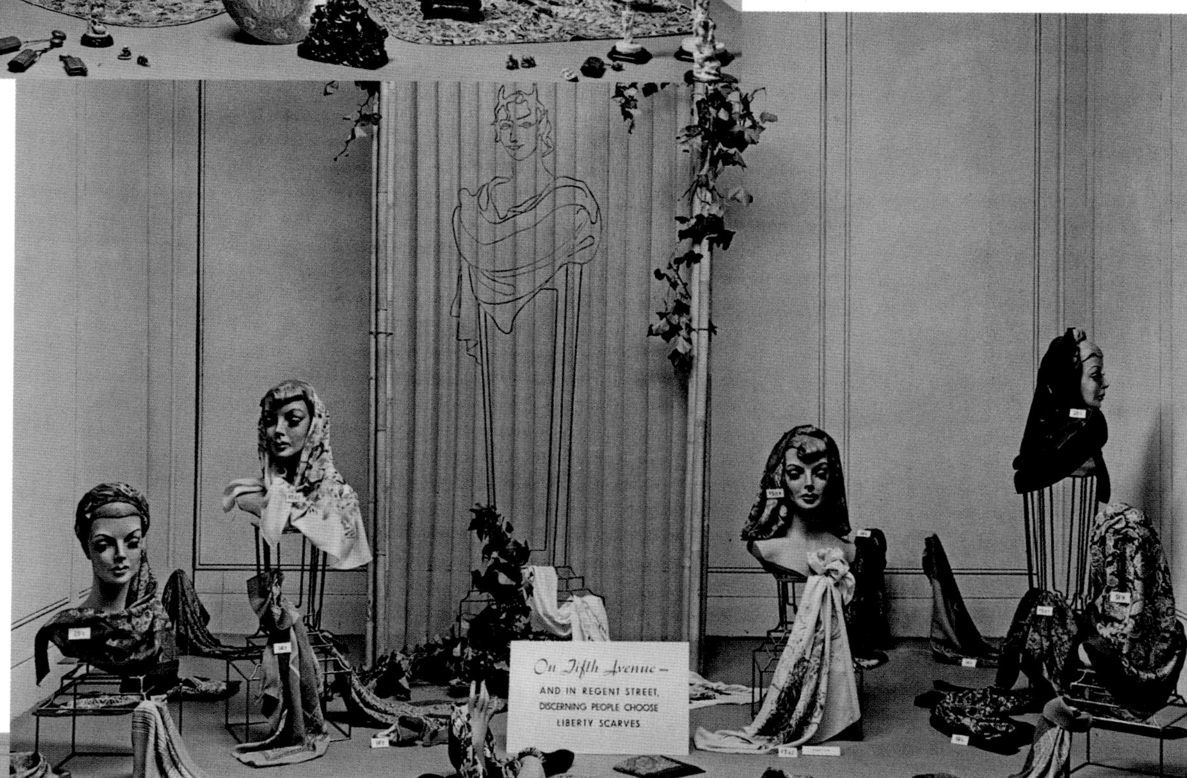

RIGHT *Here, Lucking introduces several Liberty scarves in a neo-classical setting, complete with a scarf-draped goddess and antique column.*

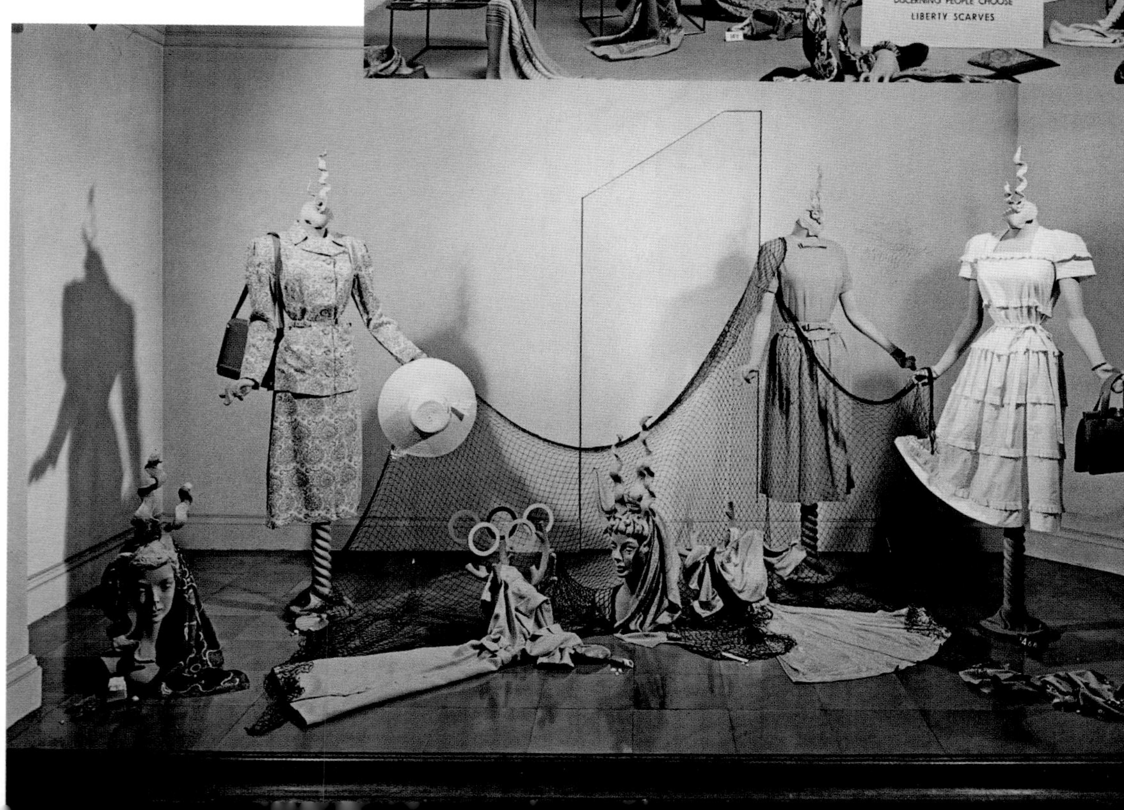

LEFT *The clothed figures and truncated heads with twisted turbans have a Dalí-esque quality in this window display, also by Lucking.*

BELOW *Two window displays from the Prints Charming exhibition held in celebration of the Liberty print in the summer of 2009. In the first, the mannequins pose in window-wide crinolines made up of hundreds of samples of Liberty-print fabrics. The models in second window below lie among undulating textures and patterns. Both displays were styled by set designer Faye Toogood.*

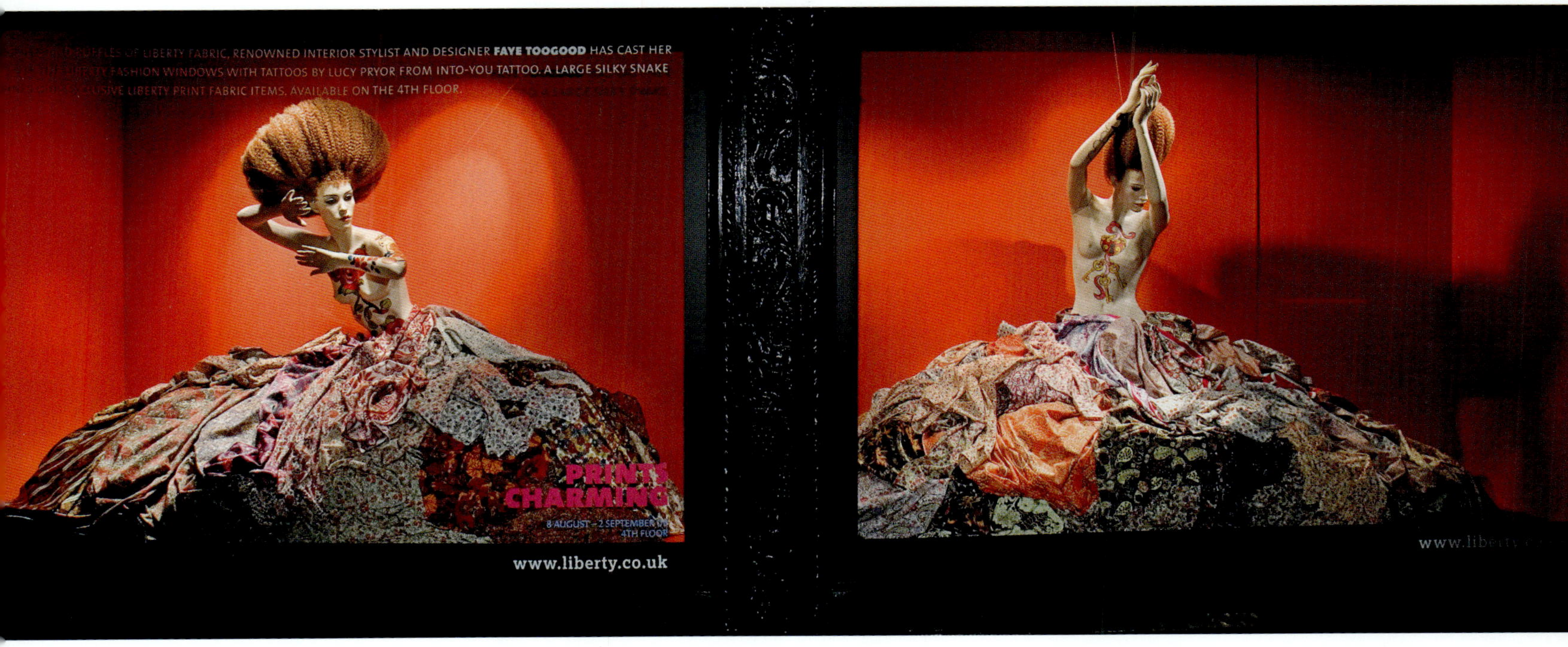

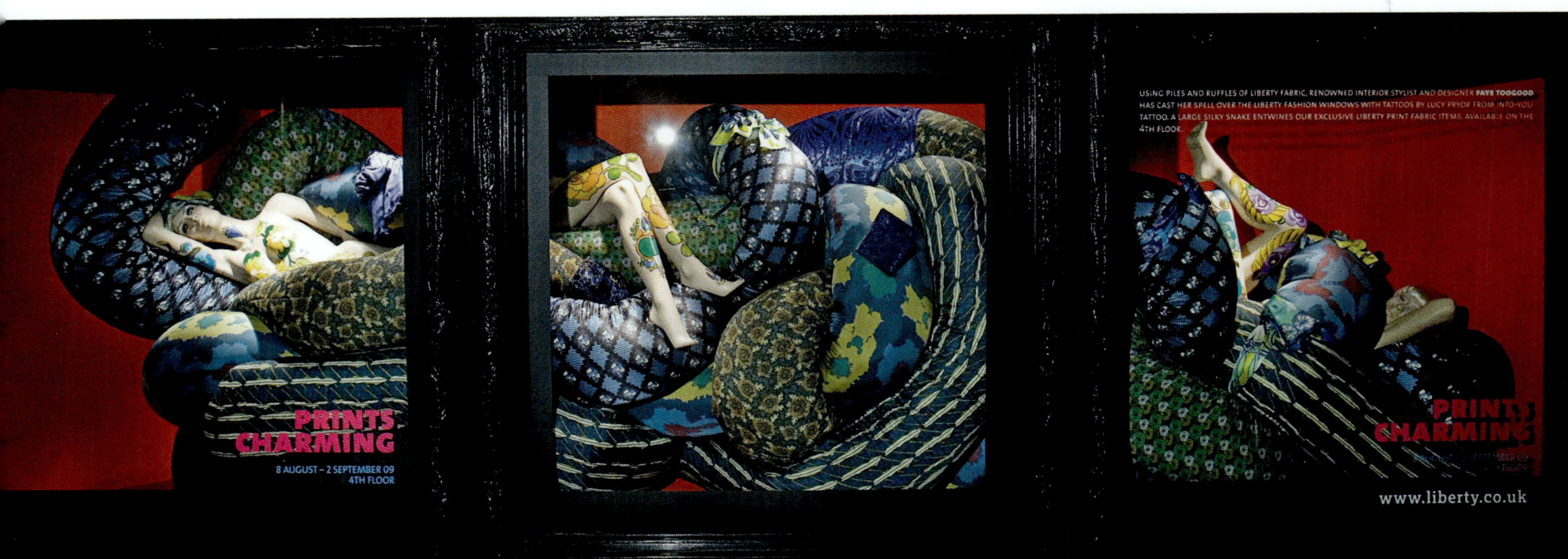

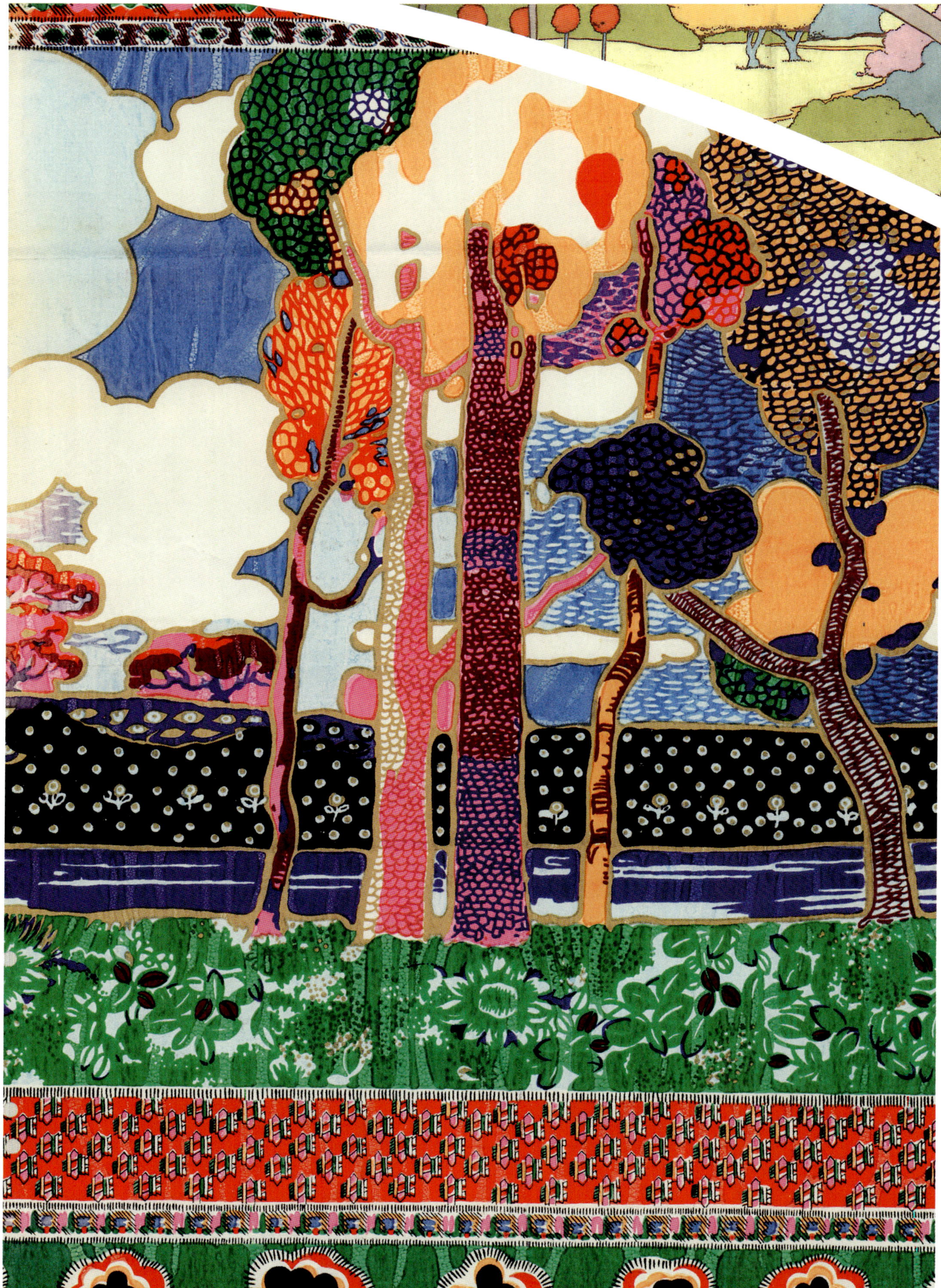

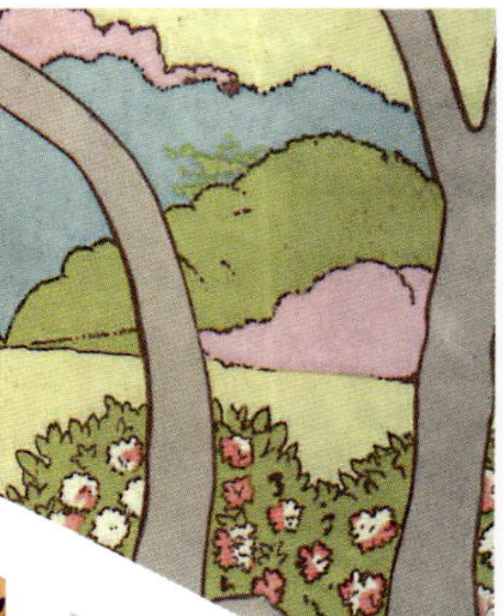

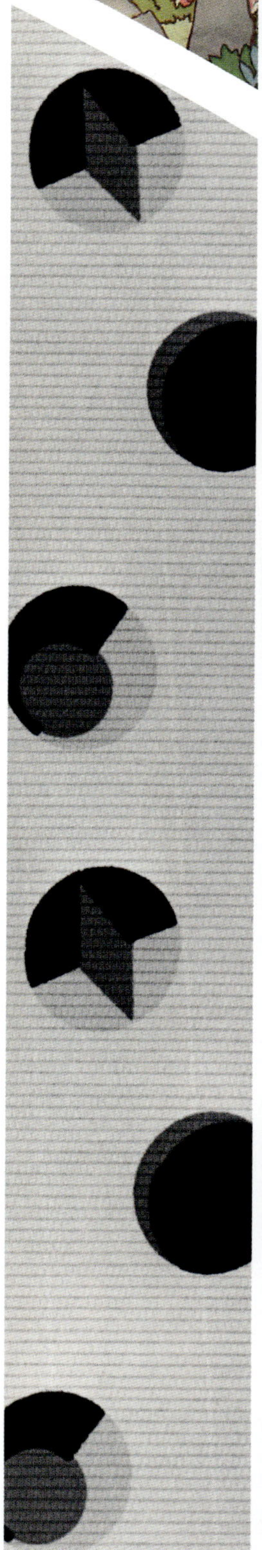

ART NOUVEAU REVISITED

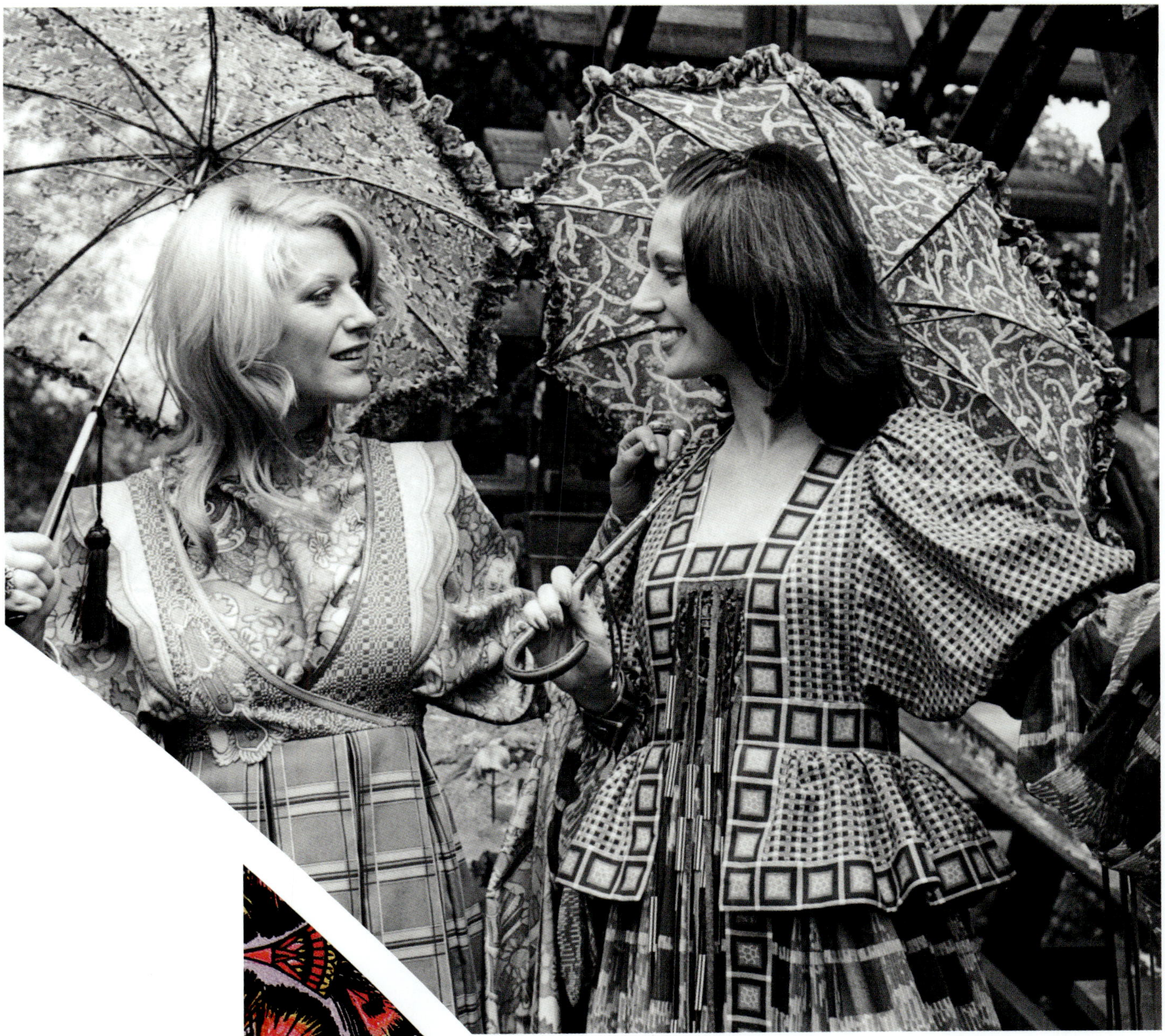

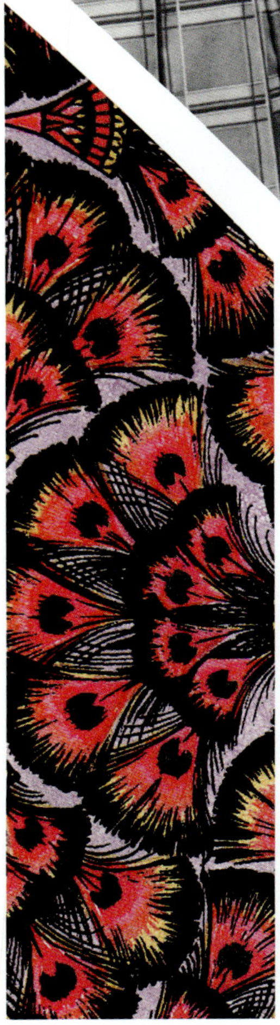

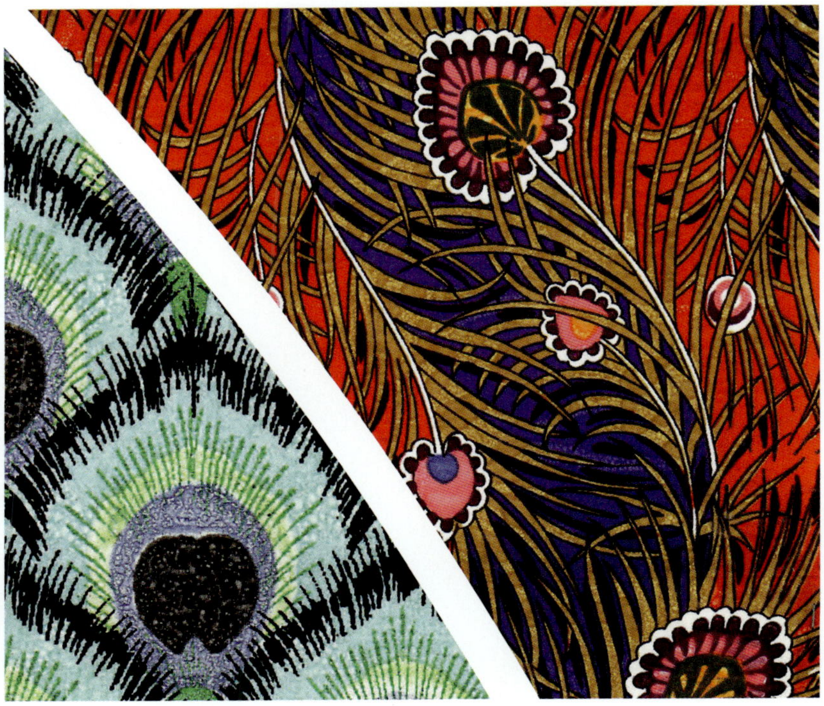

OPPOSITE
Frieze, by Bernard Nevill, 1968; Far Away, by Susan Collier, also 1968; and a geometric design by Bernard Nevill, 1969.

RIGHT TOP
Bill Gibb dress designs with textiles by Susan Collier and Sarah Campbell for Liberty, 1971–1972.

RIGHT
Two Peacock Fan prints, 1962, and the Isis print, an early-1900s archive print revived in 1968.

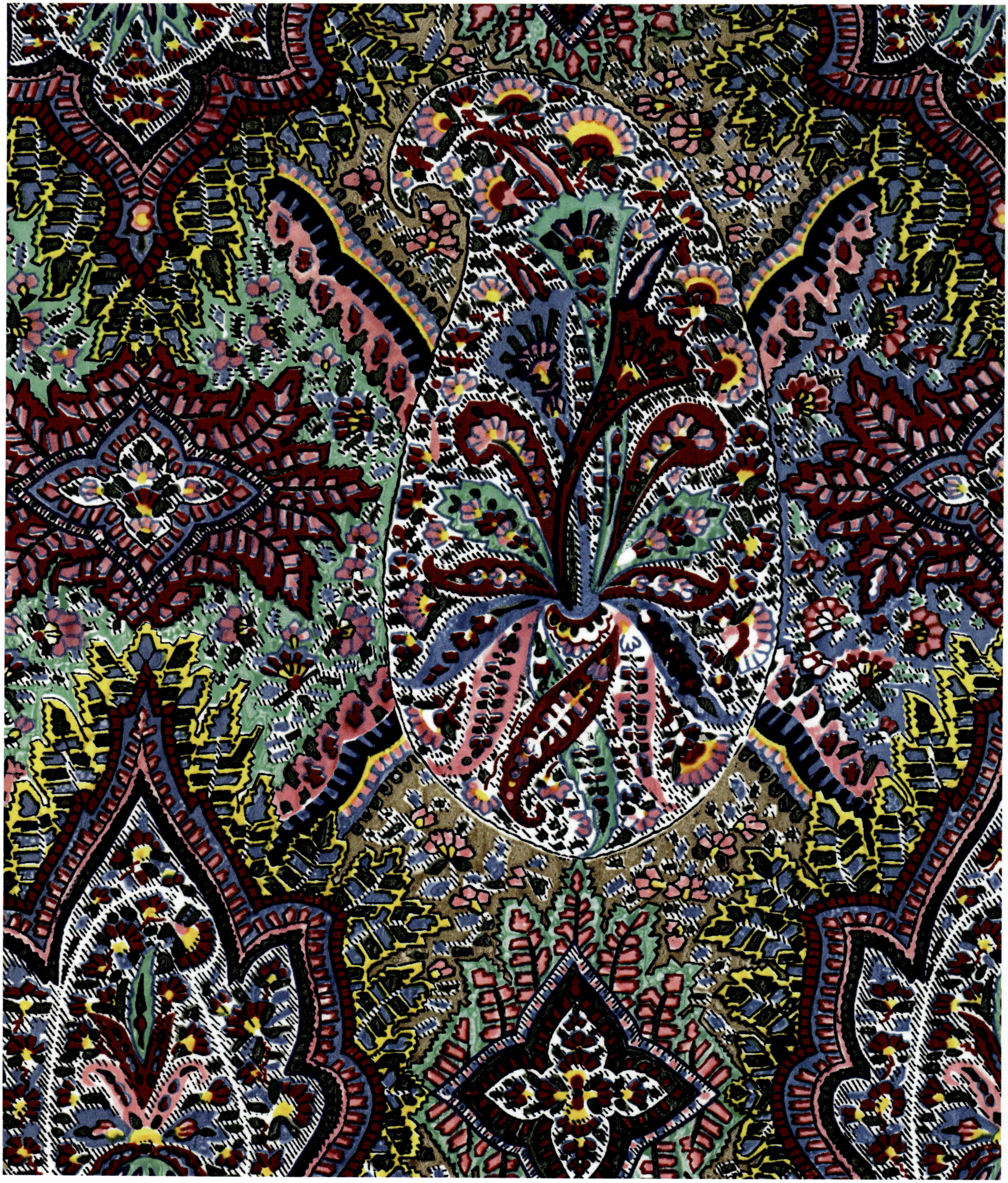

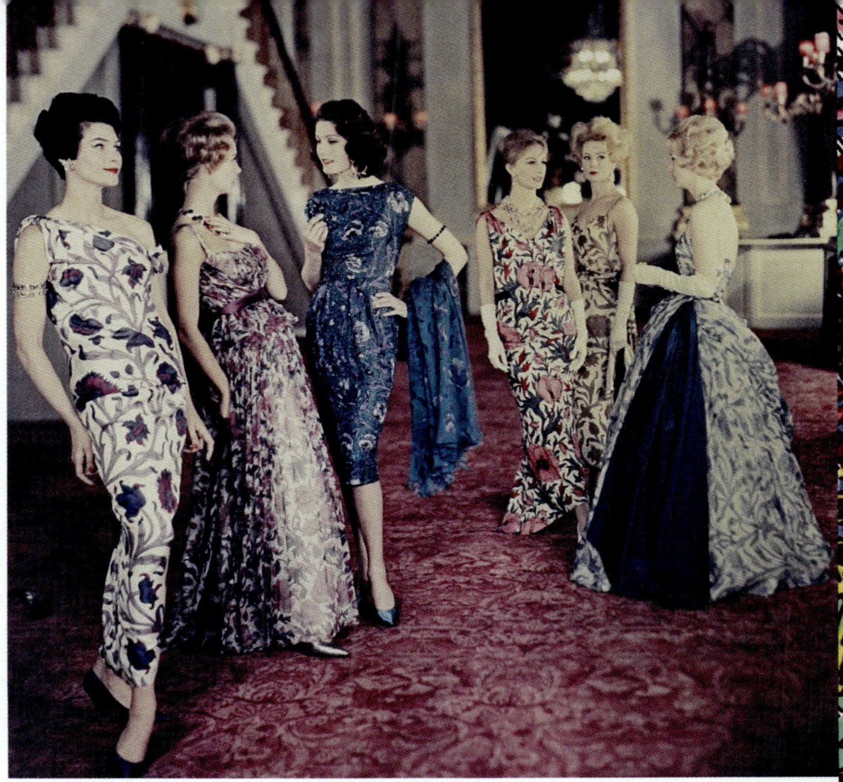

A FASHION EXPLOSION

Periods of innovation and change are frequently followed by nostalgic retrenchment, and the 1960s were no different. The culture of the 1950s had been characterized by a preoccupation with space travel, modernism and visions of "the future" as it strove to forget the horrors of World War II and shrug off dour post-war austerity. By 1960, the hard lines of modernism had begun to lose their novelty and designers had begun to revaluate the past. The tastemakers eager to find the latest trend had already started to embrace the aesthetics of a more repressed time, with Victorian nightdresses, Edwardian high-necked blouses and men's military dress jackets (later worn by the Beatles on the cover of the *Sgt. Peppers Lonely Hearts Club Band* album in 1967, designed by Peter Blake) being adopted by the demi-monde. These served as a piquant contrast to the more liberal behaviour of its wearers.

The earliest designers to start looking at the past as a source book include Liberty's Bernard Nevill and his students at the Royal College of Art, including Ossie Clark and Barbara Hulanicki of Biba, with the latter using a William Morris print to decorate her Abingdon Road shop in 1964, and Ossie Clark adopting, under the guidance of Bernard Nevill, the work of 1930s designer Lucien Lelong (1889–1958) as an inspiration.

The original Art Nouveau (New Art) was a movement that emerged between the 1890s and World War I. Taking as its inspiration the sinuous lines of nature – while exaggerating, extending and stylizing them – the movement was primarily concerned with the idea of freedom from the constraints of formal art. Art Nouveau had continued to bubble under the surface as a design inspiration throughout the twentieth century, with the Surrealists in particular paying homage during the 1930s. However, this interest exploded into full-blown cultural omnipotence with the advent of two extremely influential exhibitions in Paris and New York dedicated to the turn-of-the-century art movement. In 1959, the Museum of Modern Art (MoMA) had a show entitled "Art Nouveau – Art and Design at the Turn of the Century", and a year later, the Museum of Modern Art in Paris put on an exhibition of "Les sources du XXe siècle".

Given its famous association with late nineteenth- and early twentieth-century design, Liberty was perfectly positioned to provide the inspiration and the materials with which to satisfy this hunger for the old. Liberty's designers had to hand the most comprehensive archive of turn-of-the-century prints in Europe, which could be plundered for both inspiration and reworking.

ABOVE *During the Art Nouveau revival of the 1970s, designers including John Cavanagh, Pierre Balmain and Bud Kilpatrick all featured fabrics from the Lotus collection of prints designed by William Poole for Liberty. Here, models wearing dresses from the collection pose in the Crush Room at the Royal Opera House.*

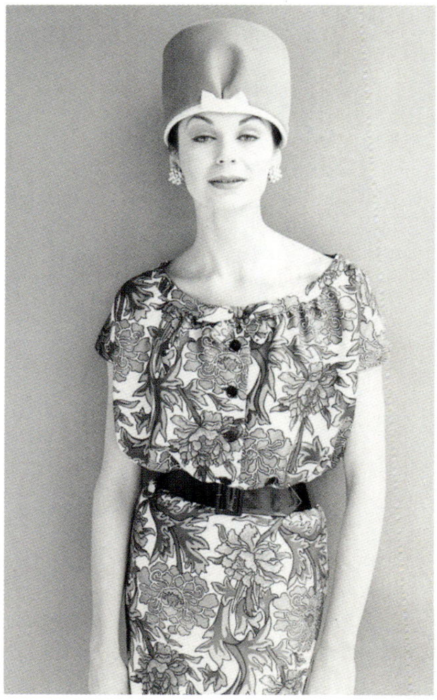

RIGHT *A 1960s silk dress designed by John Cavanagh, in two shades of green, black and white, using the Liberty Agatha print, a revival of a late-1890s Liberty furnishing design.*

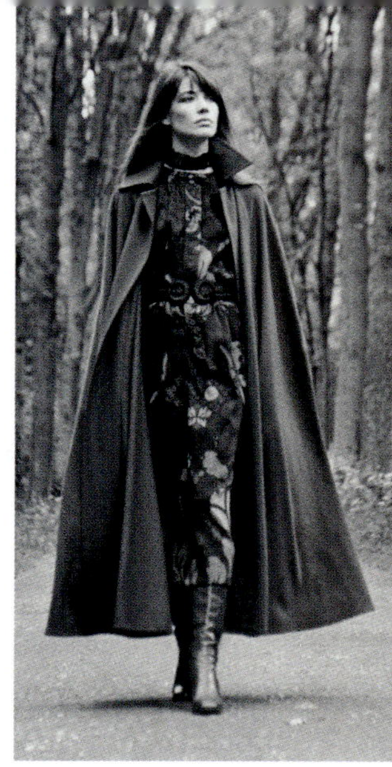

LEFT *French fashion icon and singer Françoise Hardy wears a Liberty wool challis floral print dress and a long cape by Yves Saint Laurent, 1970.*

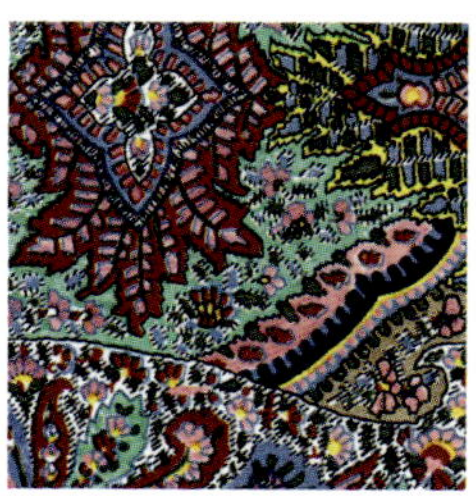

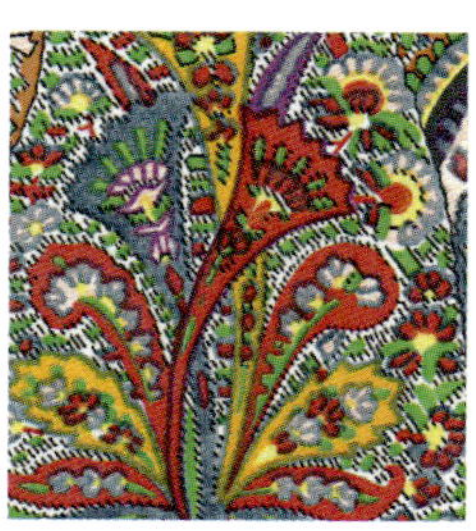

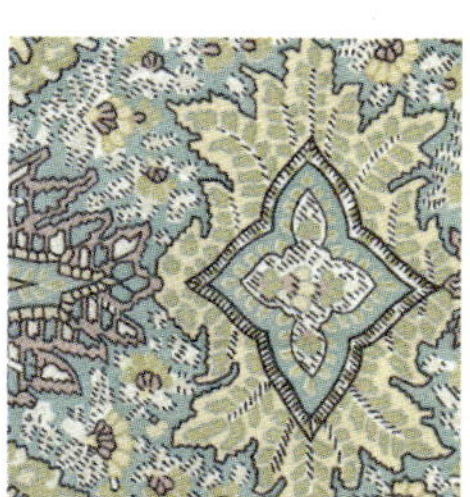

ABOVE *First created in the late nineteenth century, the Stockton design of these Tana Lawn prints was revived in 1969 and 1975.*

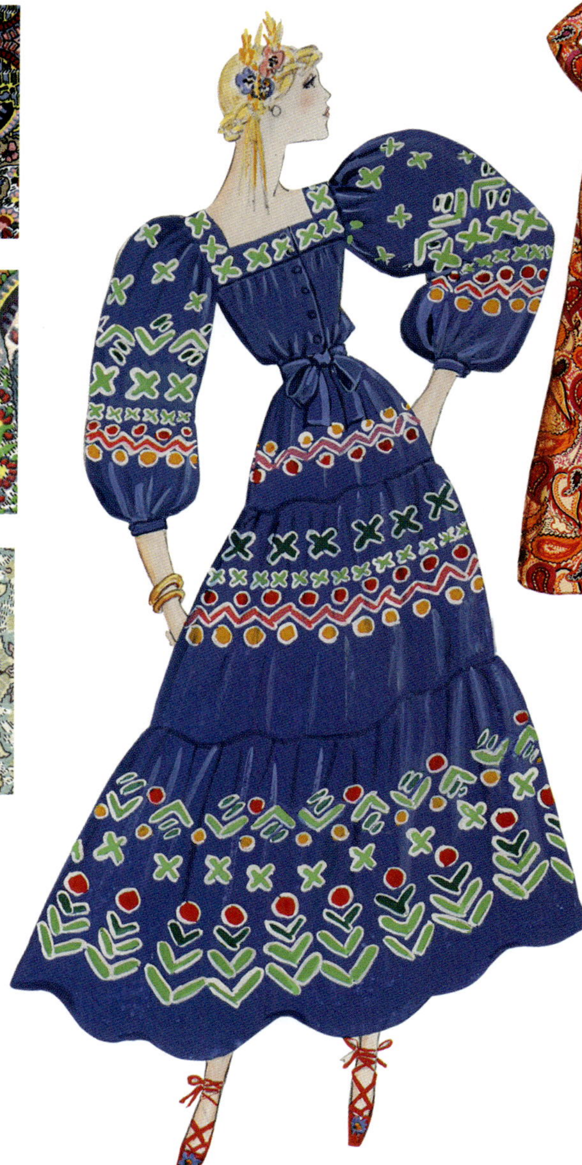

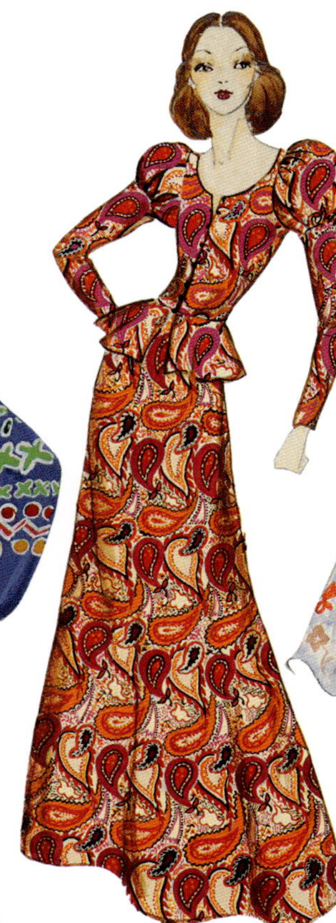

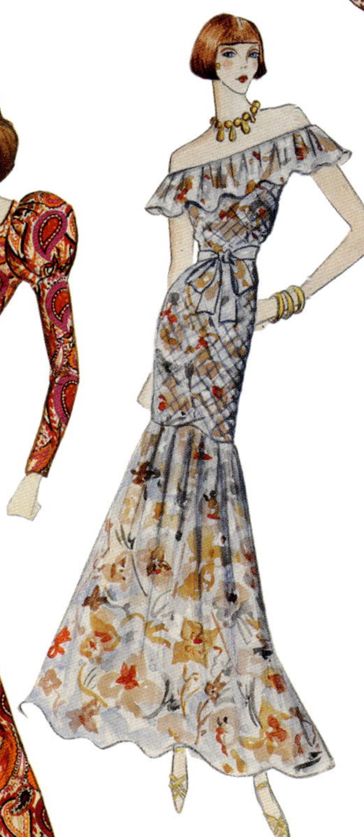

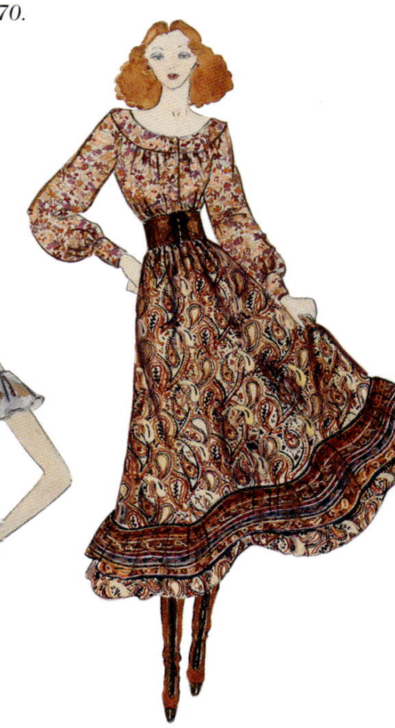

LEFT TO RIGHT *Influential French designer Yves Saint Laurent popularized Liberty fabrics for both his couture and prêt-à-porter ranges, which were first implemented in 1969. All of the garments shown here are from Yves Saint Laurent's Liberty fabric designs.*

1. *A Mexican-inspired full-sleeved dress with border print from 1973.*

2. *Yves Saint Laurent fashions a swirling psychedelic paisley print into a peplum jacket and maxiskirt in 1970.*

3. *An off-the-shoulder all-over print design from 1974.*

4. *A full-skirted "peasant-style" dress from 1970.*

5. *Two 1940s Revival dresses from 1974, featuring small-scale prints.*

6. *A 1966 scoop-necked high-waisted maxidress.*

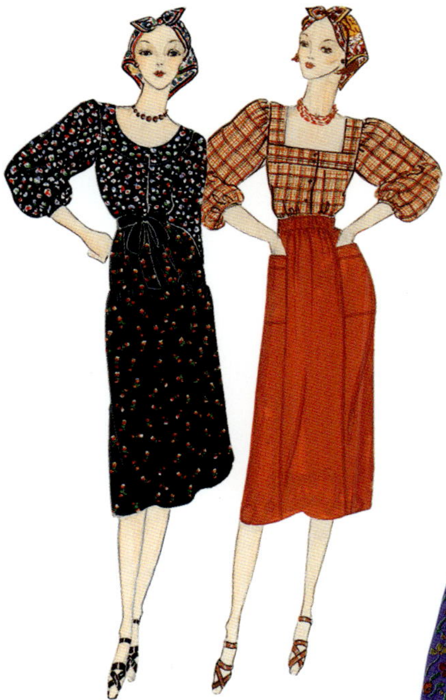

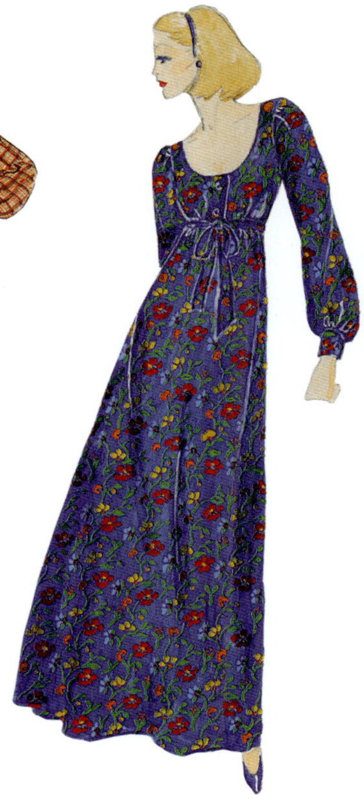

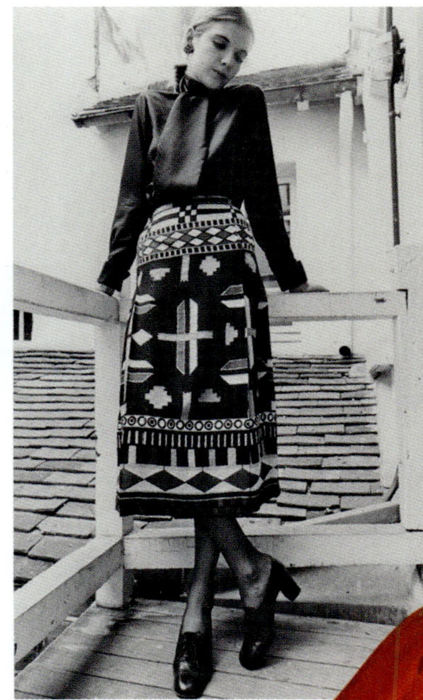

LEFT AND BELOW *Yves Saint Laurent is credited with marketing the first maxiskirt to appear on the catwalk. He used the Macedonia print design by Bernard Nevill for this pleated skirt, also seen in the illustration below.*

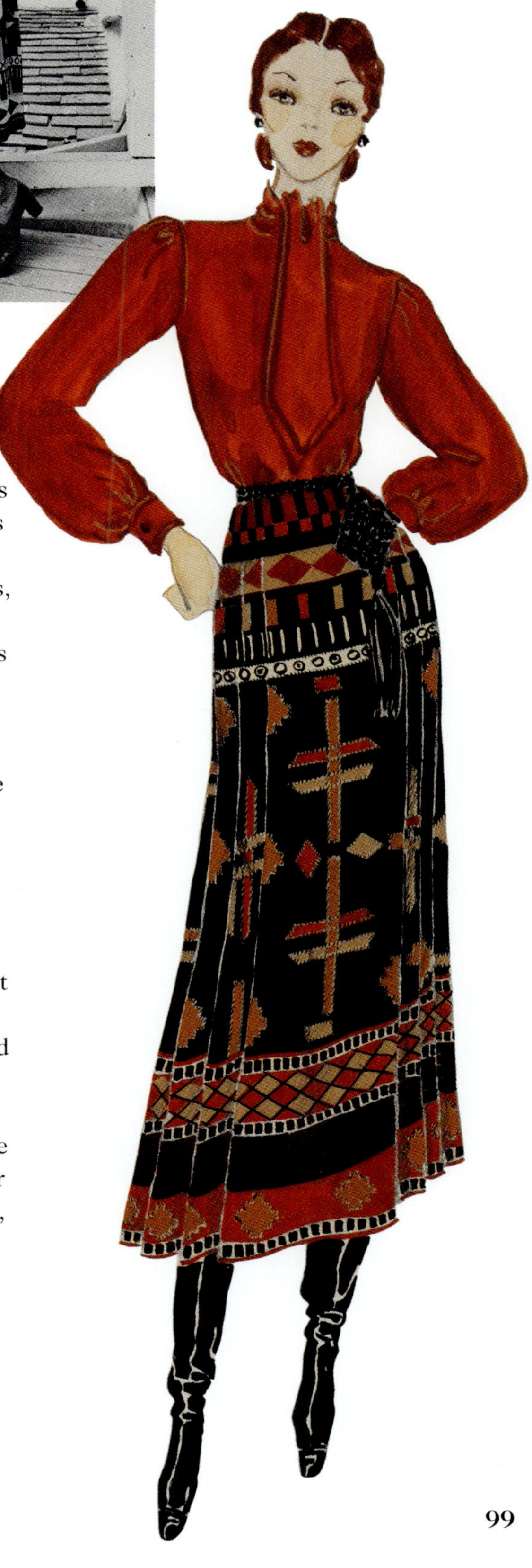

In 1960, Liberty's fabric department launched, with great fanfare, the first Lotus collection – the boldest statement yet that Art Nouveau was worthy of attention. The origins of the collection are slightly muddied, with the apocryphal story, that some samples had been found in a dusty corner of the office, being a particularly appealing version of events, or that William Poole, an assistant printmaker at Merton, had come back from the Paris Art Nouveau show fired up with inspiration that this was what Liberty must start making immediately. What is certain is that in 1960, the board decided to use these original block prints to produce a range of designs. They would be executed in the best fabrics in order to seduce the high-end couture houses, which would garner widespread press coverage and, in turn, lead to the mass-market adoption of the fabrics.

The original Victorian designs by Henry Napper and John Scarratt Rigby were reproduced exactly as they had first appeared (although screen-printed, not block-printed) while being brought up to date by the use of various modern colourways, including a bold monochrome. In spring 1960, Liberty held a fashion show that showcased the designs of various couture houses that had adopted the Lotus fabrics, including the more established couture houses such as the Fontana sisters, Arnold Scaasi, Givenchy and Christian Dior, and the new breed of young designers such as Foale and Tuffin and Mary Quant.

The fabulous success of the first Lotus collection heralded the adoption of Art Nouveau in all areas of design. The organic lines of Art Nouveau could be found in the curved silhouette of Verner Panton's S chair, and the sinuous figures, arabesque lines and colours of Alphonse Mucha in the early psychedelic prints by design collective Hapshash and the Coloured Coat from the mid-1960s.

As the decade progressed, designers – led to a large extent by Bernard Nevill and his students – looked to other art movements for inspiration, with Art Deco, the Jazz Age and the Orient all having their place under the spotlight. In the 1970s, Liberty fabrics, especially Tana Lawn, continued to be used by such prominent fashion designers as Bill Gibb, Yves Saint Laurent and Jean Bousquet at Cacharel, who promoted their Liberty print dresses in romantically atmospheric advertising campaigns by the photographer Sarah Moon.

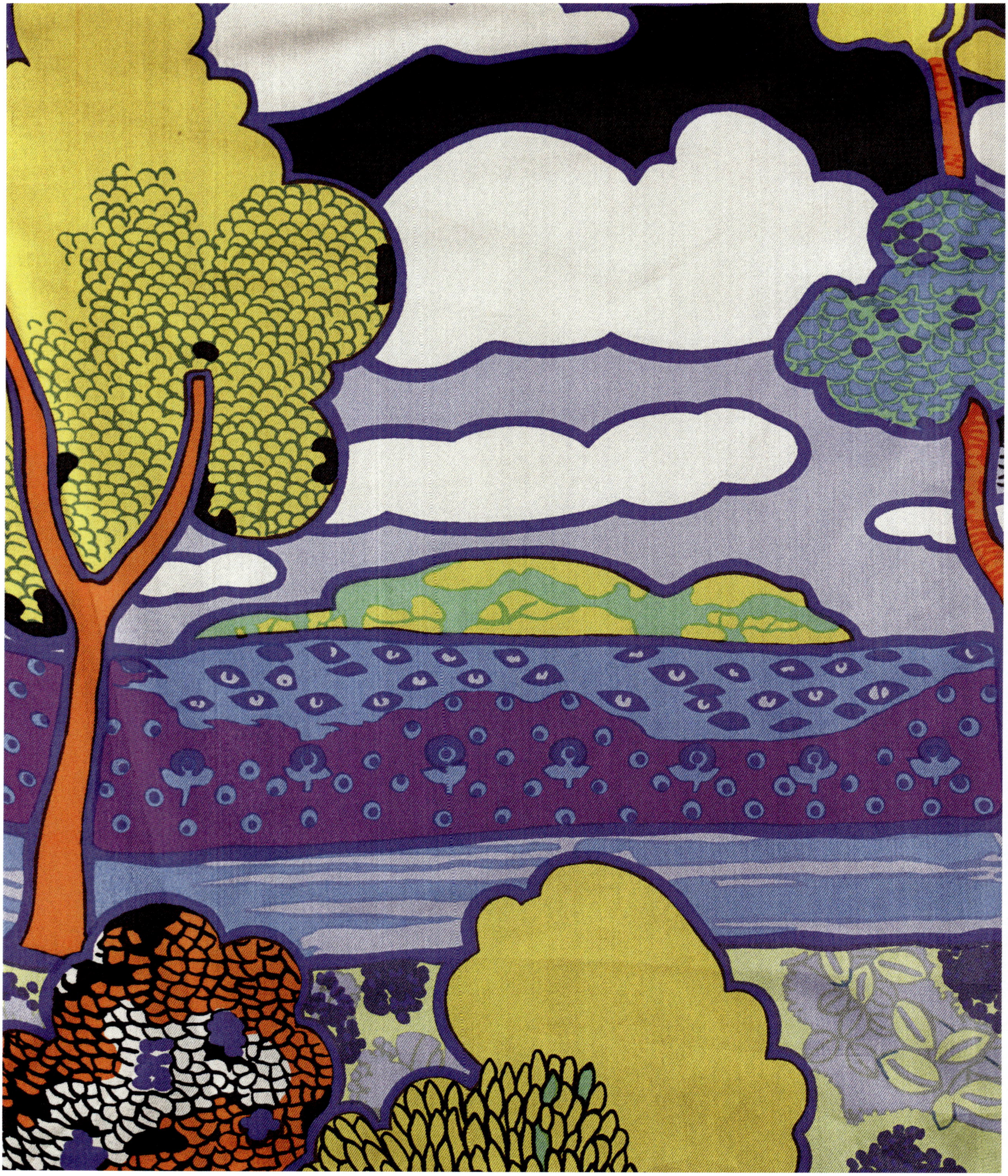

BERNARD NEVILL & SUSAN COLLIER

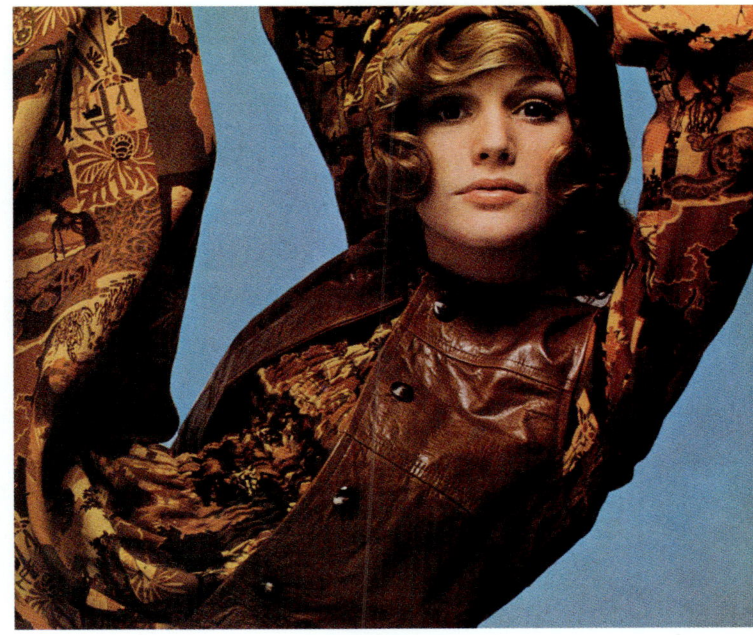

ABOVE *Designed by Mog in 1969, this maxidress features a richly coloured Liberty print in wool challis, designed by Bernard Nevill.*

The two names most synonymous with Liberty print design are undoubtedly Bernard Nevill and Susan Collier, both of whom were key designers for the store in the 1960s and 1970s, and both of whom made an enormous contribution in shaping the house style of both Liberty and modern print design as a whole.

The career of Bernard Nevill (b. 1934) is inextricably linked with Liberty. Having studied and taught at both St Martin's College of Art and the Royal College of Art, he became, in 1960, consultant designer for Liberty, breathing new life into their traditional dress and furnishing prints and enabling them to keep pace with, and ultimately influence, the fashions of "swinging" London. Nevill looked closely at late nineteenth- and early twentieth-century designers such as William Morris and the couturier Madame Vionnet (1876–1975) in order to find something new and relevant. He seemed to be able to predict with remarkable accuracy what might resonate with contemporary consumers of design. He is most well known for spearheading the Art Deco revival with his Jazz collection of 1964, but perhaps his greatest success came in 1968 when Yves Saint Laurent created his iconic and groundbreaking maxiskirt using Nevill's Macedonia print.

Susan Collier (1938–2011) also had a long career association with Liberty, before leaving in 1977 to set up Collier Campbell Ltd, her own design company with her sister Sarah Campbell (although they had been working as Collier Campbell since 1968). Known for her vibrant and joyfully painterly prints, her name is synonymous with the florals and paisleys in Tana cotton Lawn for which Liberty is famous. Unlike Nevill, Collier was self-taught, gaining experience working with renowned graphic designer Pat Albeck before being taken on by Liberty as a freelance designer in 1961, and eventually taking over from Nevill as lead design consultant in 1971. From this position of influence, Collier worked to ensure Liberty followed her preferred aesthetic of hand-painted designs and she embraced the handmade and haphazard, creating mass-produced fabrics that retained the marks of the creative process – a visible brushstroke or an uneven line.

Up to 1971, Liberty prints had been produced in limited runs for couture designers. Collier's legacy of innovation and commercial genius was to make these designs available to all through mass production as furnishing, accessories and dress fabric so that customers could decorate both themselves and their homes with Liberty prints.

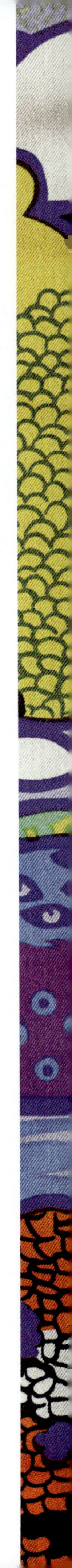

OPPOSITE *Equally formalized, Frieze, by Bernard Nevill from 1968, is graphically bolder, with a typically Art Deco-inspired colour palette.*

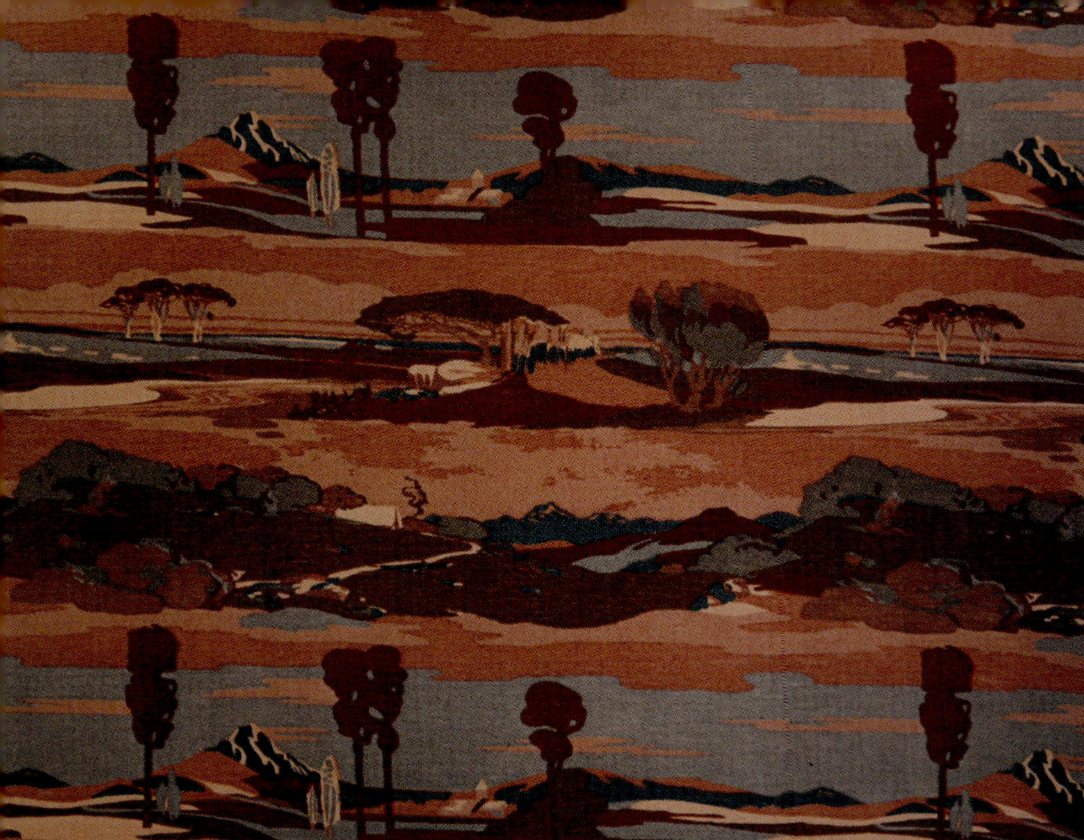

LEFT *The colour palette of brown and pink in this Landscape print by Bernard Nevill anticipates the 1970s trend away from psychedelic hues into a more subtle palette.*

BELOW *Susan Collier's 1968 Far Away design is a minutely observed yet highly stylized landscape, evocative of the 1920s fashion drawings of illustrator Helen Dryden.*

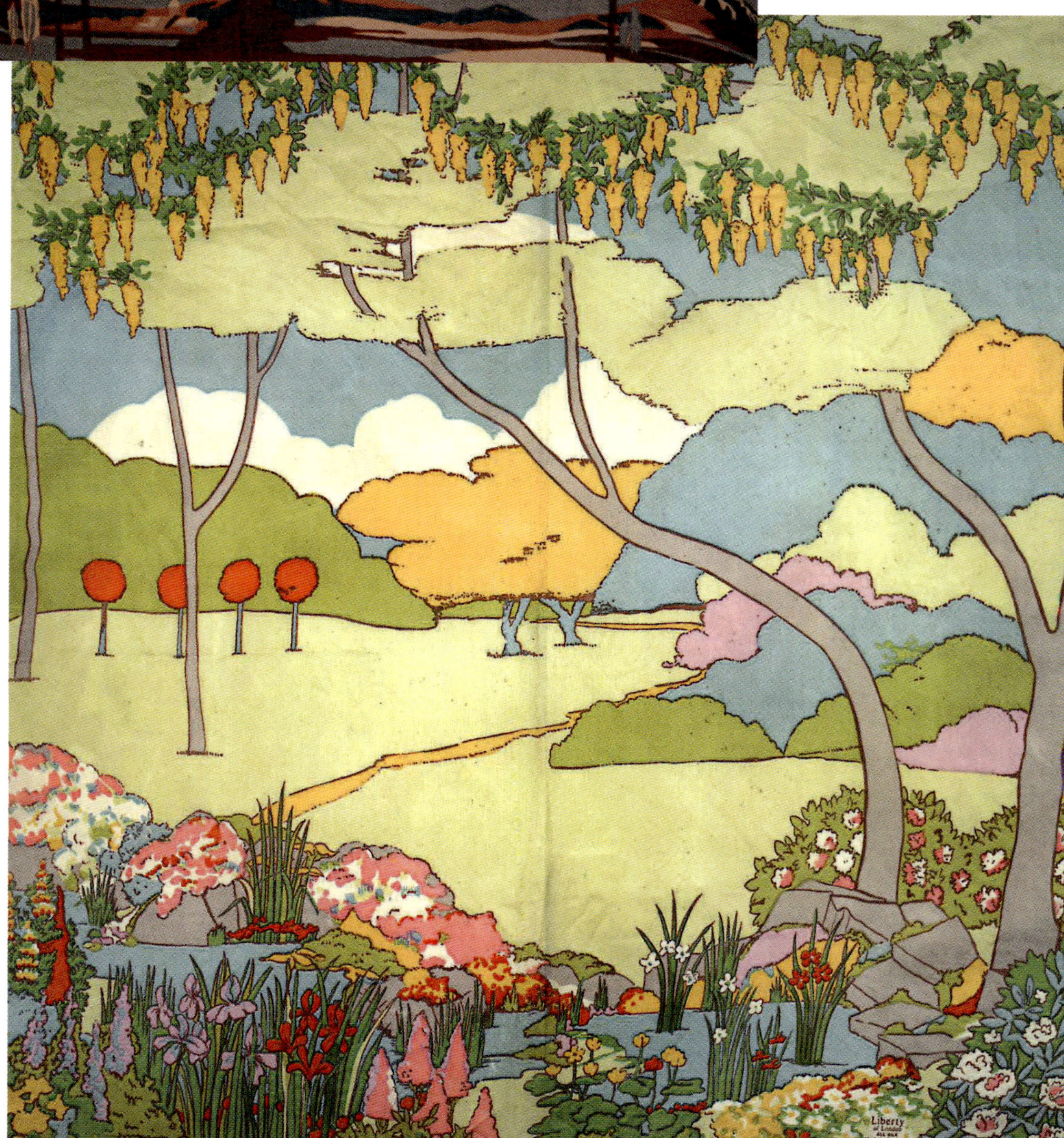

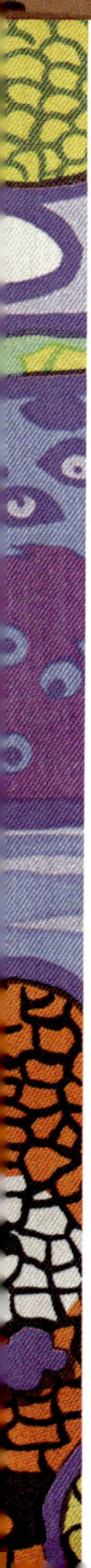

BELOW *Epitomizing the glamour of the Côte d'Azur, Vacances (also called Cunard) by Bernard Nevill in 1968, features all the accoutrements of international travel, with collaged images redolent of 1930s travel posters.*

RIGHT *Preempting the 1970s Art Deco revival and the "Odeon" style of the 1930s, Grace Coddington models a 1930s-inspired dress designed by Leslie Poole in a setting styled by Bernard Nevill and featuring fabrics from his Jazz collection. Photography by Barry Lategan.*

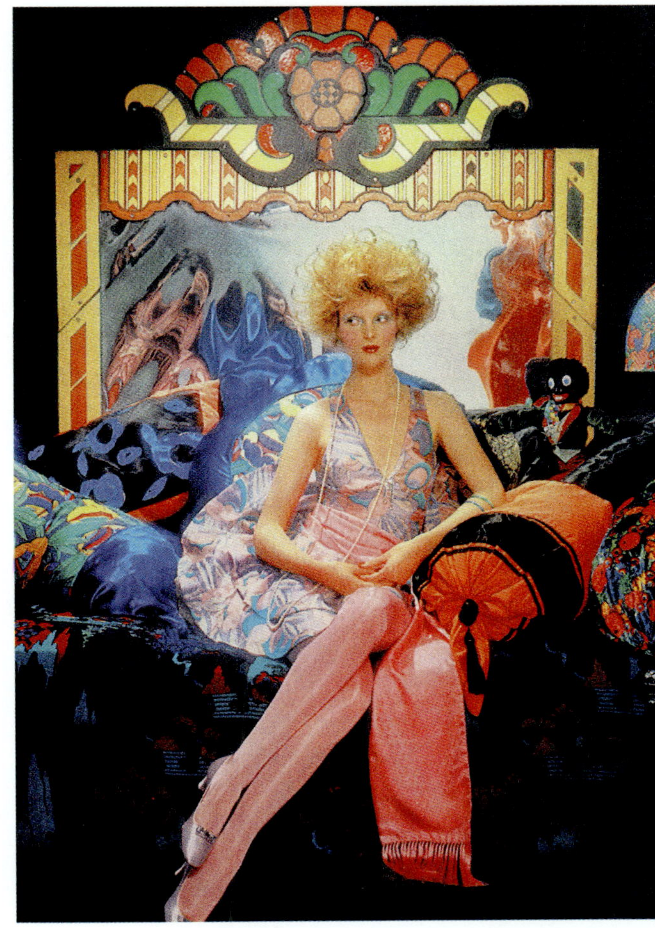

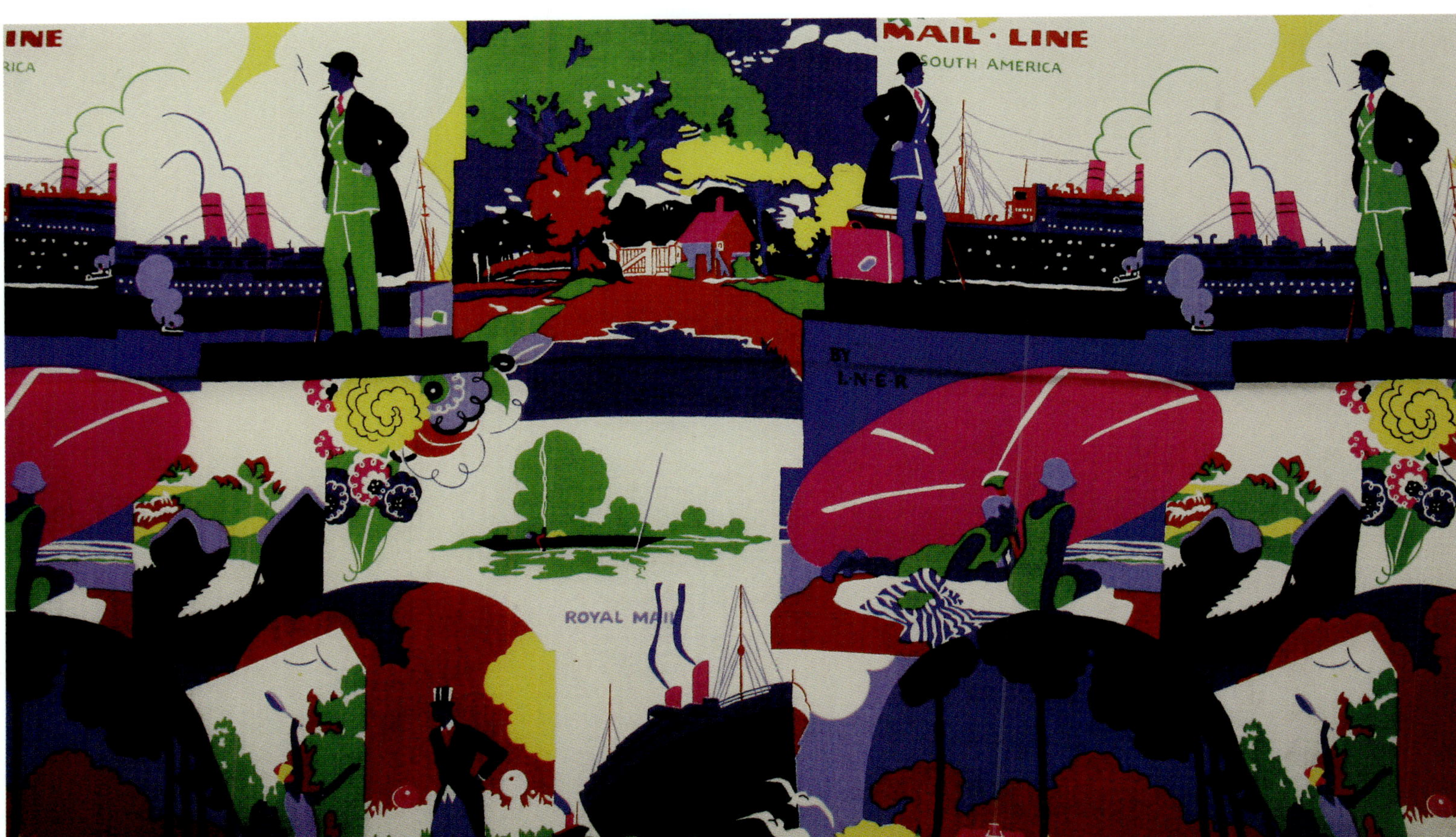

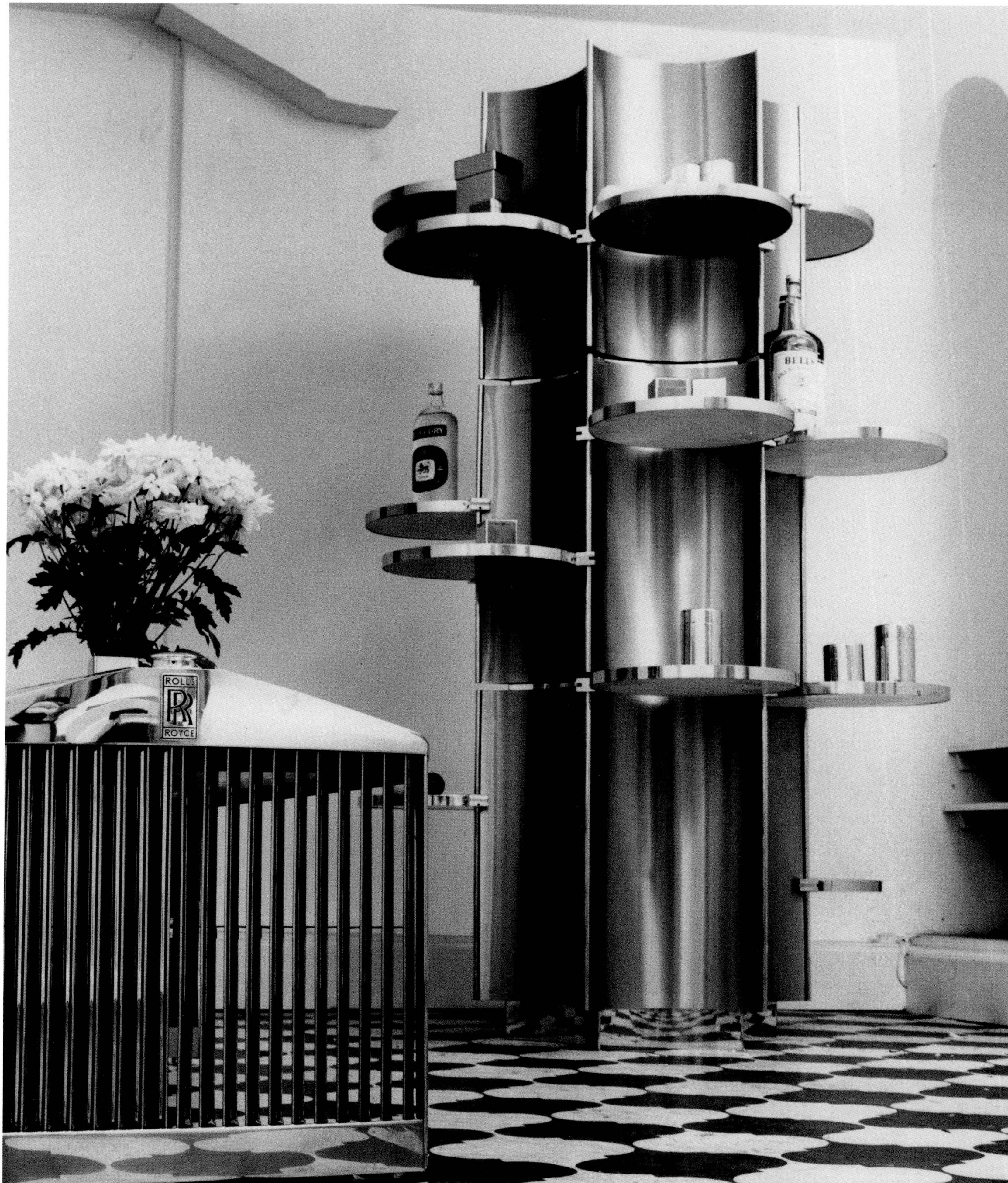
ROLLS
ROYCE
BELLS

FURNITURE DESIGN

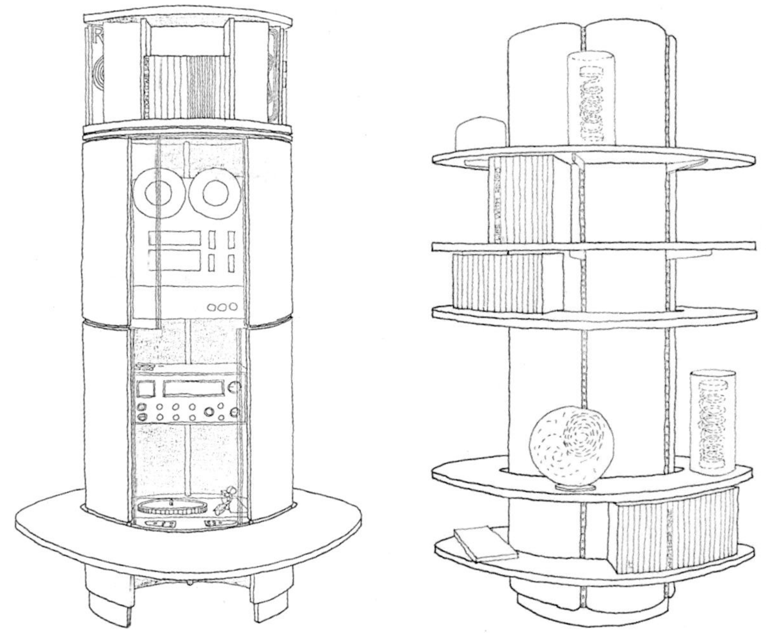

In 1971, Liberty decided that a revamp of its furniture department was required in order to replicate the success that the print department had been enjoying. This new marketing strategy, based on the idea of having a series of occasional high-profile exhibitions within the store in order to generate publicity and increase footfall, was set in motion with a showcase of the work of newly formed design company RoR.

RoR produced high-end, luxe objects suitable for the home of a millionaire musician. This was no surprise, since one of the "R"s in the name belonged to Ringo Starr, who had joined forces with established designer Robin Cruikshank (head of design at Apple Corps) to produce a series of pieces for his new home in 1969. These objects, including a stainless-steel fireplace and a hi-fi tower, were reproduced and exhibited in a specially painted showroom within the Regent Street store. The most talked-about piece was the coffee table designed by Ringo Starr, which was made from two Rolls Royce car radiator grilles.

The exhibition was a triumph, generating a great deal of press coverage. The success of the show resulted in Liberty continuing to use an exhibition programme as a key marketing strategy until well into the 1990s. In 1991, the furniture department revived the process of commissioning and producing its own-label furniture for the first time since before World War I – excluding the pieces created for the Centenary in 1975. Swedish designer Helene Tiedemann was commissioned to create a dozen pieces, to be made by British craftsmen. The collection was called Liberty I, suggesting the first of many, and was characterized by its solidly natural materials and its evocation of Arts and Crafts with a modern sensibility.

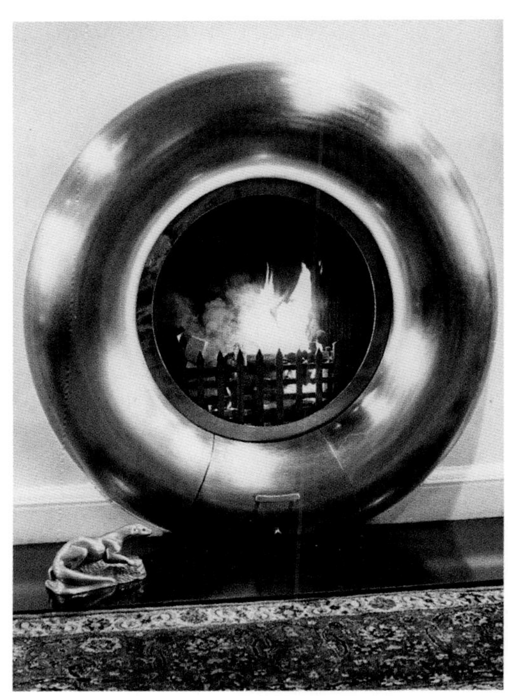

ABOVE *Original sketches for a hi-fi unit and a cylindrical shelving unit in polished steel designed by Robin Cruickshank, and produced in conjunction with British Steel.*

OPPOSITE AND LEFT *Steel fireplace (left), metal shelving unit with adjustable leaves (opposite), and a corner of the infamous Rolls Royce coffee table (opposite), seen in situ at the 1971 exhibition of RoR furniture.*

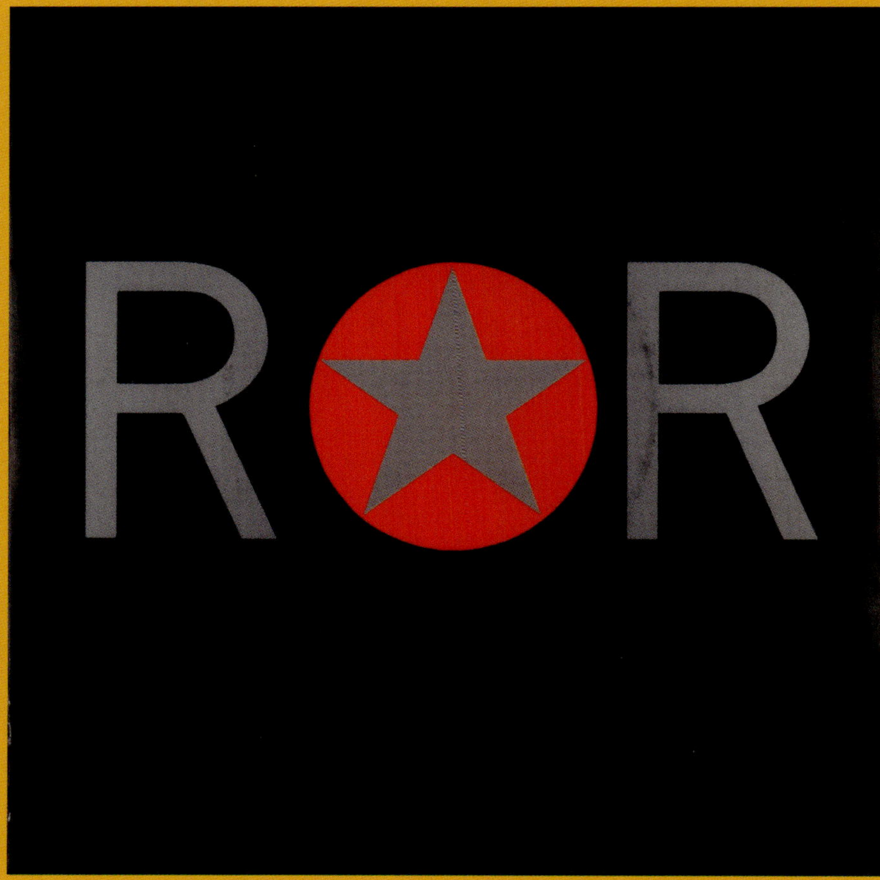

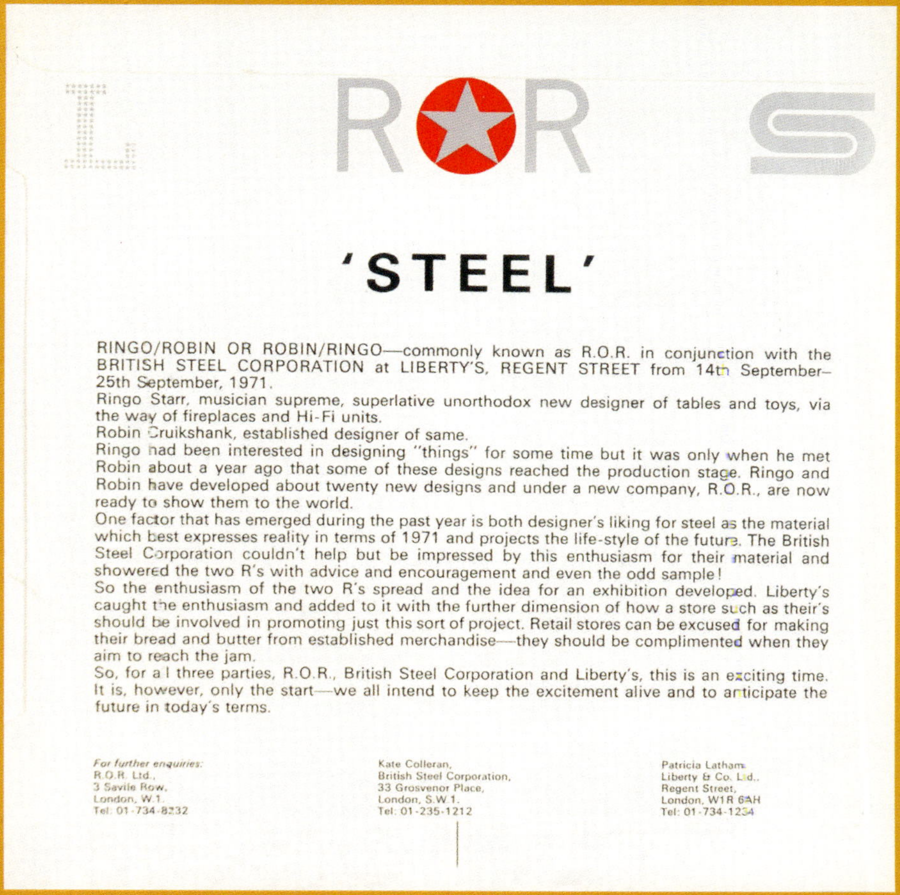

R★R

'STEEL'

RINGO/ROBIN OR ROBIN/RINGO—commonly known as R.O.R. in conjunction with the BRITISH STEEL CORPORATION at LIBERTY'S, REGENT STREET from 14th September–25th September, 1971.

Ringo Starr, musician supreme, superlative unorthodox new designer of tables and toys, via the way of fireplaces and Hi-Fi units.

Robin Cruikshank, established designer of same.

Ringo had been interested in designing "things" for some time but it was only when he met Robin about a year ago that some of these designs reached the production stage. Ringo and Robin have developed about twenty new designs and under a new company, R.O.R., are now ready to show them to the world.

One factor that has emerged during the past year is both designer's liking for steel as the material which best expresses reality in terms of 1971 and projects the life-style of the future. The British Steel Corporation couldn't help but be impressed by this enthusiasm for their material and showered the two R's with advice and encouragement and even the odd sample!

So the enthusiasm of the two R's spread and the idea for an exhibition developed. Liberty's caught the enthusiasm and added to it with the further dimension of how a store such as their's should be involved in promoting just this sort of project. Retail stores can be excused for making their bread and butter from established merchandise—they should be complimented when they aim to reach the jam.

So, for all three parties, R.O.R., British Steel Corporation and Liberty's, this is an exciting time. It is, however, only the start—we all intend to keep the excitement alive and to anticipate the future in today's terms.

For further enquiries:
R.O.R. Ltd.,
3 Savile Row,
London, W.1.
Tel: 01-734-8232

Kate Colleran,
British Steel Corporation,
33 Grosvenor Place,
London, S.W.1.
Tel: 01-235-1212

Patricia Latham
Liberty & Co. Ltd.,
Regent Street,
London, W1R 6AH
Tel: 01-734-1234

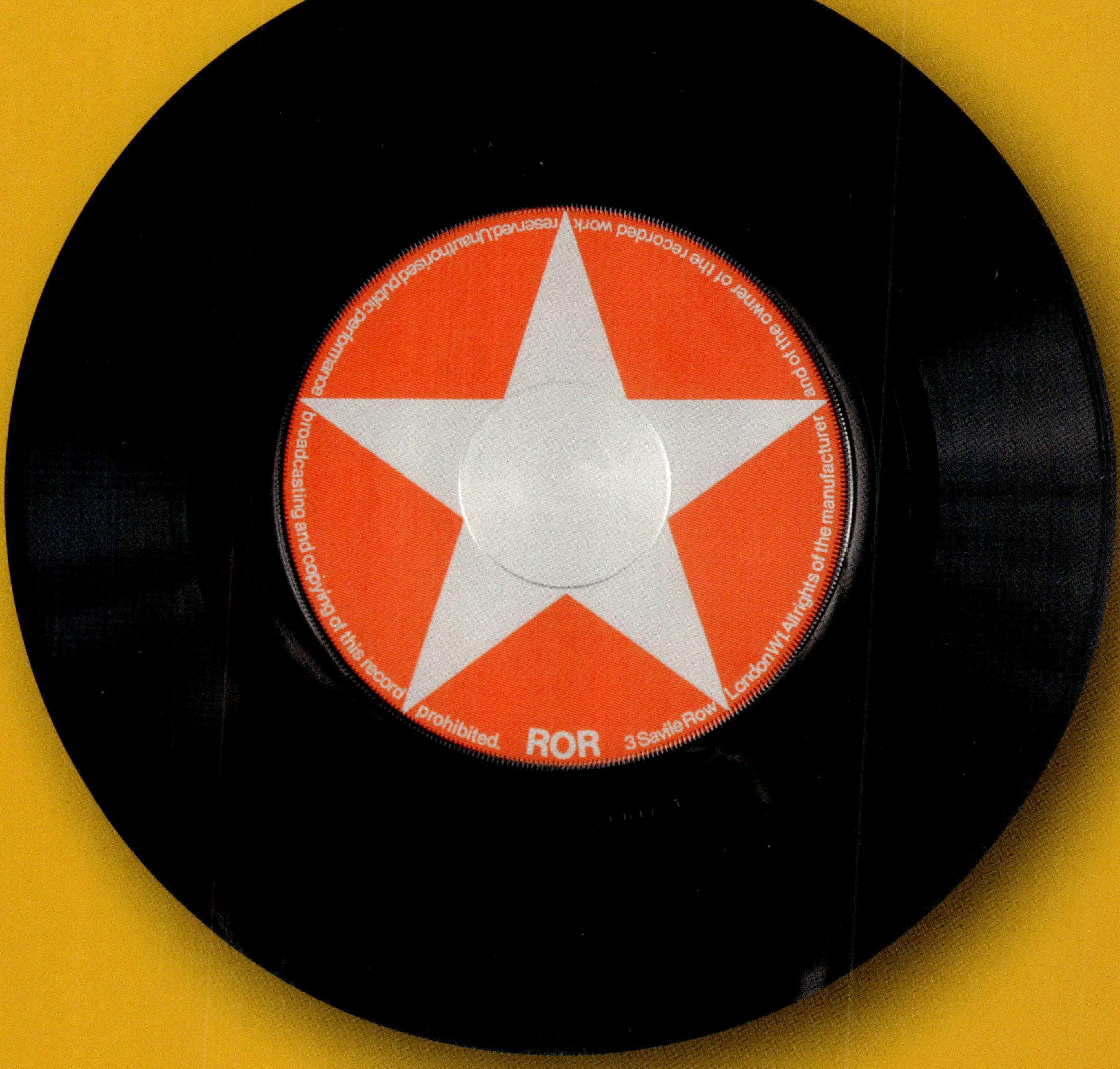

PROMOTIONAL RECORD
13 SEPTEMBER 1971
Invitation to the Ringo or Robin (RoR) furniture exhibition at Liberty, capitalizing on Ringo Starr's musical connections.

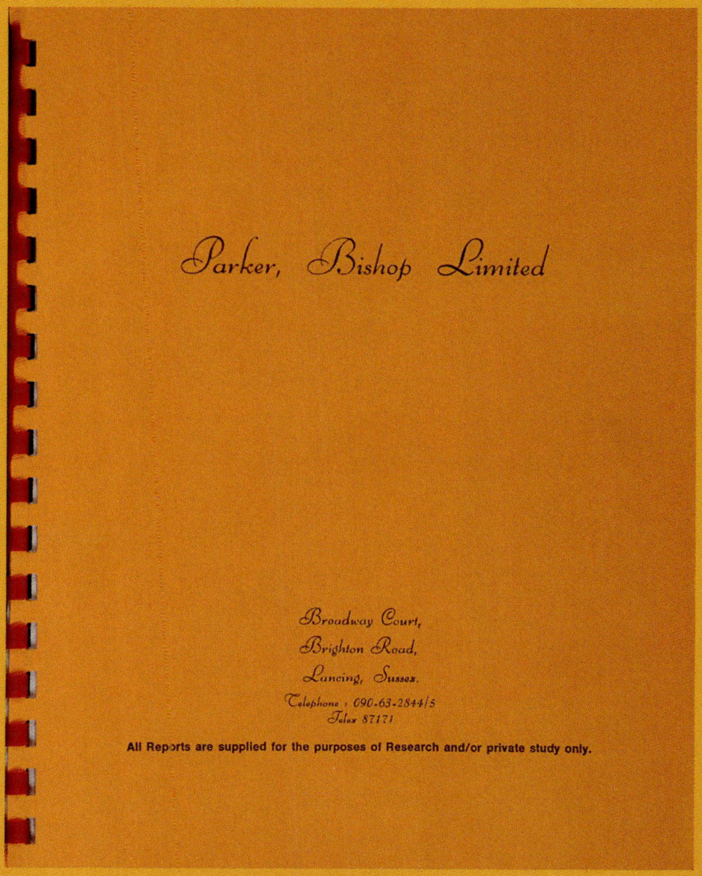
Parker, Bishop Limited

Broadway Court,
Brighton Road,
Lancing, Sussex.
Telephone : 090-63-2844/5
Telex 87171

All Reports are supplied for the purposes of Research and/or private study only.

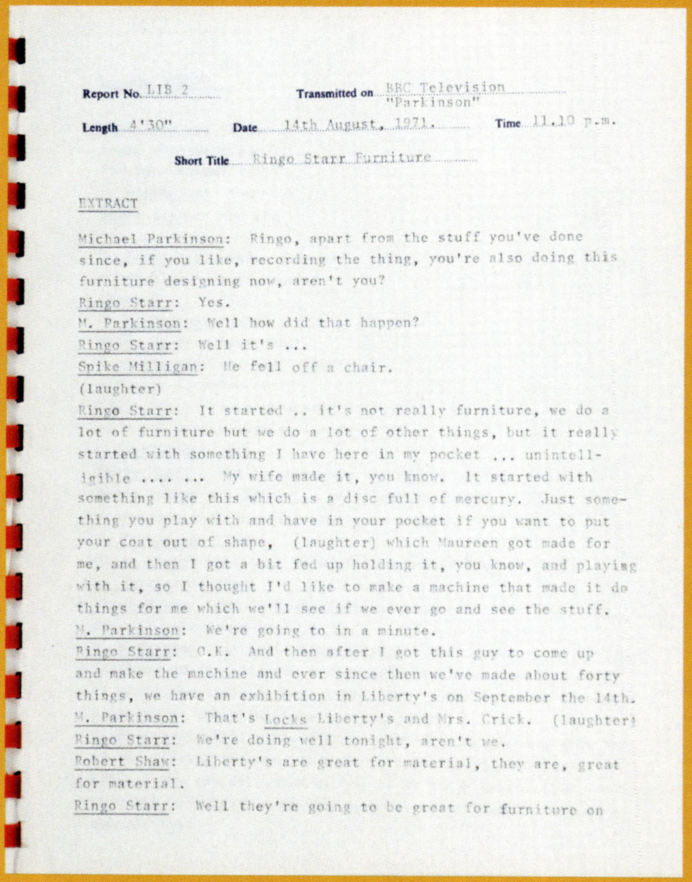
Report No. LIB 2 Transmitted on BBC Television "Parkinson"

Length 4'30" Date 14th August, 1971. Time 11.10 p.m.

Short Title Ringo Starr Furniture

EXTRACT

Michael Parkinson: Ringo, apart from the stuff you've done since, if you like, recording the thing, you're also doing this furniture designing now, aren't you?
Ringo Starr: Yes.
M. Parkinson: Well how did that happen?
Ringo Starr: Well it's ...
Spike Milligan: He fell off a chair.
(laughter)
Ringo Starr: It started .. it's not really furniture, we do a lot of furniture but we do a lot of other things, but it really started with something I have here in my pocket ... unintelligible .... My wife made it, you know. It started with something like this which is a disc full of mercury. Just something you play with and have in your pocket if you want to put your coat out of shape, (laughter) which Maureen got made for me, and then I got a bit fed up holding it, you know, and playimg with it, so I thought I'd like to make a machine that made it do things for me which we'll see if we ever go and see the stuff.
M. Parkinson: We're going to in a minute.
Ringo Starr: O.K. And then after I got this guy to come up and make the machine and ever since then we've made about forty things, we have an exhibition in Liberty's on September the 14th.
M. Parkinson: That's Locks Liberty's and Mrs. Crick. (laughter)
Ringo Starr: We're doing well tonight, aren't we.
Robert Shaw: Liberty's are great for material, they are, great for material.
Ringo Starr: Well they're going to be great for furniture on

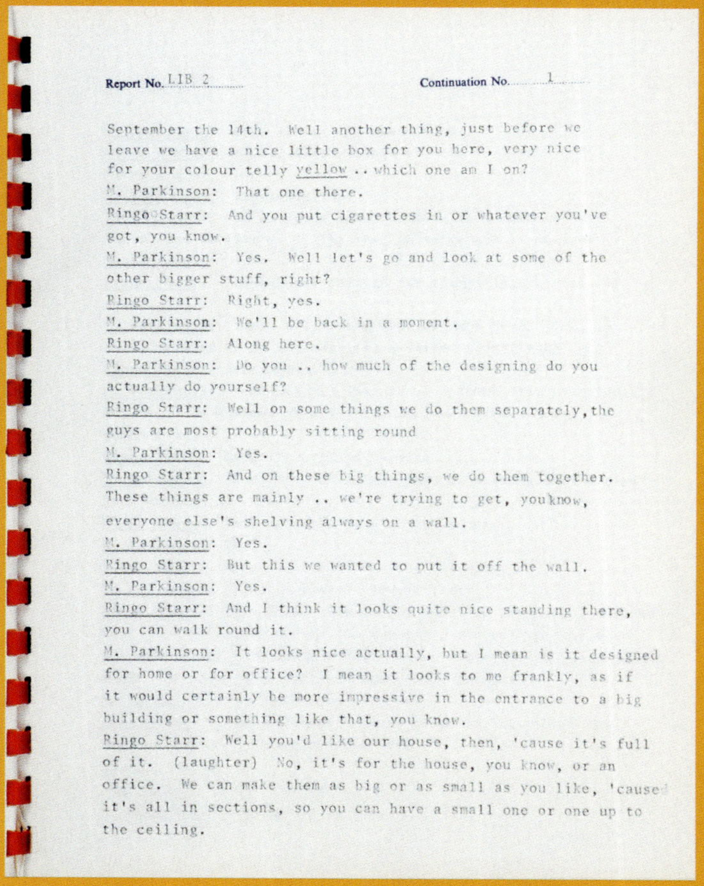
Report No. LIB 2 Continuation No. 1

September the 14th. Well another thing, just before we leave we have a nice little box for you here, very nice for your colour telly yellow .. which one am I on?
M. Parkinson: That one there.
Ringo Starr: And you put cigarettes in or whatever you've got, you know.
M. Parkinson: Yes. Well let's go and look at some of the other bigger stuff, right?
Ringo Starr: Right, yes.
M. Parkinson: We'll be back in a moment.
Ringo Starr: Along here.
M. Parkinson: Do you .. how much of the designing do you actually do yourself?
Ringo Starr: Well on some things we do them separately, the guys are most probably sitting round
M. Parkinson: Yes.
Ringo Starr: And on these big things, we do them together. These things are mainly .. we're trying to get, youknow, everyone else's shelving always on a wall.
M. Parkinson: Yes.
Ringo Starr: But this we wanted to put it off the wall.
M. Parkinson: Yes.
Ringo Starr: And I think it looks quite nice standing there, you can walk round it.
M. Parkinson: It looks nice actually, but I mean is it designed for home or for office? I mean it looks to me frankly, as if it would certainly be more impressive in the entrance to a big building or something like that, you know.
Ringo Starr: Well you'd like our house, then, 'cause it's full of it. (laughter) No, it's for the house, you know, or an office. We can make them as big or as small as you like, 'cause it's all in sections, so you can have a small one or one up to the ceiling.

Report No. LIB 2 Continuation No. 2

M. Parkinson: Gets rid of the mantelpiece.
Ringo Starr: And all these things we did, well Robin does these ...
M. Parkinson: Paperweights.
Ringo Starr: Now everyone has something on a desk or on a table, and we like .. I like them to shine and so does he.
M. Parkinson: Yes.
Ringo Starr: These boxes just to put things in, they're all shiny.
M. Parkinson: Yes. Well let's move on down here. You, in fact, trained as an engineer for a while, didn't you?
Ringo Starr: Four years.
M. Parkinson: Four years. This is .. I think this is unusual, but we'll talk about this later. It looks like a dalek, doesn't it?
Ringo Starr: Aye, it's called Charlie.
M. Parkinson: Charlie. Of course this is a thing that's really interesting.
Ringo Starr: This is a bit of bankrupt stock.
M. Parkinson: Yes?
Ringo Starr: Aye. Well this is mine actually.
M. Parkinson: This is yours? You did that?
Ringo Starr: When Rolls were having all that trouble, I thought well I'll pull them out of the quagmire, and use up some of the stock, and we built this Rolls Royce table, which costs just under the price of a fully fledged Rolls actually.
M. Parkinson: How much does it cost?
Ringo Starr: This is about - shout at me if I'm wrong, Rob - twelve hundred? Twelve hundred Rob?
Robin: Yes.
Ringo Starr: Yes, I'm right.
M. Parkinson: You're right, yes.

Report No. LIB 2 Continuation No. 3

Ringo Starr: And that's because of the radiators. But the great thing is trying to get the radiators.
M. Parkinson: Yes.
Ringo Starr: Because you have to 'phone up some guy and he runs in with them in a sack, throws them on the floor and says 'give us the money', and runs out again. (laughter) 'Cause you're supposed to have a Rolls before you can buy one.
M. Parkinson: What are you designing stuff that's costing twelve hundred quid for, though, Ringo, I mean it's true, a lad from Liverpool, you know.
Ringo Starr: Well this one is that price because it's these radiators are expensive, you know, and to get them made, most of the stuff that .. they're so expensive because we use, you know, heavy steel, stainless steel and things like that, but we do make a few cheap things for about five hundred. (laughter)
M. Parkinson: Can we have a look at this now, it's ...
Ringo Starr: Ah this is .. well this thing, you see, see those little things there ..
M. Parkinson: Where's the camera, wait a minute, let me get, yes.
Ringo Starr: Are a tiny one of these, and you press the magic button and pray it goes.
M. Parkinson: It's going.
Ringo Starr: And it goes up there on the spiral, runs down there, and comes back in here, you see, and goes up again. Now that's very exciting. (laughter)
M. Parkinson: Why is it very exciting?
Ringo Starr: Well you don't have to do anything but look at it. (laughter) It's great when we let the baby play with it, and she tries to watch it and she's going ... 'cause it's too fast for her, you know.

Report No. LIB 2 Continuation No. 4

M. Parkinson: Did you invent that one?
Ringo Starr: Aye. But he built it, you know.
M. Parkinson: Yes.
Ringo Starr: And he sort of does the electrics and things like that.
M. Parkinson: Let's have a look at this thing here.
Ringo Starr: Now this is a nice thing. This again, is because everyone has a record player, even if they buy a box they shove it up against the wall, you know, and I wanted to get away from boxes anyway, stand it up and make it shine, and let's see what we have here.
M. Parkinson: You've got one of these in your house, too, have you?
Ringo Starr: Yes, this one came from my house.
M. Parkinson: Really?
Ringo Starr: Yes, yes.
M. Parkinson: Must be a big house.
Ringo Starr: Yes it is a big house. Well I've only got three kids, not like Robert with twenty five. (laughter) (extract from Beatles record)
Well that's about it, you know. All these nice things. These spirals we're trying to do, we're having a lot of trouble because when they cool the spiral breaks.
M. Parkinson: What do you reckon about that then?
Robert Shaw: That's what I'd like to do most.
M. Parkinson: What?
Robert Shaw: Oh I'm sorry we were talking about ...
M. Parkinson: We're not interrupting anything, are we?
Ringo Starr: Can we take any orders?
Robert Shaw: We were talking about gardens.
M. Parkinson: About gardens?

...oOo...

TRANSCRIPT
14 AUGUST 1971
Transcript of the conversation discussing the RoR exhibition, between Ringo Starr, Michael Parkinson and Spike Milligan on the BBC television programme Parkinson.

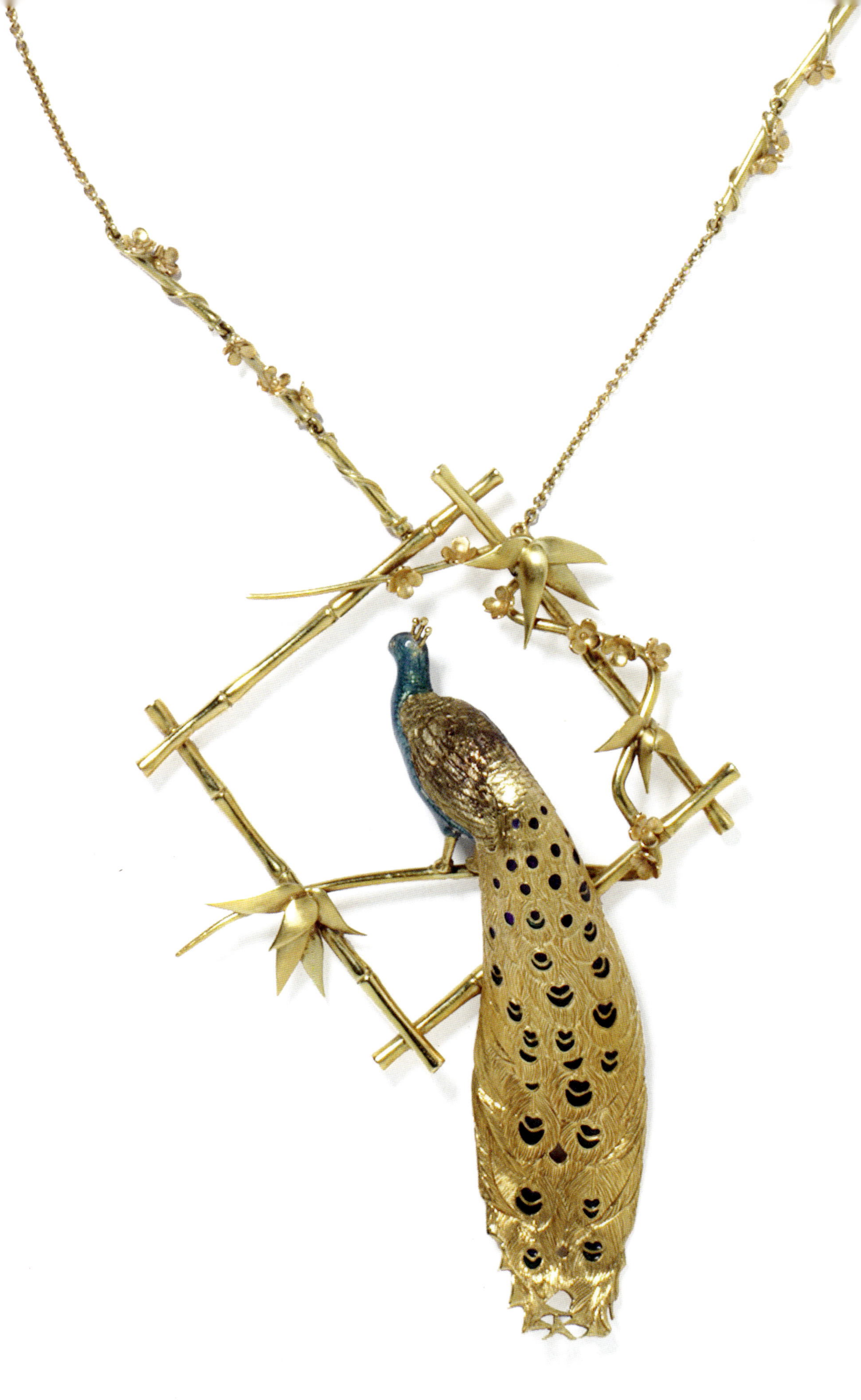

THE 1975 CENTENARY

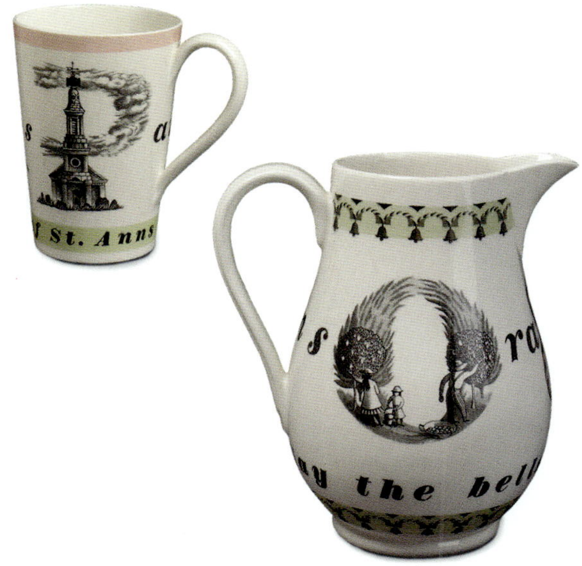

LEFT *A mid-twentieth-century lemonade set comprising an earthenware beaker and jug designed by Richard Guyatt, with a transfer-printed decoration on the theme of "oranges and lemons". Made by Josiah Wedgwood & Sons Ltd, Etruria, for Liberty & Co.*

BELOW *Marked "Liberty & Co. 1875–1975" and designed by Susan Collier, this commemorative ceramic bowl is decorated with bamboo stalks and stylized bamboo leaves on the inner rim. The floor of the bowl features a single butterfly.*

After a century of trading, the board of directors felt it was appropriate to commemorate Liberty's anniversary in a grand manner in order to consolidate past success and reposition the brand in the modern retail world. Therefore, in 1975, a joint exhibition was held at both London's Victoria and Albert Museum – a temple dedicated to the decorative arts – and within the store itself, showcasing key pieces from Liberty's past, focusing in particular on the various Arts and Crafts designs on which the store had built its reputation. Arresting window displays were also used to illustrate how the store had captured the spirit of each era while emphasizing the strength of the Liberty brand.

In addition, the centenary was celebrated commercially with the reissuing of past designs and the commissioning of new artefacts that acknowledged Liberty's past. These new commissions included a centenary mug designed by William Adams, produced by British heritage company Wedgwood, and a new range of dining furniture by British designer John Makepeace. The reissues included fabrics designed by Arts and Crafts luminaries Walter Crane and C. F. A. Voysey, and wallpapers by William Morris, with his Willow print wallpaper, produced by leading manufacturers Osborne & Little, proving one of the most popular.

The exhibitions served to underline Liberty's importance in design history over the preceding century by emphasizing the key role it had played in the material culture of Britain and also internationally. The centenary served to provide a focus on what had made Liberty a success and also provided a confident platform from which to plan the future.

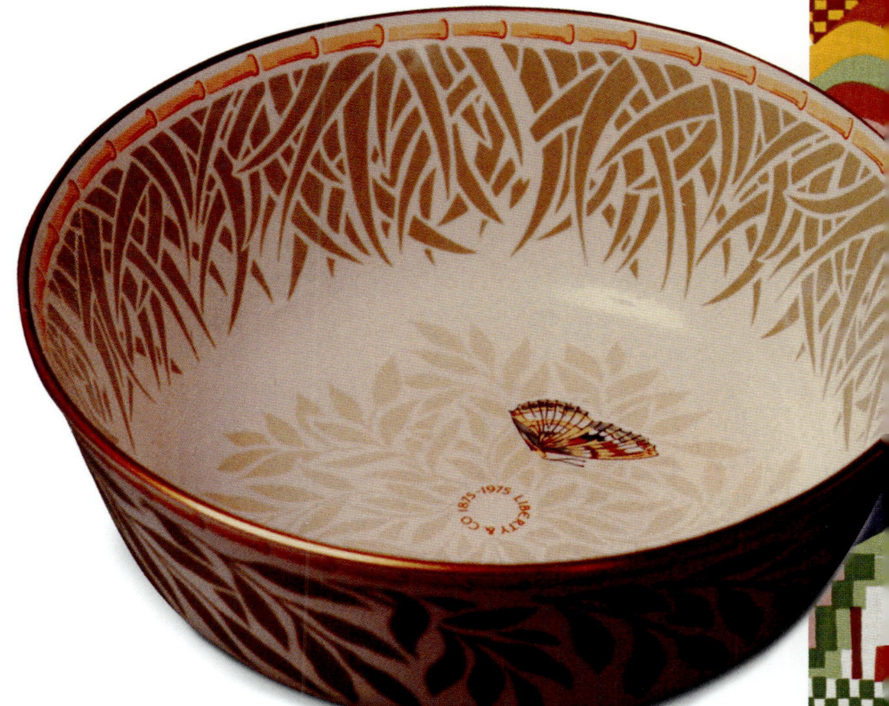

OPPOSITE *Acknowledging Liberty's historic role as an Oriental emporium and commemorating the centenary of the London shop is this gold and enamel necklace, featuring a gilded peacock – the symbol of the emporium since the store's inception.*

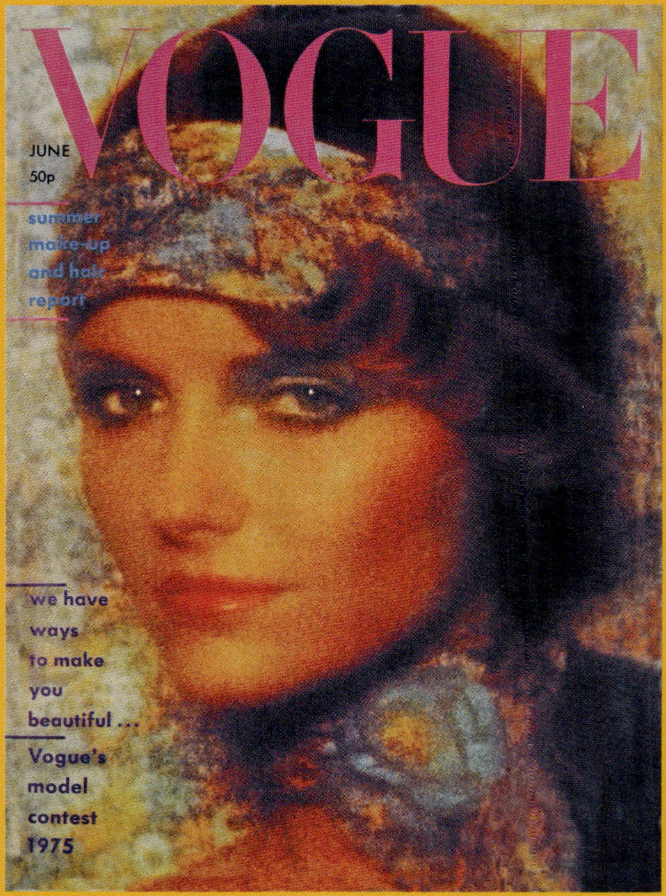

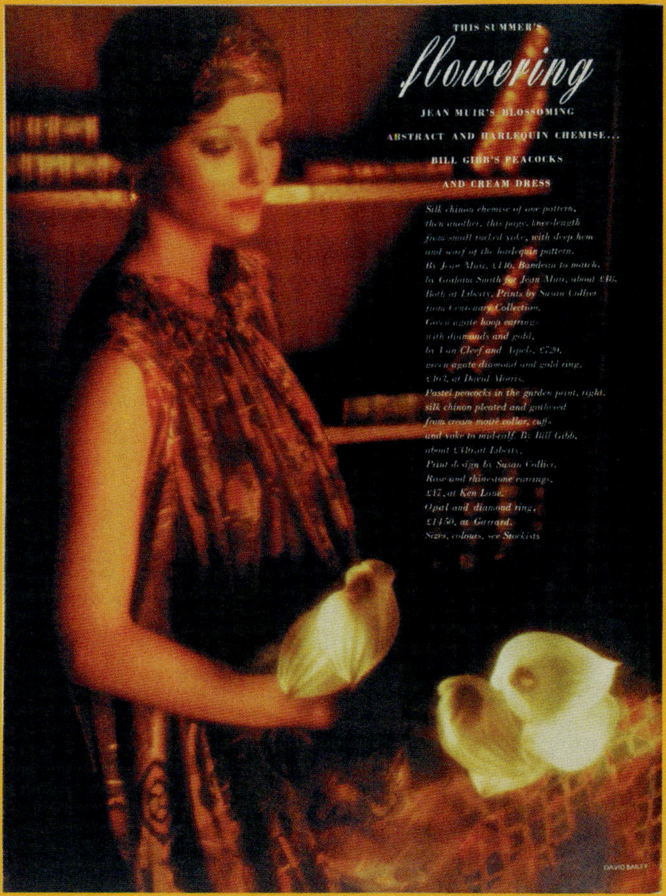

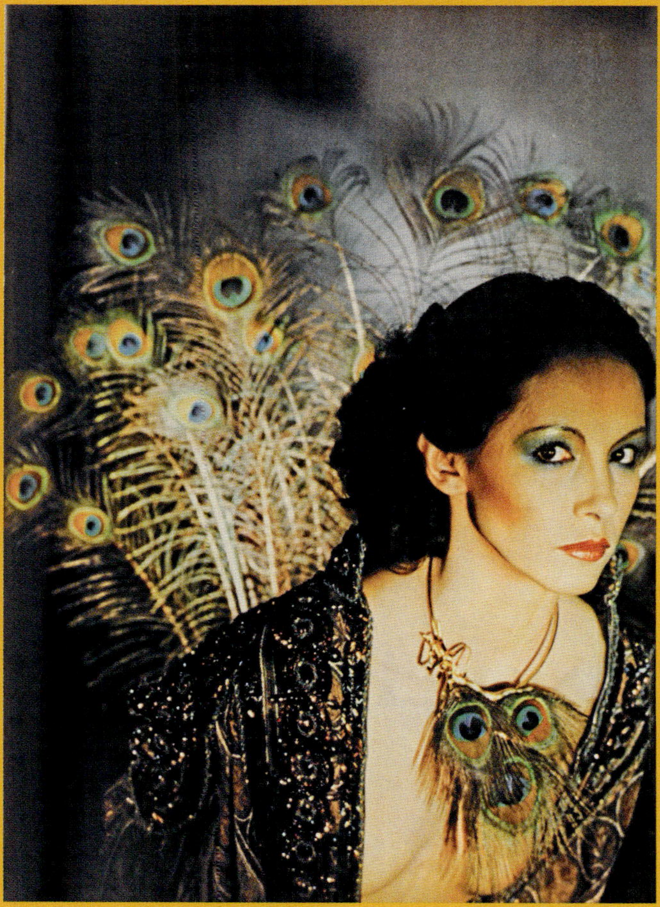

VOGUE MAGAZINE
JUNE 1975
Liberty's centennial issue in Vogue magazine with the strapline, "One Hundred Years of Bringing You Flowers" featured furnishings and fashions.

AT THE SIGN OF THE PEACOCK FEATHER

Liberty QUALITY CENTENARY

Think of Liberty and you think perhaps of a fine-drawn, brilliantly-coloured flower print lawn. Think again, it is and has been lots more; porcelain, lacquer, brass, bronze, silver, silk, embroidery, Kelims, Kakemos, earthenware, glass, costume, oriental, mediaeval, whole worlds, whole gardens of interior design. Liberty history is one hundred years of craft, and of such nostalgia for this that even the most timeless examples often demonstrate nostalgia for nostalgia for nostalgia. Turning circles, it is a pretty story, and also the story of the remarkable Arthur Lasenby Liberty, Victorian merchant adventurer, man of particular taste and style, who travelled the globe with his wife, Emma Louise, in search of the authentic and beautiful, treated his staff with liberal consideration, knew men like William Morris but put science and technology to the service of Art.

The heyday was from the start, May, 1875, when Arthur Liberty opened half a shop at 218a Regent Street and called it East India House. The fashionable and aesthetic world transferred their devotion from the Oriental Warehouse he had been managing for Farmer & Rogers down the street. Whistler, Ruskin, Burne-Jones, Watts, Rossetti, all the pre-Raphaelites came to discuss Art and rustle through the Indian tussores, nothing else was as perfect for draping their models. Wilde and other languid fellows wandered the oriental delights and posed as new consignments of Japanese fans or Mr Liberty's favourite blue and white porcelain were unpacked. Liberty fashion became a fever. Du Maurier and Beerbohm caricatured it. Paris loved Liberty (and Liberty responded by opening Maison Liberty in 1890). Liberty agents persuaded the Indians to use a wider loom. In this country Arthur Wardle began fast-dyeing the silks in "reds so soft that even the most rubicund wearer cannot vulgarise them", wrote "Sylvia's Home Journal" in 1879. "Greens and blues so indefinite it is difficult to class them as greens and blues." Liberty's windows showed these in rainbows against white—a shock in mid-Victorian days of the drab and meretricious. By 1881 there was a print works on the Wandle, across from William Morris', producing very Indian prints. The same year Liberty designed costumes for the first production of "Patience"; they had produced the cream of greenery yallery in their Umritza cashmere of 1849. Arthur Liberty loved the stage and whole theatres were given the Liberty treatment. Liberty sold furniture, the Thebes stool and sideboard, Moorish designs, the ever popular bamboo, and built a larger shop, Chesham House, which was a maze of electrically lighted tiny rooms. They ran Moorcroft's Barumware pottery, costumes designed under the guidance of E. W. Godwin—always airing his views on health and freedom in Modern Dress, and Kate Greenaway clothes for children; Isadora Duncan took one of these outfits to Paris, loved Liberty and had the taste to end her life at the end of a Liberty scarf.

As the Aesthetic Movement waned the Celtic renaissance came into bloom. The year 1899, the Art Nouveau that Liberty patronised through lines like their Cymric Silver and Tudric Pewter was exemplified by great designers like Archibald Knox and Rex Silver of Silver Studios. Arthur Liberty disliked the excesses of German Art Nouveau, he called it the Squirm, but must have been flattered by the Italians who named theirs Stil Liberty.

Through Edwardian times Liberty style spread with agencies from Tokyo to Tasmania, houses for maharajahs, grand hotels in Budapest and Genoa. Arthur Liberty was knighted in 1913. The war came and went, Arthur Liberty died and his nephew Captain Ivor Stewart-Liberty inherited. The 1920s arrived and, ignoring modern style, Liberty looked back again and went totally Tudor, their new building of 1924 a monument to the principles of mediaeval guilds, built of oak and teak timbers from HMS Hindustan and Impregnable, the interior with ancient Tibetan temple hangings suspended from the highest balcony, the staff in Tudor costume, and ex-naval ratings to polish the floor and woodwork every night. Their vast workshops turned out impeccable linenfold panelling, their fabric departments sold faded cabbage rose and fawn union, peacock, paisley and pheasant prints, and the new rich cried out for more. Jewellery was oriental, tasselled necklaces with carved jadite pendants, Egyptian too, on the opening of Tutankhamen's tomb. The new inner sanctum for jewellery had an iron gate and Queen Mary sofa; Queen Mary also came Christmas shopping and for years bought the same three-and-sixpenny cushion cover.

The '30s were quiet and flowery, ditto the '40s, it wasn't until the '50s that Liberty hoisted a contemporary banner and from Festival of Britain time sold abstracted fabrics, Venini glass, Leach pottery, Richard Guyet's lemonade set, design by Alvar Aalto, Arne Jacobesen, Gio Ponti. They had a Modern Furniture department, a Young Liberty department and windows by Eric Lucking. In 1958 came another renaissance. William Poole saw an Art Nouveau exhibition, took out the old swatches and had them recoloured and recreated for the silk screen process; 300 not 30 yards of fabric could be run in a day; 25 blocks for one scarf was not possible but "Liberty can always afford the fourth or fifth colour", and that makes the difference. There are names to be remembered: Blair Pride, Martin Battersby and his Poiret/Bakst range (Poiret had lapped up Liberty fabrics when he came to London in 1909). Bernard Nevill, Liberty designer of the '60s, who culled the archives with knowledge and invention, producing his Art Nouveau, his Jazz collection (modern art at last), the Bo Peep arcadia of his 1968 landscapes, and inspiring the best designers of the '60s from Saint Laurent to Tuffin & Foale, Hechter, Cacharel of the ready-to-wear.

Turning circles and describing new ones, Liberty's hundred years and now can be seen in the store, and by reading Alison Adburgham's "Biography of a Shop" (Allen & Unwin, July 24, £2·95). And by calling on the Victoria & Albert after July 31 for their Liberty exhibition, which includes an oriental bazaar built from the original plans, with objects matching near as dammit those in the real 390 catalogues they hold; many seminal items like the Thebes stool; a floppy brown velvet beret just like Bunthorne's, and the good news that gathering in so much, 900 items edited to 500, the Victoria & Albert has been able to write Liberty history in finer detail, making accurate attributions, particularly in the Aesthetic and Art Nouveau periods when Liberty artists were anonymous. Walter Crane, Lindsey Butterfield, C. F. A. Voysey, Arthur Wilcock, Arthur Wilshaw, Jessie M. King, Oliver Baker, Archibald Knox, almost all the great names are there.

Liberty is still a family concern, Arthur Stewart-Liberty is chairman, and there's a strong feeling for the whole tradition. It is Liberty London, Liberty Manchester, Liberty of London Prints, Liberty in Amsterdam at Mertz. It is Susan Collier's fabrics, her wallpapers and tiles for the new Liberty interior. Mick Milligan's bamboo, flower and peacock jewels, a peacock feather scarf, a new scent called Emma Louise, Art Nouveau glass, John Makepeace furniture, blooming china, blossoming clothes and, any minute, a new Eastern Bazaar. In order to grow new feathers the Liberty peacock has been eating its own tail again; some of these feathers, very charming, you have seen before, some not, lots are on these pages.

ANTONIA WILLIAMS

SIGNED WITH THE PEACOCK FEATHER . . . *Ib Jorgensen's caftan, right, feather print from the 1887 Liberty original (in the V & A exhibition). £339, to order. Mick Milligan's centenary necklace, £320. Both at Liberty. Peacock feather eyes: Max Factor Geminesse Enriched Glowing Shadows: Sunny Green, Burnished Gold, Rainbow Blue with Navy Cake liner and mascara. Fragile Beige Enriched Moisturising Fluid Make-Up, Tawny Blush Transparent Cheek Colour, Transparent Highlight Finishing Colour. Rich Bronzewood Frost Lip Colour. Make-up by Douglas Young. Hair by Pat at Vidal Sassoon.*

ERIC BOMAN

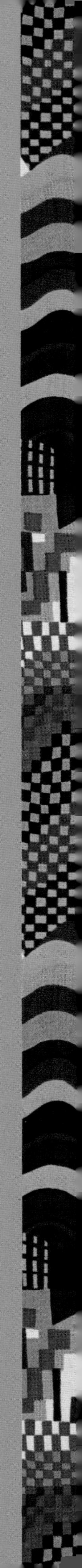

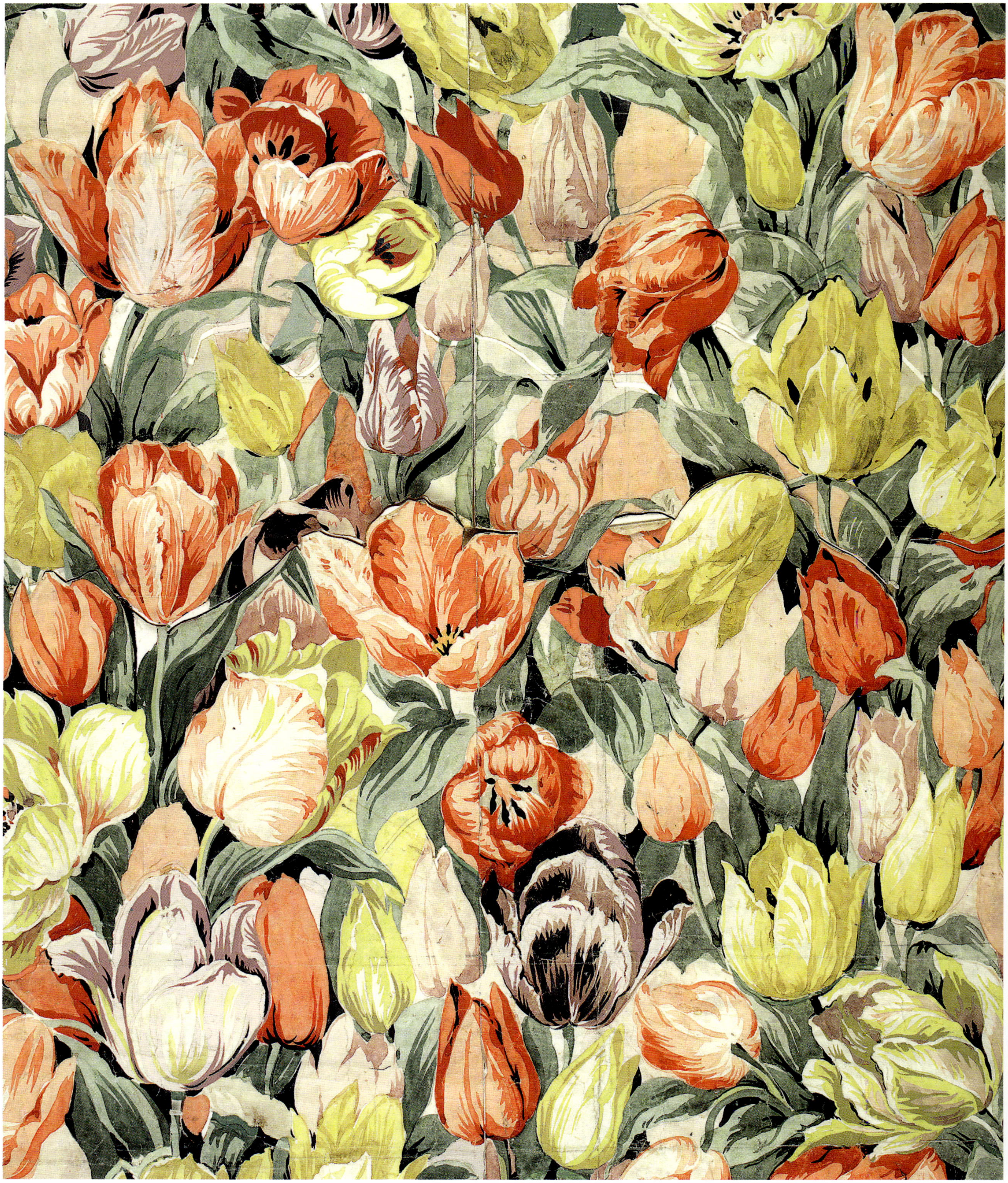

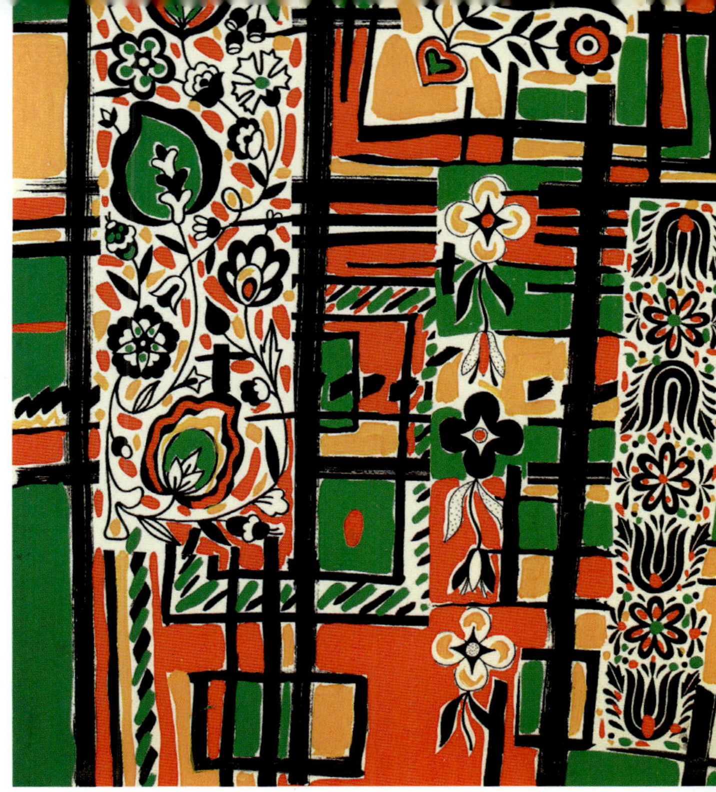

ABOVE *A Liberty print designed by The Cloth collective in 1987 and produced in 1992.*

POSTMODERN PRINTS

Design in the 1980s was an eclectic mix of styles and influences, which can be placed under the banner of postmodernism. The steel, chrome and curved pastel graphics of an Art Deco revival vied with the brash, bright colours of the Memphis school, while the influence of Japanese design and culture was also an emerging trend. There was also a concurrent interest – or rather a continuation of interest – in the country house aesthetic, with overblown florals and chintzy fabric decorating the more conservative and traditional homes.

Liberty played a key role in promoting a new wave of entrepreneurial designers and manufacturers during this period. At the centre of an emerging print movement in Britain was a collective of designers comprising Fraser Taylor, Brian Bolger, David Band and Helen Manning, known as The Cloth. In the summer of 1985, Liberty showcased work from The Cloth in a series of window displays that showed off the expressive graphic prints and mixed-media designs that the collective favoured. In terms of in-house fabric design, one of Liberty's more successful ranges from this period was the Celtic collection, produced in 1982, and a collection inspired by medieval stained glass by decorative artist Richard Peduzzi, in the same year.

However, the creation of new designs within the Liberty print department did not continue at the same pace as it had done in the 1970s. For the Liberty store, the 1980s and 1990s were more about consolidating and maintaining its reputation as the destination for avant-garde yet commercial design. One of Liberty's key marketing strategies during this period was to stage a series of collaborative and complementary exhibitions with the Victoria and Albert Museum in London. The masterstroke here was tapping into the appeal of buying something that was considered untouchable by virtue of being a museum exhibit. By selling the same products that were being displayed in South Kensington, Liberty was also subliminally suggesting that the pieces for sale were worth collecting – as though a piece of design history was being purchased.

While the interior of the shop showcased the chosen designs, the exterior was decorated with eye-catching windows and sculptures. One of the most striking was the spectacular display created to celebrate the Russian Christmas exhibition of 1989, in which exquisite Liberty-themed Russian dolls appeared in the windows and ornate onion domes decorated the store entrance. Another key show was Memphis Meets Liberty in 1983. The groundbreaking Memphis–Milano design group that specialized in reworking 1950s

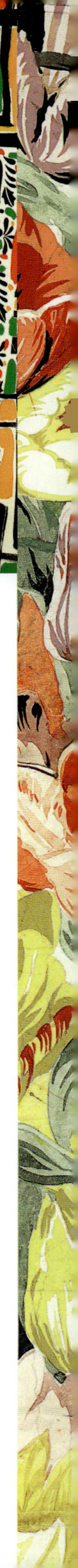

OPPOSITE *First created in 1971, Adele, also called Tulips. This all-over, one-directional print design, featuring meticulously described florals, continued in popularity, evident in its revival in 1989 and again in 1996.*

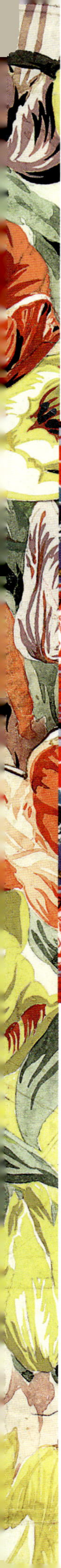

RIGHT *A paisley print by Richard Peduzzi for Liberty, designed in 1978 and printed in 1981.*

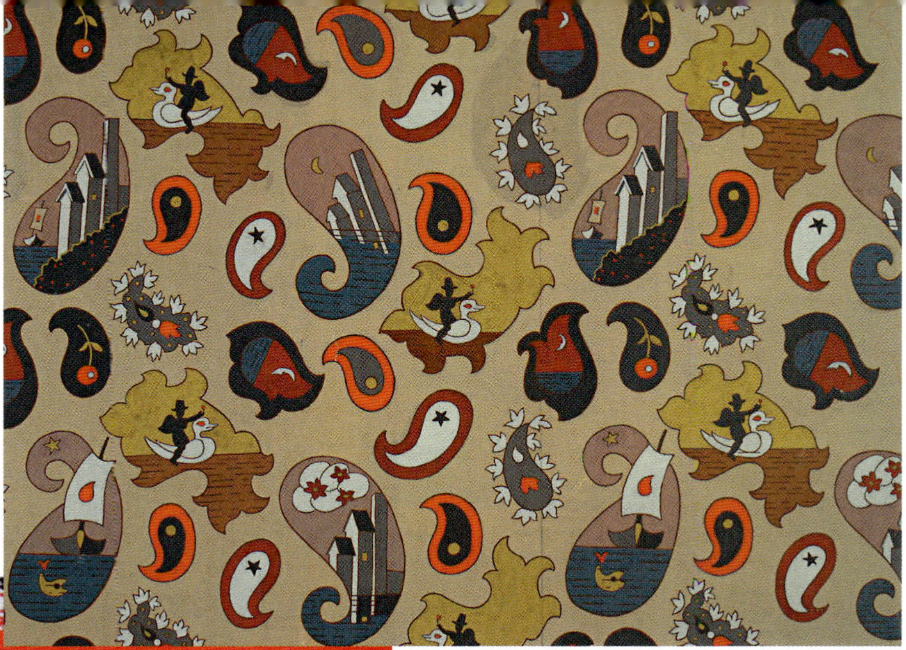

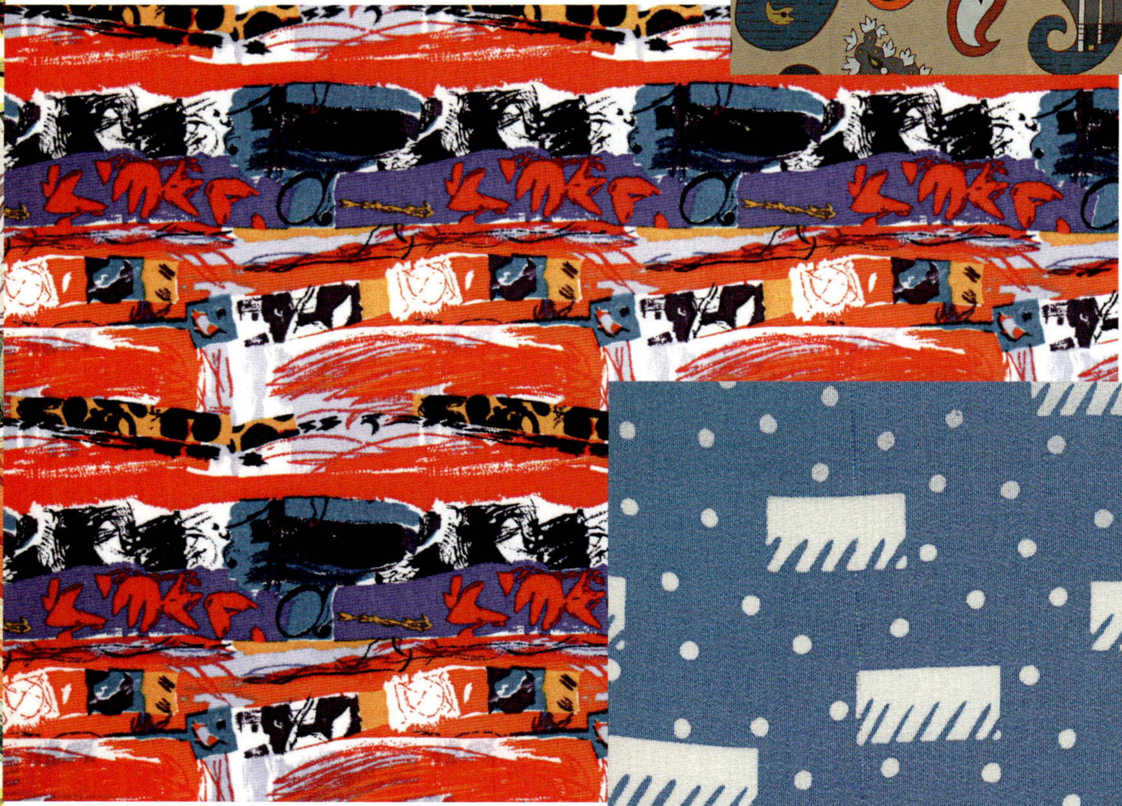

ABOVE *Mixed-media Fantasy print of collaged paper and felt-tipped pens in an 11-colour screen-print design by Liberty, 1985.*

RIGHT *Produced in 1988 and 1992, the one-colour Edinita print is redolent of 1930s geometrics.*

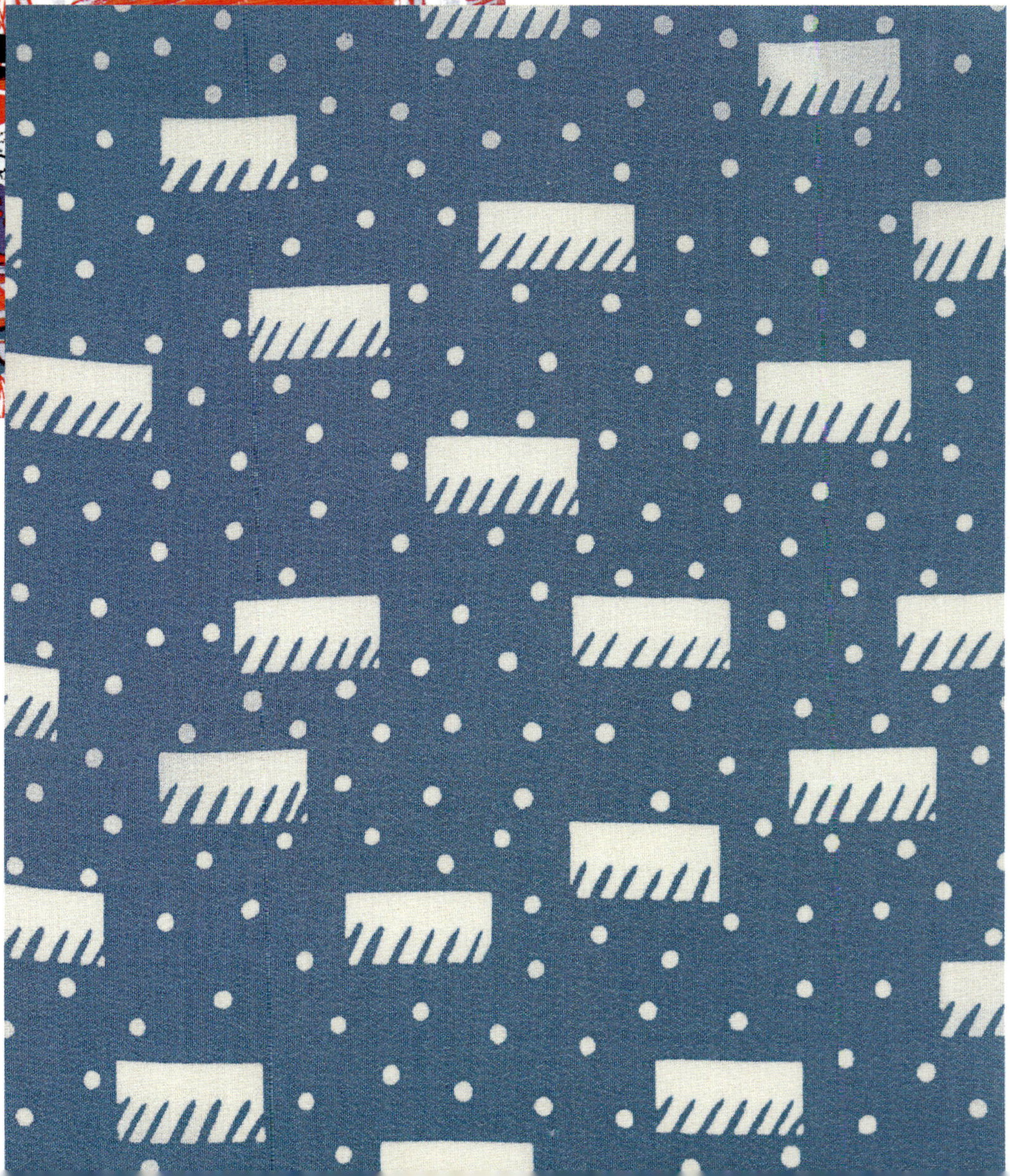

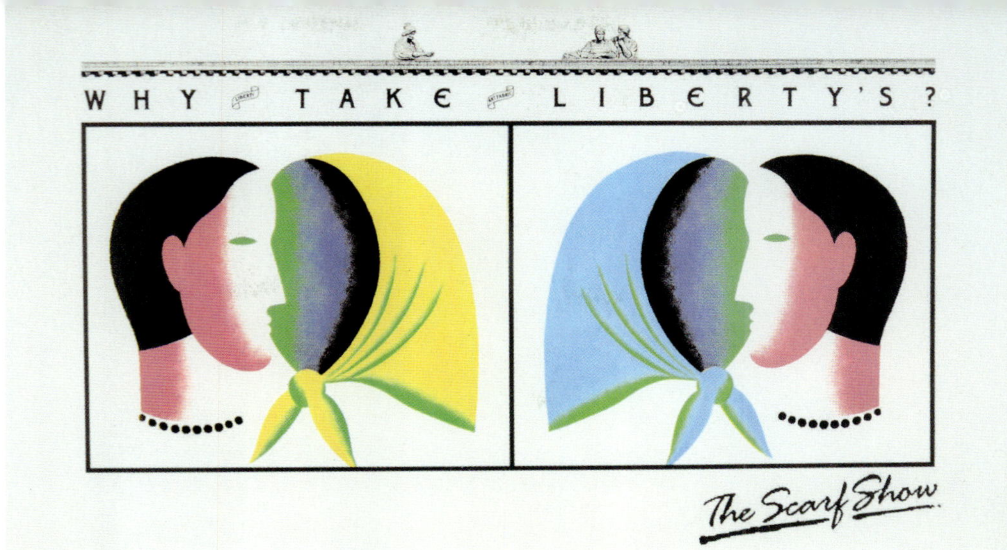

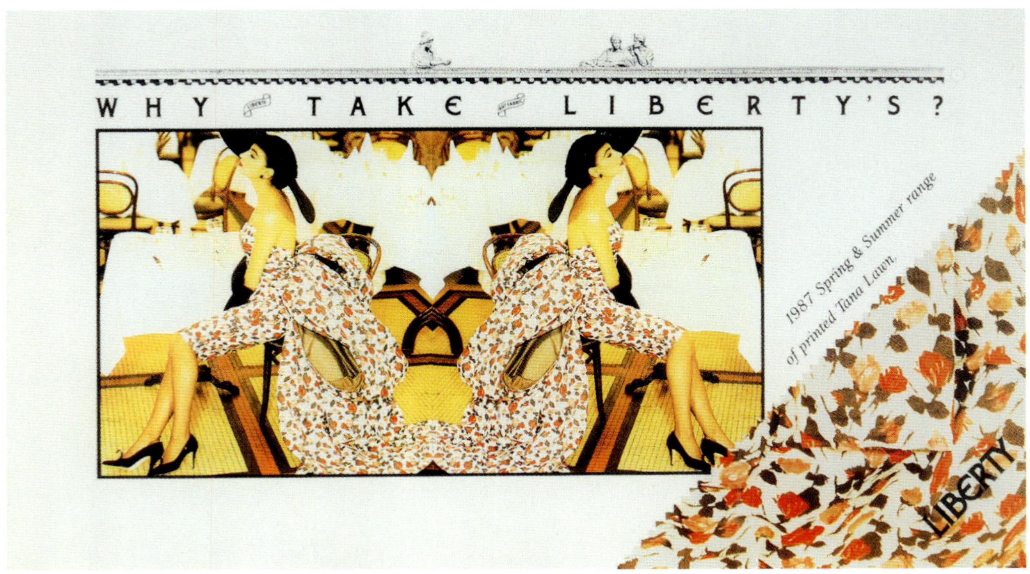

LEFT *Two invitations: one advertising The Scarf Show, October 1987, and the other the S/S 1987 Tana Lawn range.*

Americana prints and mixing Pop Art with Art Deco, produced a range of distinctive furnishing products, examples of which were displayed in room sets. However, by far the most influential exhibition – emblematic of Liberty's long-standing relationship with Japanese design – was the Japan at Liberty exhibition in 1980. Again, in collaboration with the Victoria and Albert Museum, Liberty spearheaded the 1980s interest in all things Japanese – including its ceramics, technological advances, food and, of course, its fashion. It took the rest of the world two years to catch up – with the first showing of collections by Japanese fashion designers, including Yohji Yamamoto, Issey Miyake and Rei Kawakubo, in Paris in 1982 finally catching the eye of the Western press.

This exhibition was a chance for Liberty to re-engage with its reputation as a key importer of Eastern design artefacts. The store was transformed outside by a mock pagoda and neon sign over the Regent Street entrance and the windows were full of spectacular displays. Further strengthening the historical link with Japanese design, the arrival of a Muji outlet within the store in 1991 meant Liberty was now stocking objects characterized by their functionality and simplicity – a striking contrast to the excesses of designs from Liberty's past.

The 1980s and 1990s were characterized by Liberty's attempts to find a balance between celebrating its heritage and building on its history of innovation and invention. Through re-engaging with its reputation as a key importer of design artefacts and underlining the company's skills as purveyors of key pieces of design history, Liberty ensured its place as an arbiter of taste in a competitive market.

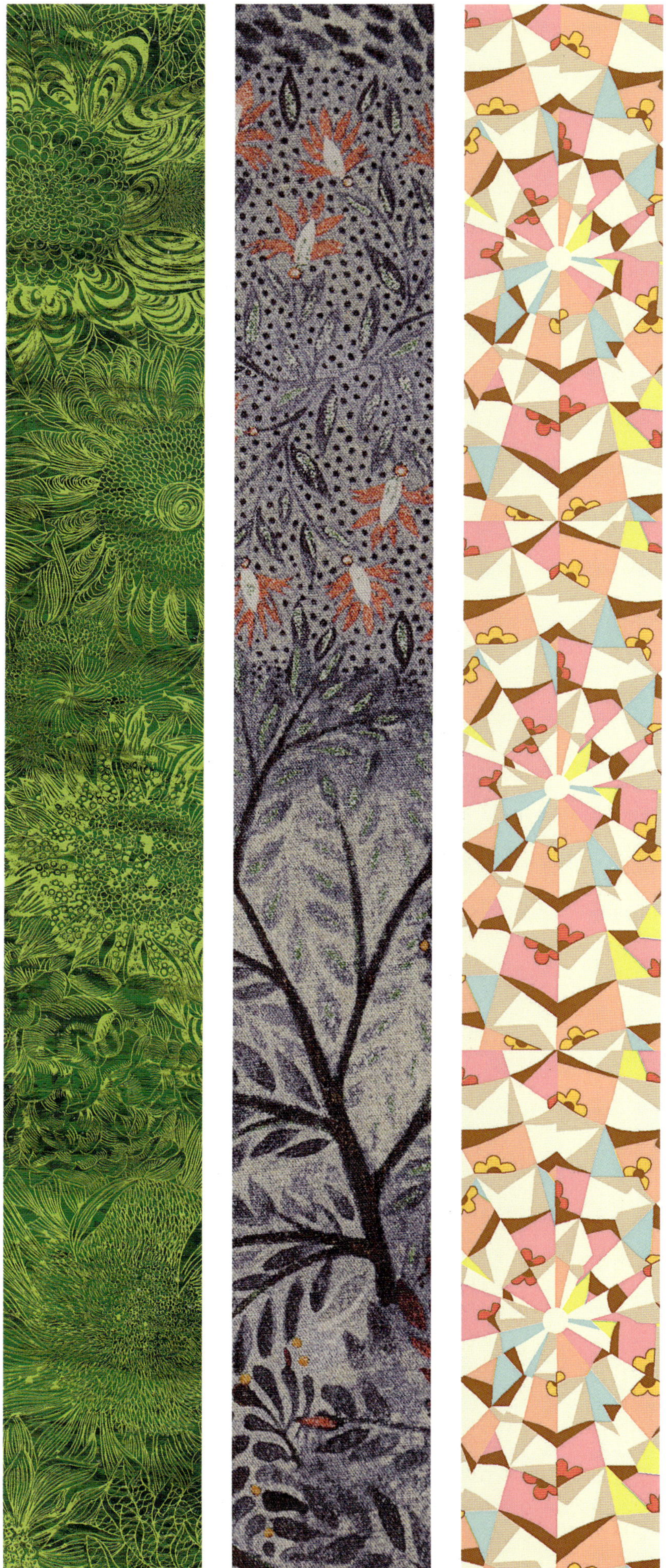

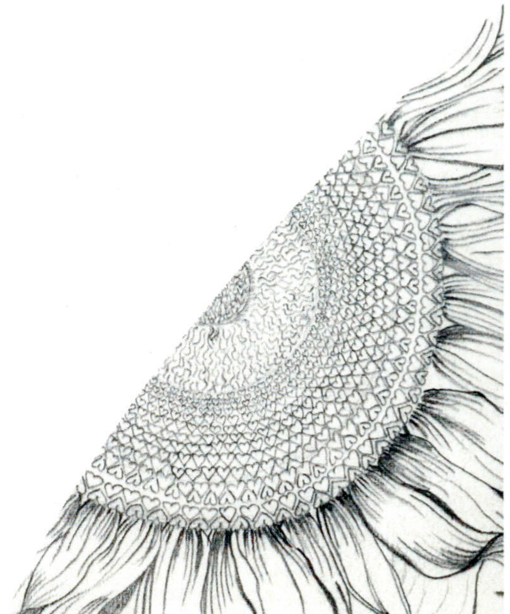

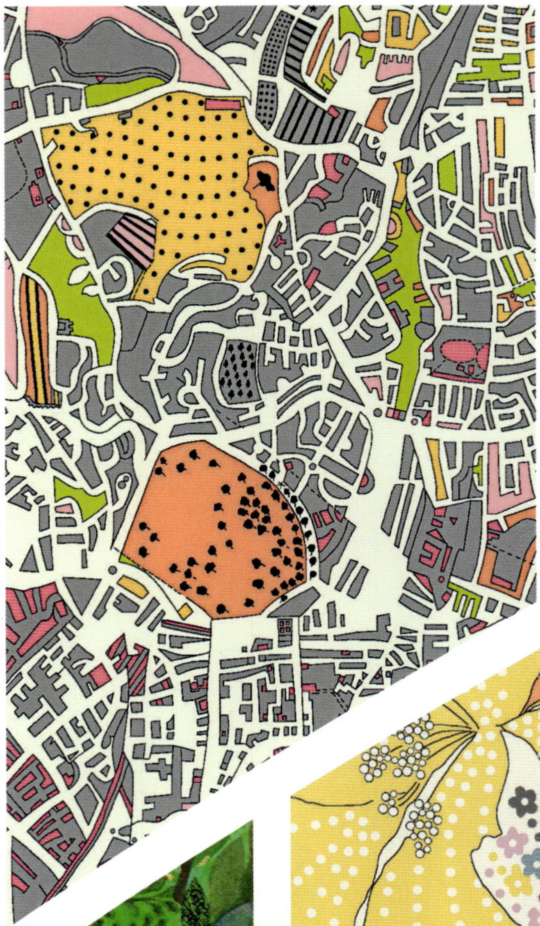

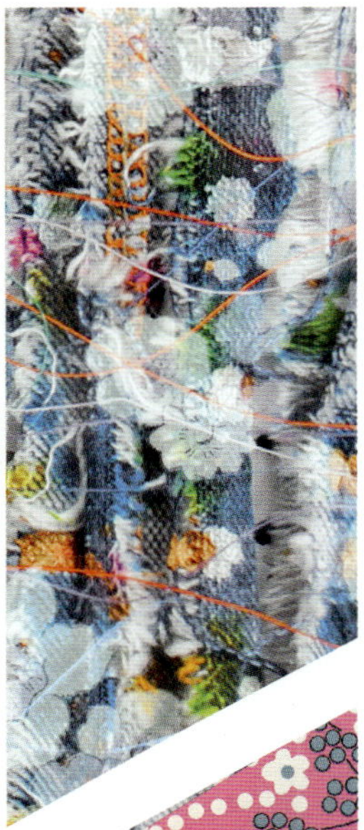

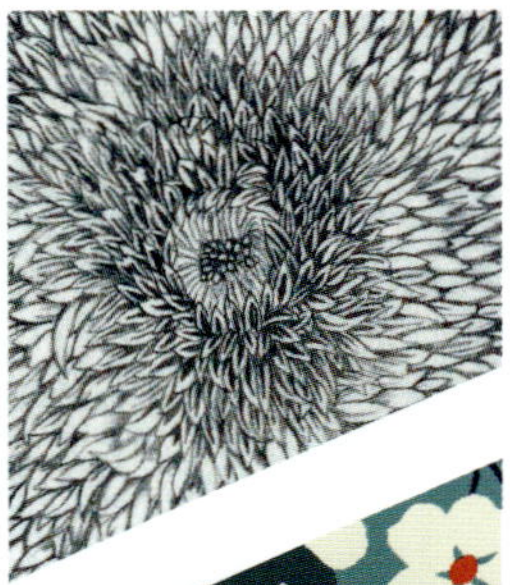

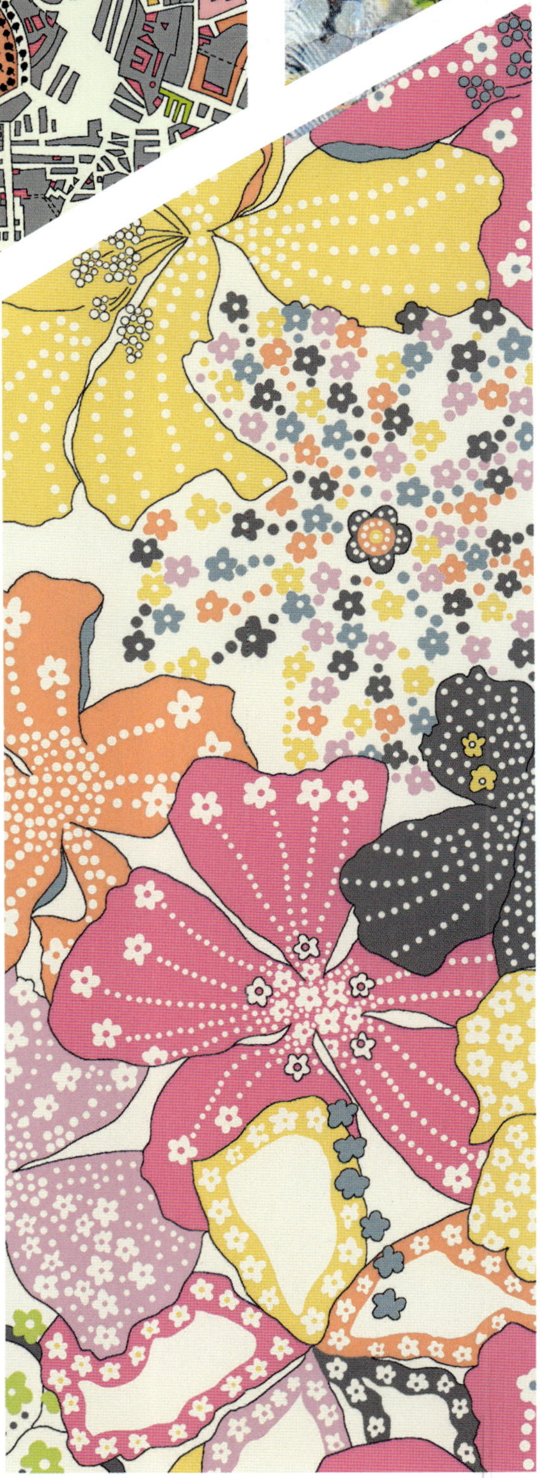

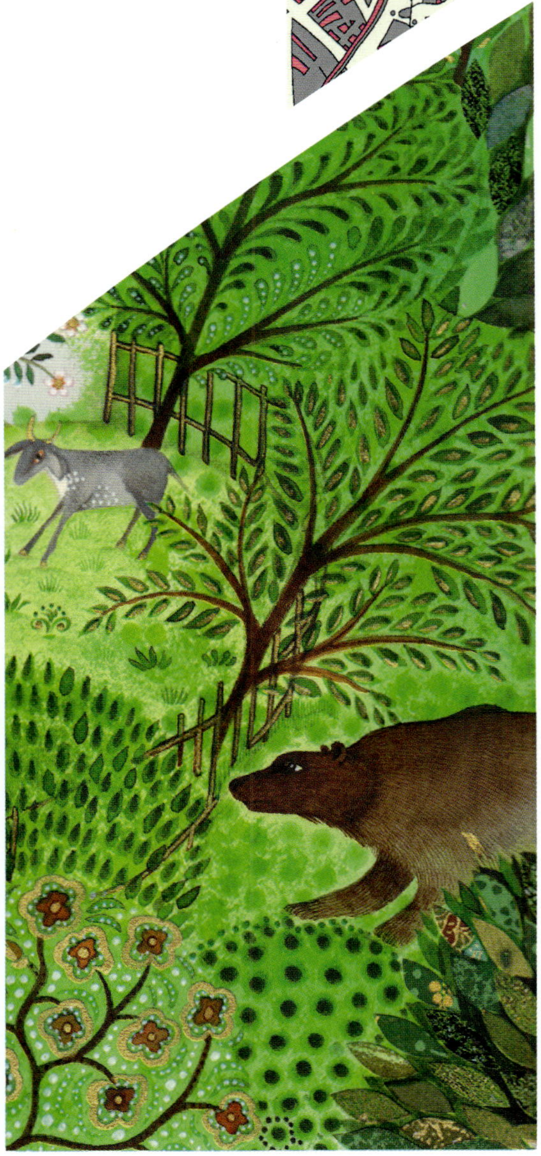

NEW DIRECTIONS

OPPOSITE
Liberty Art Fabrics, including May Rose, Ray and Poppy's Patchwork, and an original sketch for the Susanna print.

THIS PAGE
Clockwise, from top left: Sydenham Palace; Holly; Susanna; Mitsi; Mauve; and the original Ray design.

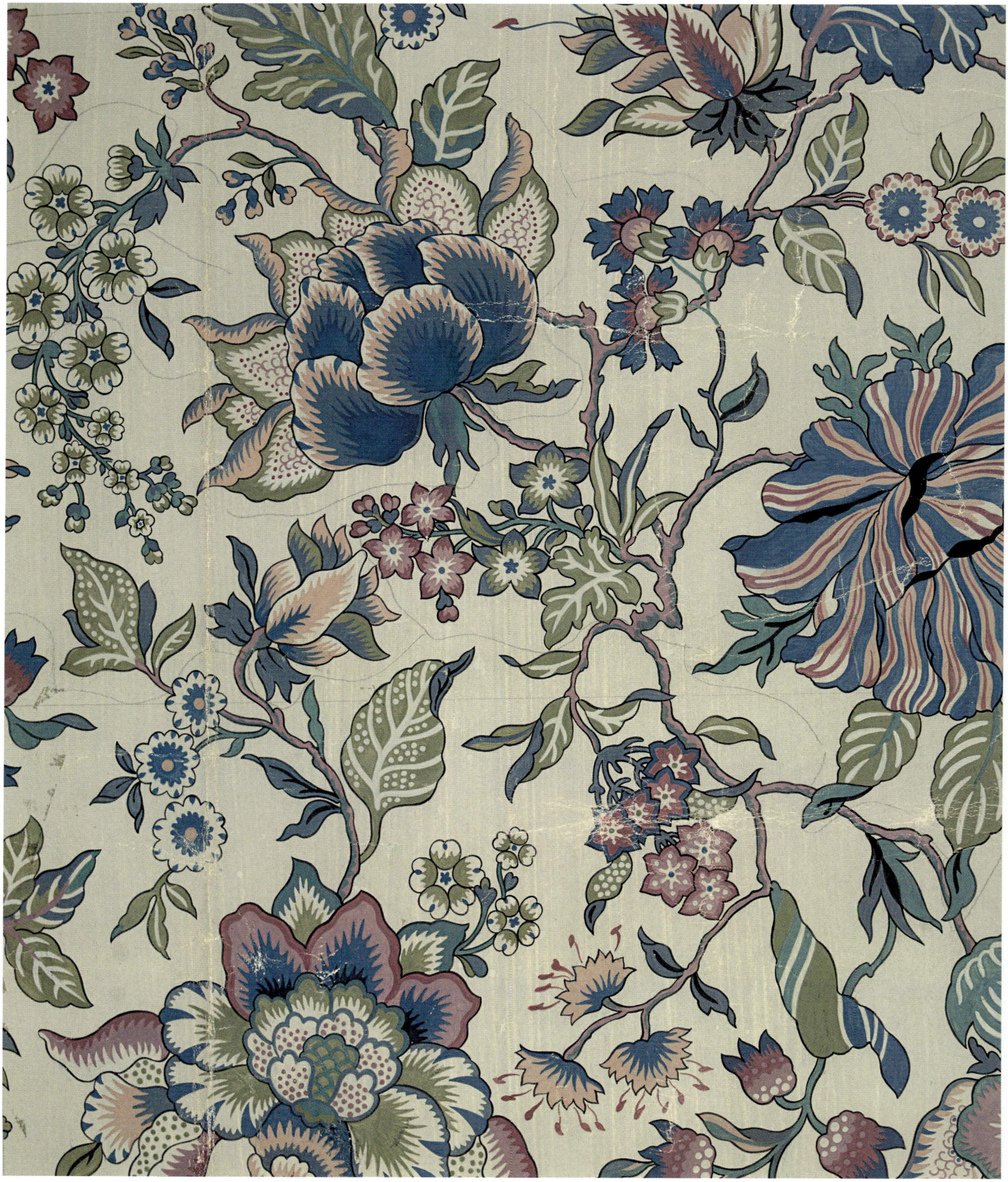

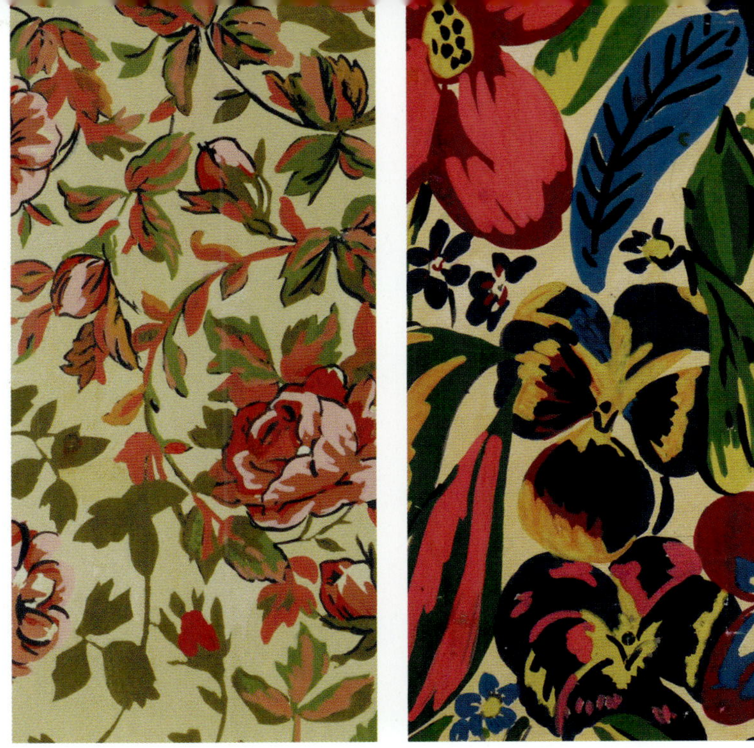

THE DESIGN STUDIO & ARCHIVE

ABOVE *During the 1990s, patterns were coloured in by hand. Each artwork was sent to the printer together with hand-painted swatches of every colour featured for accurate colour matching.*

The advent of the twenty-first century heralded the start of a new and exciting era for the design department of Liberty Art Fabrics that continues to this day. Renowned for its intelligent use of colour, detailed prints and beautiful fabric bases, the cutting-edge textile design studio today thrives on innovation and individuality, and is regarded as a trend leader in the fashion and textile industry.

In the latter years of the twentieth century, the design studio's output comprised a range of hand-painted prints that were produced on Tana Lawn, Varuna Wool or Country Cotton, or were used for craft fabric or scarves. These prints were created using existing designs or those supplied by out-of-house designers, which were simply "coloured in" by hand. With working methods similar to those in an old-fashioned artist's studio, designers painted at big drawing boards illuminated only by daylight bulbs. Starting with a photocopy of a print outline, the designer would first create a background to paint over using a white or tinted wash. This would be wiped over the design with a sponge before the chosen colours could be filled in. A square of every colour used within the final design had to be painted up and sent to the printers for colour matching. A strip of the finished design, hand-painted swatches and the paint recipes for each colour used were kept for future reference.

By spring 1999, once the modern archive had been established to catalogue the heritage designs and make them accessible to the creative team, the studio made its first steps into designing new prints again. Mainly based on 1930s designs, these collections were instinctive, rather than being defined by a narrative or theme as they are today, and adhered to a tried-and-tested formula of small florals on Tana Lawn – inherently associated with Liberty – with a few paisleys and conversation pieces.

Since that period, the design process has gained more structure. Each year there are around 40 new designs in the fashion fabric range, divided into four or five groups or design stories with a common theme or source of inspiration. Although drawing and painting remain integral, technological advances have enabled other print processes and methods of mark-making, such as mono-printing, photography and collage, to be explored, as well as digital techniques. Whatever the method used in a print's creation, the final stages require it to be in a digital format to be sent to the printers for producing the screens and for the colouring processes. In addition to new, seasonal prints Liberty Art Fabrics offer a selection of popular classic designs, some of which have been selling continuously for more than 30 years, with periodic colour changes.

RIGHT *This hand-painted artwork was the basis for a large-scale design of swirling flowers and foliage printed on Varuna wool in 1993.*

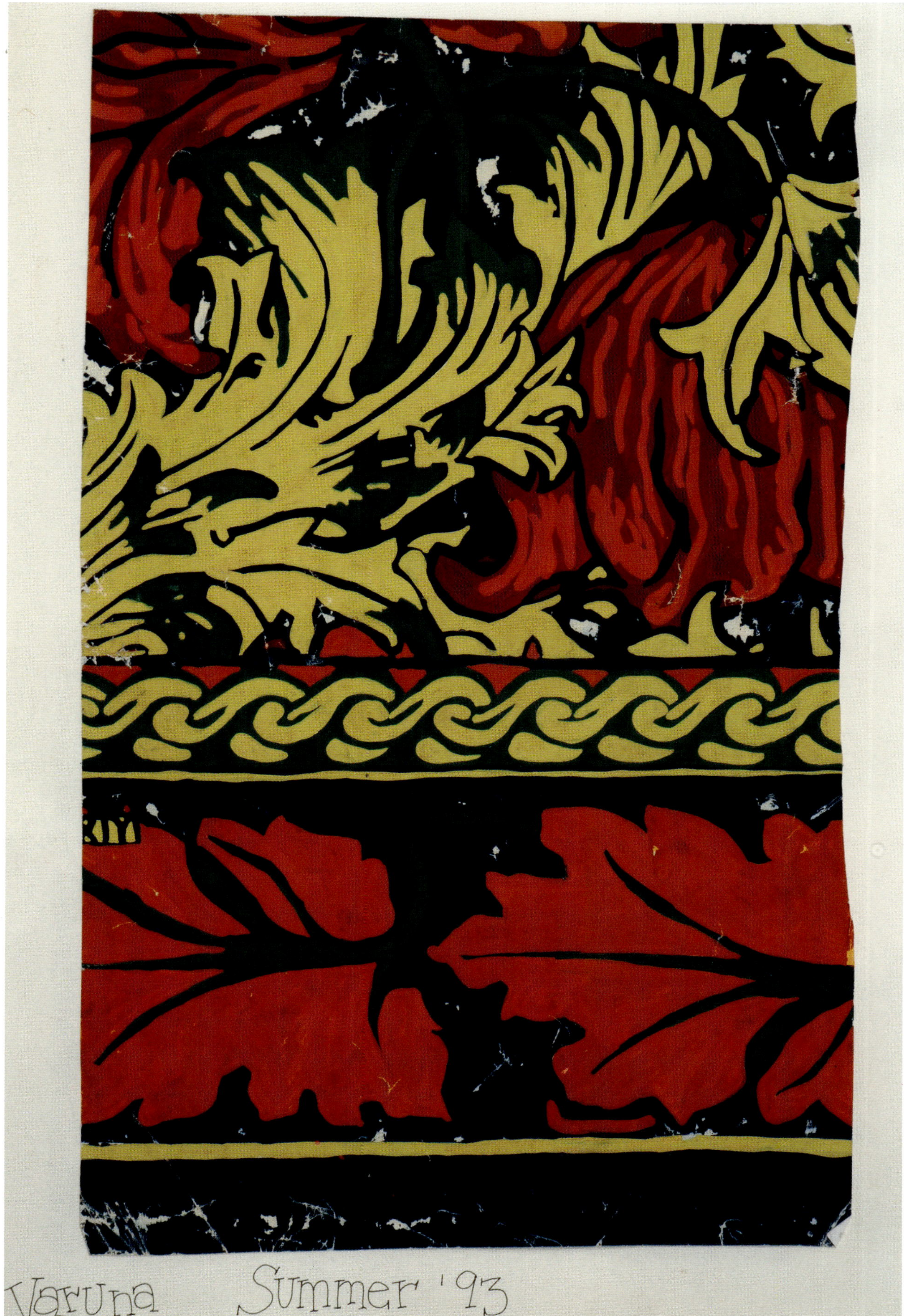

THIS PAGE *The first seasonal collection created using the newly catalogued archive was launched for S/S 1999, when historic designs such as Nina, Georgiana and Marcus (left to right) were reworked and recoloured by the in-house design studio to produce fresh, new prints.*

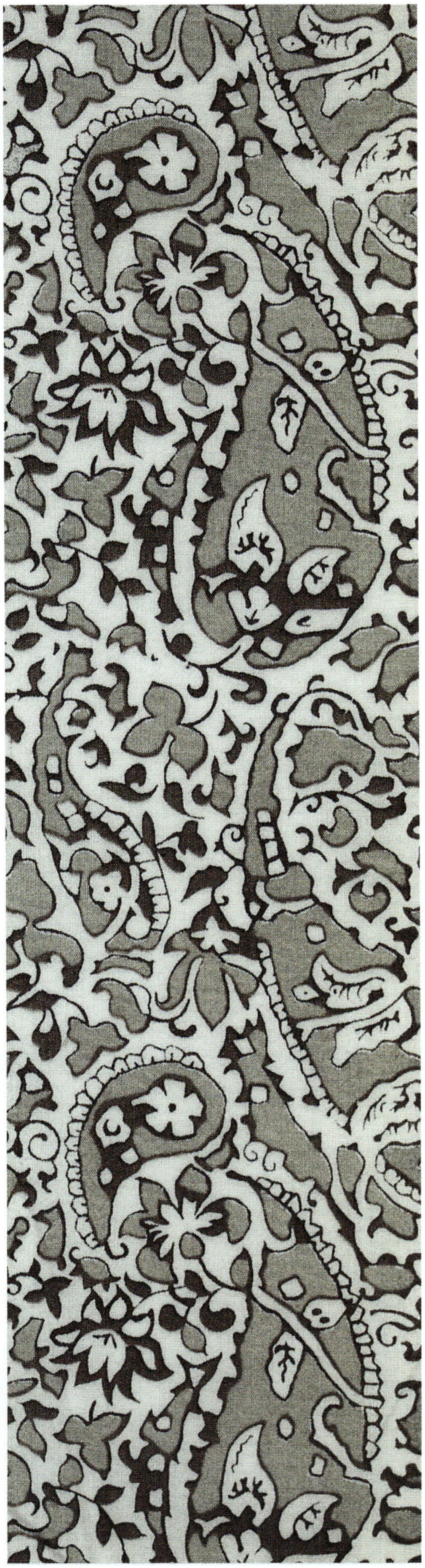

SNUG

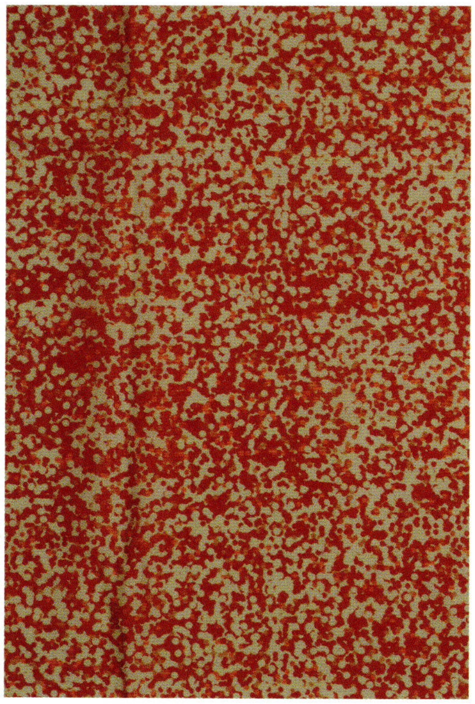

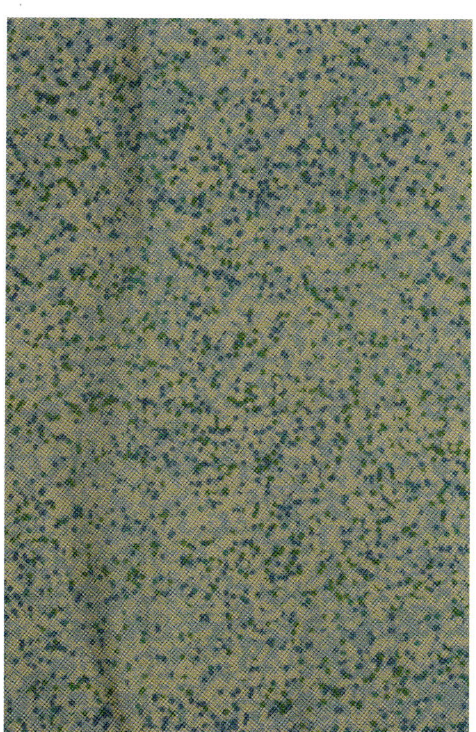

ABOVE *The first digital print created by Liberty, Snug was included in the S/S 2001 collection and became one of the bestsellers, earning it a place in the classic collection for more than 10 years.*

MARK

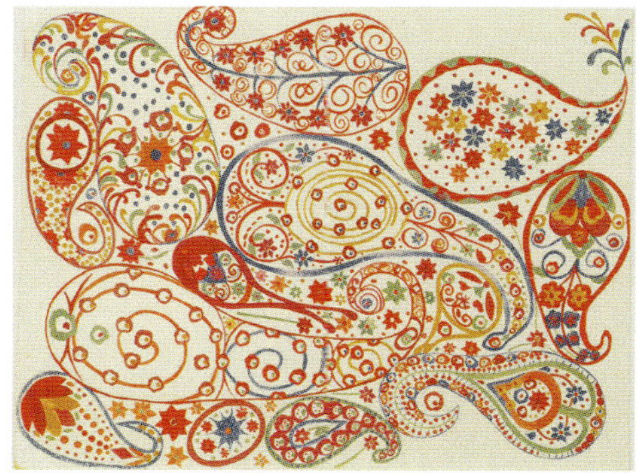

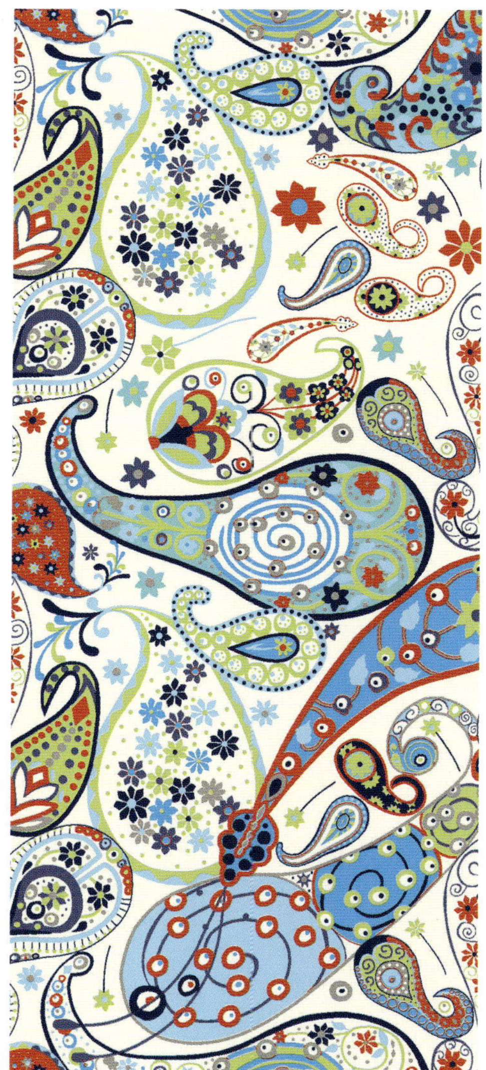

ABOVE *This contemporary paisley, based on Islamic calligraphy, was hand-painted and pieced together on the computer for A/W 2001. The versatile design has been rescaled and produced in many different colourways since. The original painting is shown (top).*

CHRISTELLE

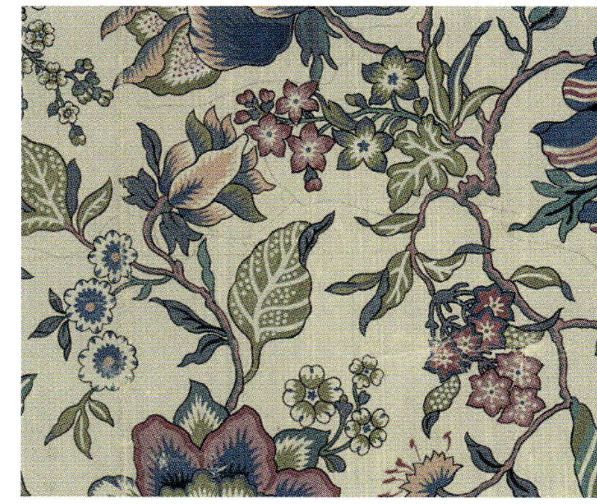

ABOVE *This traditional print of flowers and foliage for A/W 2001 is now exclusively used for the Liberty of London collection in a range of colourways.*

JACKY

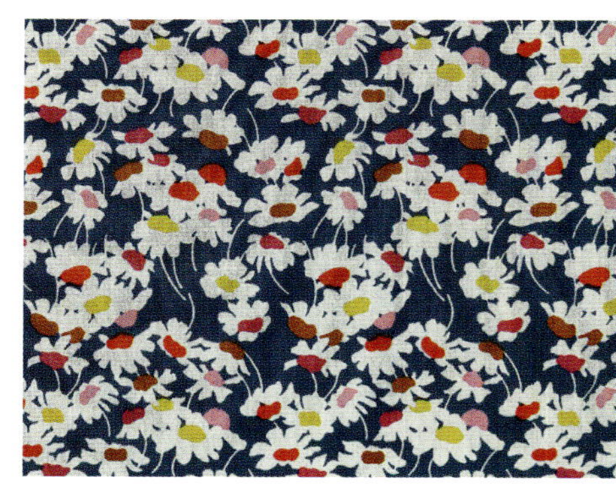

ABOVE *The two examples of this simple floral design created for A/W 2001 illustrate how different a design can look when it has been rescaled and recoloured.*

SUSANNA

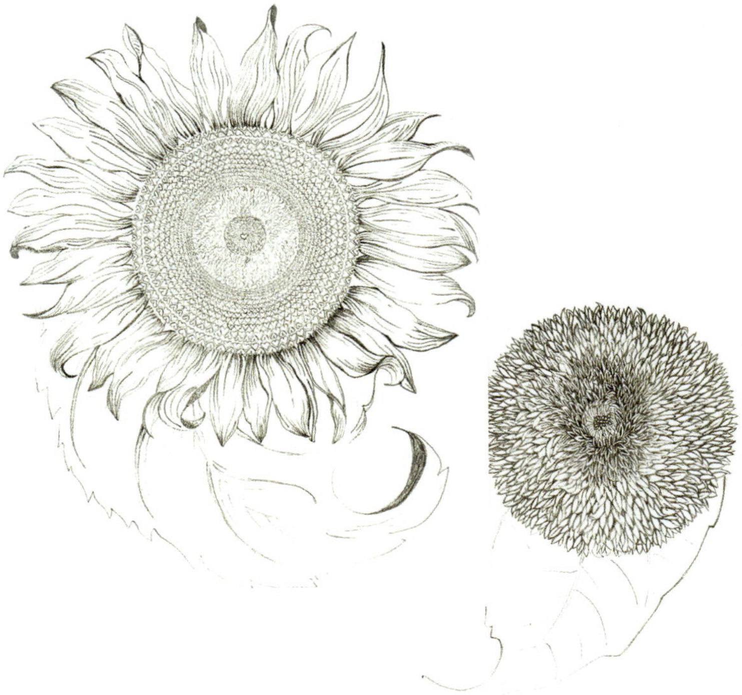

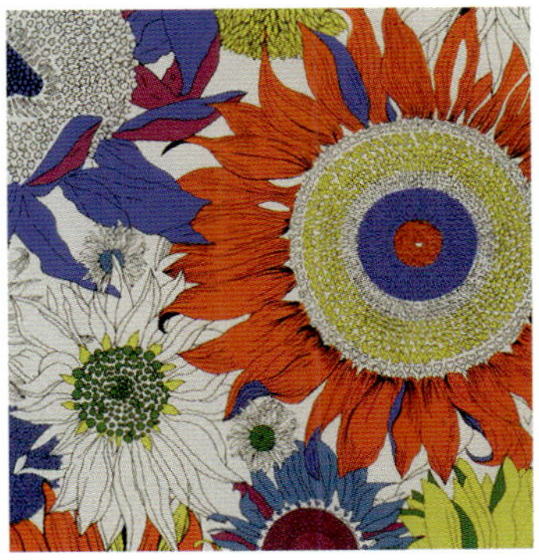

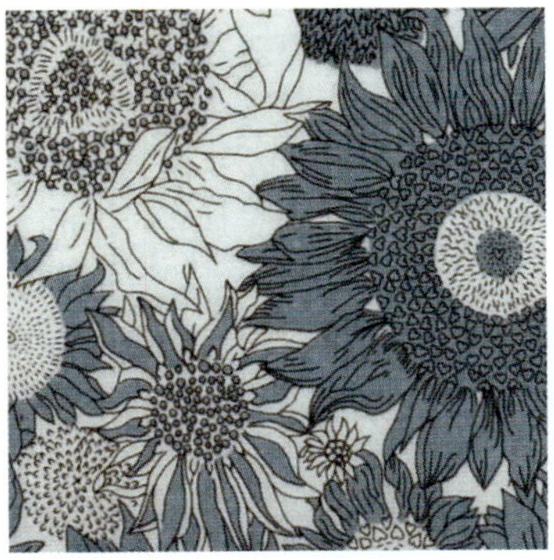

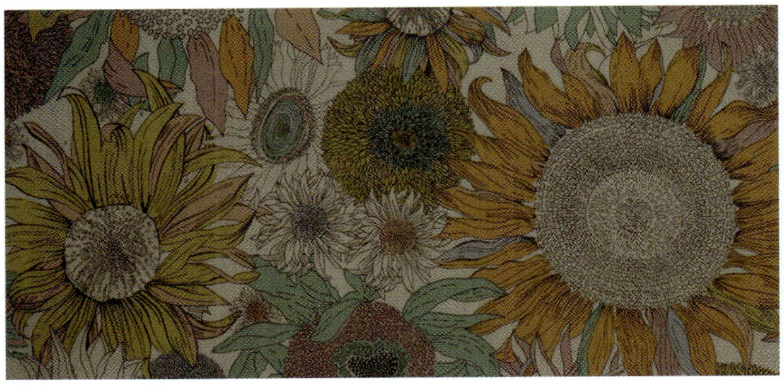

ABOVE *Created in-house as part of the Sunspot group for S/S 2005, Susanna has been reinvented many times, and is shown here reproduced in high, low and mid tones. The original drawings (top) have been adapted and redrawn to create the rescaled patterns, such as the Small Susanna version, because when a design is dramatically reduced in scale, much of the original detail is lost.*

BRONTE

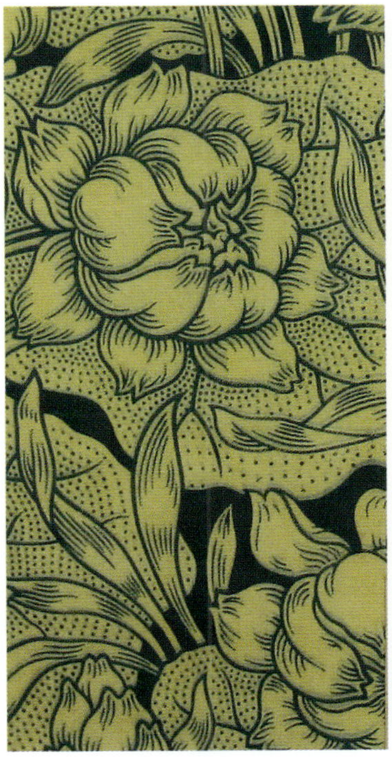

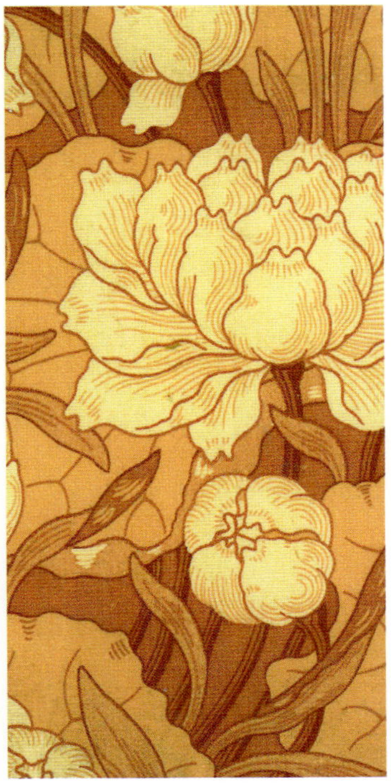

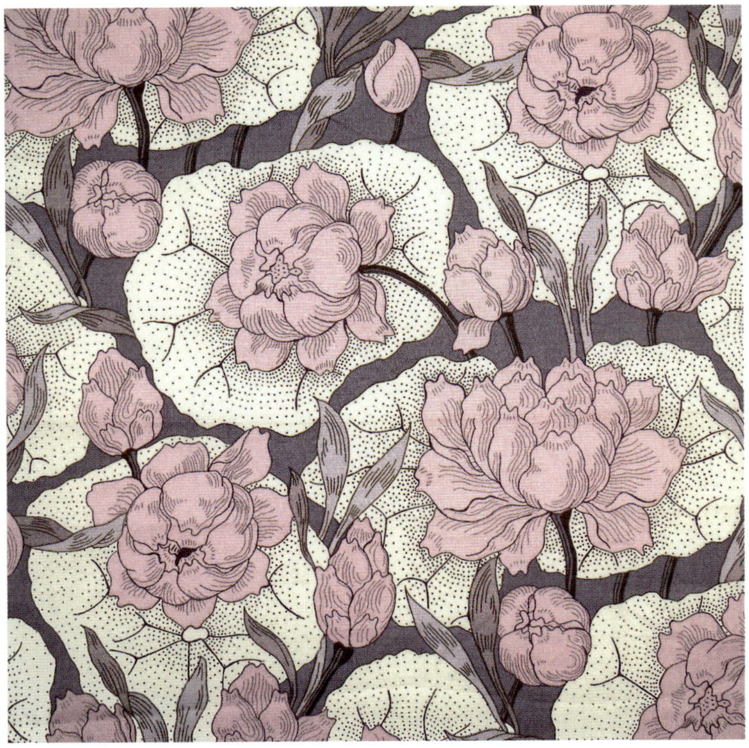

ABOVE *Bronte, shown here in a soft pink and lilac colourway, is a great example of a print that has been created by using elements from two different archive pieces (top) that have been worked together to form a new design.*

WILLIAM

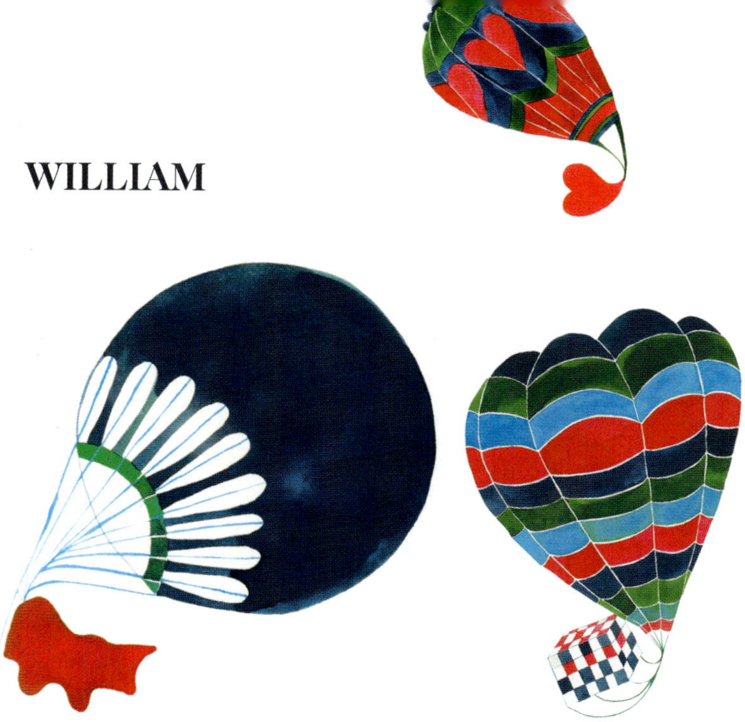

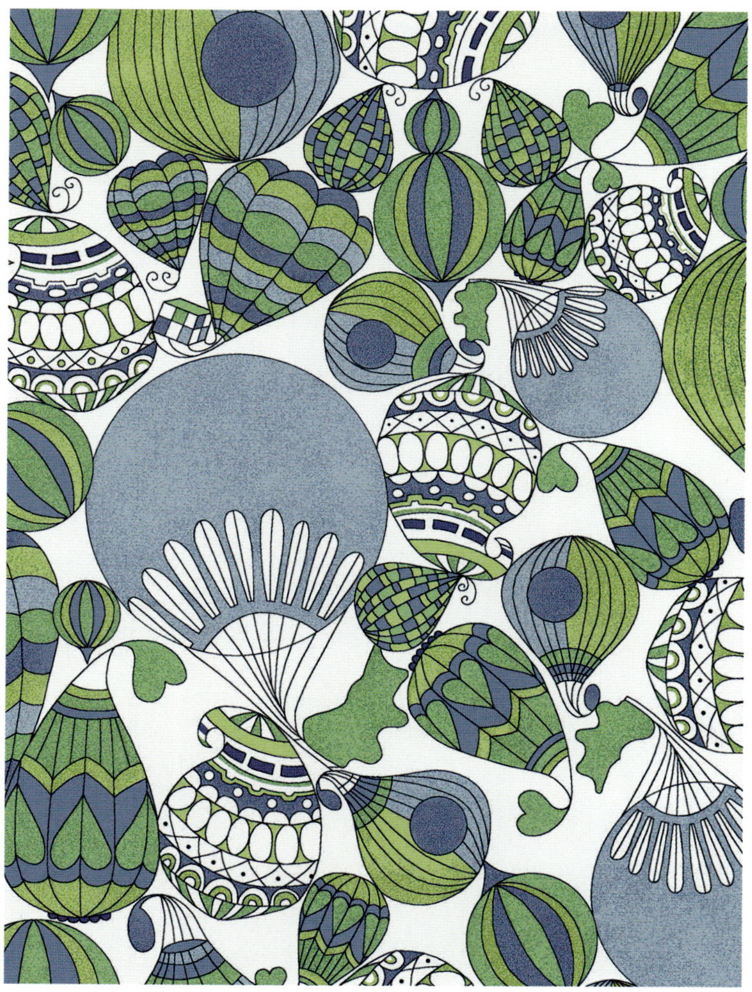

ABOVE *Created in the studio for A/W 2005, the uplifting, geometric William paisley design, featuring motifs inspired by hot-air balloons, is still being used for childrenswear.*

MIM

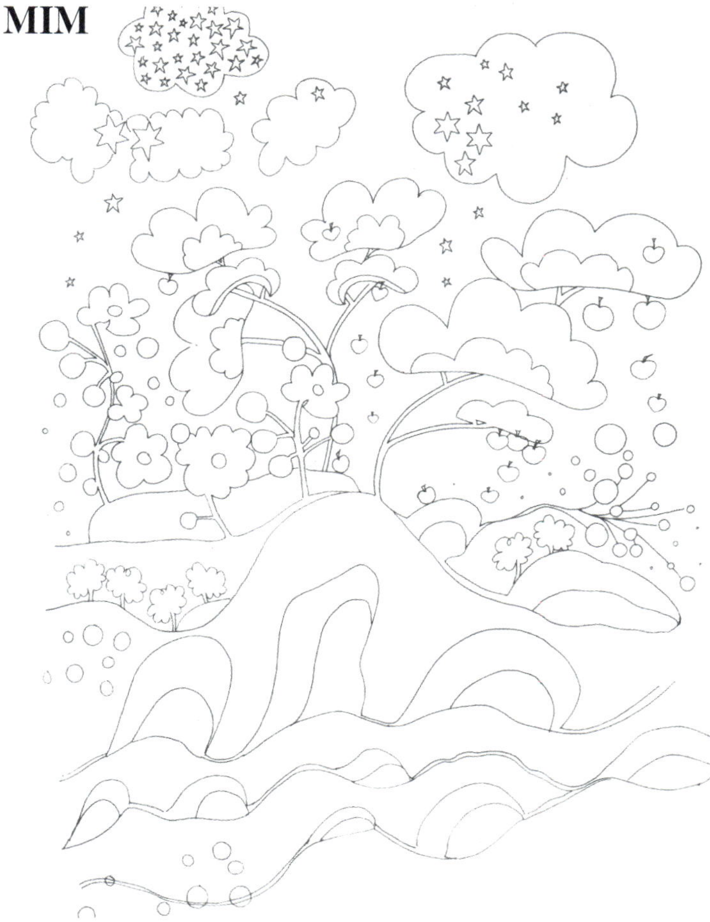

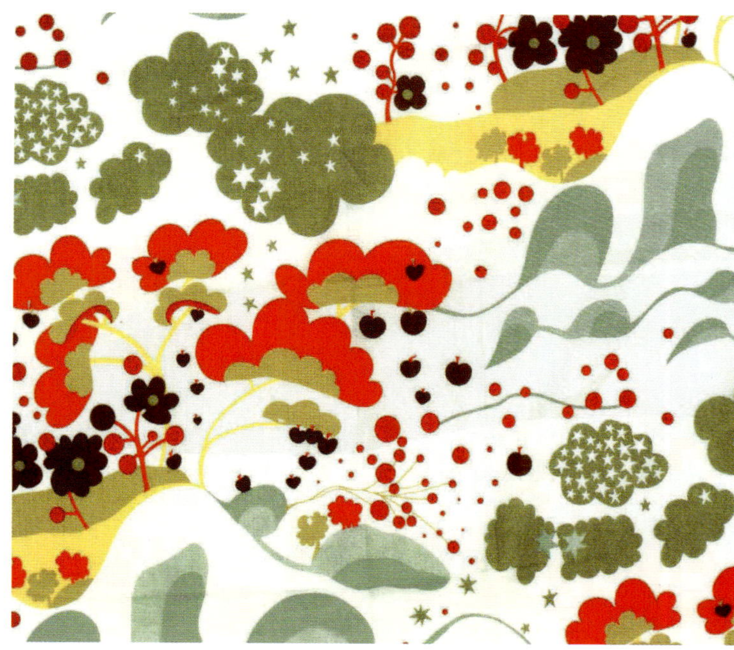

ABOVE *Inspired by a design created for fashion label Paul Smith, and based on an archive print with a 1970s vibe chosen by them, Mim has also been used for a collaboration with the Hello Kitty brand.*

STEVE

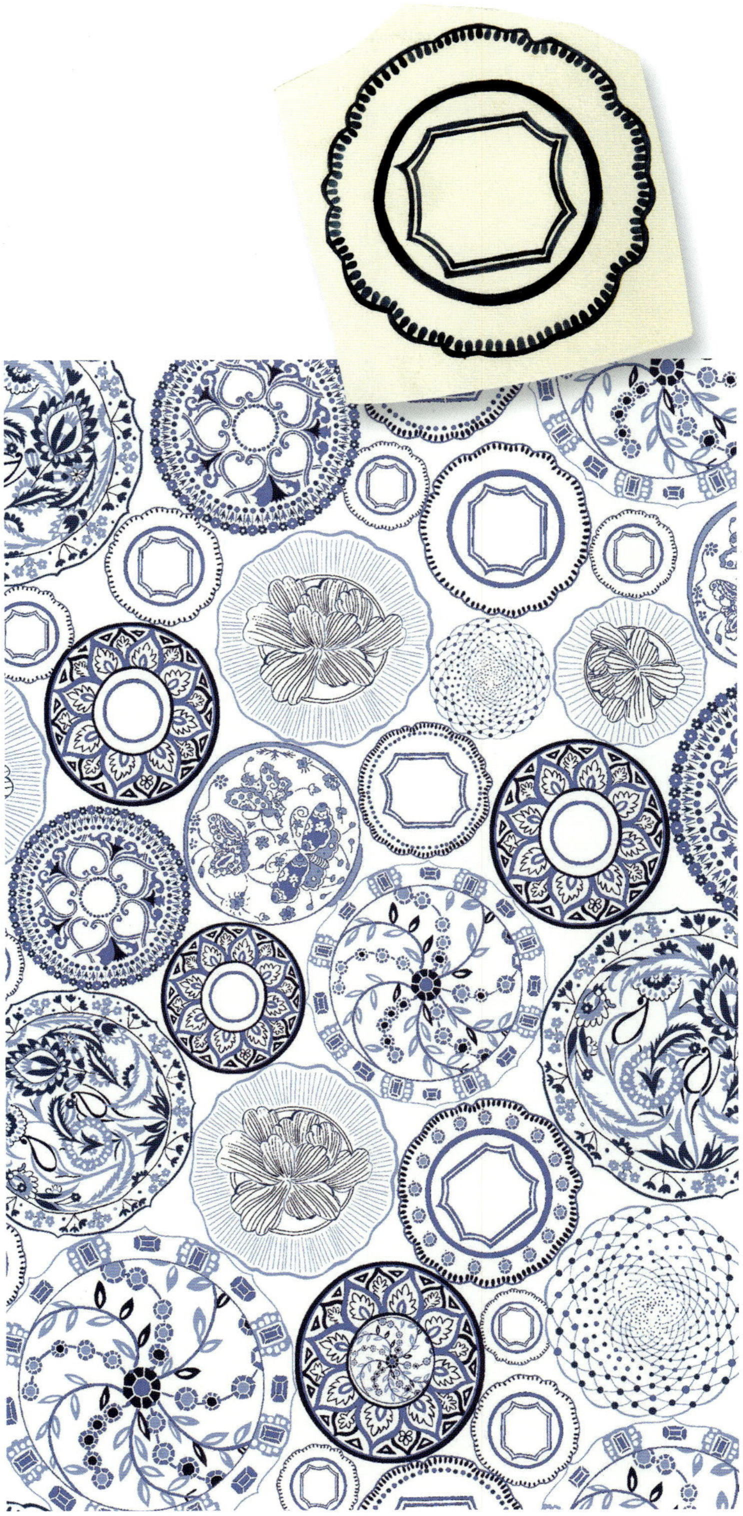

ABOVE *The Steve plate design was a bestseller, produced as part of the A/W 2005 collection.*

JOSEPHINE

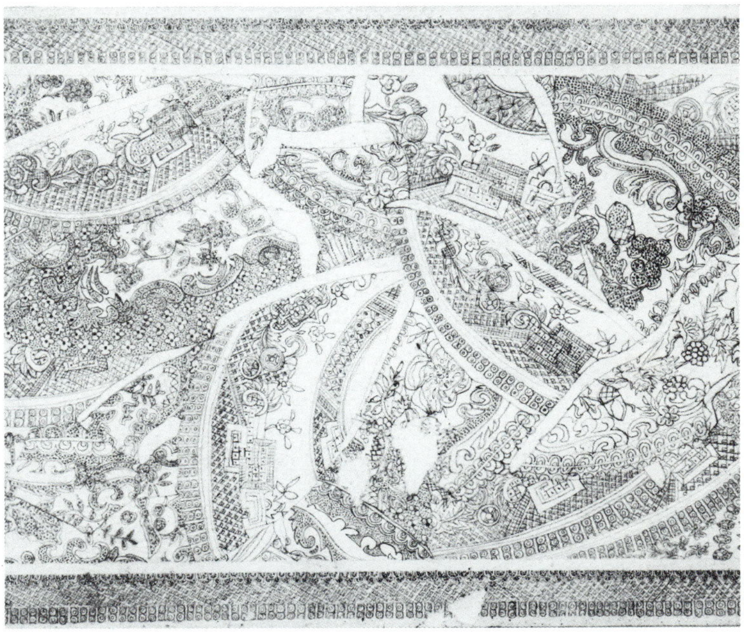

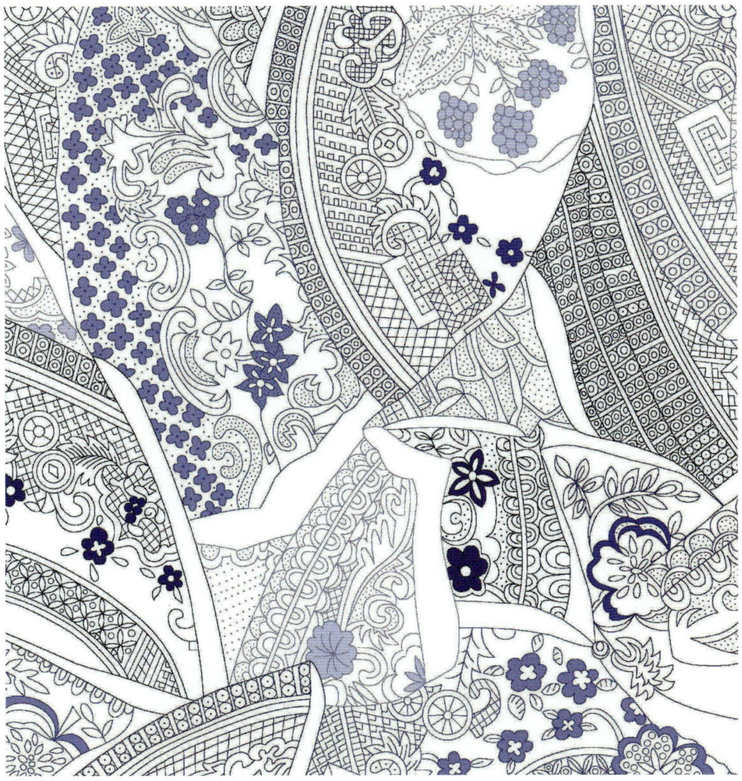

ABOVE *Josephine is the broken-plate version of Steve, illustrating that objects can be as beautiful fragmented as when they were whole. The original broken plates pencil sketch (top) was first hand-drawn in the early 1990s.*

MAUVE

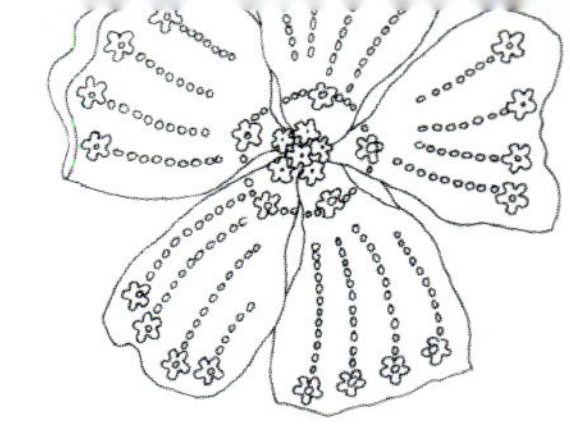

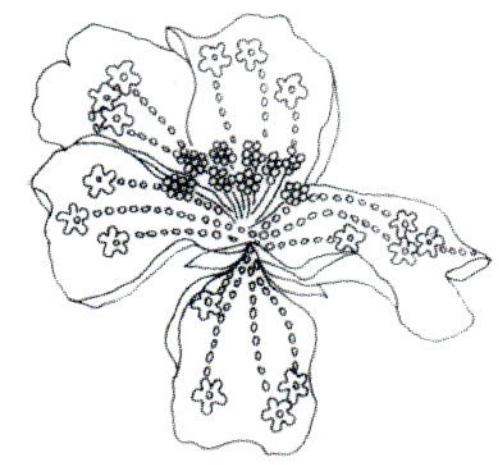

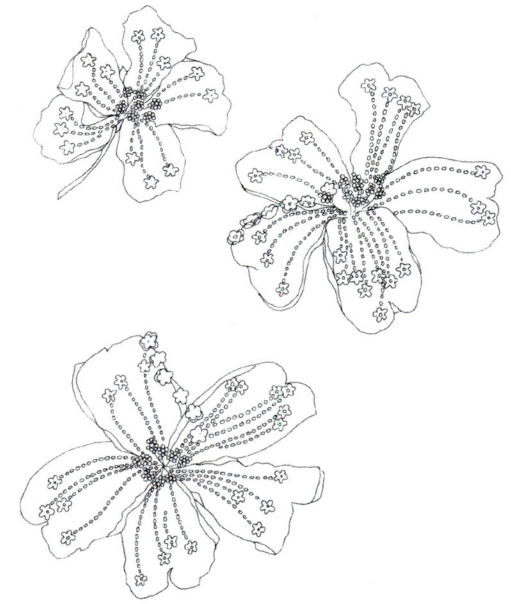

BELOW *Research is a huge part of the creative process, and the original scrapbook for the Floral Alphabet collection of S/S 2008 shows how initial sketches, tear sheets and other visual inspirations for the concept were collated.*

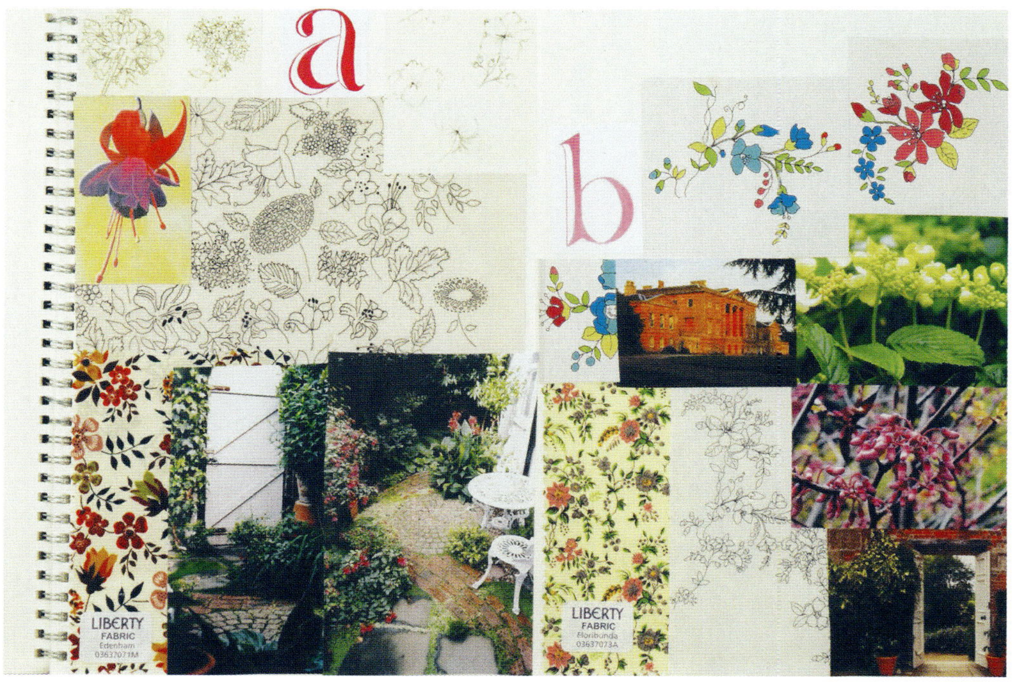

Inspiration for the collections comes from many sources and in many forms – from art galleries and exhibitions, music and film, markets and ornaments, stories and photographs, places and people, memories and life experiences. Keeping a fresh and inspiring perspective on design is crucial and the creative team considers research trips an important aspect of their work. For Spring/Summer 2008, the designers visited various gardens for inspiration and the result was Floral Alphabet. It consisted of groups of small prints (based on the structure of classic Liberty florals) with names beginning with letters A through F; medium shrub florals each began with a different letter G through M; large garden florals were based on flower names beginning with the letters N through S; and textures took names with letters T through Z. The colour stories were based on different dye shades used to print Liberty fabric.

For Autumn/Winter of the same year, the seasonal colour palettes were inspired by an eclectic collection of National Trust houses: the Georgian Uppark, the Neo-Classical Osterley, the Arts and Crafts Wightwick Manor, the Jacobean Bateman's and the 1940s Modern 2 Willow Road. Five design stories were then devised from a study of the key periods in Liberty's design history: 1880–1910, 1930s, 1950s, 1960–1970s and 1990–2000. Key archive prints were chosen from these periods and transformed into exciting and original new designs. The result was a mixture of fashion prints – florals, paisleys and geometrics – in varying scales and textures.

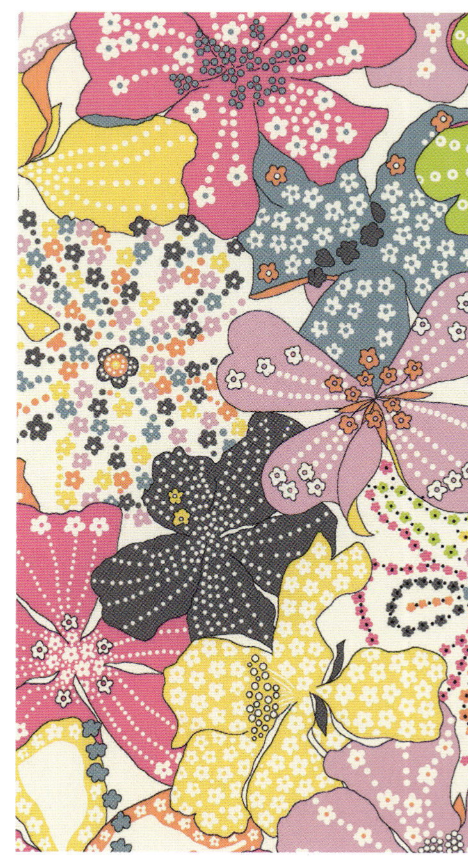

ABOVE *M is for Mauve. The inspiration for this feminine print for S/S 2008 was icing-sugar mallow flowers (the French form for "mallow" being* malva *or "mauve") and sequins. The delicate detailing on the fragile petals is evident in the original drawing (top) as well as in the final print.*

BASILDON PARK

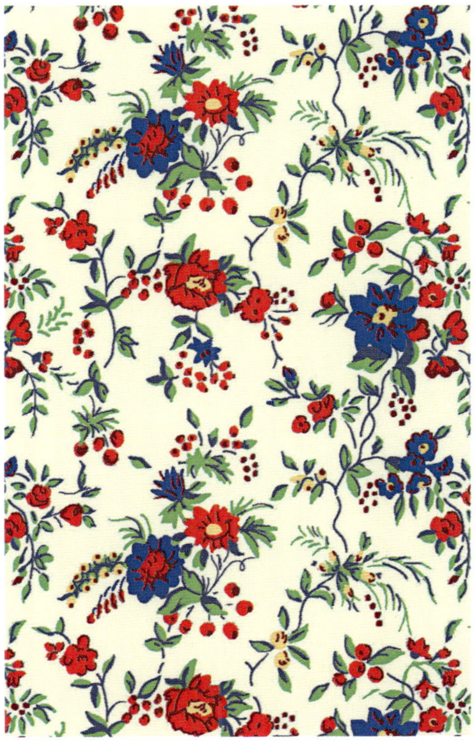

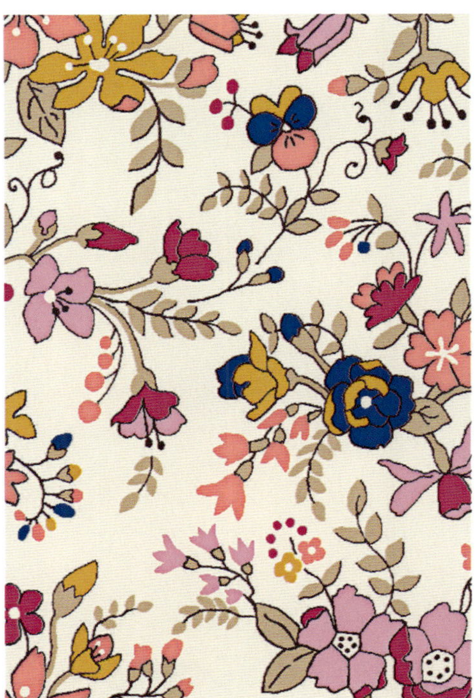

ABOVE *B is for Basildon Park, the S/S 2008 design (bottom) inspired by the classic Floribunda Tana Lawn print (top), a delicate floral designed by Allan Thomas in 1982.*

MITSI

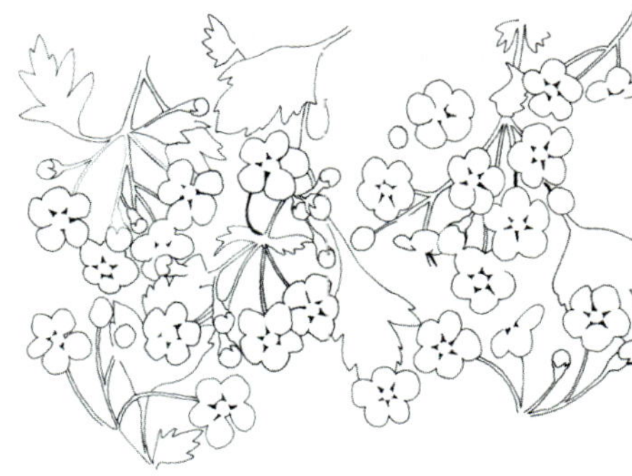

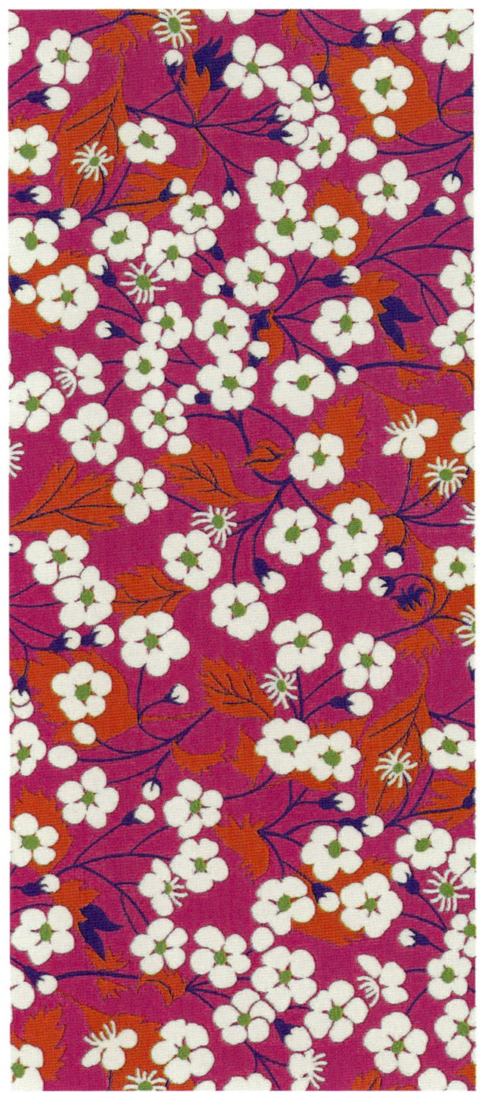

ABOVE *One of the prints in the 1950s design story, and based on a 1950s archive print, Mitsi features stylized blossom flowers, here with a hot-pink background and orange foliage. It was created for A/W 2008.*

LULU BERRY

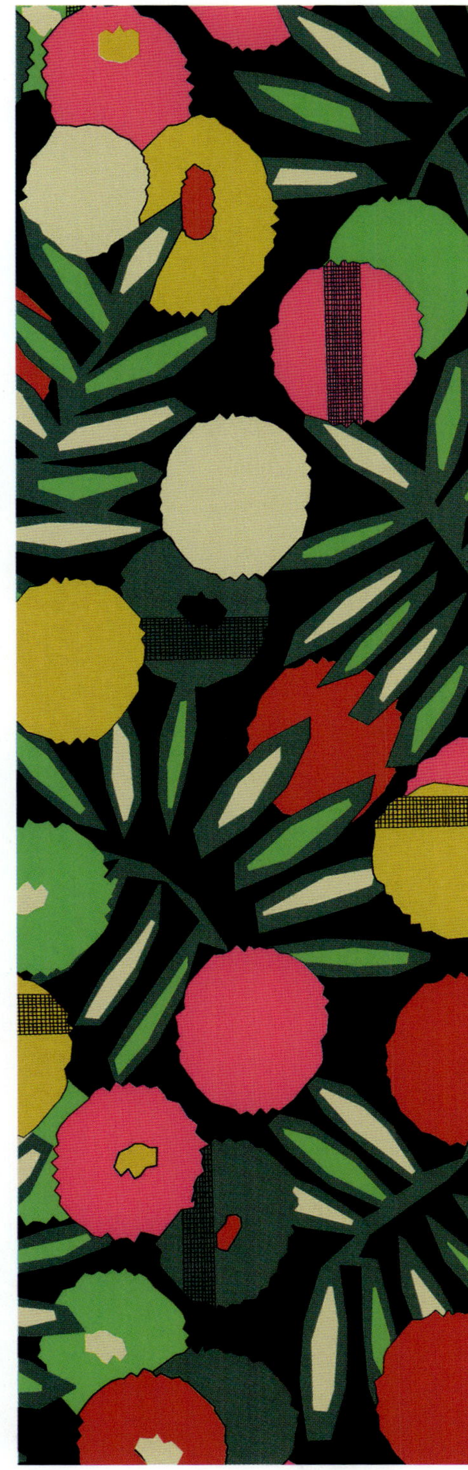

ABOVE *This woodcut berry print from the 1990–2000 design story for A/W 2008 is worked in a bold, modern colour palette.*

RIGHT *Pictured here as his transvestite alter ego, Claire, Turner Prize-winning artist Grayson Perry produced four subversive fabric designs for the A/W 2009 collection.*

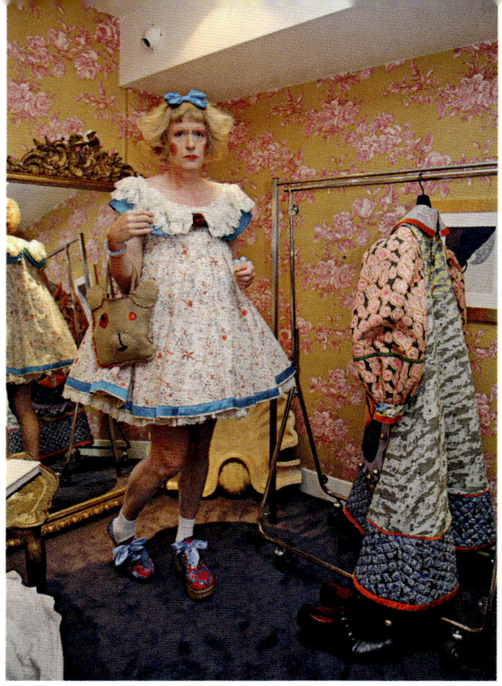

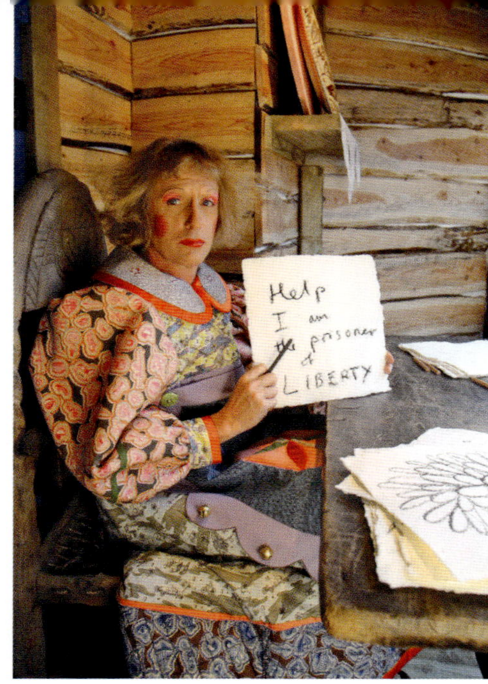

Liberty Fabrics often works closely with leading contemporary artists and designers from a wide range of disciplines to conceive new prints. These collaborations inject the design department with new bursts of creativity, and the fresh approach initiated by someone from outside the department often results in fabric collections with a very different mood.

The first season that Liberty Fabrics collaborated with artists was Autumn/Winter 2009, when six artists – Grayson Perry, Anj Smith, Simon Hart, Paul Morrison, Mike McInnerney and Michael Angove – were invited to design prints that were subsequently displayed in the Prints Charming exhibition held on the store's fourth floor. These artists all had disparate styles, favoured media and working methods, and they each expressed themselves in singular and personal ways, resulting in a unique and innovative collection of prints.

Grayson Perry, the Turner Prize-winning ceramicist, had often used Liberty prints in dresses he had designed for his alter ego, Claire, so he was delighted when four fabrics – Sissy, Cranford, Flo and Philippa – were produced from his initial sketches that reflected aspects of past, present and future society. An amazing craftsman, Perry is also an accomplished artist and drew everything in repeat himself.

For the next year's Autumn/Winter collection in 2010, the designs and colours were inspired by and embraced the culture, history, nature, art and architecture of Japan, and fused tradition and technology. It included collaborations with both British and Japanese artists, including Nigel Waymouth, Akira Minagawa and Tsumori Chisato.

BELOW *Cranford (left) was inspired by the popular BBC drama and featured a dense crowd of bonneted heads. Sissy (right) depicts "gendered toys", clothes and objects in a nursery-like print.*

BELOW *The tangle of bicycles with a 1950s feel (left), named Philippa, after Perry's wife, was inspired by a statement made by H. G. Wells with which Perry agreed: "Whenever I see someone riding a bicycle I have hope for the world." The final print, Flo (right), named after Perry's daughter, features an apocalyptic landscape of burning planes and buildings, dead trees and gravestones populated by teddy bears, rabbits and other toys.*

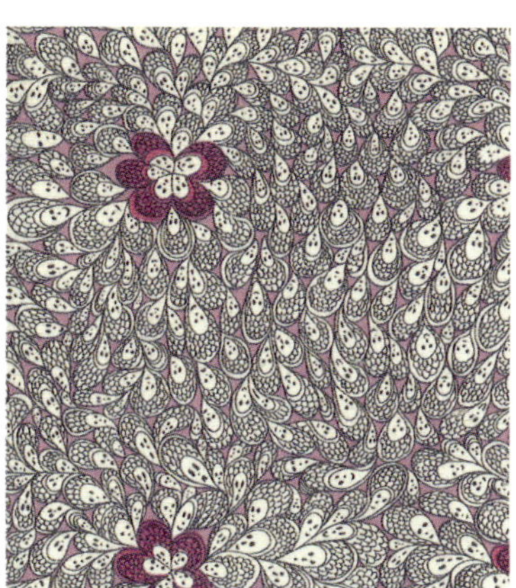

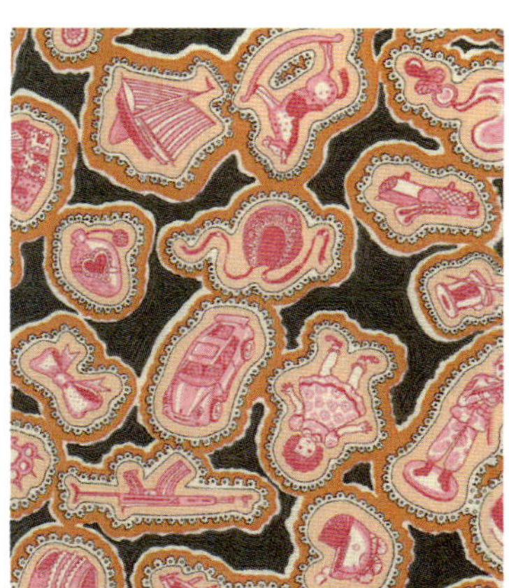

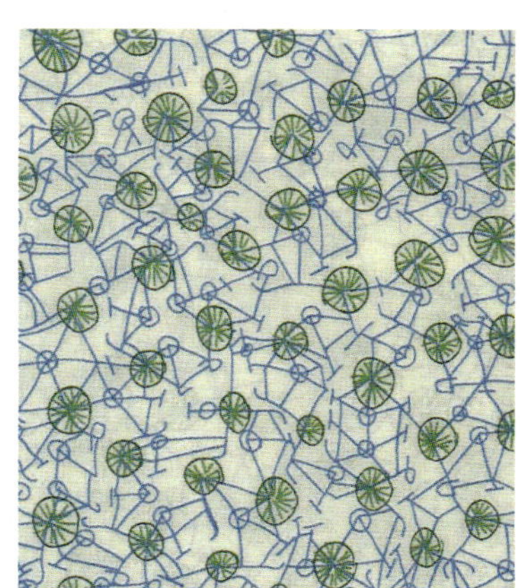

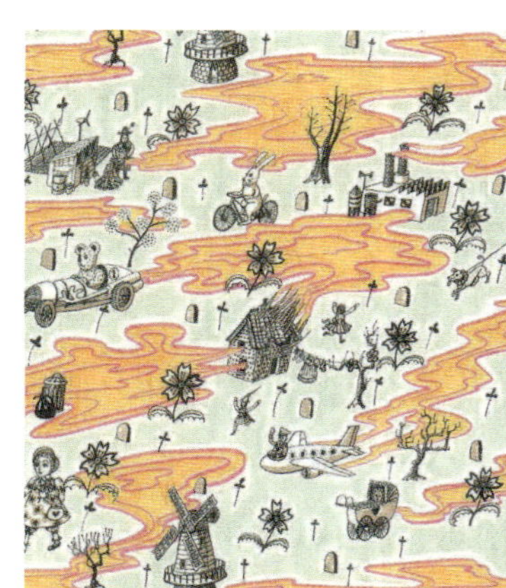

DETRITUS

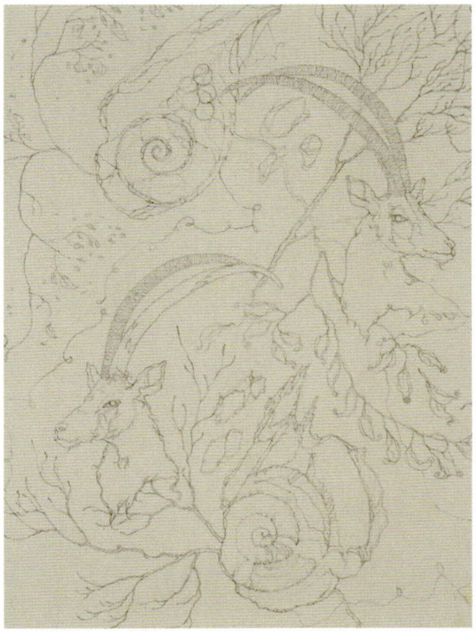

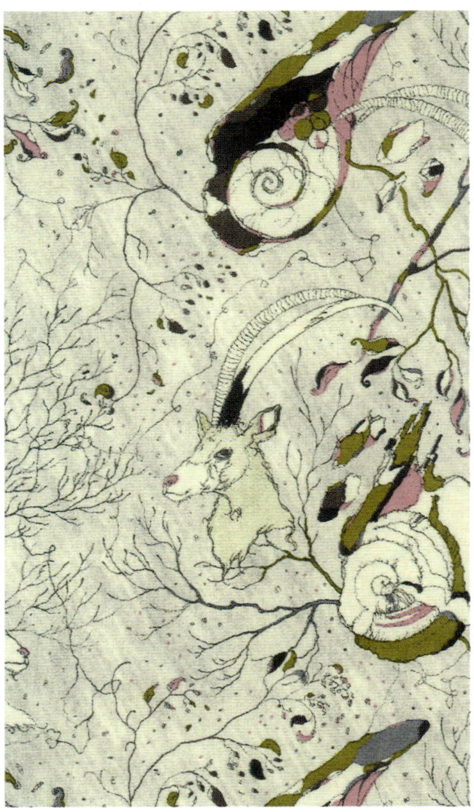

ABOVE *Surrealist painter Anj Smith drew the original sketch for this design in pencil and then coloured it in. Detritus, A/W 2009, was inspired by both George Saunders' satire* Pastoralia *and memories of the kitchen curtains of Smith's childhood, which featured repeated stag motifs.*

SLEEPING ROSE

"I am thinking back on today's light of the sun while hearing your breathing of a sleeping person that there is next to me. 'It will be good to be rainy tomorrow.' I talk it to the wind, and good night."

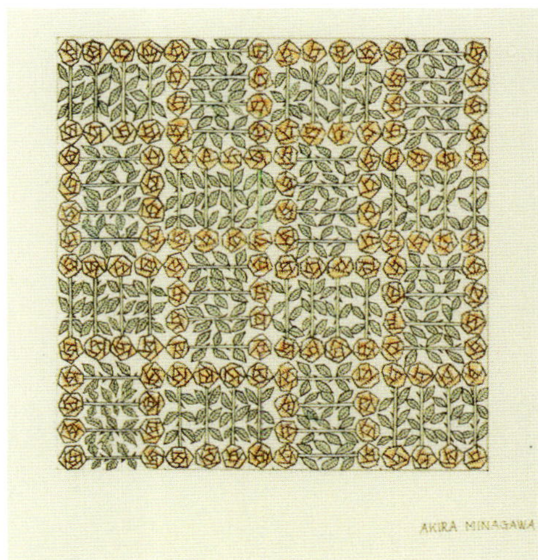

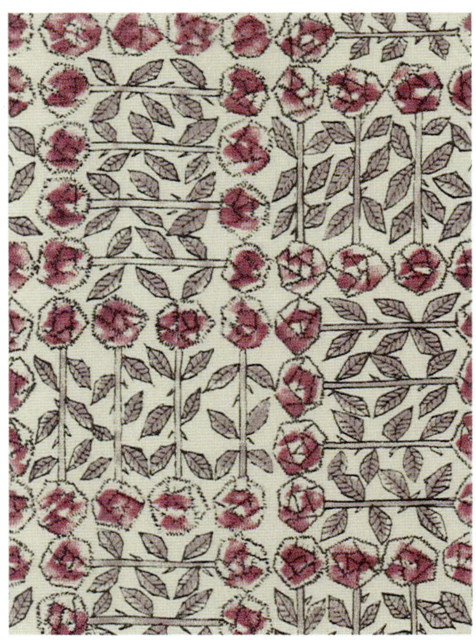

ABOVE *The Japanese theme for A/W 2010 included Sleeping Rose, created with intricate lines of coloured pencil, watercolour washes and ink, by Akira Minagawa, fashion designer and founder of the brand Mina Perhonen. The verse was written by him to accompany the print.*

AKINOBU

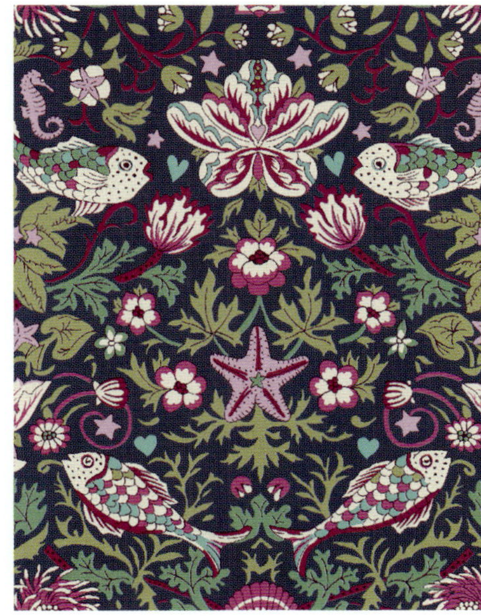

ABOVE *This A/W 2010 design is based on a classic Liberty print, Strawberry Thief, that was reworked by Japanese fashion designer Tsumori Chisato.*

HIRO

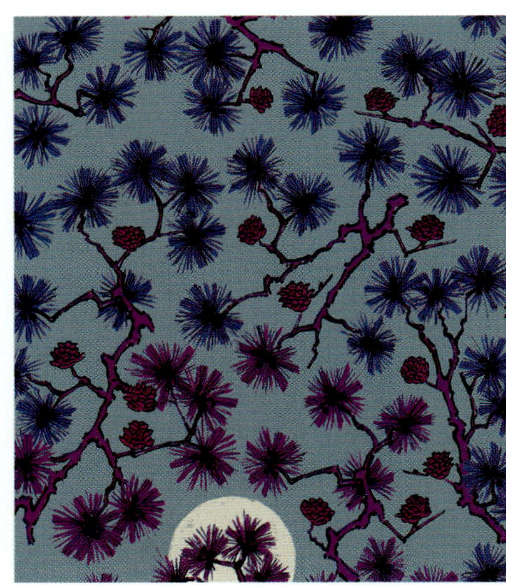

ABOVE *For A/W 2010, British designer Nigel Waymouth's single painting was separated into two designs: Martina, a floral, and Hiro, depicting the moon.*

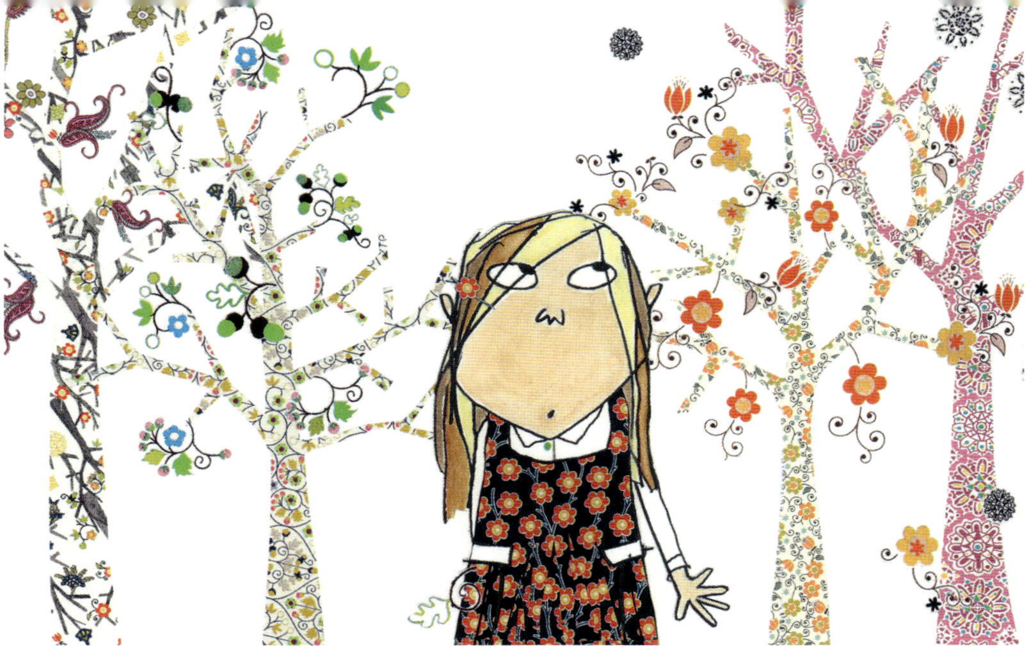

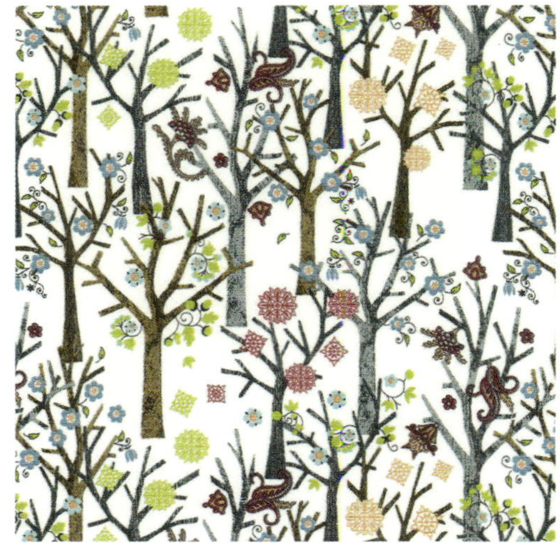

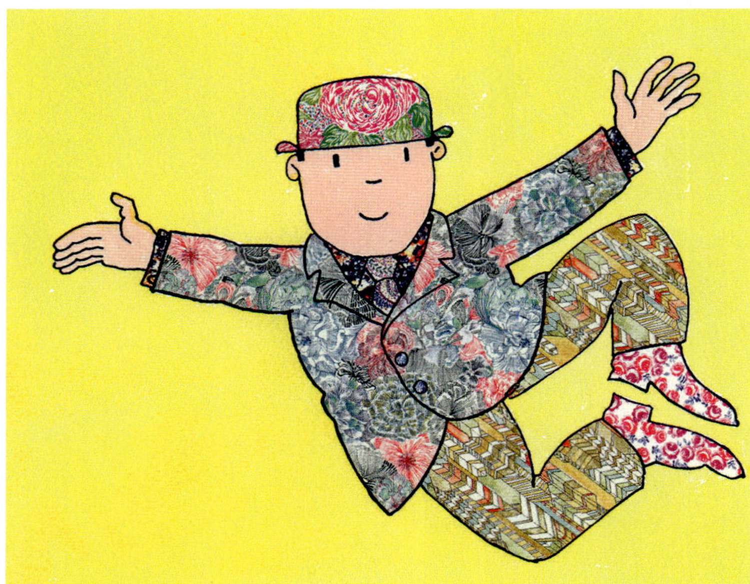

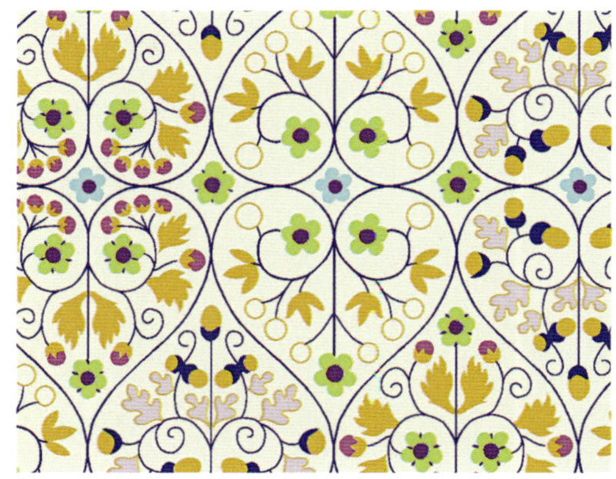

ABOVE *The original Clarice Bean artwork by Lauren Child (top left) was created using a collage of original archive Liberty prints, from which new prints were recreated: Tuesday Trees (top right) and Delfie (bottom).*

ABOVE *David McKee's character Mr Benn leaping for joy, dressed from head to toe in a gorgeous array of colourful Liberty prints.*

Inspired by the amazing, imaginative artwork found in children's books, the Storybook Collection for Spring/Summer 2011 was created in association with famous illustrators, including Lauren Child – creator of *Charlie and Lola* and *Clarice Bean* picture books – Brian Wildsmith, Jane Ray, Emma Chichester Clark and David McKee – creator of Mr Benn, who provided the original spark of an idea for this collection.

Each illustrator was asked to come up with an original piece of artwork and a quote, which inspired the design of one or more new prints. Emma Chichester Clark's lovely chidren's book *Eliza and the Moonchild* inspired a series of prints, while Brian Wildsmith's space rockets were embellished with the ditsy floral print Rania and his boats had sails patterned with Ebs, a design based on a mass of striped ties. With David McKee, the idea was that Mr Benn would go into a changing room at Liberty and come out dressed in an array of prints and embark on an adventure. The collection also included a collaboration with the Hello Kitty brand.

The Autumn/Winter 2011 collection, based on musical influences, combined the creative talents of the in-house design team with renowned musicians and artists who were passionate about the print collection. A truly original compilation of vibrant prints was designed, inspired by great British music and rock 'n' roll, from flower power anthems of the 1970s to 1950s rock and blues, 1990s acid house and the Brit-Pop movement.

ORNITHOLOGY

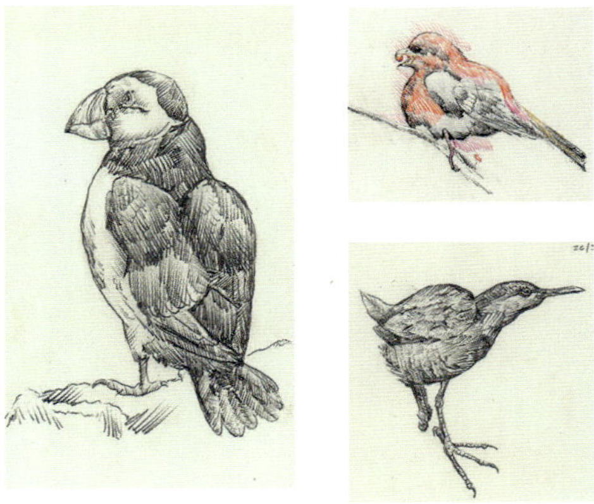

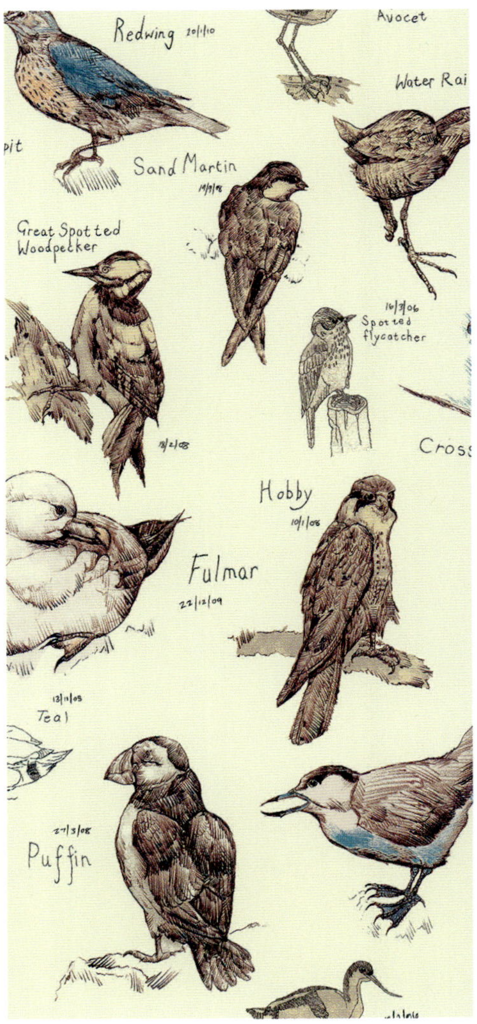

ABOVE *The Ornithology print for A/W 2011 was designed from sketches by Edwyn Collins (top), who is best known for fronting Scottish rock revivalists Orange Juice. In 2005, while recovering from a severe illness, Collins drew a bird a day, each of which has been used in this remarkable print.*

DANCING LADIES

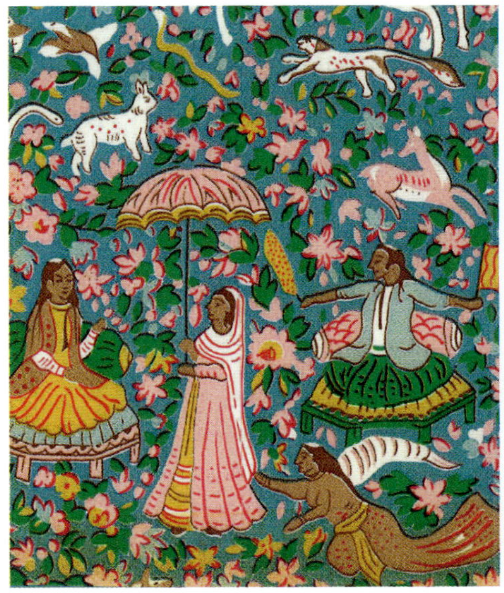

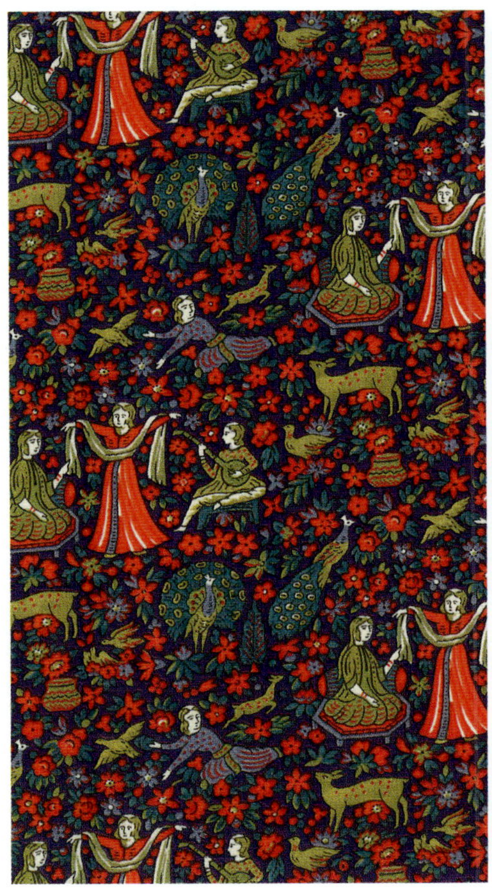

ABOVE *For A/W 2011, singer Florence Welch of Florence & The Machine selected archive Liberty prints Dancing Ladies (top, with A/W 2011 version below) and Grace to reinterpret into modern prints. Dancing Ladies is a traditional floral with figures reminiscent of Indian Miniatures, a style previously popular in the 1920s and 1930s.*

THORGERSON

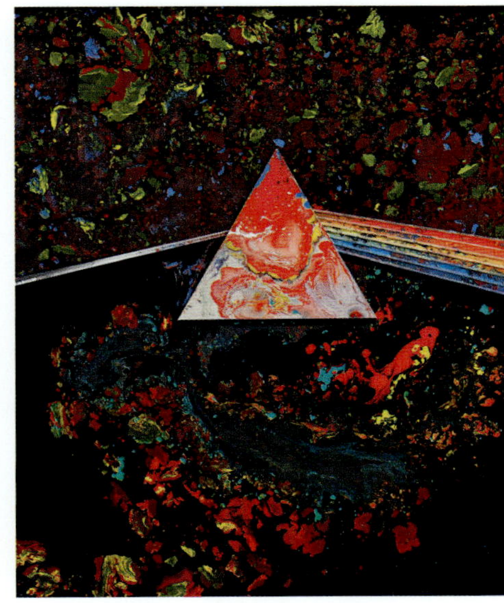

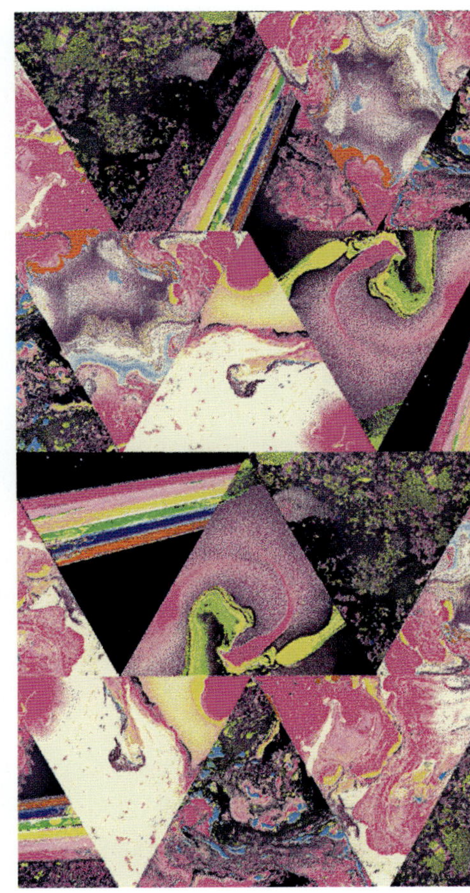

ABOVE *The late graphic designer Storm Thorgerson, who famously designed Pink Floyd's* Dark Side of the Moon *album cover, created an original painting (top), which was developed into an iconic prism graphic for Liberty's A/W 2011 collection (bottom).*

MY LITTLE POSY

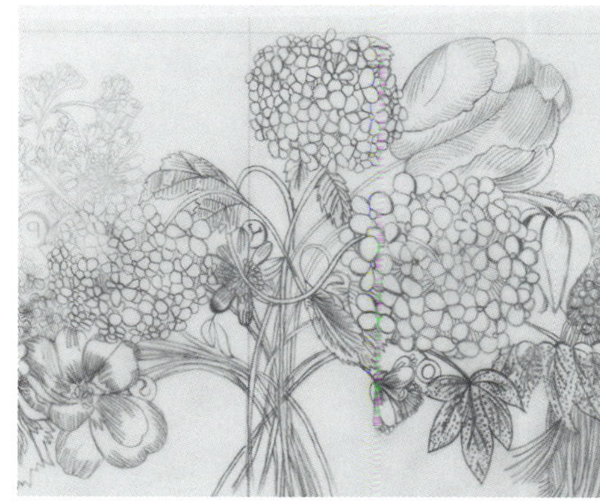

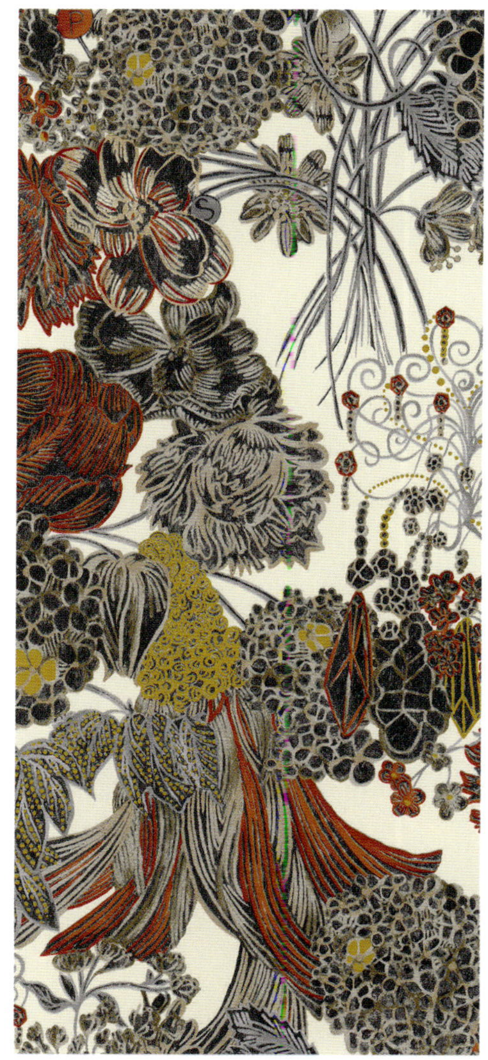

ABOVE *Part of the Glencot House collection for S/S 2012, this design comprises an antique posy created from framed documents, bedroom key tassels, chandeliers, ceramics, Glencot flora and old typewriter keys. It has been painted in the style of an old woodblock print.*

Archives, antiques and costume design were the inspirations for the Spring/Summer 2012 collection, with colour palettes based on the blue-and-white ceramics in the V&A and the British Museum, and on mood boards created by prominent figures in the worlds of fashion, art and antiques – Zandra Rhodes, Isabel Saiz, Martin Miller and Frances Pritchard. There were five design stories, and for the first time the design studio collaborated with high-profile designers working in textiles, costume and set design. The Archive collection was made up of reworked designs chosen from the Liberty archive or inspired by antiques.

Another series of designs evolved from a three-day drawing excursion to Glencot House, a magnificent Jacobean-style Victorian mansion in Somerset owned by antiques guru Martin Miller. The house's beautiful grounds and elegantly theatrical interior, filled with exotic antiques and ancient curiosities, provided a rich source of inspiration, from the glorious gardens to the antique embroideries and even an old patterned chair in the drawing room. The sketches that were made and the photographs that were taken during the trip ultimately generated a collection of highly successful prints.

The third design story of the season was inspired by a visit to Manchester's Whitworth Gallery under the guidance of Frances Pritchard, curator of textiles. Another was inspired by paintings at the National Gallery, chosen by the gallery's Business Development Manager Isabel Saiz for their bold, striking textiles, elegant and romantic blooms, abstract timeless florals and wild impressionist style. The final story comprised five designs inspired by film, selected from an annual collaboration with Central Saint Martins College of Art and Design.

Illustrating the diversity of design from season to season, the concept for the Autumn/Winter collection of the same year was a celebration of innovative textile design through an exploration of the broad spectrum of textile techniques, such as block-printing, weaving, needlepoint, embroidery and screen-printing. The colour palettes were created by digitally enhancing hues from previous seasons and merging entire colour boards to create interesting new shades. The five design stories were Weave, Xylography (block-printing), Printing and Dyeing, Embellishment, Recycling and Digital.

The Embellishment collection focuses on three-dimensional decoration, so print designs were created to represent embroidery, appliqué, needlepoint and lacework. For this group of patterns, the design team worked with Raymond Honeyman, who is best known as a designer for Erhman tapestries. He paints up every one of the 50,000 stitches that make up his needlepoint designs, believing that creating a beautiful piece of artwork is as much a part of the process as the beautiful end product. The first design Honeyman sold after graduating, Snowdrops, was bought by Liberty.

ELEVENSES

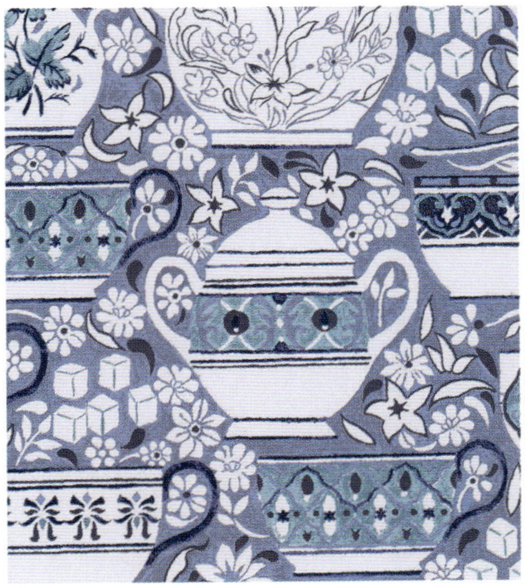

ABOVE *This charming print was inspired by afternoon tea at Glencot House while they sketched. It was loosely based on the "Dancing Ladies" print.*

GLENCOT HOUSE

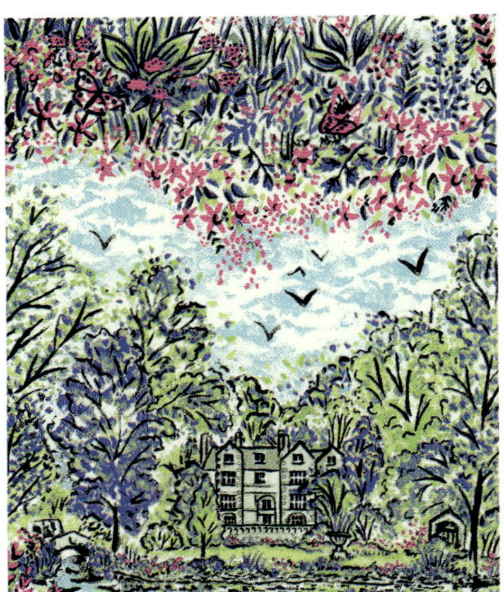

ABOVE *An adjoining field offered the perfect vantage point for painting Glencot within its landscaped gardens. The resulting print is a modern take on a toile de Jouy.*

PAISLEY CASCADE

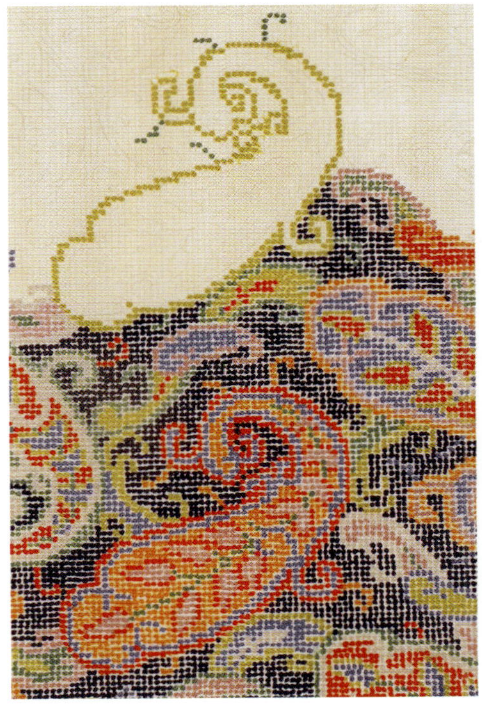

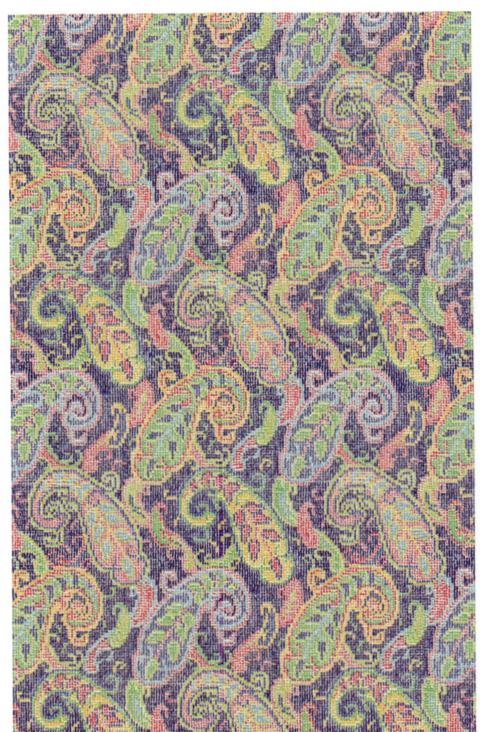

ABOVE *As part of the Embellishment story for A/W 2012, Raymond Honeyman hand-painted 22,000 dashes of colour to represent a needlepoint paisley. He even drew up the grid on which he painted the design. The original artwork is shown (top) with the finished print below.*

RAINBOW ROSE

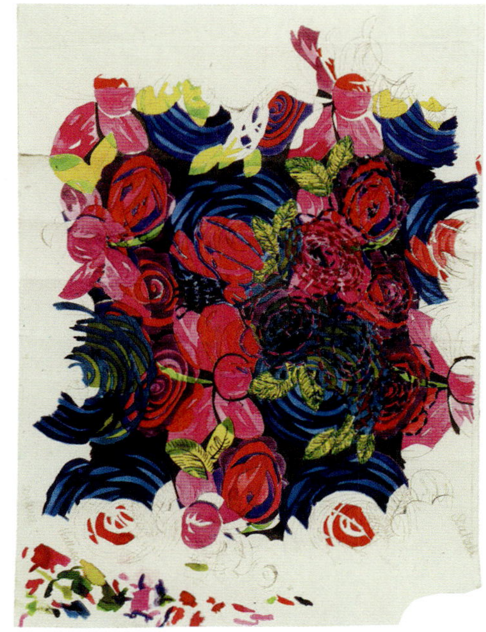

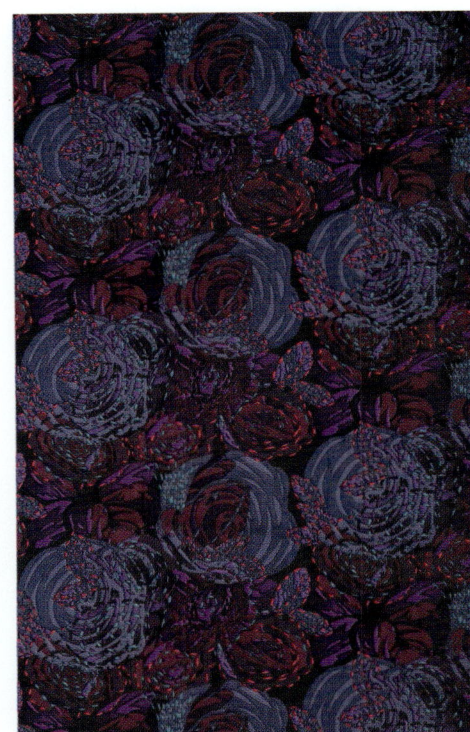

ABOVE *Another print from the Embellishment group, Rainbow Rose is a hand-painted design inspired by Arts and Crafts embroidery with naïve hand-stitching in deep, rich hues.*

GRENVILLE

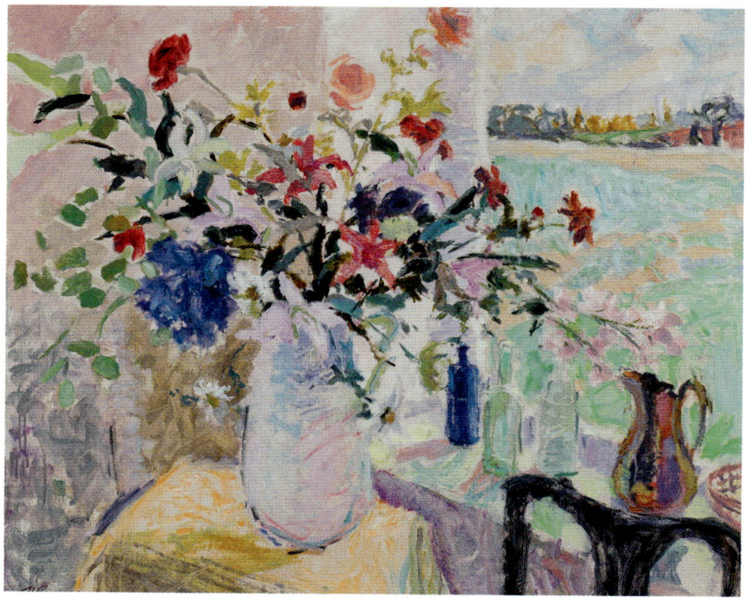

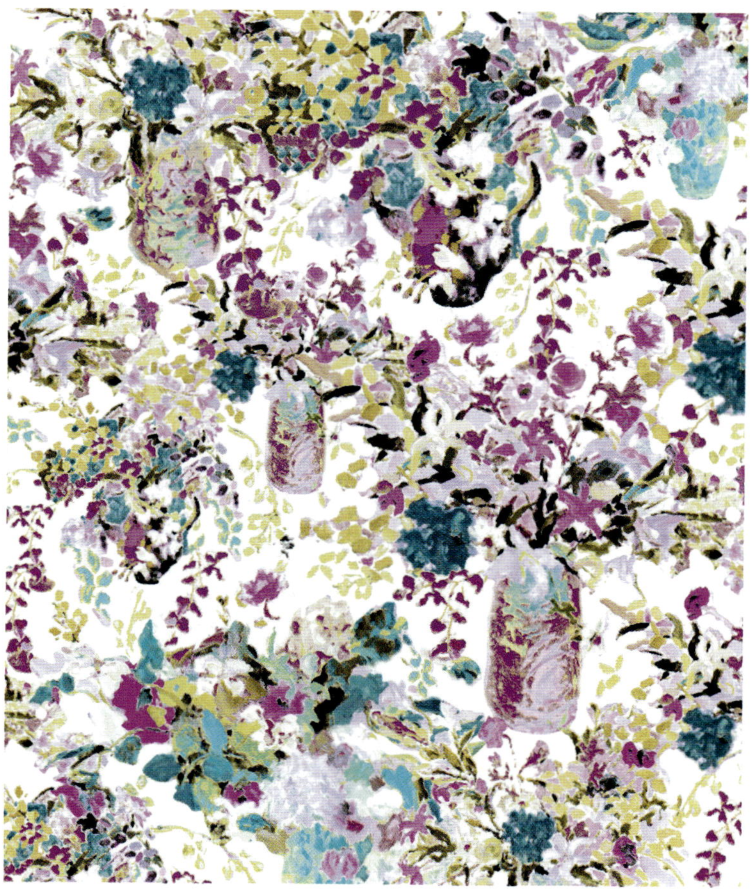

ABOVE *Tresco, one of the Isles of Scilly, is a Mecca for artists such as the botanical painter Hugo Grenville. Created for the S/S 2013 botanical collection called Flower Show, the digitally printed fabric incorporates the vase of flowers from his original painting (top).*

TRESCO

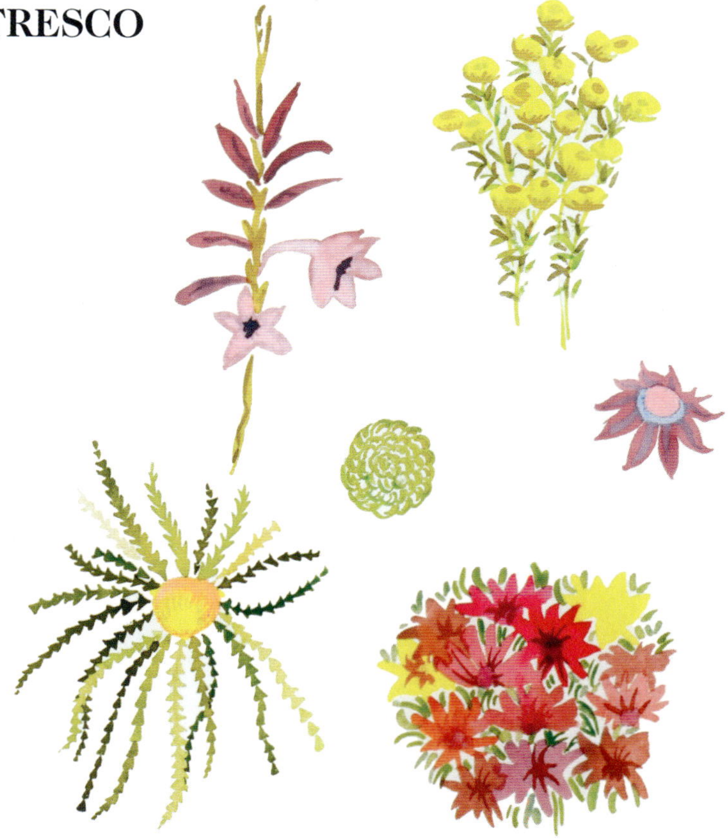

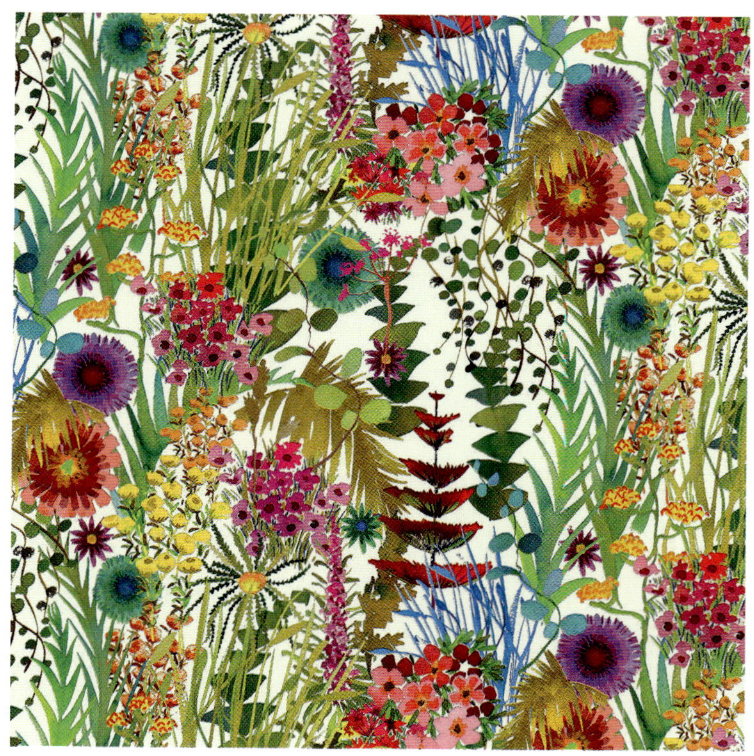

ABOVE *Also for S/S 2013, this lush, verdant print, teeming with colourful flowers, ferns and succulents, was created using watercolour and ink studies of a range of flora growing in the windswept sand dunes of Tresco and the landscaped borders of the Abbey Garden.*

JOY & SORROW

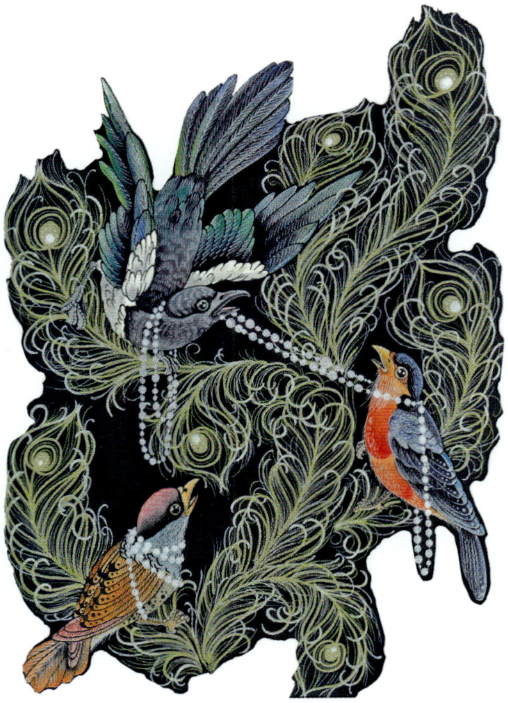

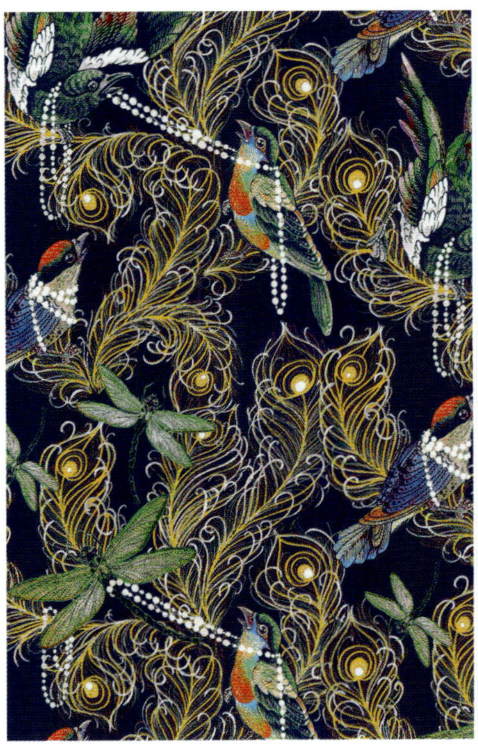

ABOVE *For A/W 2013, tattoo artist Mo Goppoletta collaborated on designs to represent the sense of touch. Derived from Goppoletta's fascination with the dark magic of nursery rhymes, the birds symbolize the Liberty peacock. Other elements were inspired by 1920s Liberty prints.*

MANNING

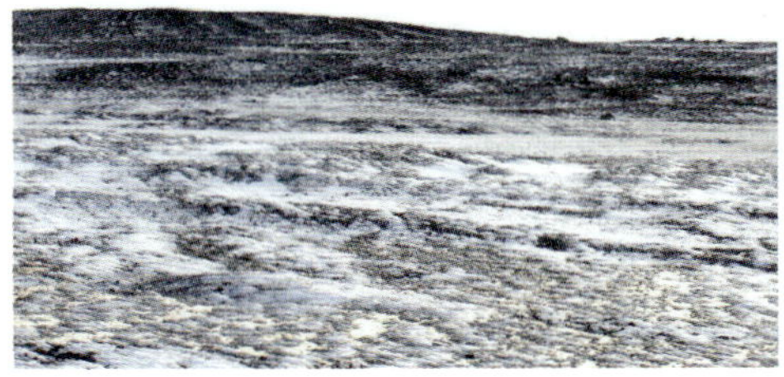

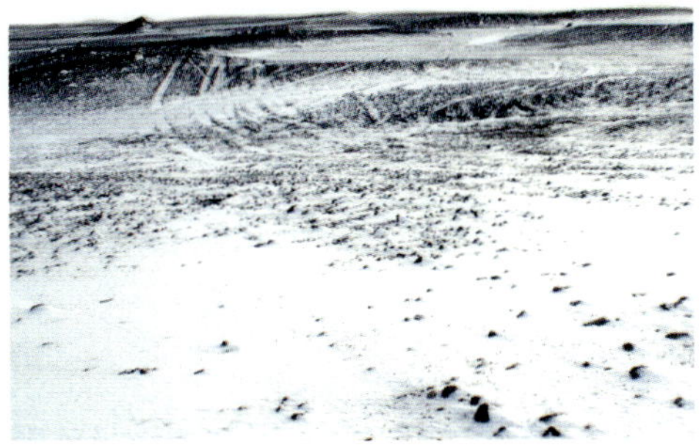

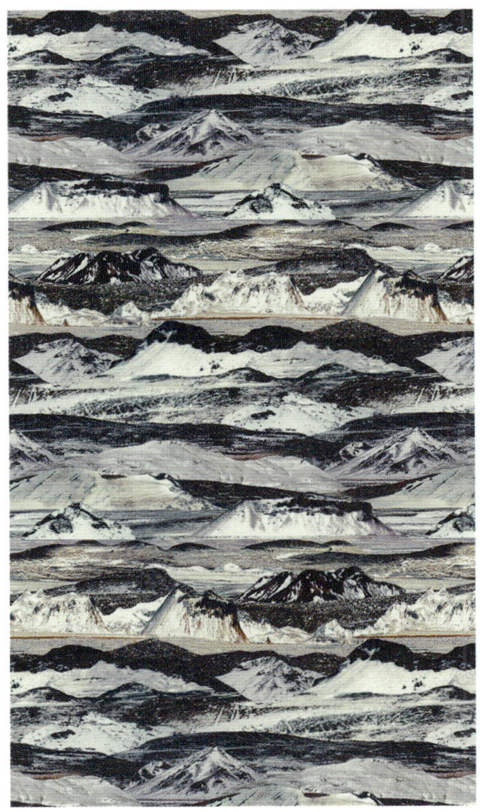

ABOVE *The dramatic scenery of glaciers, mountains, waterfalls, geysers and snow-covered fields inspired the Iceland First Seen collection for A/W 2013, based on the sense of sight. This digital design was created with photographs that the design team took during their trip.*

RAINBOW SALAD

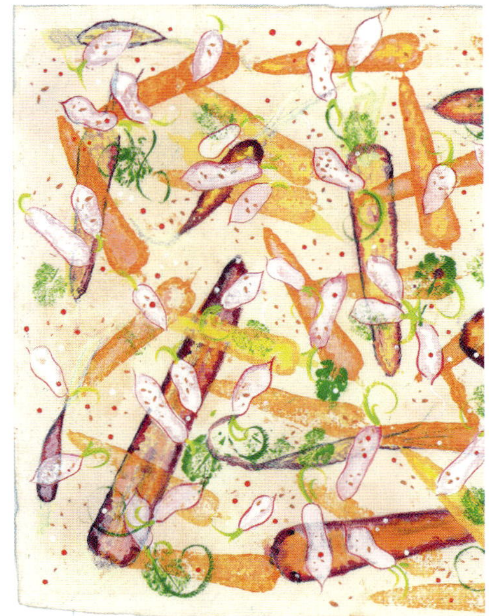

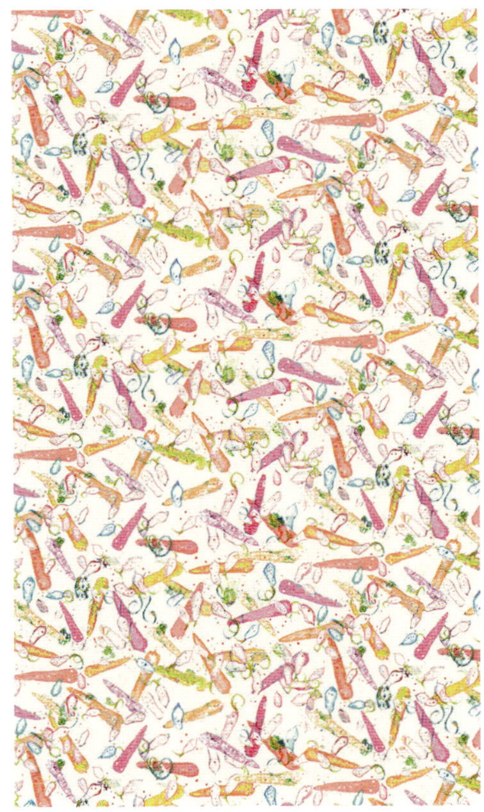

ABOVE *Chef Jamie Oliver collaborated on the A/W 2013 designs relating to the sense of taste. The motifs for this tweed-effect fabric, a digitally printed recipe for Rainbow Salad, were created with carrots and radishes pressed by Jamie and his team.*

ATRIUM

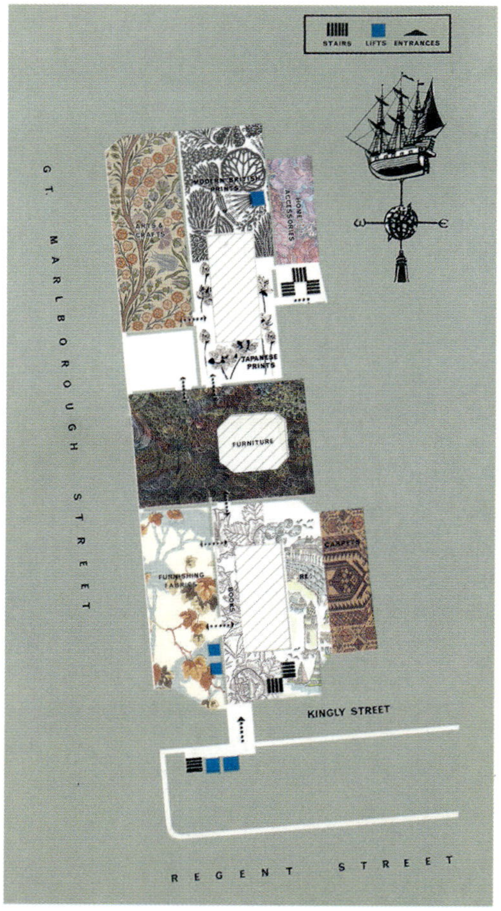

ABOVE *A reworking of an archive floor plan from the 1970s reflects the layout of the flagship store at the time when the S/S 2014 collection was conceived, with individual prints associated with each department in the shop.*

A Gallery of Print is the apt name for the Spring/Summer 2014 collection of 40 limited-edition prints created and curated by the Liberty Art Fabrics design studio, with a number of these designed in collaboration with guest artists and designers. The collection transforms the flagship store into an art gallery, with a print that represents each department on the shop floor.

The six design stories came about by exploring all corners of the Liberty store, from textiles, furniture and fashion to jewellery and ceramics. The designers' briefs were selected from a "lucky dip" of Liberty Print envelopes, which directed them to different departments where they drew what they saw or were inspired by. Some prints were created from original artworks, while others began with an archive print, referencing various periods and global styles from Liberty's history. For example, Poppy's Patchwork, representing the haberdashery department with its portrayal of an intricate patchwork quilt, was created from an archive print that was originally produced as a scarf in 1975. Forget-me-nots, however, representing the handbag room, is a contemporary conversational print featuring the contents of a Liberty lady's handbag.

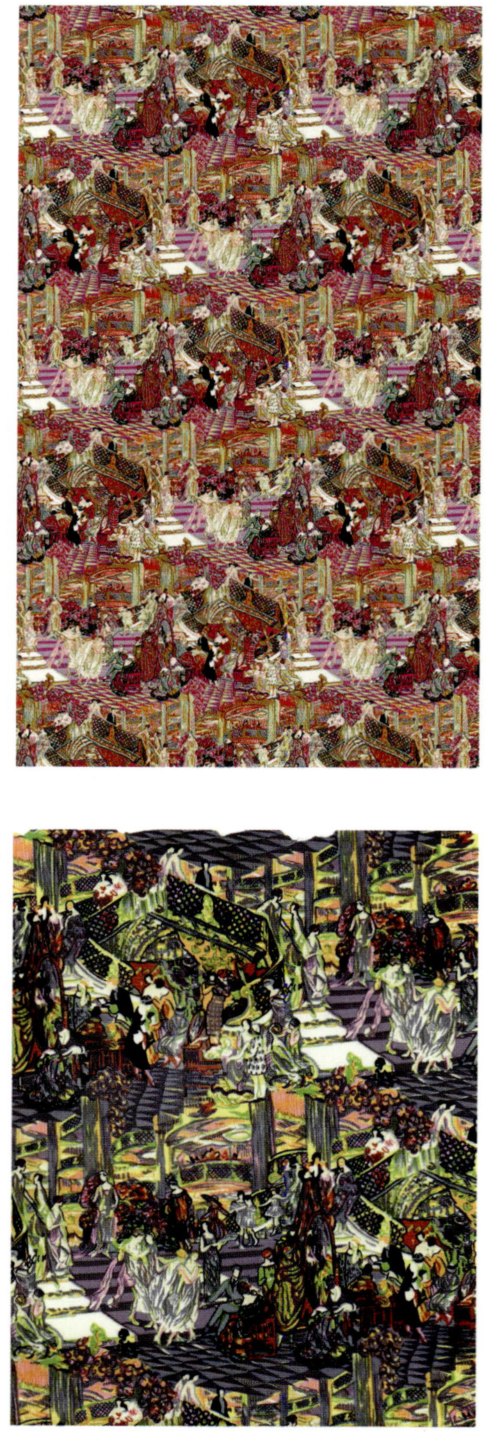

ABOVE *Representing the decadent and theatrical atmosphere of the central atrium of the Liberty department store, this design for S/S 2014 (top) was based on an archive print from 1972 (bottom), which in turn was based on a book illustration.*

ESTELLA & ANNABELLE

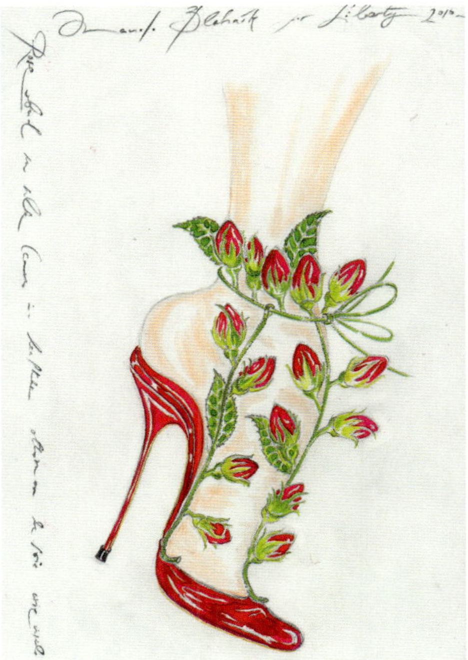

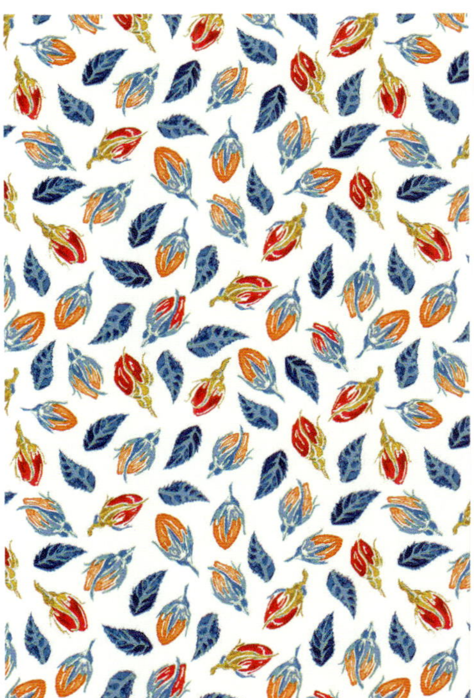

ABOVE *Liberty's second floor is dedicated to food, fashion and footwear; Estella & Annabelle represents the shoe department. The original artwork (top) of this exquisite design of scattered rose buds (bottom) was hand-painted by the shoe designer Manolo Blahnik.*

HOLLY

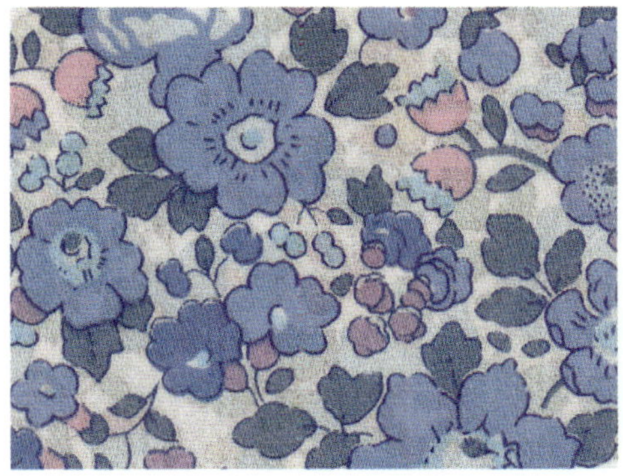

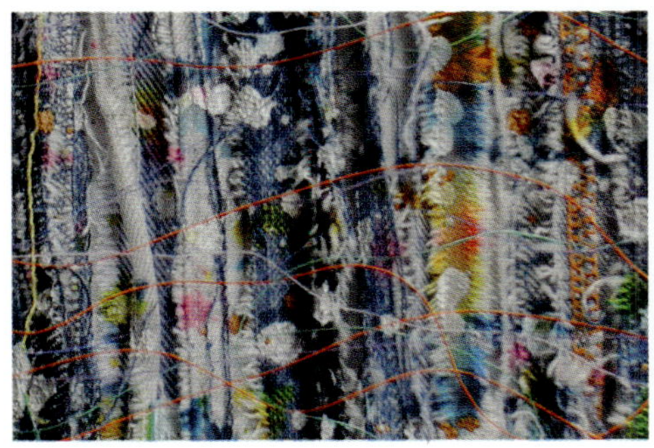

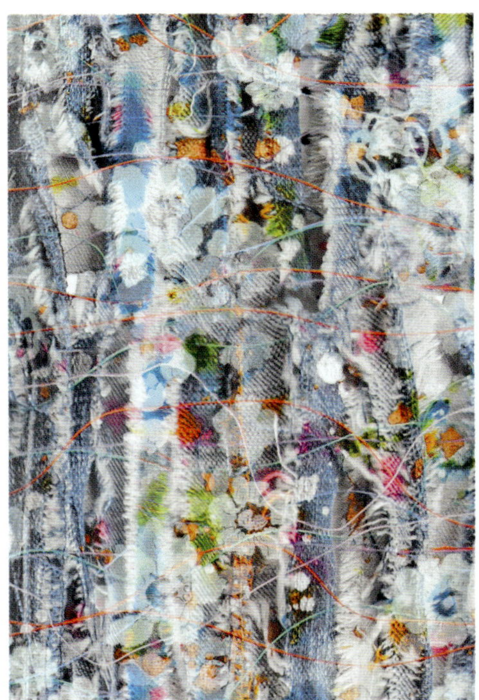

ABOVE *The first floor is dedicated to fashion, and Holly (bottom) represents Denim and Casual Wear. The creative process involved ripping pairs of jeans into strips and covering them in multi-coloured ink droplets (middle). The result was then manipulated digitally, working in elements of the floral print Betsy (top), originally designed in 1933.*

PTOLEMY

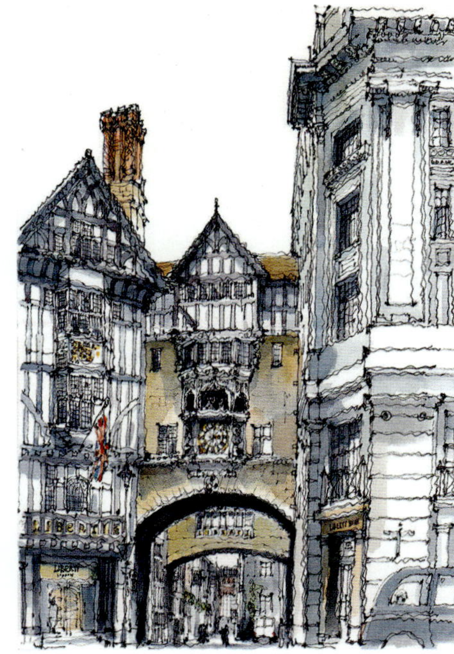

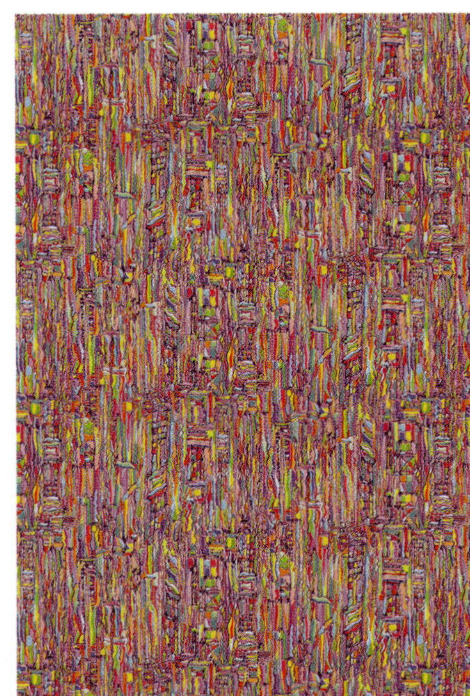

ABOVE *Ptolemy Dean, Surveyor of the Fabric of Westminster Abbey, has been painting and sketching Britain's architectural heritage for more than 25 years. The geometric print named after him (bottom) represents Liberty's famous façade as seen through the fuzzy TV screen that he remembers from his childhood in the 1970s. The print was based on his original watercolour (top).*

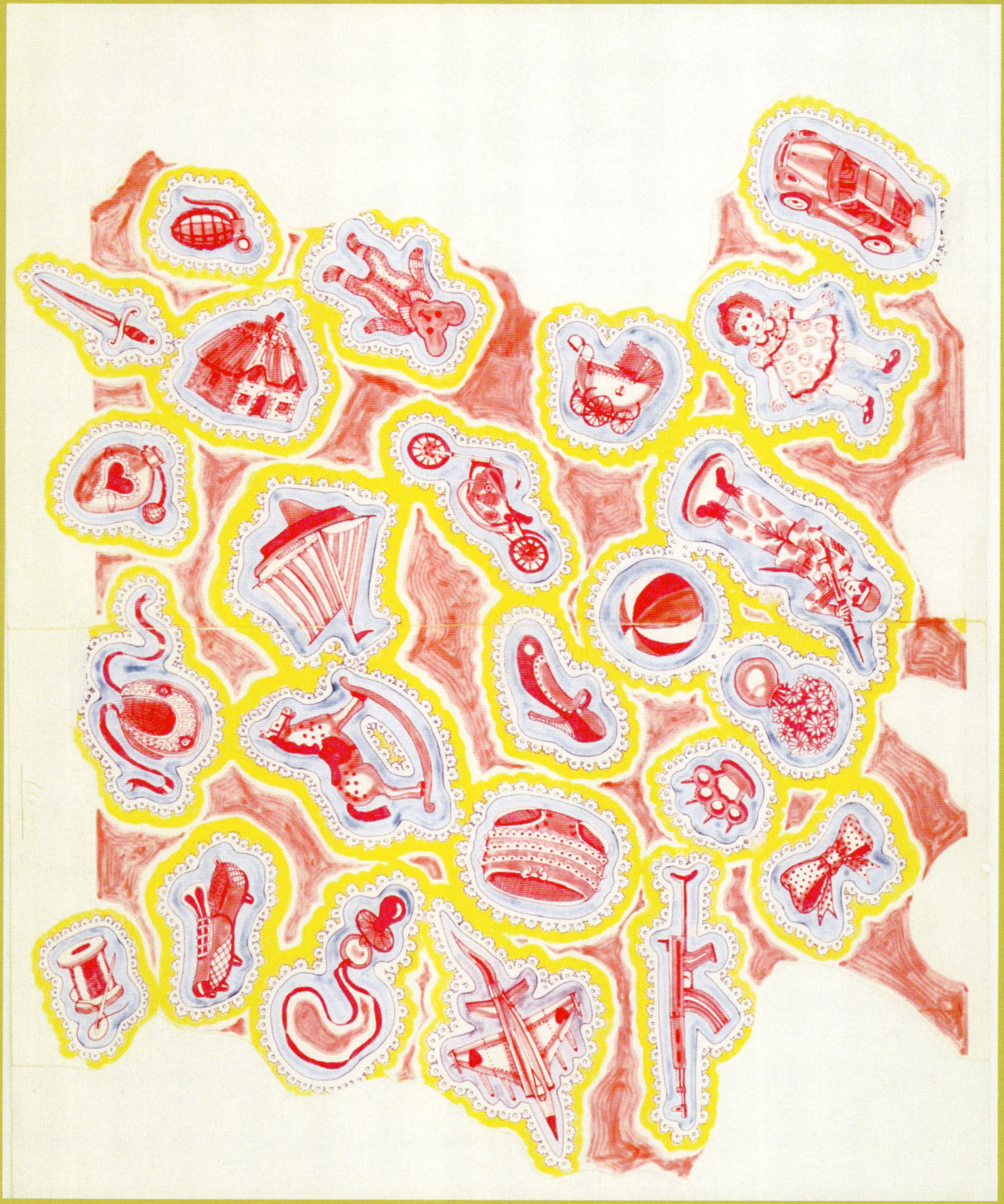

GRAYSON PERRY SKETCH FOR SISSY, 2009

Facsimile of an original sketch for the Sissy print by Grayson Perry.

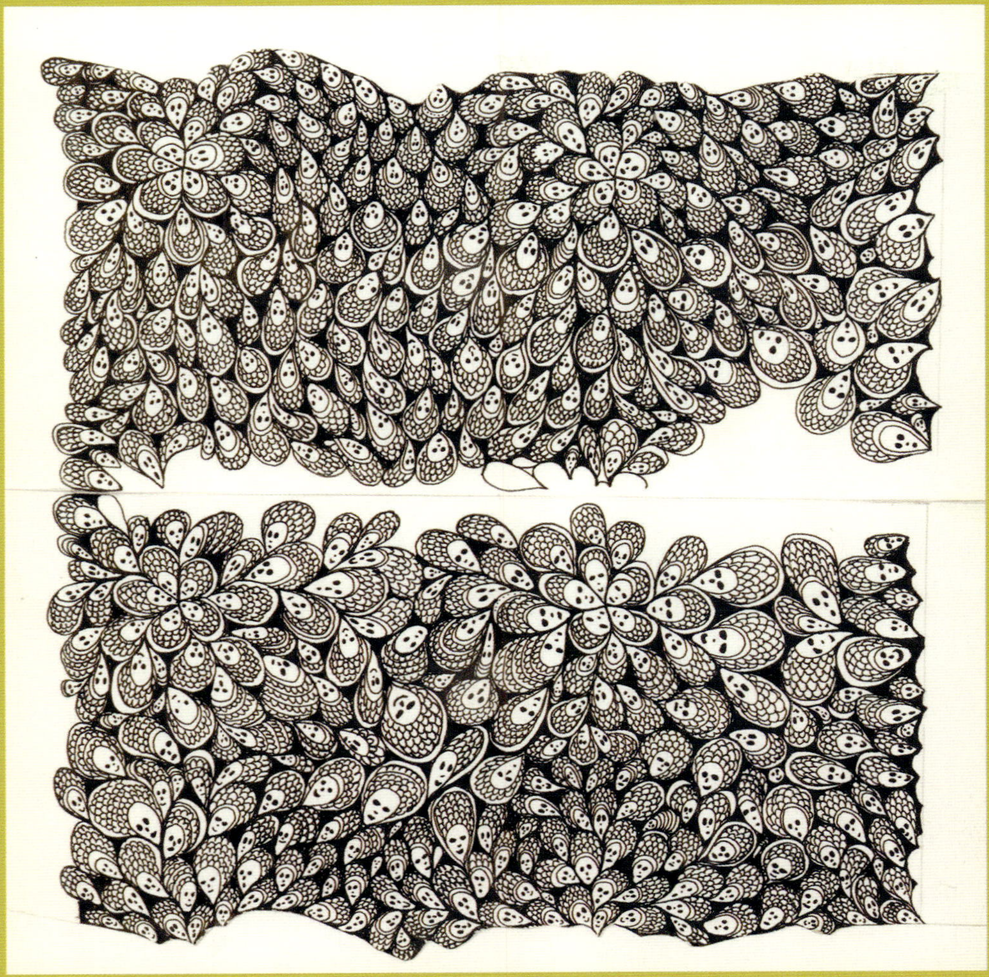

GRAYSON PERRY SKETCH FOR CRANFORD, 2009

Facsimile of an original hand-drawn pen drawing by Grayson Perry, showing the repeat pattern of the Cranford print.

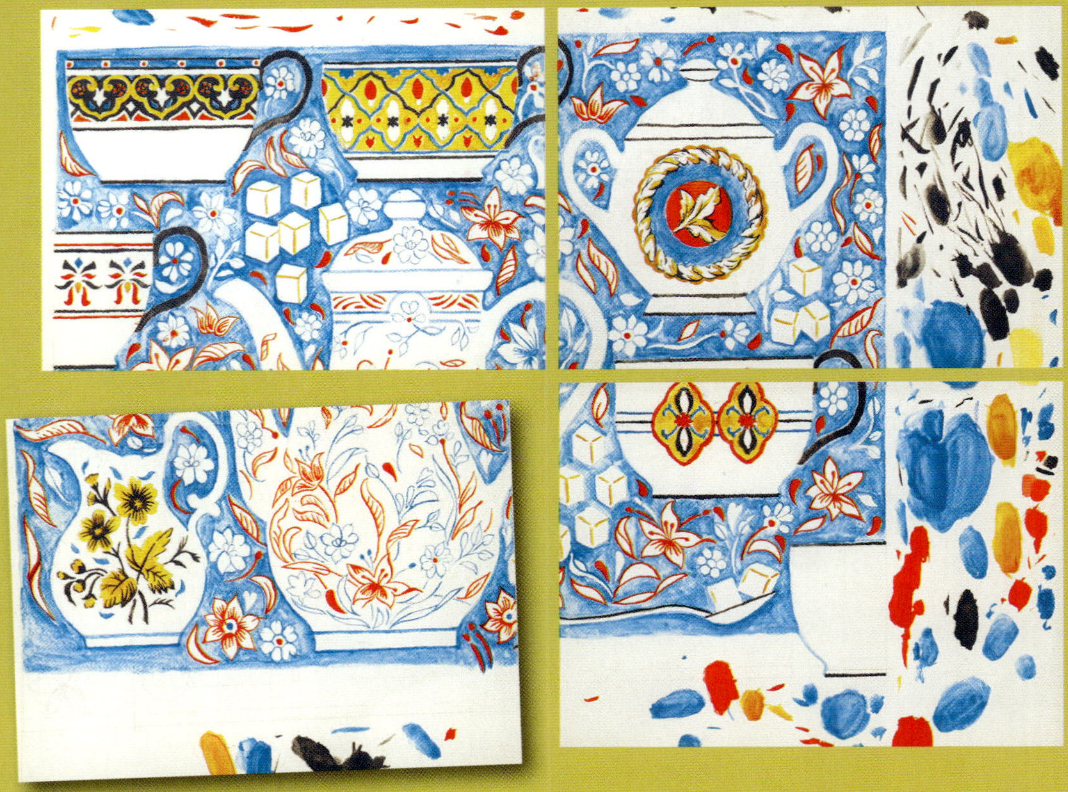

SKETCH FOR ELEVENSES, 2012

A hand-painted drawing worked over four sheets of paper for the Elevenses print by the Liberty Design Studio, inspired by afternoon tea during a trip to Glencot House in Somerset.

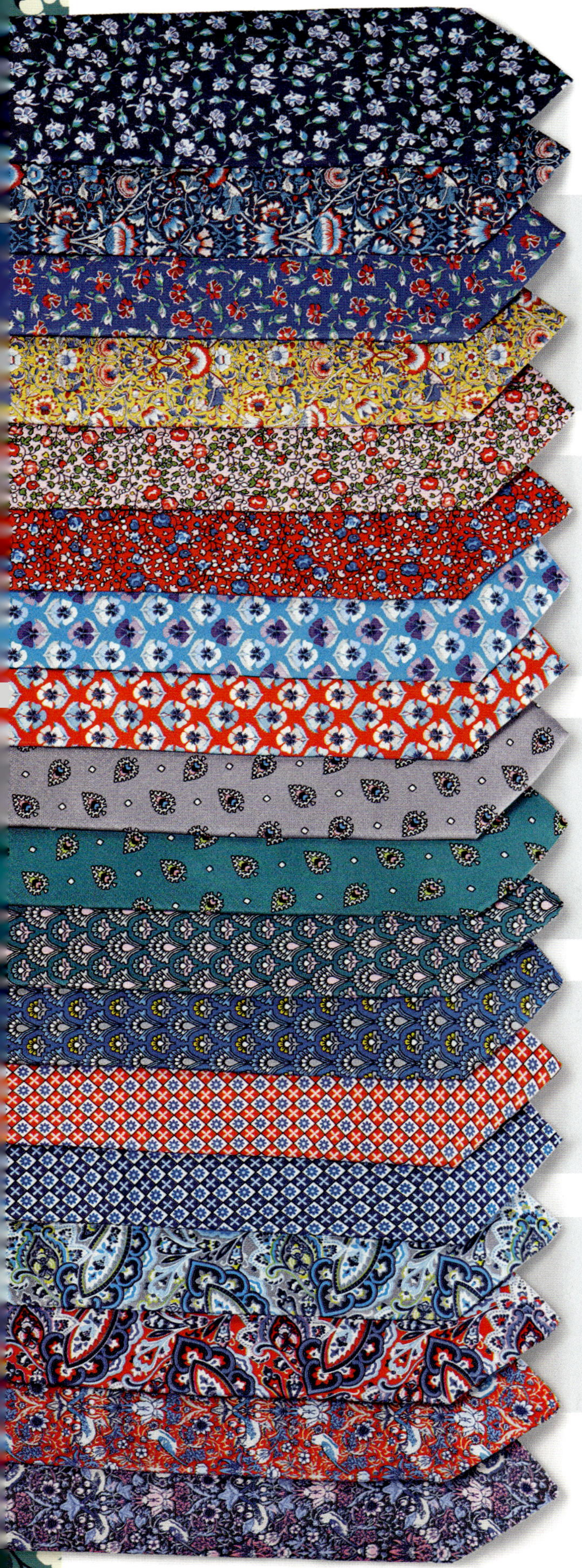

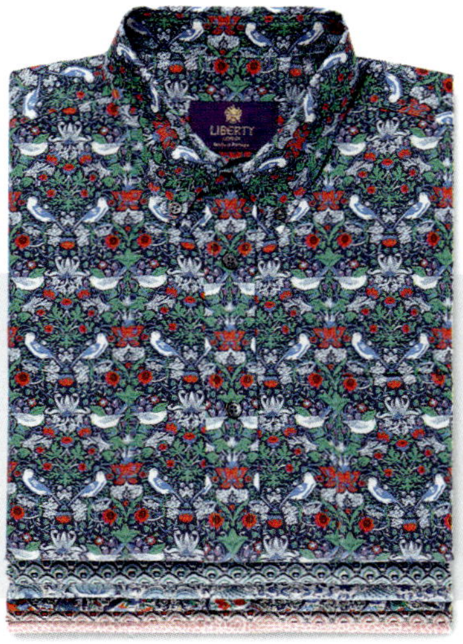

LEFT *Liberty of London's menswear includes classic cotton shirts featuring iconic floral, paisley, geometric, abstract and conversation prints. Each season, different archive prints are introduced and reworked in the new colourways.*

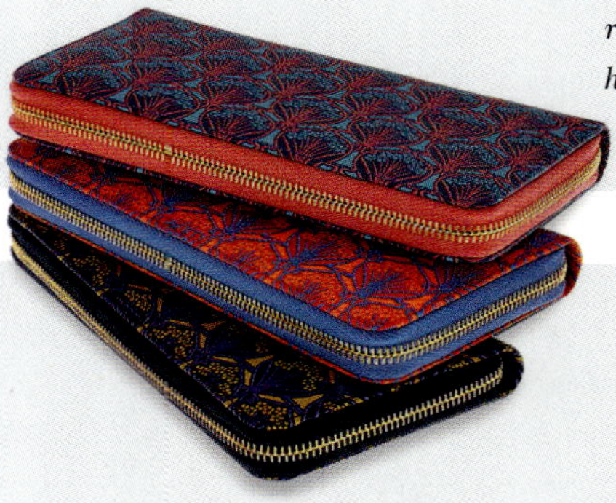

LEFT *The small accessories range by Liberty of London has undergone a recent relaunch and includes a collection of must-have items in classic Liberty prints.*

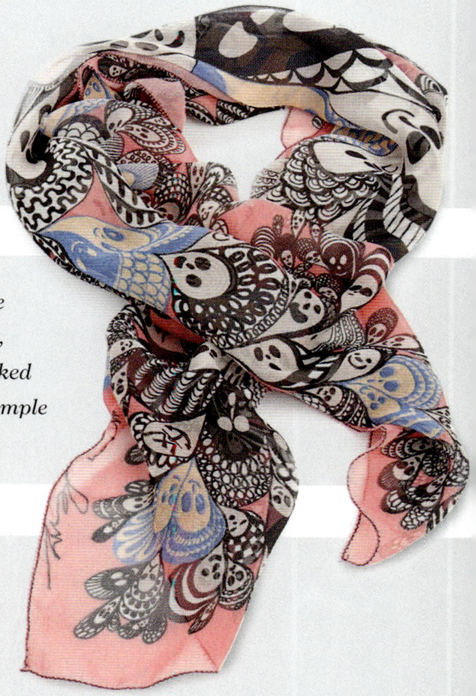

RIGHT *Liberty's artistic scarf collection is one of the things for which Liberty is best known, with exquisite new designs as well as reworked archive prints created each season. This example is designed by artist Grayson Perry.*

LEFT *Together with scarves, colourful printed ties by Liberty of London have remained steady sellers throughout Liberty's history. They were originally block-printed at Liberty's factory in Merton before being transferred to the silk-printing works of David Evans.*

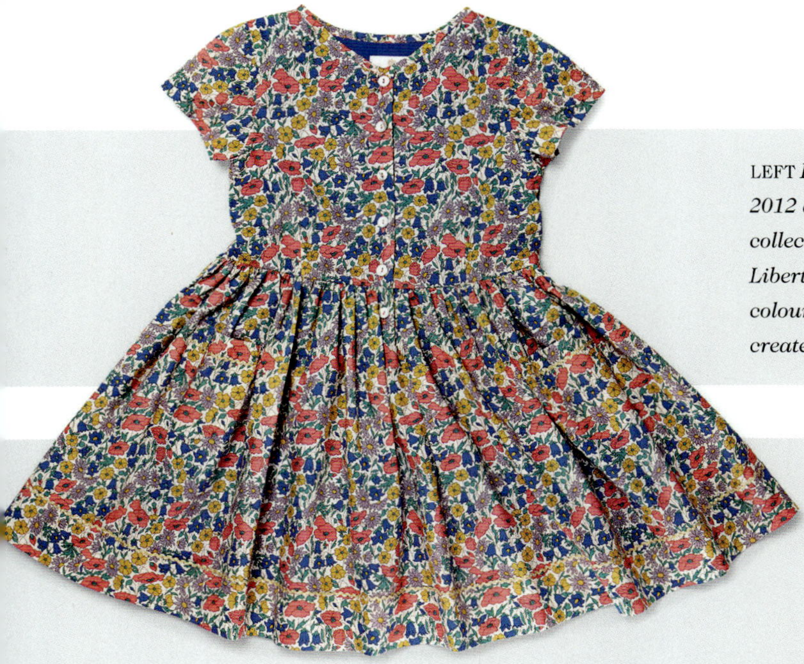

LEFT *Little Liberty was relaunched in 2012 and includes a beautiful capsule collection of quintessentially British Liberty of London childrenswear in colourful and imaginative prints created in the Art Fabrics design studio.*

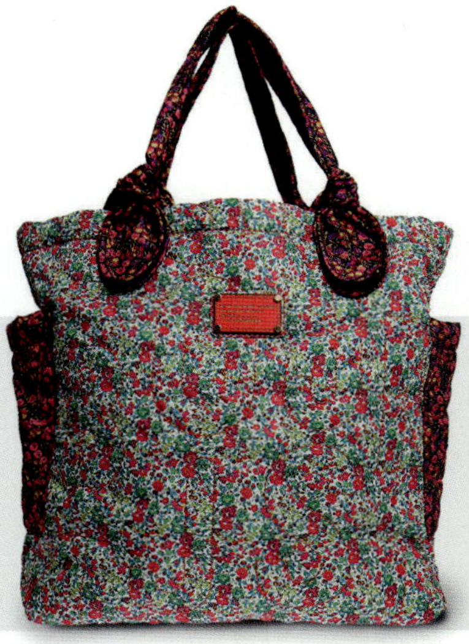

ABOVE *A bag from the Liberty Pretty Nylon collection from S/S 2013. It features two prints, Emma & Georgina (the floral) and Wiltshire Berry (the trim), selected by the team at Marc by Marc Jacobs from Liberty's Classic collection. Each shape in this limited edition range of accessories features Marc Jacobs' name in stitching across it.*

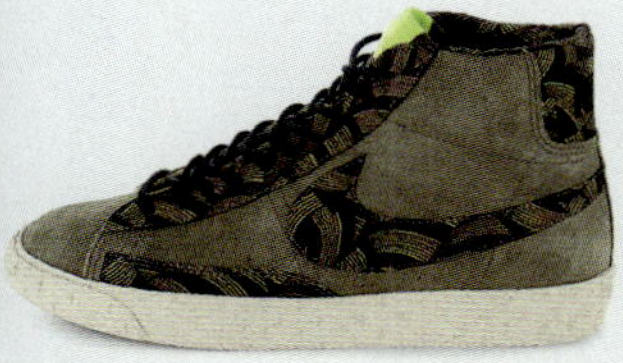

LEFT & BELOW *Nike and Liberty have teamed up successfully for several seasons to reinvent some of the sportswear brand's favourites in signature Liberty prints – from classic florals, such as Kate Ada (bottom right), to Brian Wildsmith's Model Planes designed for the S/S 2011 Storybook collection (left). Liberty have also collaborated with French brand L'Espadrille Tropézienne on a range of prettily patterned espadrilles, including Macleod (bottom left).*

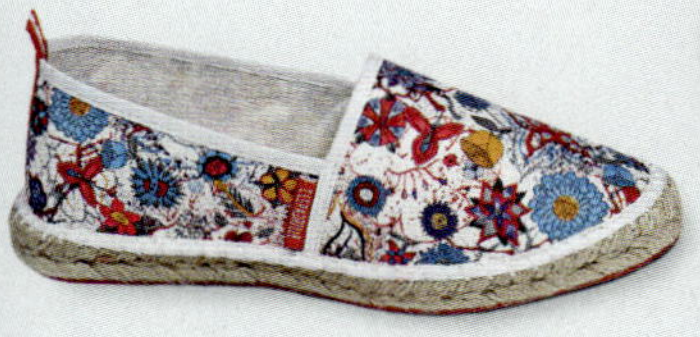

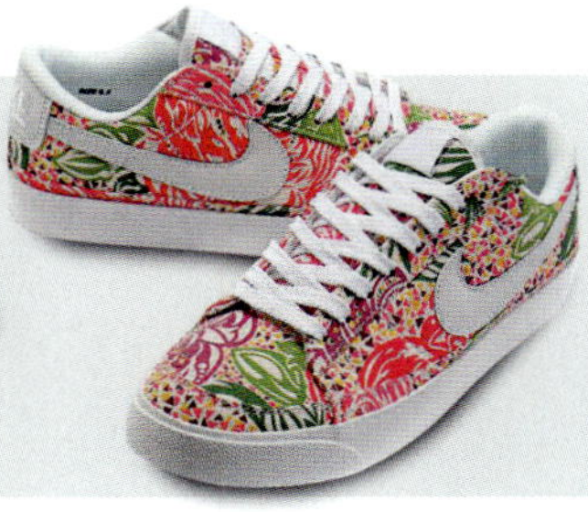

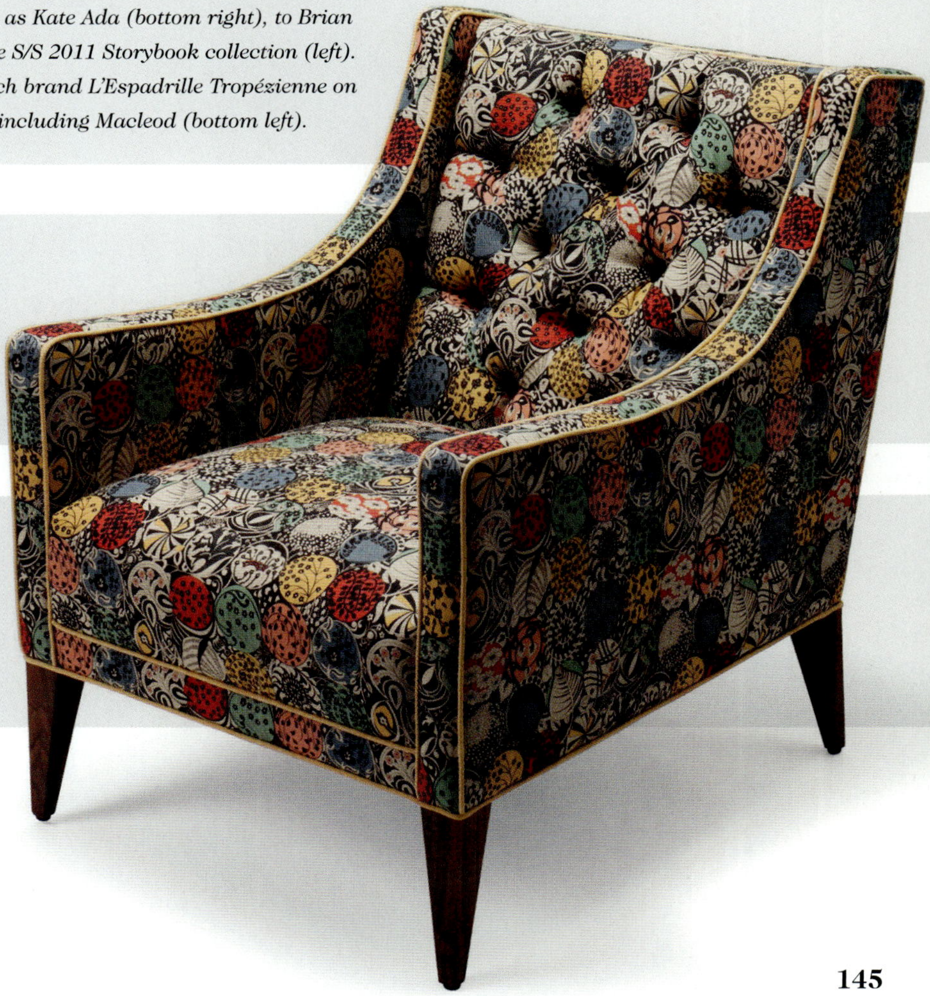

RIGHT *Stuart Scott's timeless Sartor armchair has been upholstered in September Roslynd linen union with contrast yellow piping. The multi-coloured print is from Liberty's 2012 debut Jubilee collection of furnishing fabrics.*

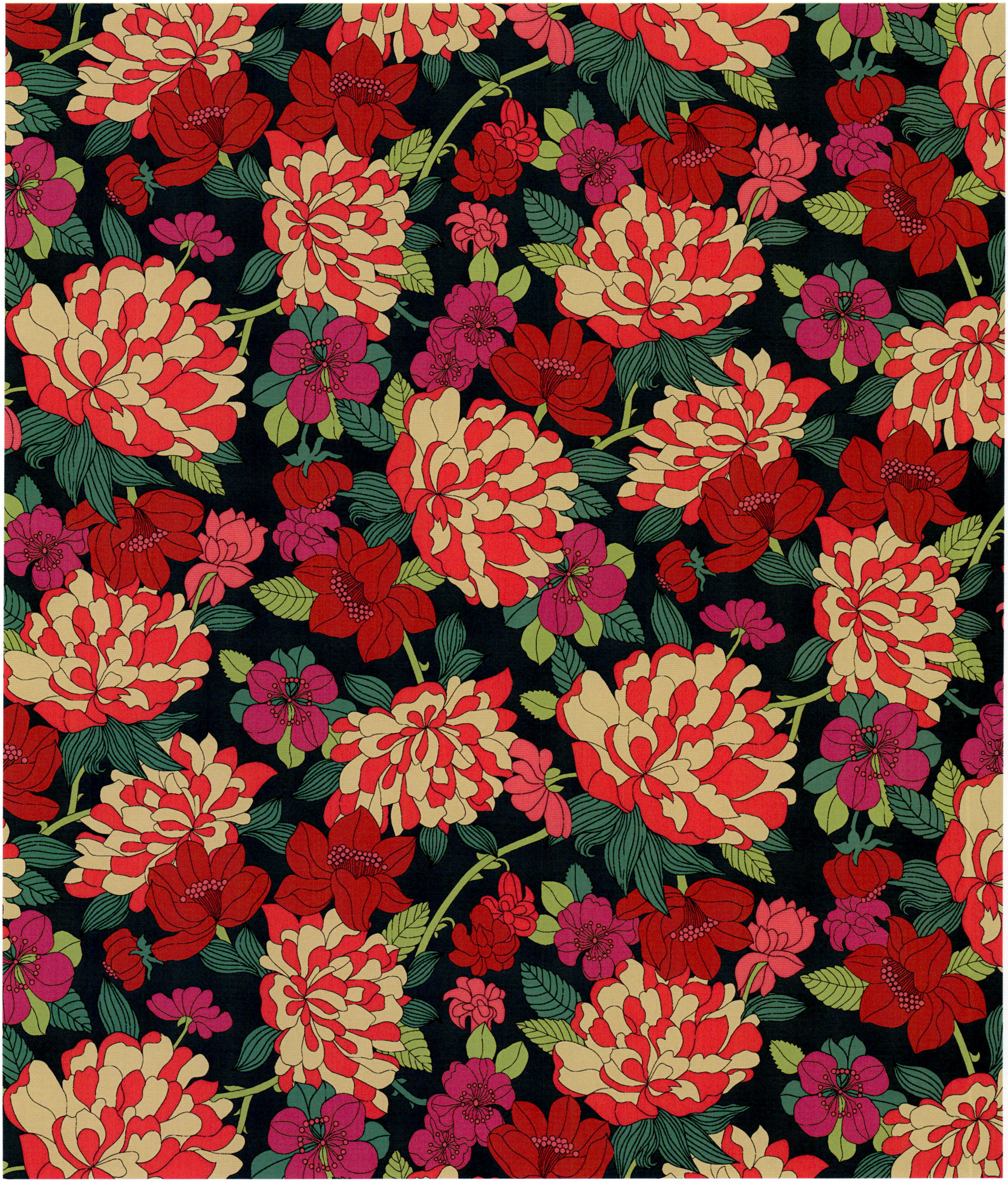

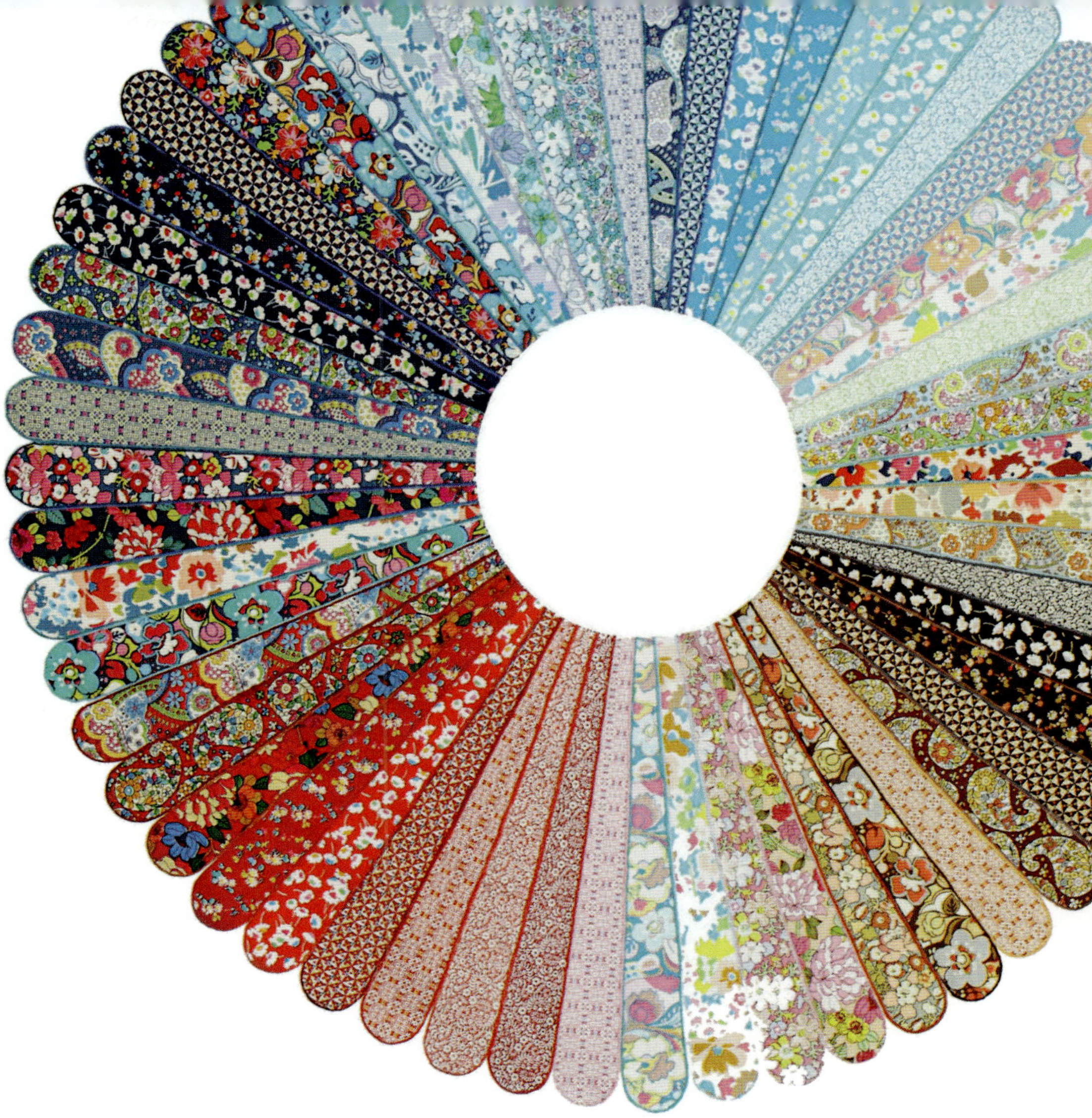

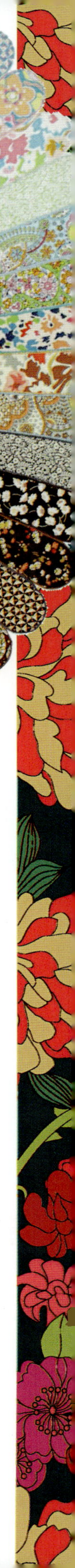

LIFESTYLE FABRICS

Liberty Lifestyle Fabrics, launched in 2012, provides a collection of exciting Liberty prints in a range of cottons that are perfect for patchworking, quilting, crafting and sewing projects. As with the fashion fabrics, the Liberty archive provides a rich source of heritage designs that are reworked and reinterpreted to create a new collection each season.

Bloomsbury Gardens was the first collection of 11 prints inspired by the rich cultural history and architecture of London's Bloomsbury district, with its beautiful garden squares brimming with plants and flowers. The area gave its name to the Bloomsbury Group of English intellectuals in the early 1900s, whose members included writers Virginia Woolf and E. M. Forster, and artists Duncan Grant and Vanessa Bell. The second collection of craft-weight cotton fabrics was inspired by the Art Nouveau movement and specifically the work of architect and designer Charles Rennie Mackintosh, a major exponent of the style. Liberty designs captured the spirit of the Art Nouveau movement to such an extent that the two were inextricably linked and in Italy known as "Stile Liberty". Consequently, the Liberty archive provided a rich source of inspiration for the eight designs produced in four colour palettes and the collection was named Stile.

ABOVE *Liberty patterns have always played with the full colour spectrum, pairing both bold contrasts and sublte complements.*

CATHERINE

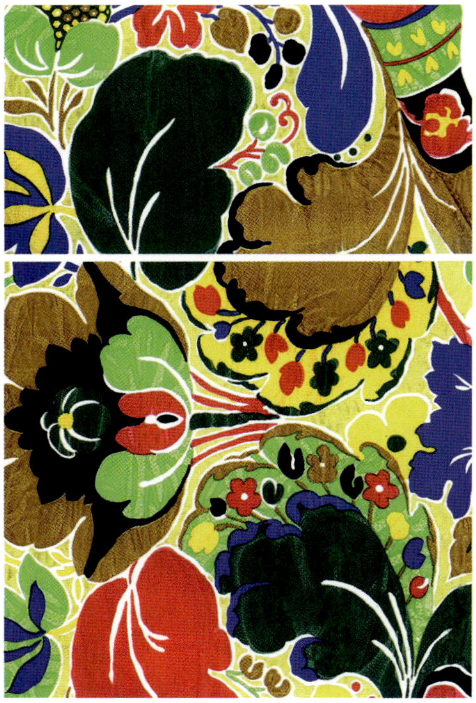

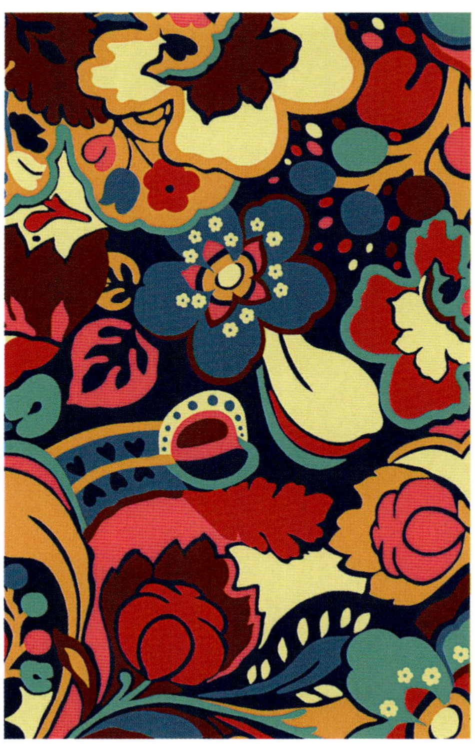

ABOVE *Part of the Bloomsbury Gardens collection, this colourful floral print (bottom) is a reworking of a design created for Liberty in 1969 and printed in 1971 (top). It was inspired by a screen in Duncan Grant's studio, painted by the artist in the 1930s.*

COPELAND

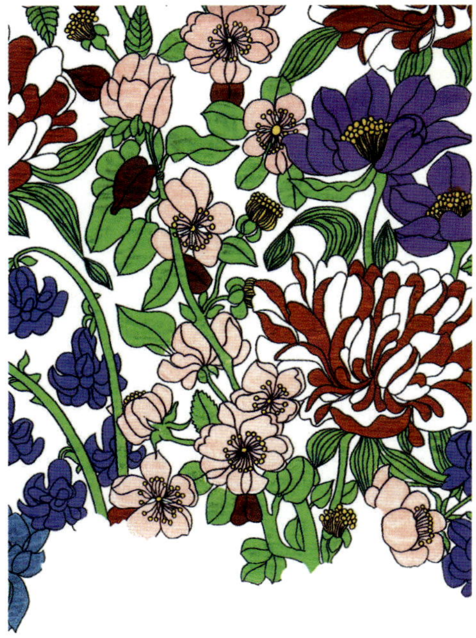

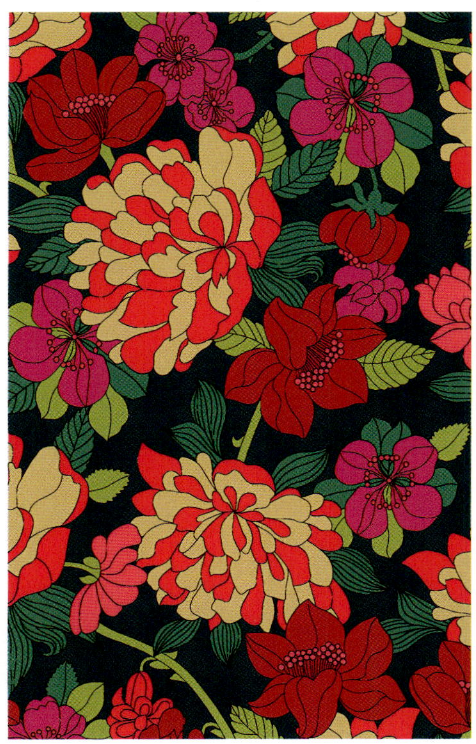

ABOVE *This print (bottom) represents the bouquets of flowers seen on the more traditional upholstery at Charleston, former home of Vanessa Bell and Duncan Grant. It was based on a Liberty archive print designed in 1965 and originally printed at Merton (top).*

DOROTHY

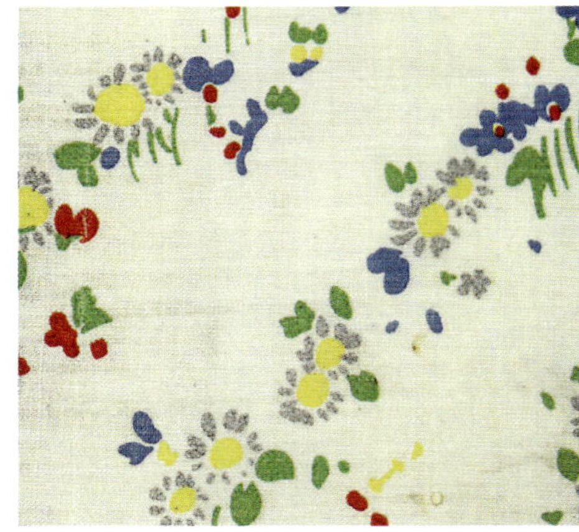

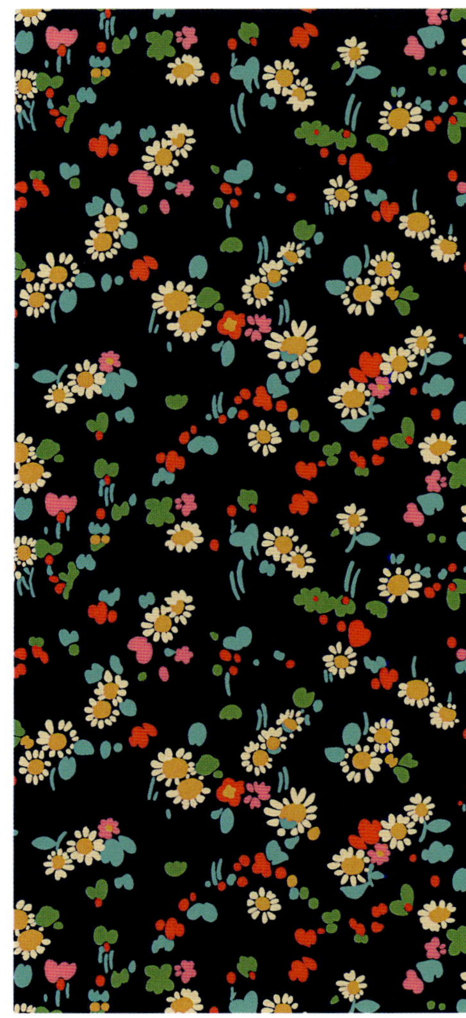

ABOVE *Flowers and abstract shapes (bottom), adapted from a design created for Liberty in 1937 (top), float on a background designed to represent a fabric created by Duncan Grant, Grapes, and used to upholster Venetian chairs at Charleston.*

RENNIE

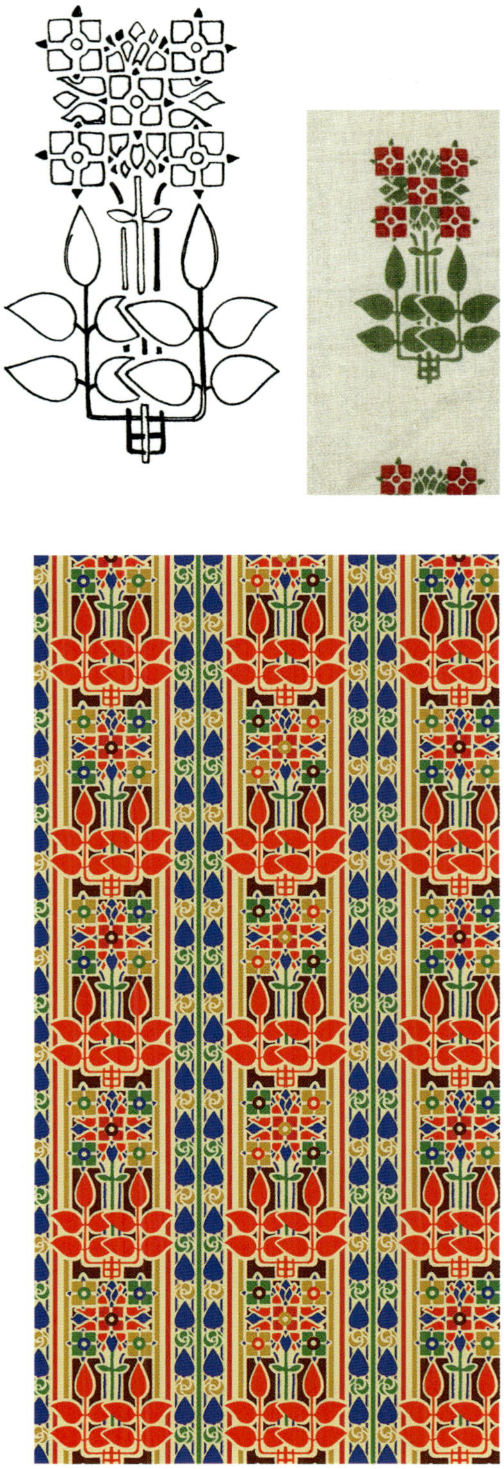

ABOVE *A Liberty archive design from the Art Nouveau era (top) has been reworked and added to (bottom), reflecting elements from the Willow Tea Room in Glasgow, which was designed by Charles Rennie Mackintosh, one of the major influences of the Stile collection.*

WELLS

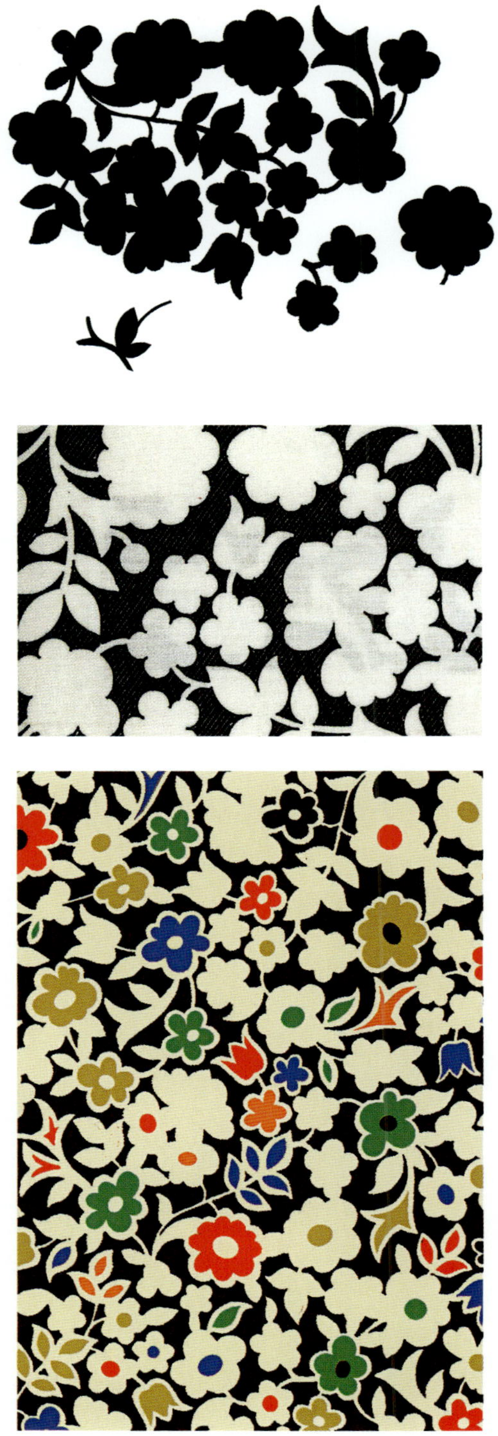

ABOVE *An original monochrome archive print from 1933 (middle) was reworked (top) for the Stile collection to incorporate more elements and a vibrant colour palette, while still retaining the simplicity of this pretty design.*

HERBERT

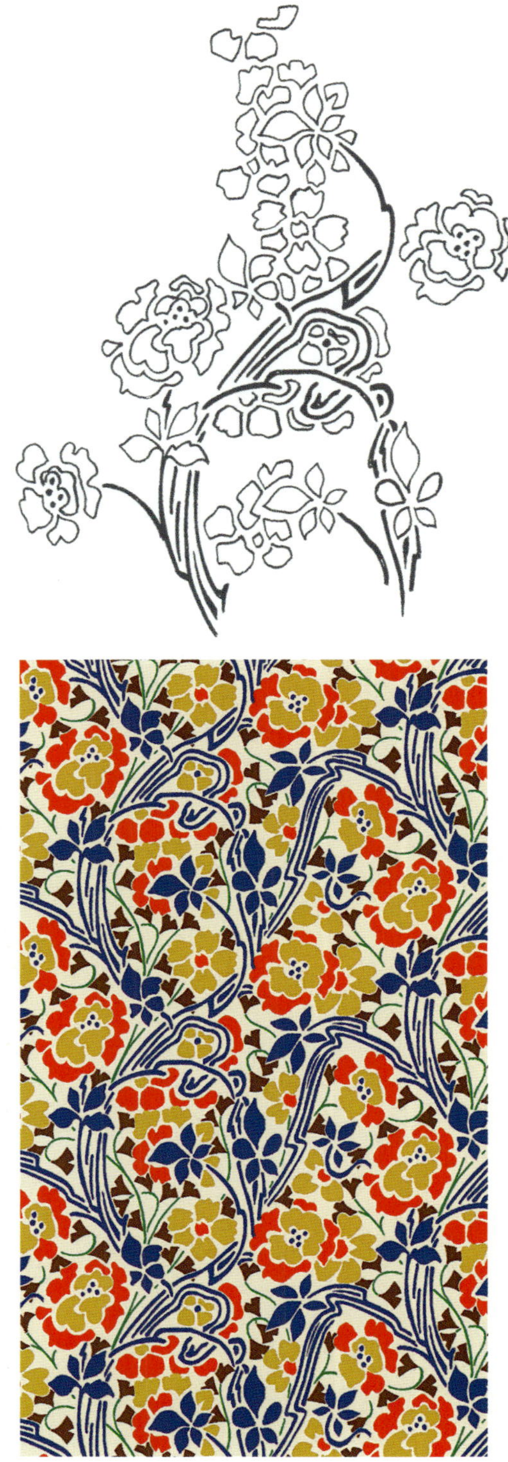

ABOVE *The vivid blooms on swirling stems that make up this energetic Stile print were based on an archive design produced for Liberty in the early 1900s (top), with additional elements incorporated and a rich colour palette applied.*

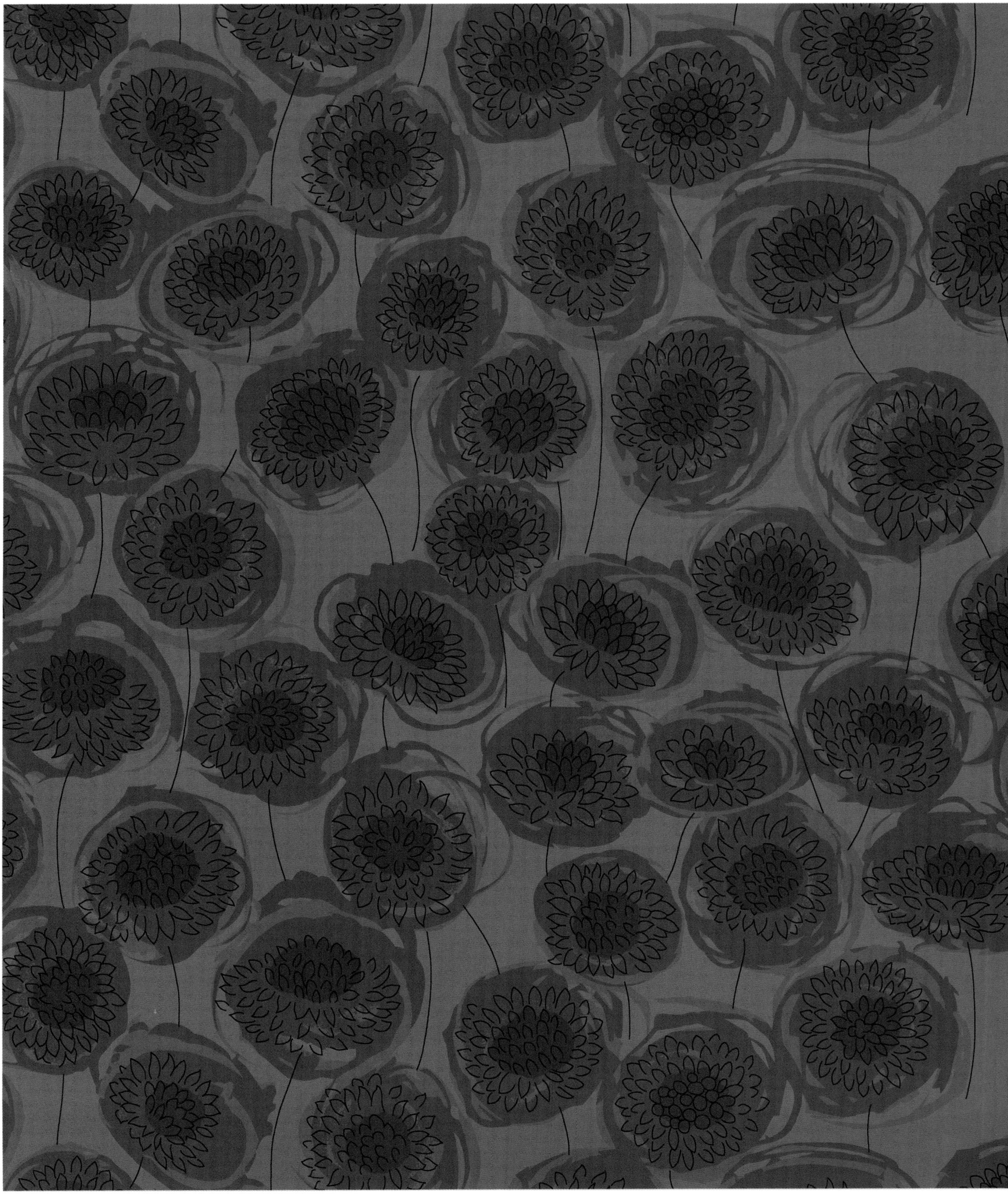

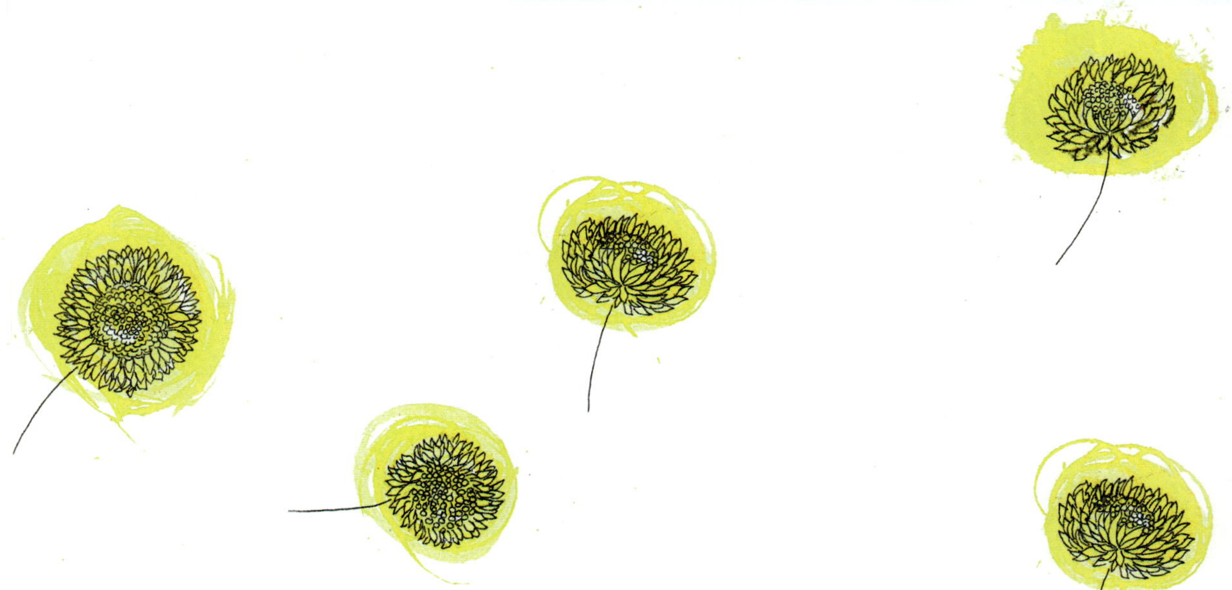

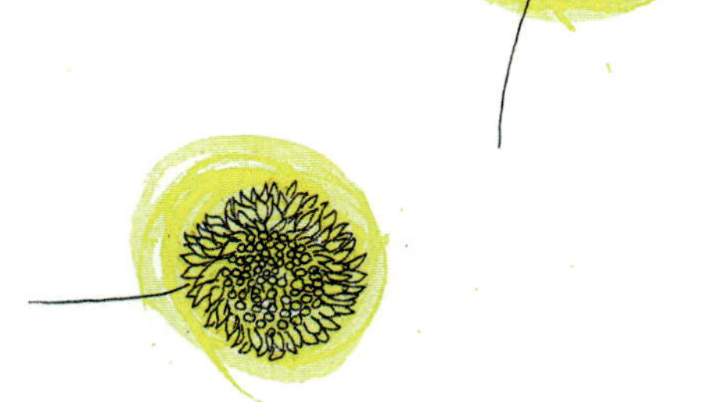

FURNISHING FABRICS

Liberty has a strong history in the production of innovative home furnishings, but for many years the rights to its archive prints – a rich source of inspiration – were licensed to manufacturers Osborne & Little. Liberty has now brought them back in-house, and in 2012, celebrated the launch of its first home furnishings collection for 15 years.

Designed by the Liberty Art Fabrics studio and manufactured in England, the debut Jubilee collection comprised high-quality linens, cottons and velvets featuring an eclectic selection of prints that represent all the different styles indelibly associated with Liberty. This quintessentially British collection has the distinctive Liberty spirit, derived as it is from heritage prints influenced heavily by nature, art and architecture. Bold Oriental fruit and foliage patterns, detailed cartography, and Art Nouveau- and William Morris-inspired prints sit alongside traditional paisleys, stylized roses and classic Liberty florals. For example, the Hardy Wingback armchair, pictured overleaf, is upholstered in the iconic Ianthe, which was originally created as a wallpaper border by an Art Nouveau French designer around 1902, first printed for fashion in 1967 and then reworked as a furnishing fabric for the Jubilee collection.

The Nesfield collection, launched in 2013, was the first wholesale collection and was accompanied by a complementary range of wallpapers and paints. The collection was named after the landscape architect William Nesfield, who, it is believed, was a friend or acquaintance of Arthur Liberty. The colour stories were inspired by his most famous gardens, including Castle Howard and Kew Gardens. Many of the prints within this beautiful, bohemian collection were created from designs that have also been reworked for fashion fabrics, including the classic peacock-feather print Hera, William Morris's Merton Sunflower and Tresco-inspired Xanthe Sunbeam. Based on original research and eschewing the vagaries of interiors fashions, the Liberty home furnishings range continues with its own distinctive identity.

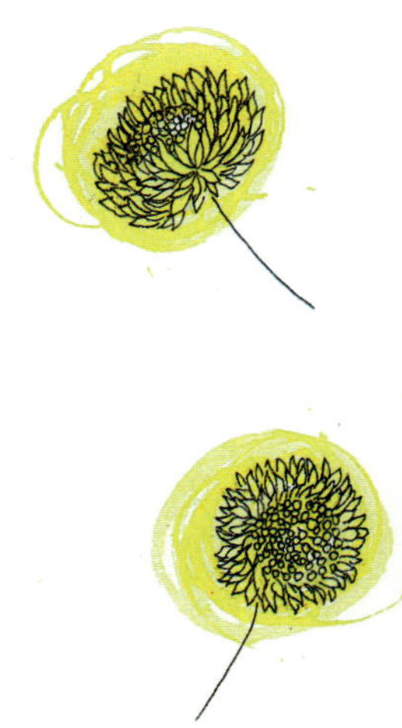

OPPOSITE *Field of Xanthe Sunbeams, from the Nesfield collection, is derived from hand-painted sketches (right) of scattered tansy flowers that surrounded the Abbey Garden on Tresco.*

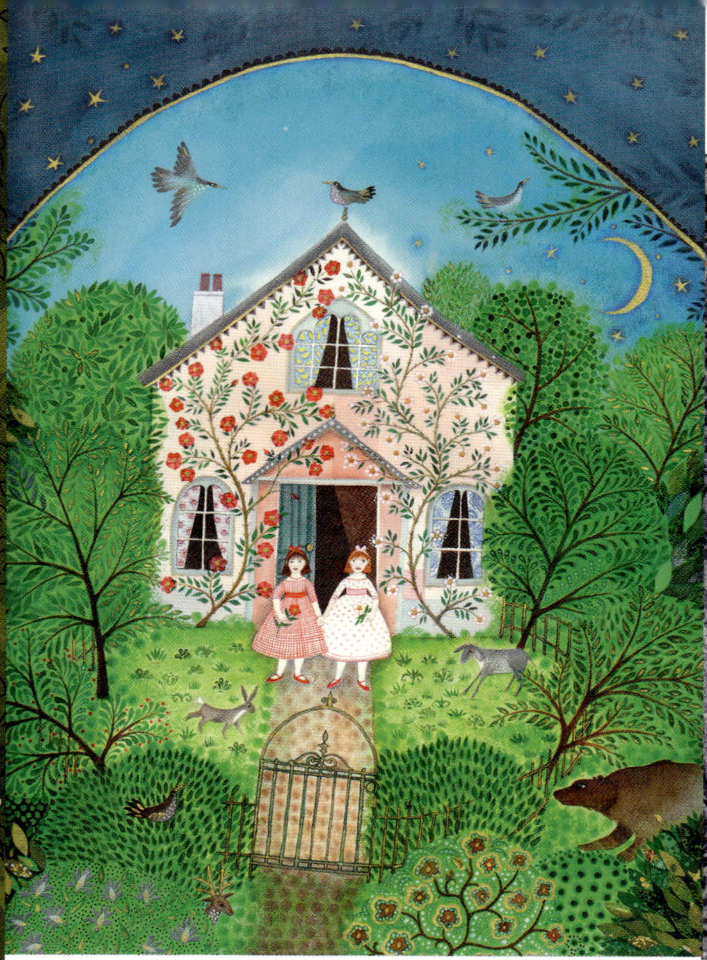

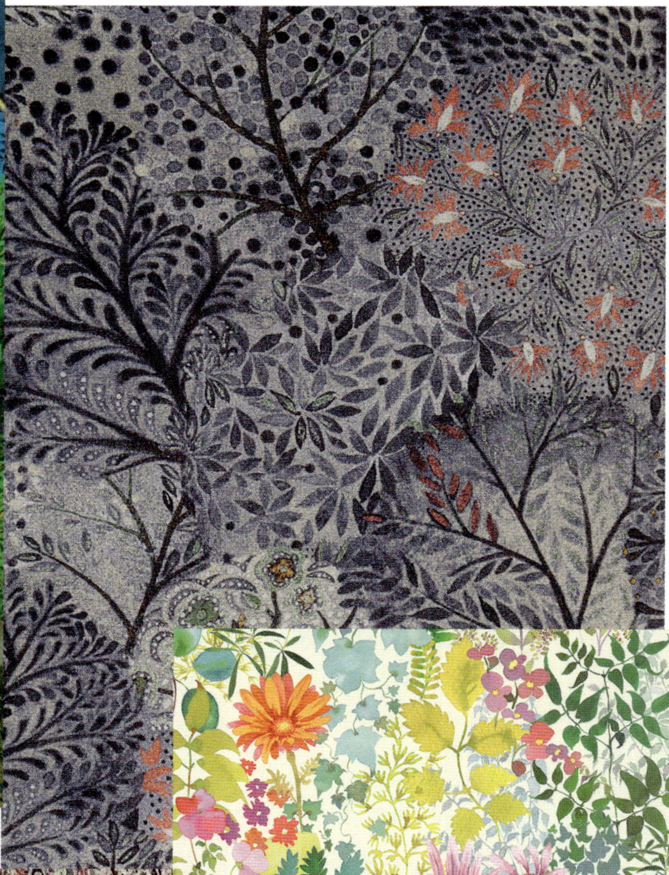

LEFT *Ray (far left) was inspired by an original artwork by author and illustrator Jane Ray entitled* Snow White and Rose Red *(left), commissioned as part of the S/S 2011 Storybook collection.*

OPPOSITE *The Hardy Wingback armchair, with Ianthe print.*

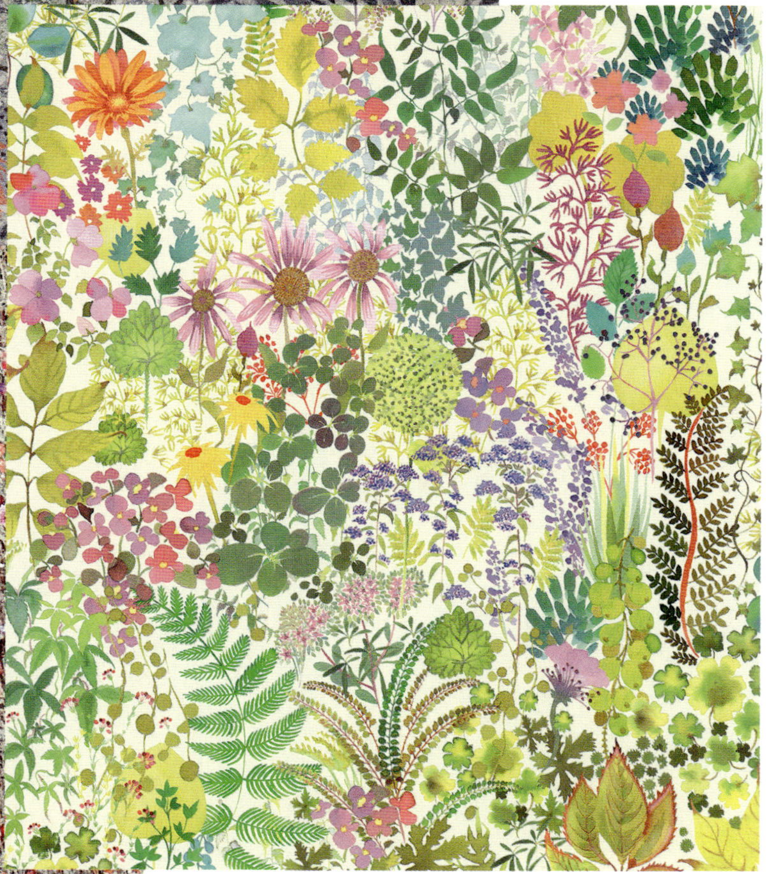

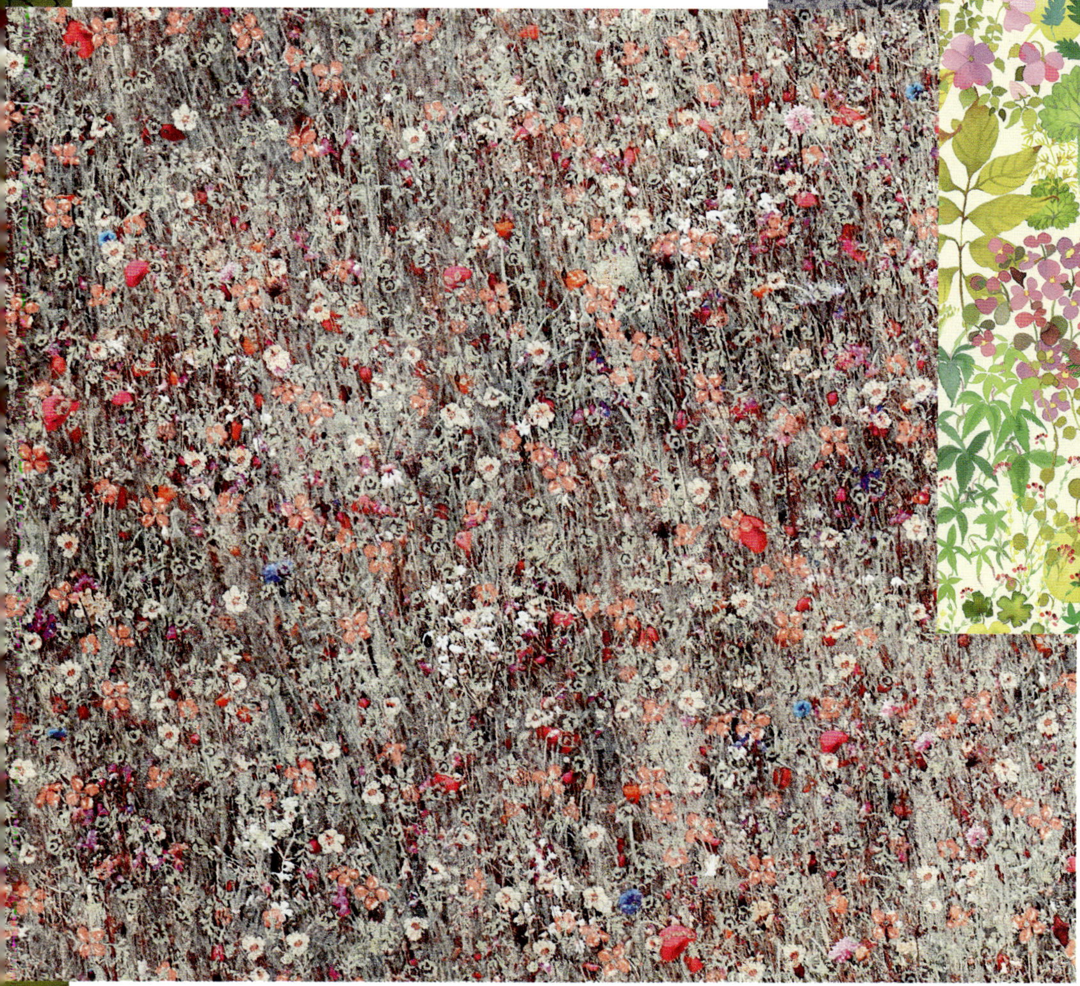

ABOVE AND LEFT *Floral Mawston Meadow (left) was based on a photograph of a Cornish meadow with the classic Meadow print added. Fresco (above) was inspired by a hand-painted walled garden in France.*

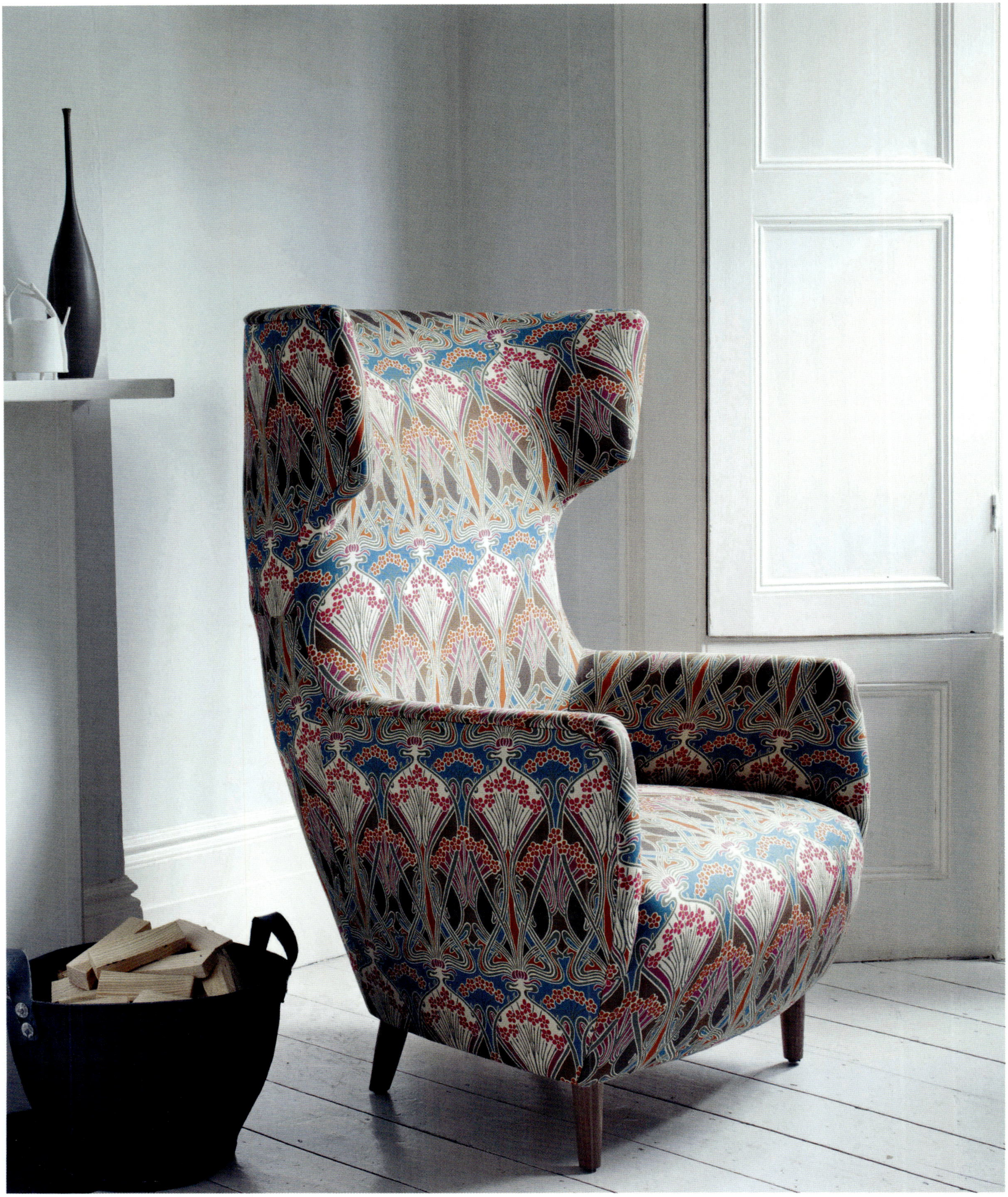

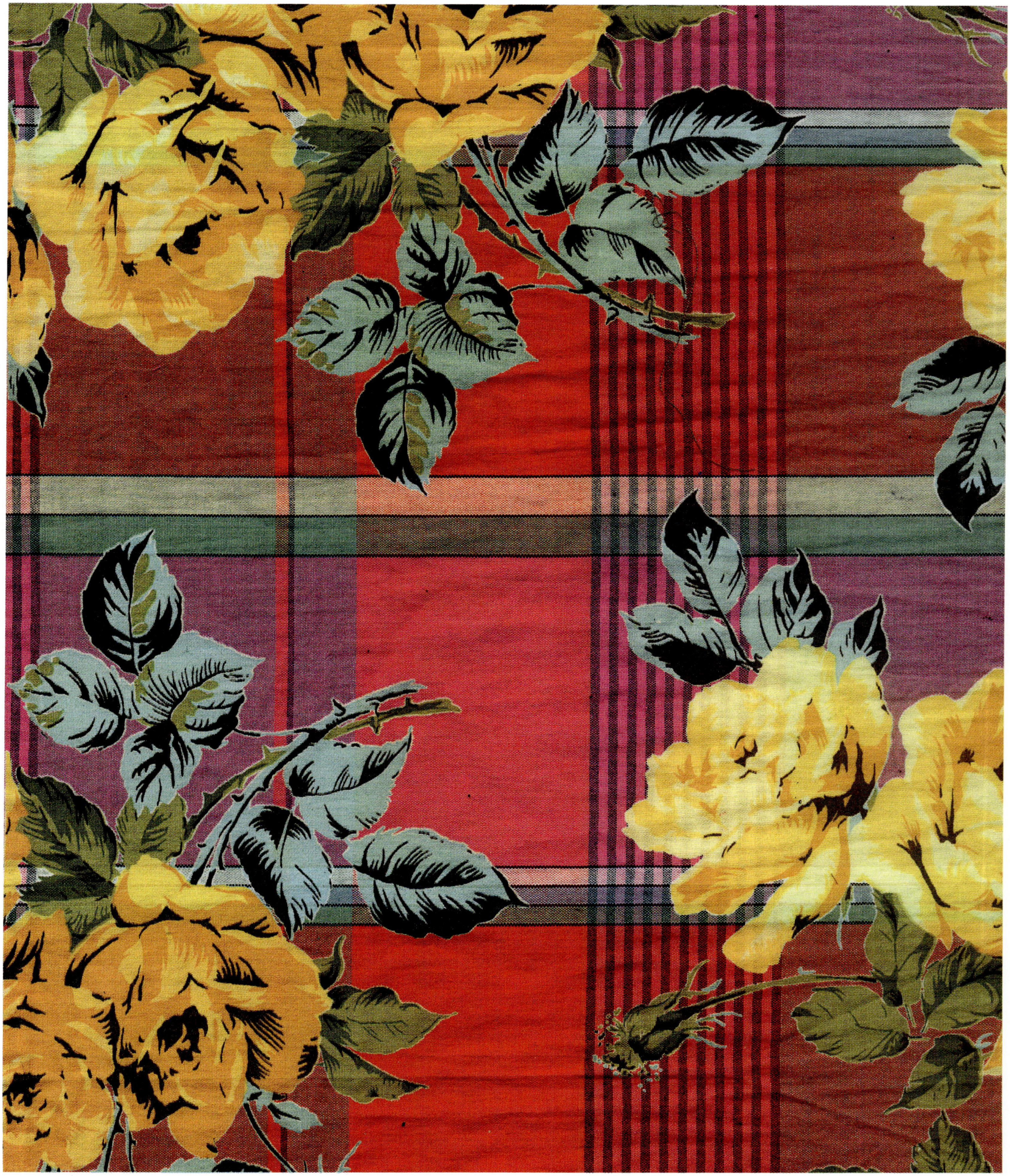

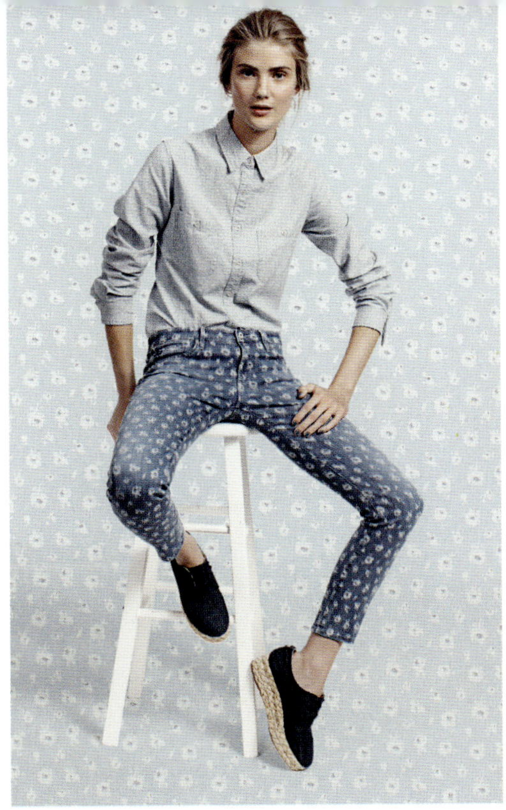

LEFT AND BELOW *Indigo denim was launched exclusively by AG Adriano Goldschmied Jeans in 2012. Classic Liberty designs are printed onto a variety of traditional indigo denims. The finished garments are then washed in various chemicals to expose the designs, creating finishes that range from deep indigo with a crisp, light design to pale, vintage indigo with a subtle, barely-there design.*

INNOVATION

Remaining at the forefront of the textile industry is a driving force at the heart of Liberty's continued success, and innovation is crucial to the growth of the brand. Since 2008, two talented fashion-textile designers have headed up a dedicated innovation programme within the Liberty Art Fabrics department, working closely with printers, weavers and other textile artisans to create new and innovative products that will appeal to fashion leaders – both existing Art Fabrics customers and new customers. Bringing together a diverse range of textile skills – base-cloth development, design, printing, washing and finishing – the new fabrics range from everyday indigo denim to occasion fabrics such as silk organza. One of the most successful is Linford Fleece, a 100 per cent cotton, brushed-back fleece, printed with the edgiest of Liberty designs and colourways, which has been used by popular, young fashion brands Supreme and Acne. Other successes include Lomond Nylon, the finest-quality Italian nylon printed with Liberty designs and given a silk-like finish, used widely for sportswear, outerwear and accessories, and a truly quintessential British project that involved the merging of two very traditional brands, Harris Tweed and Liberty, to produce exquisite woollen cloth for premium outerwear.

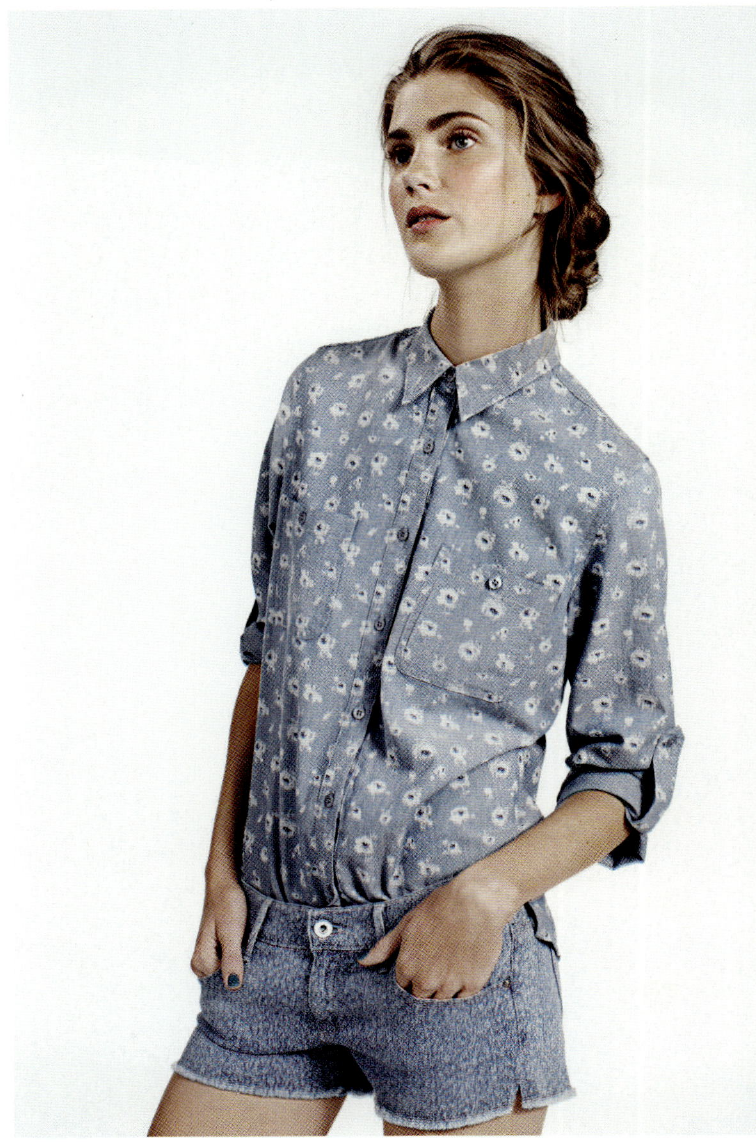

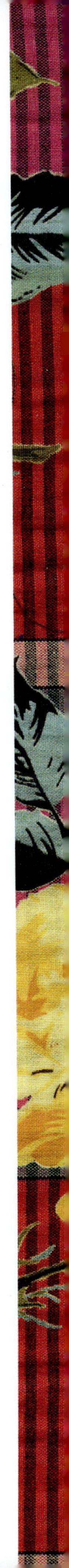

OPPOSITE *Madurai Check is woven in vivid shades in Madras, India, which is then overprinted with traditional Liberty florals. This red Madras check and yellow rose print is an example of two traditional textiles working together.*

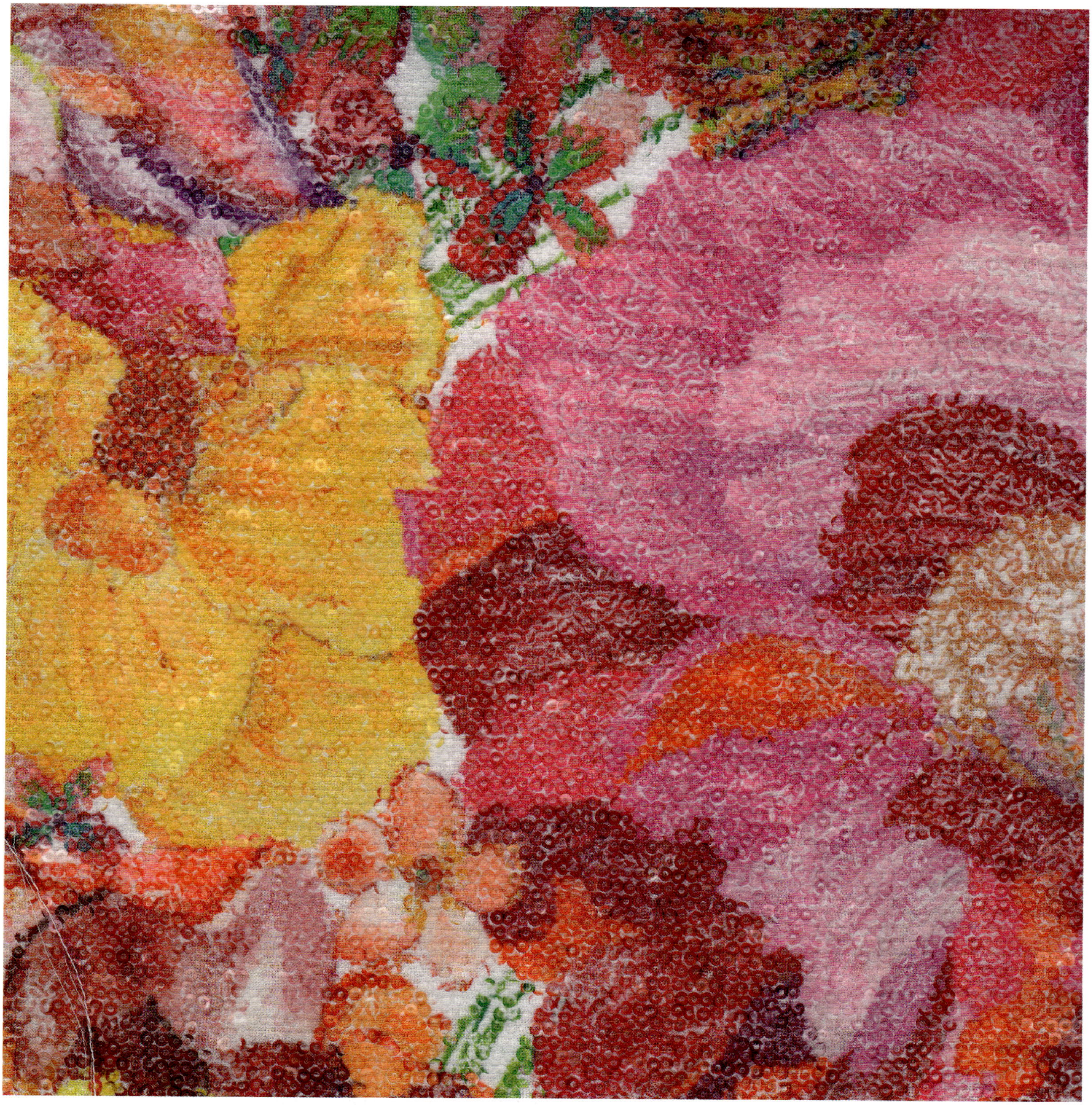

ABOVE *Marina Seaflower Sungleam Sequins is an example of a sumptuous occasion fabric. Such fabrics are used to create fashion pieces for womenwear and childrenswear, including the Liberty London range.*

OPPOSITE *Milla is shown here on Tana Dobby fabric, but is also available on Tana Crepe, a softly draping fabric created from the same fine-gauge Egyptian cotton used exclusively for Tana Lawn.*

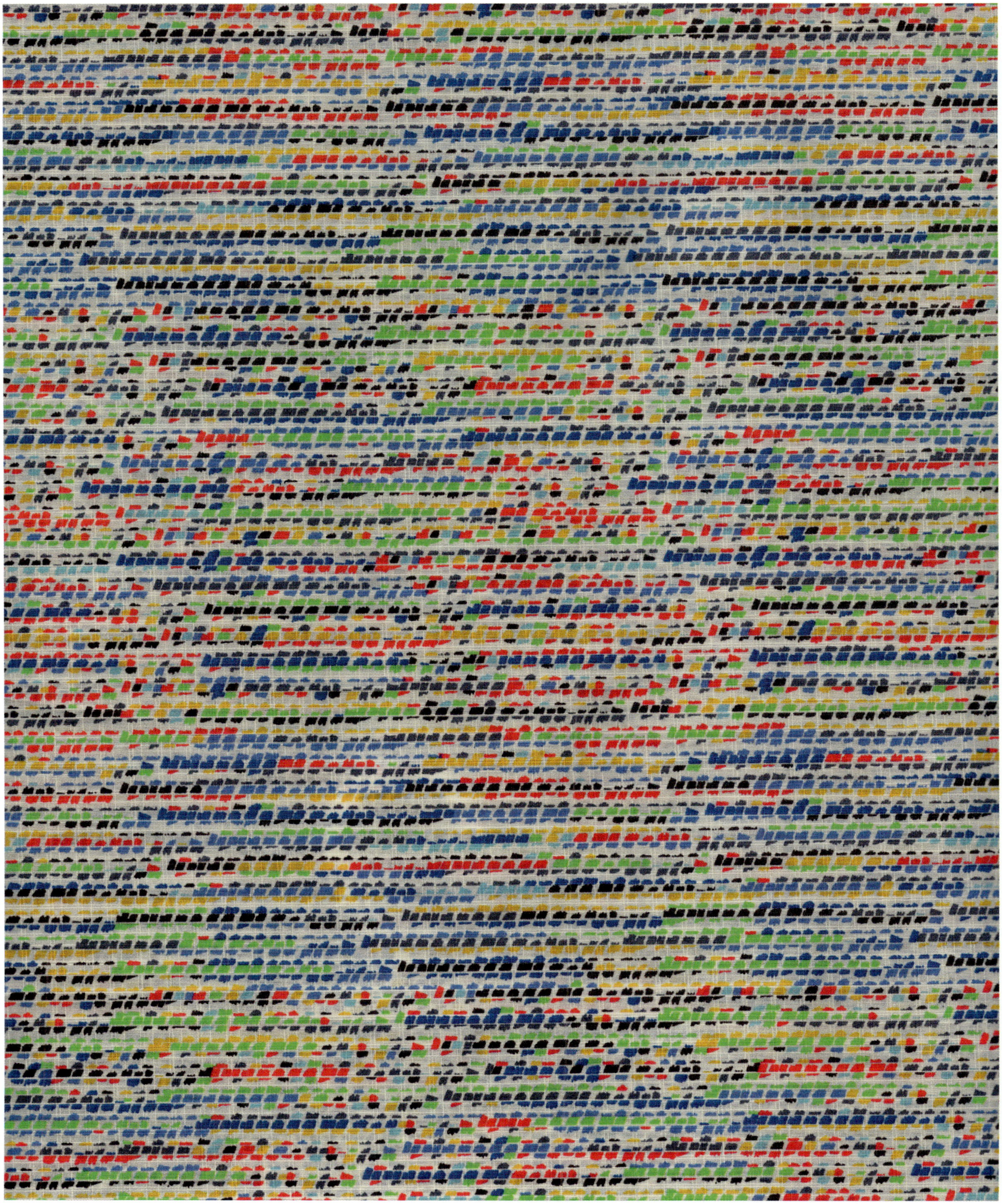

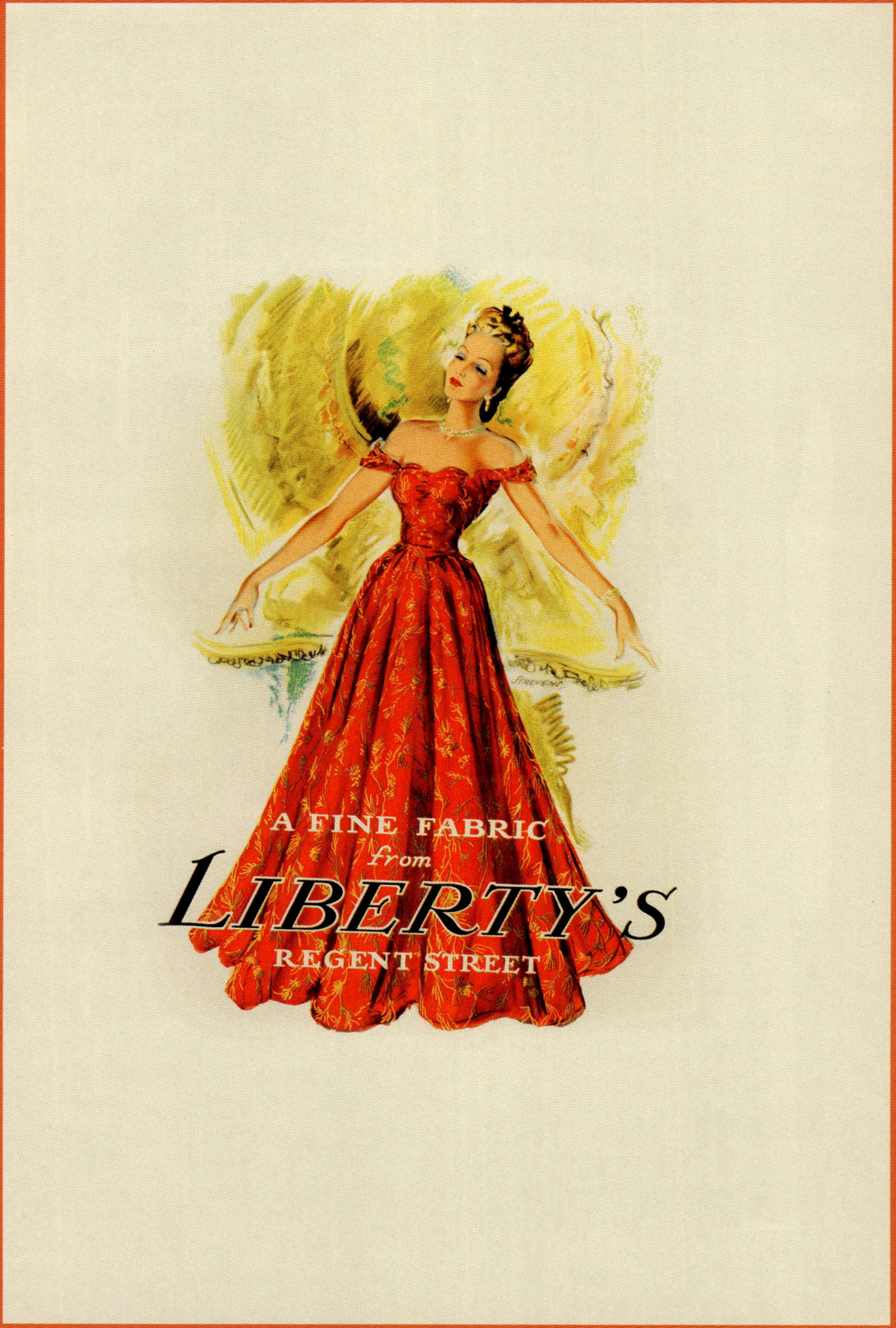

Posters advertising Liberty fabrics for daywear and eveningwear in the 1940s.

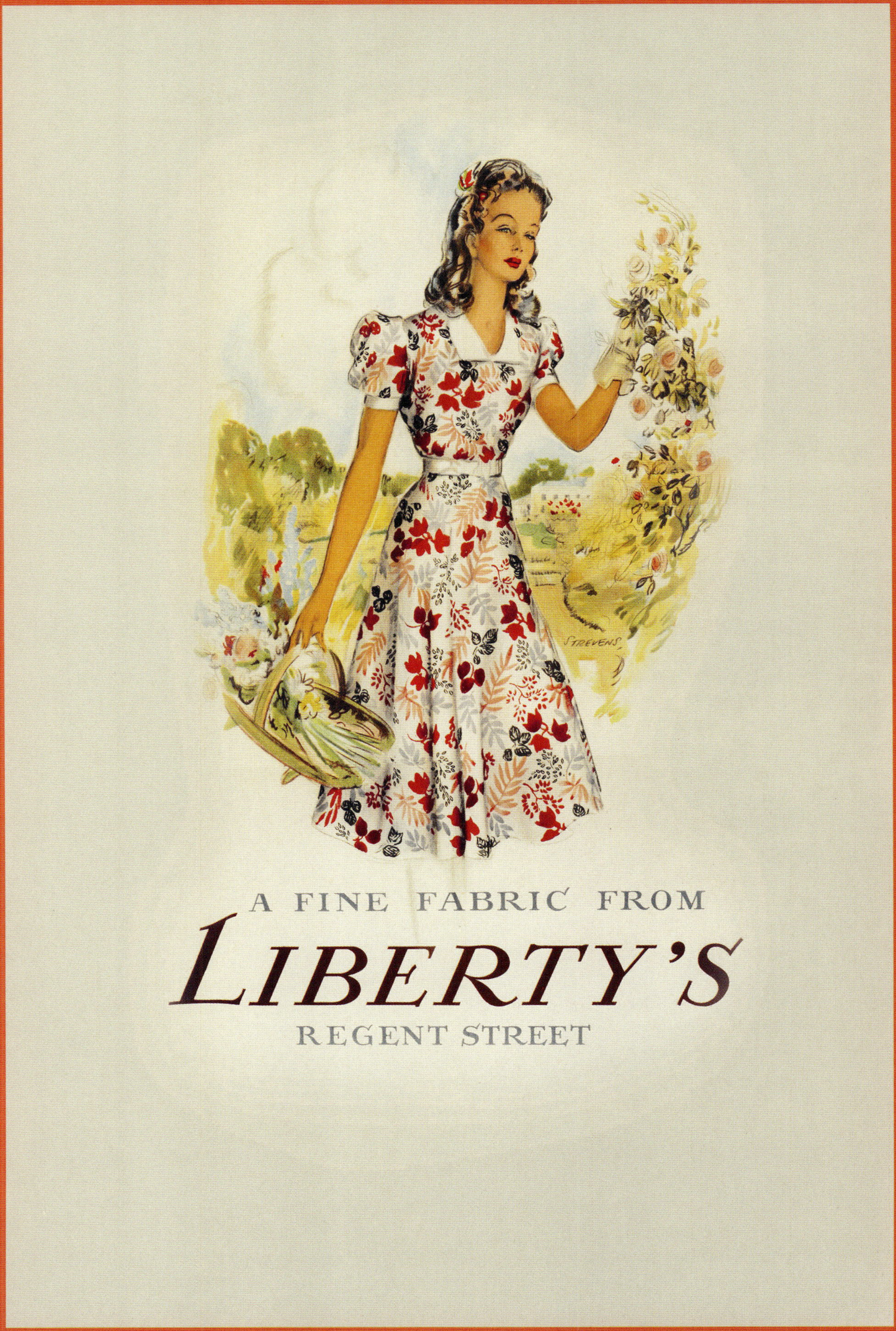
STEVENS
A FINE FABRIC FROM
LIBERTY'S
REGENT STREET

CREDITS

Special Acknowledgments:

Current Heads and Directors of Design Departments featured within the 'New Directions' section:
Kirstie Carey – Managing Director of Liberty London & Liberty Art Fabrics.
Anna Buruma – Archivist.
Emma Mawston – Head of Design for Liberty Art Fabrics.
James Millar – Head of Accessory Design Liberty London.
Louise Scott-Smith - Head of Childrenswear Liberty London.

The Liberty Arts Fabric Design Studio designers featuring in the 'New Directions' section:
Sheona Quenby; Sally Kelly; Polly Overton; Sholto Drumlanrig; Robin Hulme; Sholto Drumlanrig; Keighley Shepherdly; Carrie Osborne; Edward Forster; Meera Sleight; Duncan Cheetham; Daisy Spurrier; Laura-Maria Arola, Lauren Wallace, Rupal Patel.

The Liberty London Studio designers featuring in the 'New Directions' section:
Dominique Devaux; Alexandra Overton; Bethan Silverwood; Tamara De Peon.

Picture Credits:

The publishers would like to thank the following sources for their kind permission to reproduce the pictures in this book.

Key: t=Top, b=Bottom, c=Centre, l=Left and r=Right

All photographs reproduced in the book have been taken from the archives of Liberty Ltd, except for the following:

4l Westminster City Archives; **4c** Westminster City Archives; **4l** Getty Images/Chicago History Museum; **5cl** Westminster City Archives; **8** © Carlton; **10** © Carlton; **11tr** Westminster City Archives; **12l** Westminster City Archives; **13** Westminster City Archives; **14** Westminster City Archives; **15** Westminster City Archives; **17** Westminster City Archives; **18** Westminster City Archives; **20t–21t** Westminster City Archives; **22tl** The Bridgeman Art Library/ Photo © The Fine Art Society, London/Private Collection; **22br** Westminster City Archives; **23l** Museum of London; **23r** Westminster City Archives; **24** © Victoria and Albert Museum, London; **25** Westminster City Archives; **26-27** Westminster City Archives; **27** Private Collection / Photo © The Fine Art Society, London, UK / Bridgeman Images; **29** © Tate, London 2011; **30l** Museum of London; **30c** Getty Images/Chicago History Museum; **30r** Scala/Art Resource/ The Metropolitan Museum of Art; **31** Westminster City Archives; **32-41** Westminster City Archives; **43** Kerry Taylor Auctions; **44** Scala/Art Resource/The Metropolitan Museum of Arts; **45l** © Victoria and Albert Museum, London; **45r** Westminster City Archives; **46-47** Westminster City Archives; **49** Westminster City Archives; **51t** Westminster City Archives; **52l** © Victoria and Albert Museum, London; **53 clockwise from top left** Liberty Ltd; Liberty Ltd; Westminster City Archives; Patch Rogers www.gallery.acfc.co.uk; Patch Rogers www.gallery.acfc.co.uk; Liberty Ltd; Westminster City Archives; Bonhams; Westminster City Archives (final 4); **54** Patch Rogers www.gallery.acfc.co.uk; **55** Westminster City Archives; **56-57** Westminster City Archives; **60bl** Patch Rogers www.gallery.acfc.co.uk; **60cb** Patch Rogers www.gallery.acfc.co.uk; **60br** Patch Rogers www.gallery.acfc.co.uk; **61l** Patch Rogers www.gallery.acfc.co.uk; **61r** Patch Rogers www.gallery.acfc.co.uk; **64t** (b&w illustrations) Westminster City Archives; **65l** (b&w illustrations) Westminster City Archives; **64-65** (jewellery) Patch Rogers www.gallery.acfc.co.uk; **68** (jewellery) Patch Rogers www.gallery.acfc.co.uk; **68-69** (b&w illustrations and sketchbook) Westminster City Archives; **70-71** (jewellery) Patch Rogers www.gallery.acfc.co.uk; **70-71** (b&w illustrations and sketchbook) Westminster City Archives; **72** © Victoria and Albert Museum, London; **74-75** Bonhams; **78** © Victoria and Albert Museum, London; **79** Westminster City Archives; **83** Westminster City Archives; **84** © Victoria and Albert Museum, London; **85tl** Westminster City Archives; **86-89** Westminster City Archives; **91** Westminster City Archives; **92** Westminster City Archives; **94r** Westminster City Archives; **95t** Westminster City Archives; **97** Westminster City Archives; **98tl** Westminster City Archives; **98tr** Corbis/Condé Nast Archive; **98-99** (colour illustrations) Westminster City Archives; **99tr** Westminster City Archives; **101** Mary Evans Picture Library/National Magazine Company; **102t** Westminster City Archives; **103t** Barry Lategan; **104-105** Westminster City Archives; **106-107** London; Westminster City Archives; **108-109** London; Westminster City Archives; **110** © Victoria and Albert Museum, London; **111b** Westminster City Archives; **112-113** Westminster City Archives; **117** Westminster City Archives; **118c** Liberty Ltd, courtesy of Jane Ray; **119bl** Liberty Ltd, courtesy of Jane Ray; **126br** Liberty Ltd, courtesy of Paul Smith; **130** Grayson Perry; **131l** Liberty Ltd, courtesy of Anj Smith; **131c** Liberty Ltd, courtesy of Mr Minagawa; **131tr** Liberty Ltd, courtesy of Tsumori Chisato; **131br** Liberty Ltd, courtesy of Nigel Waymouth; **132tl** Liberty Ltd, courtesy of Lauren Child; **132bl** Liberty Ltd, courtesy of David McKee; **133l** Liberty Ltd, courtesy of Edwyn Collins; **133r** Liberty Ltd, courtesy of Storm Thorgerson; **135c** Liberty Ltd, courtesy of Raymond Honeyman; **136tl** Hugo Grenville; **137tl** Liberty Ltd, courtesy of Mo Coppoletta; **137r** Liberty Ltd, courtesy of Jamie Oliver; **139tl** Manolo Blahnik; **139tr** Liberty Ltd, courtesy of Ptolemy Dean; **140-141** Grayson Perry; **142l** Camera Press; **143r** Camera Press; **152br** Liberty Ltd, courtesy of Mark Mawston; **152tr** Liberty Ltd, courtesy of Jane Ray; **155** AG Jeans; **158-159** Westminster City Archives.

Every effort has been made to acknowledge correctly and contact the source and/or copyright holder of each picture and Welbeck Publishing Group Limited apologises for any unintentional errors or omissions, which will be, corrected in future editions of this book.